Autonomy and Ideology

Autonomy and Ideology

Positioning an Avant-Garde in America

EDITED BY **R. E. SOMOL**

THE MONACELLI PRESS

First published in the United States of America in 1997 by
The Monacelli Press, Inc.
10 East 92nd Street, New York, New York 10128.

Frontispiece photograph of Philip Johnson and all photographs of conference, participants, and attendees copyright © Dorothy Alexander

This book documents the conference "Autonomy and Ideology: Positioning an Architectural Avant-Garde in America, 1923–49" hosted by the Canadian Centre for Architecture, Montréal, with the Columbia Graduate School of Architecture, Planning, and Preservation, New York, and the Museum of Modern Art, New York; held on February 1, 2, and 3, 1996, at Columbia University and the Museum of Modern Art; organized by Phyllis Lambert and Peter Eisenman; and convened by R. E. Somol.

Library of Congress Cataloging-in-Publication Data
Autonomy and ideology : positioning an avant-garde in America / edited by R. E. Somol.
p. cm.
Proceedings of a conference in honor of Philip Johnson held in Feb. 1996 in New York City.
Includes bibliographical references.
ISBN 1-885254-59-8
1. Avant-garde (Aesthetics) — History — 20th century — Congresses. 2. Architecture, Modern — 20th century — Congresses. 3. Architecture, Postmodern — Congresses.
I. Somol, Robert.
NA680.A94 1997
724'.6 — dc21   97-28418

Printed in Hong Kong

Designed by
COMA New York / Amsterdam
Cornelia Blatter and Marcel Hermans

Preface

This publication results from an important conference intended to reopen the debate on the development of architectural discourse in America from 1923 to 1949 and to position for the first time a broad range of European polemical strategies in a North American context. The conference honored the key role of Philip Johnson in the culture of architecture for three-quarters of this century. Hosted in New York City in February 1996 by the Canadian Centre for Architecture with the Columbia University Graduate School of Architecture, Planning, and Preservation and the Department of Architecture and Design of the Museum of Modern Art, the conference was organized by Peter Eisenman and me and convened by Robert Somol. Presenting new issues, which to date have remained unexamined, debate included discussion of the motivation of practitioners of the avant-garde in America and the extent to which they were interested in form rather than in the philosophical, political, and economic underpinnings of the European movement.

In welcoming participants to Columbia University on February 2, 1996, remarks by Bernard Tschumi, dean of the Graduate School of Architecture, Planning, and Preservation, placed the school in the context of the period of this conference. Introducing the session held the following morning at the Museum of Modern Art, Terence Riley, chief curator of the Department of Architecture and Design, presented the institution's relationship to the origins of the avant-garde. Their texts are included in this volume as is my introduction to the conference, "Kirstein's Circle: Cambridge, Hartford, New York, 1927–1931." Robert Somol's introduction explains our use of the term *avant-garde*, the argument presented to the participants, and the issues they addressed.

I would like to express my appreciation to the institutions who supported and helped to organize this event: the Museum of Modern Art; the Graduate School of Architecture, Planning, and Preservation, Columbia University; and the Canadian Centre for Architecture. I would also like to thank those who made this conference possible: my colleagues Peter Eisenman and Robert Somol, as well as Terence Riley and Bernard Tschumi; and those who have provided essential support: Peter B. Lewis, the American Friends of the Canadian Centre for Architecture, Lily Auchincloss, Mr. and Mrs. Gustavo Cisneros, Agnes Gund and Daniel Shapiro, Mr. and Mrs. Ronald S. Lauder, Emilio Ambasz, Marshall S. Cogan, the Leo and Julia Forchheimer Foundation, Joseph E. Seagram and Sons, and Victoria Newhouse.

PHYLLIS LAMBERT   *Director, Canadian Centre for Architecture*
Montréal, July 1996

9

BERNARD TSCHUMI

In this brief introduction, I would like to place Columbia's Graduate School of Architecture, Planning, and Preservation in the context of the period of this colloquium. I do so to try to accentuate the kind of controversies that are both normal and, indeed, almost normative at Columbia. For example, every semester, when we invite a number of lecturers to speak, they are free to organize their arguments as they choose; we do not try to refocus the content of their talks. In the same way, when Phyllis Lambert asked us if the school would be agreeable to a colloquium organized as a joint venture between the Canadian Centre for Architecture in Montreal, the Museum of Modern Art in New York, and itself, we did not try to rearrange the conceptual coordinates of the discussion. Any colloquium involving speakers the likes of Philip Johnson, Beatriz Colomina, Colin Rowe, Peter Eisenman, Rem Koolhaas, and Sylvia Lavin, among others, is bound to attract controversy. Controversy is, historically speaking, a part of Columbia's way of life.

Much of the current history of the School of Architecture at Columbia—its tensions, paradoxes, and ambiguities, its frustrated energies and occasional strokes of genius—can be traced back to the early antagonism between Charles McKim, the practitioner, and William Ware, the academic. But if we look at the subsequent period, namely the one that is the subject of this colloquium, other themes begin to emerge: how, for example, changes in the architectural profession used to have a profound effect on the work in schools of architecture. Today, we tend to say the opposite, that it is the work in the schools that influences the newer development in the profession. I will speak through a series of collaged quotations or excerpts originating from research done more than ten years ago by Rosemarie Bletter, Judith Oberlander, Diane Boas, and Kenneth Frampton. [1]

In the mid-1920s, projects assigned to students reflected the beaux-arts legacy of the profession at the time, including its links with the American Academy in Rome, which was founded by McKim. Projects were called "an Egyptian Barge," "a Mayan Temple," "a Romanesque Church," or "an English Banquet Hall," to cite a few examples. Rosemarie Bletter quotes a student of the time: "As I was completing my architectural studies in 1927 . . . we had at Columbia a sort of insulated academic background—so much so that none of the instructors or professors would even talk about the International Style, the Bauhaus, or what was going on in Europe. . . . It was only in one lecture that we were told about it. . . . We were almost taken in, as if we were going to be told some dirty stories. 'We'll tell you about it, but you better forget it. . . .'"

As Bletter has stated, the situation reflected the prevalence of the beaux-arts system of education at the time: "Many of the professors who were teaching at Columbia had either themselves spent some time at the Ecole des Beaux-Arts in Paris, or had attended American schools where this teaching method was quite common in the late nineteenth and early twentieth centuries. . . . [Morris] Lapidus [the student quoted above] believed that [his] professors at Columbia had been so reticent about Le Corbusier, De Stijl, and the Bauhaus because they were all fighting for their professional lives. They probably realized full well that the new European style would upset everything that they had learned and stood for. Understandably, they did not spend time to proselytize it. . . . The Art Deco exhibition in Paris of 1925, produced an even stronger reaction. . . . Columbia students as well as the profession at large took note. . . . It was the kind of modernism that American architects, steeped in the Beaux-Arts tradition, could feel quite comfortable with."

Dean William Boring retired from the School of Architecture in 1933 and Joseph Hudnut, professor of the history of architecture, became acting dean. Bletter writes that "At the same time, [Columbia] President Butler appointed a committee with, among others, Wallace K. Harrison, William F. Lamb (of Shreve Lamb & Harmon) [who later designed the Empire State Building], and Ralph Walker (of Voorhees, Gmelin & Walker) to study possible changes for the school's curriculum. Hudnut's own annual report of July 1934 coincided with many of the revisions recommended by the commission. Most importantly, design courses were to be more realistic and down-to-earth than the highly idealized and occasionally far-fetched design problems assigned under the Beaux-Arts method. Projects were now to be considered in relation to a specific site, something that had not been done under the older method. Design was no longer to be geared as closely as in the past to the competitions of the Beaux-Arts [system] . . . and both beginners and advanced students were to work together in groups with specific 'Studio Masters.' The Studio Masters [the equivalent of our studio critics today] were not to be responsible to each other, thereby, presumably, allowing for the development of a much greater variety of approaches within the School." The new program began in fall 1934. Bletter cites one student, Theodore Roohdenburg, explaining the change and the shock: "For one who had toiled over the niceties of a problem in superimposed classic orders just before the summer recess, to pledge allegiance to the harsh discipline of the new 'functionalism' required considerable mental agility."

In the words of Judith Oberlander, Hudnut "outlined a series of long-term changes in his Dean's report of 1934. These included . . . a course in urbanism, housing, and the planning of cities; professional courses in the industrial arts . . . 'so that Columbia may become the most important center for this work in the United States.' Of all the changes envisioned by Hudnut, the most radical dealt with the administrative structure, the location, and thus the purpose of the School."

As Bletter writes, "Columbia did in fact get a sampling of the avant-garde education when, coinciding with Hudnut's changes in 1934, Jan Ruhtenberg was hired to teach architectural design. Ruhtenberg had received his education in Germany. In 1931 he briefly worked for Mies van der Rohe at the Berlin Building Exposition. Ruhtenberg left Germany in 1932 and practiced architecture in Stockholm until he came to the United States in 1933. At the school, he introduced the use of transparent models made of [Plexiglas], something that, after so much emphasis on [Beaux-Arts] drafting, the students were not quite ready for."

Oberlander concludes her analysis by observing that "In his short tenure as Dean of the School, Hudnut had managed to create at least a new image of what architectural education should become, and he had been able to institute as far-reaching changes as possible within the constraints of time, faculty, and budget. Hudnut surely understood that the changes he envisaged could not be accomplished quickly." Consequently, "it is a criticism neither of Hudnut nor of his changes to say that his departure . . . somehow left Columbia in a state of confusion. The old pedagogy had been discredited, and a new pedagogy to take its place had not yet been fully instituted."

Hudnut became dean of the Harvard Graduate School of Design in 1935. He was responsible for hiring Walter Gropius for its faculty. Oberlander notes that "Hudnut's . . . working relation-ship with Gropius at Harvard has formed the basis of a rumor that Hudnut wanted to bring Gropius to Columbia"; indeed "Gropius, while in England in the early 1930's and out of work wrote to various educational institutions in the United States seeking employment. He did so at the suggestion of . . . an editor at the *Architectural Record*. The only institution to express interest was Columbia's School of Architecture, or rather Joseph Hudnut, then Acting Dean. . . . However, Ise Gropius . . . claimed that Gropius never had any intention of coming to Columbia because he felt that Columbia was not an adequately influential institution."

There are indications, however, that new changes in the area of current design were occurring in the School. Diane Boas observes that Leopold Arnaud set up an interdisciplinary studio, called the Scenic Design program, in 1935, in collaboration with the Juilliard School of Music under the direction of Frederick Kiesler: "Kiesler gave a series of lectures and under his direction architectural students [at Columbia] designed and executed sets and costumes used in several operatic performances." According to Boas, Kiesler's appointment was "clearly Arnaud's response to Hudnut's appointment of Gropius at Harvard. Arnaud recognized that Gropius would become influential in the field of applied design and he was anxious to establish his own course in Contemporary Design. Kiesler, although a romantic and innovative designer, never enjoyed a great following, and on one occasion, he perturbed the administration when his studio spent an entire semester on the design of a bookcase."

13

Bletter remarks that "An indication that the new curriculum at Columbia had made somewhat of a difference was the announcement in *The New York Times* in 1936 of a student project for a new Museum of Modern Art. It was to replace the inadequate building at 11 West 53rd Street. The students' designs were to be exhibited at the Architectural League. This project, based on an actual site, '. . . closely approximated the conditions under which architects worked.' One of the factors for a change in attitudes toward Beaux-Arts education may . . . [of course have] been the Museum of Modern Art's show 'Modern Architecture: International Exhibition' of 1932 as well as the publication in the same year of *The International Style* by Henry-Russell Hitchcock and Philip Johnson."

It was obvious that a new spirit in architectural education was in the air throughout the thirties. However, Bletter asks, "How much difference did the new curriculum at Columbia make in the end? Hudnut left only a year after the changes were instituted to assume his deanship at Harvard. Jan Ruhtenberg left the following year, 1936, to start his own office. Max Abramovitz [a graduate of the school], who had taught design at Columbia from 1930–1932 and then was at the Ecole on a fellowship for two years, on his return from Europe in 1934 found that everybody at Columbia was still 'teaching the same thing that I'd taught two years before.'" Bletter concludes that in one year only the seeds of change could be planted: "Although Hudnut instituted a new curriculum, most of the same teachers were on the faculty before and after 1934. Harvey Wiley Corbett, the Beaux-Arts trained architect, taught design before and after the change. Talbot Hamlin, the School's great teacher of architectural history, was at Columbia from the twenties onward. In 1933, he had written an essay in *The American Architect* attacking modernism called 'The International Style Lacks the Essence of Great Architecture,' a theme which he was going to continue in many of his later writings." In the words of Kenneth Frampton, Hamlin's approach, which coexisted with Hudnut's, was radically opposed to it: "Hamlin differed from Hudnut not only in his reluctance to advocate any particular modernist style, but also in his nostalgia for an idyllic, if not mythical, America that had long since passed away. Like William Morris in *News from Nowhere,* Hamlin cherished the idea of a normative architecture which would one day be, again, representative of an as yet unborn provincial democracy."

A mix between the old and the new, a constant battle of influence, had become a trademark of Columbia's School of Architecture. This has continued through this day, often in the most fertile manner. Some things change, some things stay the same.

TERENCE RILEY

Rather than presenting a definitive account of the period under consideration, I would like
to introduce this volume by briefly recalling some aspects of the Museum of Modern Art's
connection to the origins of the avant-garde. In his paper, Detlef Mertins speaks of the origins of the term *avant-garde,* specifically its military associations invoking images of struggle, of combativeness, of clearly defined forces arrayed against each other. Alfred H. Barr
Jr., the founding director of the Museum of Modern Art, was certainly a man capable of expressing himself and the museum's mission in those terms. Barr's review of Henry-Russell
Hitchcock's 1929 book *Modern Architecture,* written before the landmark book *The International Style,* comes to mind. The review was published in *Hound & Horn* that same year.
Barr writes: "Even in praising Le Corbusier or condemning Ralph Adams Cram, [Hitchcock's]
discriminating mildness is pervasive. But his caution in his last chapter—The Architecture
of the Future—is a little disappointing. . . . [In comparison to the enthusiasm of the Victorian
critic G. G. Scott], Mr. Hitchcock's prophesies seem meager, dissipated by a rather conscious, Spenglerian melancholy." Barr's clarion call for a more proactive, more critical
stance on the part of Hitchcock was heard equally by the young Philip Johnson.

15

Inspired by his readings of Hitchcock's works, including a monograph on J. J. P. Oud, his further readings of Gustav Platz's *Die Architektur der Neuesten Zeit,* fervent discussions with
both Hitchcock and Barr, and his extensive travels through Europe to see the architecture
referred to as the *neues bauen*, Johnson displayed little of the academic evenhandedness
that characterized Hitchcock's wide interests. With Barr's support, Johnson's first effort was
the "Rejected Architects" show of 1931 staged in a 57th Street storefront, which protested
the exclusion of a number of young modern architects, such as Clauss and Daub, from the
annual Architectural League exhibition. While the rhetoric of the exhibition pamphlet was
hot enough, the picketing of the League exhibition by men wearing sandwich boards saying
"For real modern architecture, see the Rejected Architects" created a furor that resulted
in widespread media coverage and George Howe and others resigning from the League in
protest. *The International Style,* published in 1932, and the near simultaneous exhibition
"Modern Architecture—International Exhibition" were, to use the military metaphor,
Hitchcock and Johnson's response to Barr's call to join the fray. Part of winning the good
fight would be making sure that people could tell the difference between "the wheat and
the chaff." Toward this end, the curators developed a polemical attitude in their writings.
Some examples can be cited:

Hitchcock on Wright: "Wright belongs to the International Style no more than Behrens, Perret, or Van de Velde. He is more akin to the man of 100 years ago than to the generation that has come to the fore since the war" (*The International Style,* 1932).

Johnson on art deco: "The Paris Exposition of Decorative Arts in 1925, with its neoclassic trappings and bizarre ornament, made a strong impression on our designers" (*Machine Art,* 1934).

Barr on the New York Skyscraper school: "Romanesque, Mayan, Assyrian, Renaissance, Aztec, Gothic, and especially Modernistic. No wonder that some of us who have been appalled by this chaos, turn with utmost interest and expectancy to the International Style" (*The International Style,* 1932).

Equally, the expressionist and the functionalist movements in Germany were heaped with scorn by Johnson, Hitchcock, and Barr alike. Together, their efforts were directed toward creating an avant-garde in American art and architecture: an organized body struggling against an equally defined body across a critical line in the sand. Considering the relatively modest scale of the Museum of Modern Art in the 1930s, Barr's success is exceptionally remarkable. The museum clearly became associated with the art of the time, the art of the now.

Mertins also refers to the "aporia of the avant-garde": the paradox that exists in the coupling of the avant-garde's longing for freedom and its invocation of discipline and organization as a means to achieve and sustain it. In this sense the radical innovation engendered by a desire for freedom and the methodical refinement suggested by disciplined development are, in fact, allied, though frequently fractious, strategies. Particularly in architecture, this oscillation between temperaments has important implications. Frank Lloyd Wright spoke of this in defining architecture as necessarily being both radical and conservative. A second oscillation comes into play. Robert Somol and others have invoked a related paradox of high and low as inspirations for art and architecture and the added problematic this conception brings to the rhetoric of the avant-garde: innovation versus refinement, high versus low. You might call this, philosophically, the double bind of the avant-garde. Yet what was and remains problematic in the abstract proved to have been less so in terms of establishing the Museum of Modern Art's early programs. The push and pull between high and low and innovation and refinement proved to be a matrix upon which Barr, Hitchcock, and Johnson, as well as their successors, could rely. Mondrian, whose work has been shown and collected since the museum's earliest years, provides an example illustrating how this matrix of issues might be said to illustrate the essence of the avant-garde, as well as of its contradictions. Making the great leap from the figural to the totally abstract, his revolutionary posture was equaled only by the absolute discipline with which he adhered to those principles over the next thirty years, his austere, lofty, even unapproachable visions capturing the messy energy of boogie-woogie jazz syncopations and New York's Great White Way within a rigorous system.

I recently had a conversation with Johnson about those early years and we began discussing the relationship of architecture and design to Barr's overall program in those years. The tentative conclusion was that Barr understood the possibility for the Department of Architecture and Design and Johnson himself, who refers to his role during the period as being the "screamer and runner-arounder," to realize Barr's unique vision of the museum. That is, the Department of Architecture and Design could negotiate the matrix of high and low, innovation and refinement, in a unique fashion. Shows like "Why America Can't Have Housing," curated by Carol Aronovici in 1934 (which actually included cockroaches in the gallery to demonstrate slum conditions), and "A Home for the United Nations: Must We Repeat the Geneva Fiasco?," curated by Rudolf Mock in 1946, were brassier in their approach than might have been acceptable for the Department of Painting and Sculpture. Similarly, Philip Johnson's "Machine Art" exhibition of 1934, based on the premise that engineers were unselfconsciously absorbing the spirit of the age and in the process creating works of art, caused a sensation for it's audaciousness as well as its media friendliness. News stories featuring photographs of the jury, which included John Dewey and Amelia Earhart (a media star in her own right), projected a serious issue—that is, what constitutes a work of art?—into the consciousness of a broad segment of the public, jolting the established art world in the process.

By some form of dispensation the Department of Architecture and Design was able to undertake certain kinds of shows that would not have been acceptable in the traditional media of the fine arts. Under the direction of Johnson, the department staged its first competition in 1933: a typography competition, the first in a long series of such competition programs featuring architecture, product design, and graphic arts. This effort prefigured the 1941 Organic

Furniture Design Competition organized by Elliot Noyes, from which Charles Eames and Eero Saarinen emerged as the leading innovators of furniture design in their day. Similarly, Philip Johnson's 1933 exhibition "Young Architects From The Middle West," which was a rhetorical response to the Chicago Century of Progress World's Fair and its art deco architecture, was unique in its time. While all curators devote a certain amount of energy to the development of younger artists, the overtly affirmative rationale of Johnson's exhibition, that is, the selection of architects for exhibition based more on promise than on accomplishment, was more speculative and more proactive than any other Museum of Modern Art program in the early years. The first of a series of exhibitions entitled "Useful Objects Under Five Dollars" (originally) then ". . . Ten Dollars," and even "Useful Objects in Wartime" was initiated by John McAndrew. The shows, begun in 1938, promoted contemporary designers by showing their works, interestingly, at Christmastime, even providing information about where they could be purchased. This mixing of high art and lowly commerce not only supported modern designers but was widely popular. Escaping the strictures of propriety surrounding other aspects of the museum's program, the genre reached its apogee during the early 1950s when a program called "Good Design," orchestrated by Edgar J. Kaufmann Jr. and coorganized with the Merchandise Mart in Chicago, appeared three times a year. The exhibitions were clearly intended to promote a new generation of designers including not only Eames and Saarinen but also Florence Knoll, George Nelson, Harry Bertoia, and a host of others. Appearing once a year at the museum, the "Good Design" shows served to introduce this new generation to a sophisticated public. The same shows appeared twice a year at the Merchandise Mart in a more overt attempt to influence American tastes by influencing the buying patterns of the nation's major furniture distributors. In a less innocent age, the department store appearances of René d'Harnoncourt, then director of the museum, to promote "Good Design" seem noteworthy. Even so, at the outset of postwar America's romance with prosperity and consumerism, his stated beliefs that a broad portion of the public might eventually come to understand the higher principles of, say, Mondrian's paintings through the "Good Design" program were no doubt sincere. These programs and d'Harnoncourt's words confirmed the Department of Architecture and Design as the avant-garde of the Museum of Modern Art's avant-gardism, a status derived not so much from a single coherent manifesto but from its deft ability to negotiate the quadrangle of high and low, innovation and refinement.

R. E. SOMOL

> I never believed in originality. . . . No, I was never an avant-garde man. It never interested me.
> — PHILIP JOHNSON

> If exchange is the criterion of generality, theft and gift are those of repetition.
> — GILLES DELEUZE

Sometime in 1963 Philip Johnson took possession of, but apparently neglected to pay for, Robert Morris's first lead relief, *Litanies.*[1] Through this act of appropriation, Johnson inadvertently instigated (or should one say "enabled"?) what would become one of the founding documents of conceptual art and an early recuperation of historical avant-garde procedures, namely Morris's properly notarized *Statement of Esthetic Withdrawal,* which declared null all "esthetic quality and content" in the construction under dispute. It is in the same spirit of give-and-take that the present essays are offered on the occasion of Philip Johnson's ninetieth birthday. Of course, if Sylvia Lavin's portrayal of Otto Rank's presentation of a copy of *The Trauma of Birth* to Freud on his birthday is any indicator, the fate of such a gift may be its ultimate reception as a "heretical departure" from the work of its intended beneficiary.

Any discussion of the economies of theft and gift, and the peculiar modes of repetition that they allow, inevitably involves the themes of title and entitlement. It is a well-rehearsed fact that, ever since its publication, the purported "authors" of *The International Style*, Henry-Russell Hitchcock and Philip Johnson, took every occasion to disavow the title under which they and the work they promoted would become renowned. Instead, this "unfortunate pseudo-title," as Colin Rowe has referred to it, was attributed to Alfred Barr, director of the Museum of Modern Art. Similarly, under the architectural dicta of *plus ça change,* the definitively inadequate title of the February 1996 colloquium in New York, "The Origins of the Avant-Garde in America," must be credited to a combination of anonymous institutional forces and presumed marketing demands. Not only, as Rosalind Krauss has suggested, is "originality" a *modernist* myth, but the related search for "origins" likewise seems perverse, particularly in the case of the avant-garde. Nonetheless, the elision of "originality" with "avant-garde" is a common one, as seen in Johnson's statement above. For the record, however, when the participants developed their contributions for the colloquium and the present collection it was in response to a brief statement entitled "Autonomy and Ideology: Positioning an Architectural Avant-Garde in North America, 1923–49," which was assumed to have been the rubric for both the symposium and the publication. While the present volume restores part of the working title, it eliminates the references both to architecture and to the dates, and therefore does not sufficiently account for the limits imposed on the essays at the outset. If this should be considered an act of editorial withdrawal, it is with the knowledge that, for better or worse, withdrawal is still not abstinence.

To focus on the question of the avant-garde in the second quarter of the twentieth century might, given common wisdom, more reasonably promote reflections about its *repression* rather than its origins. And indeed, to the limited extent that this period has been seriously considered, it has largely been characterized as a tale of double repression, advanced by two equal but opposite camps. The first repression story, supported largely by American historicists and promoters of the so-called vernacular, contends that the introduction of European modernism stifled the continued development of an authentic and native form of modern architecture that had been growing for the previous forty years. The second version of this lament suggests that the formalization of modernism as the "International Style" eliminated any avant-garde tendencies (political and aesthetic) evident in the original European context. These positions, of course, map onto the dominant politics of the postmodern, the former more pronounced in the realms of practice and the popular press and the latter most persuasively argued by those connected to the academy. While the first position fails to recognize the rise of mass culture in its nostalgia for the vernacular, the second too quickly appropriates models of modernism and the avant-garde first developed in the context of other disciplines and media. In other words, while the postmodern revaluation of architecture beginning in the late 1960s would begin to displace previous high-art forms, the discourse of other disciplines—e.g., advanced art history, literary criticism, and philosophy—would continue to explain and inform the newly elevated situation of architecture. Just as it became necessary for a generation of critics and historians in the visual arts to rehabilitate the limited conception of the avant-garde offered by literary history, it is now necessary to continue to pluralize that account by a direct confrontation with the specific requirements and possibilities provided by architectural conditions and procedures.

Today, after a thirty-year period in which the habit of architectural theorizing has finally begun to develop its own techniques and problematics, the prosthetics and assumptions appropriated from other discourses can begin to be reevaluated. While these extra-architectural methods have provided invaluable insights — and are in any case constitutive of the translation of modernism in architecture — they have also produced a series of increasingly difficult impasses and contributed to a recent climate that is unable to think beyond the dialectics of function and form, practical and theoretical, social and speculative. Unlike the disciplines and professions of other arts and sciences, architecture has invariably occupied a compromised or blurred territory, one that has often served as the site for a compensatory or colonizing investment by bordering modes of production and knowledge, and this is no doubt why so many incompatible claims are made either against it or in its name, requests that are increasingly left unfulfilled.

Nonetheless, many of the essays in this volume depart from a familiarity with what might be referred to as the recent tradition of avant-garde studies, a trajectory that stems from Peter Bürger's now canonic discussion of historical avant-garde movements (including constructivism, futurism, dada, and surrealism) as offering a critique of so-called institution art, and the extension and transformation of that analysis in the work of more recent thinkers. Briefly, in contrast to what can be characterized as modernism — with its values of originality, authenticity, contemplation, medium specificity, autonomy, and so on — the historical avant-garde project involved itself with mechanical means of reproduction, collective modes of production and reception, multimedia and between-media practices and events, and the attempt to collapse or realign the disjunction between art and life. Part of the confusion over this particular attitude to the avant-garde — which is in large measure a generational one — no doubt derives from Clement Greenberg, particularly in his too-well-known essay, "Avant-Garde and Kitsch," since what he considers to be "avant-garde" we would today call "high modern," while many of the phenomena he dismisses as kitsch — from mass culture to Surrealism — are those that for us have resonance with the historical avant-garde project.

Exactly how this project can or might intersect architecture — or how it could be translated by or through architecture, particularly in an American or postwar context — is a difficult question, but again one that has historically tended to be either too easily dismissed or too readily assumed. For example, European historians and architects of various ideological persuasion — from the neo-Marxism of Manfredo Tafuri to the metaphysical essentialism of Georgio Grassi — have continually asserted that an avant-garde is impossible in America *specifically* or in architecture *generally*.[2] Conversely, other writers, primarily American, have automatically presumed the triumph of the avant-garde through devices associated with institutions like the Museum of Modern Art. Whether celebrated or criticized, the successful importation of the European avant-garde to America is associated with devices such as the translation of painting and particularly cubism into architecture, as well as the maintenance of vertical distinctions between high and low and of horizontal distinctions between architecture and other realms (such as economics and politics), as propounded in texts like *The International Style* up to its last sentence "We have an architecture still." These devices, however, would more likely be understood today as a high modernist framework rather than an avant-garde one, and it is largely toward this latter possibility that recent revisionary histories have been directed, as indicated by the previous work of several contributors to the present volume. For example, the two alternatives that Alfred Barr specifically excludes from consideration in his preface to *The International Style*—namely, the "fanatical functionalism" of Hannes Meyer as well as the work of those "modernistic impresarios," the "American skyscraper architects"—are precisely the sources that have emerged as more instructive for contemporary concerns, the former addressed by Michael Hays, and the latter by Rem Koolhaas. In addition to recuperating politically oriented European as well as corporate American practices previously excluded from the discourse of architectural modernism, other historians have reframed central figures within the modernist narrative. Rather than situating Le Corbusier's work within a high modern tradition through analogies to painting, Beatriz Colomina locates its involvement with the mass media, particularly photography, film, and advertising. Finally, these recent revisionary histories would only have been possible alongside simultaneous neo-avant-garde design practices and institutions (for example, those of Peter Eisenman, Bernard Tschumi, and Koolhaas) that have emerged since the 1960s. One aspect of the present collection, then, has been to turn the attention of those who have worked primarily either on the European experience of the 1910s and 1920s or the American situation after the 1950s toward the formative (if invisible) "middle period," which has so far remained unformulated, despite the fact that its difficult transactions may well be responsible for the various discursive trajectories enabled for the first time in a North American context. More specifically, the primary ambition of this project has been to address two related themes: first, how can an examination of the architectural discipline open up or multiply the conventional understanding of "*the* avant-garde," a historical construct that seems to remain the limited property of art and literary history?, and second, what would this reconceptualization mean for the current politics of architectural design and theory?

Of course, from the beginning, the provisional dates of this collection were always a bit of a conceit, a ready-made tabula rasa or, perhaps closer still, a surface of the type Michael Hays attributes to Mies's Seagram Building, a screen on which the contributors have projected their historical and critical fantasies. While no consensus emerges, a chalk outline begins to take shape, one that may vaguely surround the absent figure of Johnson, that strange attractor for the event, but that more significantly serves as evidence of the themes, obsessions, and debates that cut across five generations of architectural thinkers, establishing a snapshot of the various idioms through which architectural discourse has been conducted for the last forty years: from the lapidary if not purple prose of the reminiscence to the staccato sound bites of an almost cinematic script; from the emphatically vague to the ambiguously precise; from the narrative to the critical to the projective; from the humanist to the structuralist, the psychoanalytic, and the performative. In the opening segment of the book— in the section that runs from Johnson to Rowe to Eisenman to Ockman to Linder—these genealogical lines of development and deviation are perhaps progressively most evident through the various denials, limitations, embraces, redirections, and involutions that the avant-garde project undergoes. This is not to say as well that this multigenerational discourse is not without its internal ironies: e.g., from the curious dismissal of the concept of the zeitgeist because it is too old to the defense of autonomy on the basis of external disciplines. In a curious turn that has a resonance with other discussions in the collection (particularly the exchange between Kipnis and Johnson), Paulette Singley argues for fashion as an avant-garde venue in the postwar world. Suggesting that the possibility for "ideas" (or ideology) is contingent on style, this representative of the fifth generation folds back to the first two. In other words, contained within the recuperation of "style" as a viable material for design research today, there resides the potentially unseemly aftereffect of renovating an avant-garde posture for the high modern bachelors, Johnson and Rowe. As Rowe's intellectual program and Johnson's fashionable excess collapse in a new paradigm of the "style of sincerity," Singley's tactic moves undecidedly between a theoretical apologia and a practice of viral criticism, thus exposing the predicaments of contemporary revisionism. Here, as elsewhere, ideology and autonomy emerge as complicit, correlate terms that may well serve as the prerequisite for discursive practice—and thereby the avant-garde—itself.

In raising a slightly different antinomy characteristic of the period under consideration, Francesco Dal Co, Detlef Mertins, and Mitchell Schwarzer allude to the contradiction between the techniques of science and the forms of tradition, between civilization and culture. Each in his own way suggests that the avant-garde's attempt to reframe this contradiction involved developing new modes of knowledge, new disciplines or practices, and through their respective historical accounts each calls for, if not quite enacts, a vision of the critical historian or theorist as necessarily projective. The imagination of a role where programmatic speculation and formal experimentation might be conjoined, however, has practically disappeared in today's intellectual landscape. In part, this has to do with the documentation of the "failure" of architectural experimentation offered by postmodern history combined with the more recent suspicions over "master narratives" raised by poststructural theory. The price for this critical sophistication has been an inability to engage in any speculative, generative, or projective thought. Though a perverse outcome never envisioned by the proponents of advanced design discourse, institutional forces within the architectural establishment have seized upon these insights precisely to dismiss routinely both the avant-garde *and* theory, and this current cultural alignment can be witnessed in professional magazines, recent sociological accounts of the field, and now retrenching educational institutions and organizations. A brief glance at one among many examples, the 1996 Association of Collegiate Schools of Architecture program statement, is instructive in this regard:

> Many would argue that architectural education has been paralyzed by theoretical debate and has retreated from any direct engagement with the messy reality of modern life. . . . Do we provide our students the kinds of "useful knowledge" they will need to make real contributions to the constructed environments of the next century? Do they have the cultural sensitivity and technical skills that will be necessary to reinvigorate the profession? Have zeitgeist theories, and their exhaustion as believable explanations or justifications of architectural production and form, been replaced with other effective strategies for projecting built form? . . . How is a persistence of the avant-garde to be explained? Can an architecture based on intuition and originality be sustained, or has this persistence grown to represent a newly established institutional order within architectural education and a few corners of the profession?

Here, in condensed form, are the general tenets of the current dismissals of theory and the avant-garde: the opposition of theory and "reality"; the reduction of significant forms of knowledge to the behavioral and building sciences; the confused association of the avant-garde with originality and intuition (or alternatively, the zeitgeist), and thus its condemnation as irrelevant. In the present context, any conference that takes as its point of departure the historical and contemporary issues of the avant-garde in architecture and the related forms of its theorization necessarily becomes a political gesture. As Sanford Kwinter argues in his critique of the bureaucratic rationalization that the avant-garde project experienced in its assimilation to the United States, "to speak of an avant-garde, today, is both a right and a political obligation."

As seen earlier, while European accounts have suggested that an avant-garde program was *impossible* in American architecture, a more recent native form of critique claims that it has rather been the *dominant* mode of production and must now be displaced. These polemics (sometimes Marxist, sometimes neotraditional, and invariably thoroughly preoccupied by the call to originality and origins) express the desire to block contemporary translations of the avant-garde, and mark such production as either inconceivable or redundant. Such alternatives fail to consider that it may not be possible to evaluate repetition on the basis of either formal resemblance or operative analogies given the radically transformed situation after 1950. In describing Alexander Dorner's critical and curatorial projects and their increasing affiliation to an American pragmatism as a presumed solution to the avant-garde impasse of engagement or withdrawal, Joan Ockman notes that "in postwar America, art would enter life more powerfully than the avant-gardes of the 1920s had ever imagined." This social and cultural transformation also suggests why Michael Hays posits Mies's American work as the endgame of a particular avant-garde project in architecture, the attempt to "desubjectify the aesthetic phenomena" and the simultaneous commitment to produce a resistant aesthetic experience. But Mies's immediate postwar gambit is precisely what is no longer available by 1960, "the moment when the mass culture of corporate capitalism was in the process of dismantling all vestiges of bourgeois culture's individual experience and liquidating the oppositional functions of high art,"[3] as Benjamin Buchloh describes the situation when Yves Klein projected his particular version of an avant-garde "repetition." It is probably no coincidence that at exactly the same time as Klein's production (and at the identical moment in the formative emergence of the architectural neo-avant-garde), a postwar cinematic vanguard was developing its own major precepts in the form of the *nouvelle vague*. The so-called *auteur* theory—seemingly a concept that would have been anathema to the productivist concerns of the historical avant-garde—was developed precisely to confront the new homogeneity and totalization of the commercial film industry.

If, as Beatriz Colomina suggests, what differentiates the postwar architectural avant-gardes from their predecessors is an "extraordinary intimacy with film," then it is not surprising that the tactic of developing a critical signature would be one potential area of translation, particularly since the closest analogue to the massive centralization and standardization of the postwar building establishment was that of the motion-picture industry. This potentially critical aspect of the signature, of course, constitutes what is today routinely confused and dismissed by social critics of architecture as the "star system."[4]

The particular hostility of a segment of recent social criticism toward historical and contemporary configurations of the avant-garde (and with it, questions of both form and theory) seems to be a peculiarly American phenomenon. In part this results from the common historical wisdom (regardless of whether this is evaluated as a positive or negative development) that, in its transition to the United States, the modern movement lost its social project. Sylvia Lavin's account of Richard Neutra begins to complicate this simple evaluation as she reveals a kind of instrumental reason that unfolds in the American context, a psychologizing of architecture toward the provision of microtechnologies of the self and its spatial regulation. The translation of modernism in America becomes the repository for the therapeutic, ultimately raising the expectancy of architecture's remedial capacities through extravagant presumptions and, ultimately, self-abusing confessions. In this way, the accusations made about architecture today may not be due to the validity of a convenient historical narrative where the formal subsumed the programmatic (in its broadest sense), but rather to one where psycho-social therapy came to stand in for a transformative vision of the political.[5] This begins to explain why the social critique of architecture is much more prevalent in the United States than in Europe, and how it is as much a complicit product of this period as it is a developed critique of it.

The fashioning of techniques and practices that escape the limited oppositions and dialectics typically advanced by architectural criticism and polemic — a project that might constitute one aspect of a contemporary avant-garde — requires alternative ways to think repetition. The first and most common way to conceive repetition relies on an ideal of the origin or model, an economy of identity. This typological and categorical model of repetition pervades Colin Rowe's essay on the New York Five, in which he advances his classic distinction between the alternative repetitions of *physique*-flesh and *morale*-word, form and ideology, and is equally evident in his contribution to this collection. In a clever, if perverse, reading of events in the 1920s, Rowe sets Mies aside as a kind of classic liberal and nominates the nearly forgotten figure of Peter van der Meulen Smith as "American avant-gardist Number 1." On the basis of two rather derivative and anemic-looking perspective sketches, Rowe exalts that Smith's unrealized house project of 1927 is "even by the standards of fifty years later . . . outstanding" and at that date "entirely clairvoyant in its awareness of the most recent French and Dutch innovations."[6] A thin catalog of various modern devices—as presented in its two oblique views—the project ironically begins to look like a bizarre hybrid of Rowe's antithetical models of Garches and the Bauhaus, and exhibits none of the "phenomenal" transparency or compressed and highly framed depth that he and Robert Slutzky have so convincingly associated with the former. In addition to the Smith House—which would seem to be devoid of textuality and an unlikely candidate to sustain any discursive exegesis—Rowe proposes a parallel example of an "advanced" architectural proposition, Chick Austin's "eclectic," "pseudo-Scamozzi job" in Hartford, which he posits as *almost* surreal and, one imagines, *almost* avant-garde (or at least as close as America might get). One can sense, however, that these equally weighted exemplars of advanced American experience, Smith and Austin, are merely retroactively conceived predecessors to the Whites and the Grays, thus ultimately confining repetition to a pluralist language game.

For Rowe, all repetitions are equal (repetition as identity) and entail the necessity of origins, and it is this aspect that allows them to constitute a rule-bound language. Of course, the *particular* repetitions of Smith and Austin *are* equivalent (regardless of style) in that both idealize rather than appropriate and misread their sources. In this way, they are no different from similar subsequent repetitions, such as those of Meier and Stern. Nonetheless, it is possible to imagine an alternative model of repetition,[7] one that does not rely on pointing backward or on a contractual exchange, that is neither historicist nor liberal. This aspect of repetition can be gleaned in the moments of misreading or swerving (through "accidents" of theft and gift)[8] that one ascertains, for example, in Craig Owen's description of Johnson's Glass House,[9] in the work of some of the New York Five, in Koolhaas's Villa Dall'Ava—and, for that matter, in Mies, despite Rowe's desire to exclude him from consideration. This second form of repetition exists as a continual, horizontal process of differentiating, and perhaps this is ultimately a more productive manner in which to understand the phenomena of the avant-gardes generally: that is, not as "originating" somewhere and migrating—and certainly not conditioned by the apparent presentation of a new style or on the measured sociological evidence of producing a requisite degree of "shock" — but as a function of continual cross-Atlantic translations and mistranslations — circulation without origin or end, save that of proliferating movements and connections.

Perhaps the contributions that advance this alternative repetition furthest, and that avoid the privileged oppositions that Lavin's paper begins to dismantle, are the more projective or prescriptive accounts implied by Mark Linder and Rem Koolhaas. In both cases, the chance for exceeding classic architectural antinomies (like form and word) is found in the diagram: Linder's correlation of Lacan's diagram (the interior 8) to Kiesler's Endless House, and Koolhaas's recognition of the fullest realization of a "futurist avant-garde diagram" in the Pan Am Building. Through the figure of Kiesler, Linder locates a practice that operates between and across disciplines, one that displays a conjunction of psychoanalysis and surrealism in visible contrast to the framed, optical definition of high modernism associated with Johnson, Rowe, Barr, Greenberg, and Fried. Seeming to eschew politely but deliberately the monumentality of the U.N. and the Seagram Building — the one too isolated from the city and the other too articulated — Koolhaas insinuates the improbable model of the Pan Am Building almost by default, an entity thoroughly exhausted by the urban flows it channels and utterly without redeeming articulation or detail. From Kiesler's reframing of Duchamp's *Large Glass* as at once mural-window-wall to the "disappearing act" of the Pan Am, both architectural programs similarly rely on what Linder calls tactics of mimicry and Koolhaas describes as "an apotheosis of background."

In a curious act of involution, the book ends precisely where it began, though the common sites have by now become quite unrecognizable. In her opening essay, Phyllis Lambert describes the intense cultural activity in the late 1920s and early 1930s that provided the framework for a reception of European modernism, a combination of events sponsored variously by Harvard University, the Wadsworth Atheneum, and ultimately the Museum of Modern Art. This optimistic portrait of the individual and institutional forces that risked an advanced cultural program, however, assumes a much less sanguine tone in Beatriz Colomina's conclusion:

> It would seem that experimental work in architecture today is rarely found outside the gallery or the university. The American avant-garde architect, if we still want to use the term, and I am not sure that we do, has become some kind of installation artist.

Though separated by seventy years, the institutions that historically introduced an avant-garde—the museum and the university—now appear to present a major impasse to its survival in anything but a sterilized or in vitro existence. In addition to serving as a challenge to any architectural avant-garde to move beyond the models of semiotic and institutional critique (models, incidentally, that made sense given the postwar conditions of reception and production in the museum-university complex), Colomina's final lines may also suggest that theory itself has become the latest (and perhaps the last) locus for avant-garde activity, a diagnosis that is strangely similar to Manfredo Tafuri's claim that there can no longer be a critical architecture but only a critical history of architecture. While her essay provides a largely sympathetic reading of the Eameses and their multidisciplinary practice, its conclusion may support those who call for a more "proper" allocation of roles and maintenance of boundaries: i.e., a request for architects who "do" that seemingly predefined thing called architecture. Taking her cue from Charles Eames's self-description of his withdrawal from architecture as "chickening out," Colomina bemoans those contemporary architects who are "chickening out of building" in increasing numbers. Like Duchamp's "abandonment of painting," however, it is at least possible that what appears to be an abandonment of architecture may well lead to the invention of something else, something that retroactively could transform the very definition of architecture and its opportunities.[10] In other words, it is important to distinguish chickening out from playing chicken, raising the stakes (or the levels of pleasure and terror) in anticipation of a potential collision and reconstruction.

With regard to the contemporary moment, the fact that at least part of the historical avant-garde project has been realized in the erosion or collapse of boundaries means that any contemporary practice that proposes to continue that process must engage in ever more subtle calibrations. Any large and complex event—whether an act of building or publication—is only possible due to a diverse confluence of interests, constituencies, forces, and agendas. Thus, such an event tempts a specific kind of impossibility, doomed to failure before beginning, as is the case with this book, which was only *conceivable* by its ability to serve, however improbable that may seem, as a commemorative act, a market-driven investment, and a critical project. Whether these often opposed agendas and their related idioms—nostalgia, commercialism, and critique—can comfortably coexist in this framework remains unsettled. The point is simply that it would be naive to believe that any *one* of those genres could exist in pure form, that, for example, there could ever be a "purely critical" endeavor, untainted by circumstance. Rather than dream of a lost moment of purity, one project for the contemporary avant-garde would be to advance a practice that registers—by recognizing, soliciting, realigning, and subverting—the various frames that allow it to come into being, and to provide virtual alternatives that retroactively transform their contexts. Phyllis Lambert concludes her paper on the specific forces that conspired and condensed ultimately to shape *The International Style* and what was to follow by noting that without those forces "something would have happened, but something else." The essays collected here are presented in the name of that something else.

PHYLLIS LAMBERT

Kirstein's Circle
Cambridge, Hartford, New York, 1927–1931

A culture of the avant-garde became anchored as a movement in North America due to an extraordinary concentration of intellectual activity at the end of the 1920s that can initially be characterized as an ever-expanding network of people and public events located in three centers: Cambridge, Hartford, and New York. The movement advanced and consolidated the gains of the preceding generation, which had initiated a dramatic change in taste and in expectancy about the role of art through isolated events located primarily in one city, New York. Reference points include the exhibition mounted in 1908 by "The Eight," a group of "progressive" artists organized by Robert Henri and John Sloane, which proved for the first time that a strongly anti-academic group of artists, including photographers, could attract considerable public attention.[1] At the same time, Alfred Stieglitz considered his exhibition of Matisse watercolors "the first blow of 'Modernity' in America."[2] Seeing the new work in Europe as a model for renewal, Edward Steichen, along with Stieglitz at his 291 Gallery, brought together American and European avant-garde artists between 1906 and 1914.

Additional isolated events, such as the Armory Show of 1913 and exhibitions of Katherine Dreier's *Société anonyme*, were fostered by a widening circle of intellectuals, committed aesthetes, and wealthy collectors. There is a certain resonance with the eighteenth-century British Society of Dilettanti, for whom wealth and education were the basis of membership and the grand tour a fundamental activity. Despite, and because of, their privileged positions, the Dilettanti effected a major change in the culture of art and architecture in Britain.

Similar forces coalesced at Cambridge between 1927 and 1931, and an intellectual position was established that circumscribed the program of the Museum of Modern Art in New York and the Wadsworth Atheneum in Hartford. At its center was the Fogg Art Museum, under the direction of Edward Waldo Forbes and Paul Sachs. Its dynamo was Lincoln Kirstein. In his sophomore and junior years at Harvard, Kirstein founded, with extraordinary energy, two separate cultural ventures that brought the most advanced American and European artists and writers to the public in a continuous flow. The first was the literary journal *Hound & Horn*, published in Cambridge in 1927, closely followed by the Harvard Society for Contemporary Art (HSCA), which mounted twenty-seven exhibitions between February 1929 and December 1931. My paper is intended as an introduction, setting the background for the conference and this volume.

While I was working on this paper, Lincoln Kirstein died, on January 5, 1996. This discussion therefore serves to present and memorialize the central but little-researched role he played in synthesizing the many diverse aspects of the avant-garde and new work in North America not as isolated manifestations but as a continuum of intellectual and cultural undertaking.

By the time he entered Harvard, Kirstein's self-proclaimed "avid visual appetite" had been nurtured by his mother's monochrome monographs, *Klassiker der Kunst*, and by visits with her to museums in Boston and Europe.[3] His literary affinities were developed in the Boston Public Library, where his father was chair of the board of trustees. Kirstein later wrote of the interpenetration of these two streams:

What propelled my desire to become a painter was less the instinctive physical joy of pushing paint around than a quest for the mirrored self-image of a mechanic, mastering the ways to capture human gesture, moving my hand against the flow of time. This was more a branch of literature.[4]

With his methodical training in art history, Kirstein claimed a "historical attitude" toward art: "I never felt that one school or one epoch in itself had any priority or enduring quality. I was very much interested in so-called modern art in the twenties," he claimed dyspeptically in an interview of 1986, "but my instruction in art history made me very suspicious of most of it."[5] While what Kirstein said about Alfred Barr Jr. may or may not be accurate, it seems to describe Kirstein's own attitudes in the 1920s:

> Alfred Barr had a peculiar attitude about art. . . . I never heard him make a qualitative judgment. He treated everything as if it were an ethnographical object. . . . He felt that freedom was the most important thing, and anybody could do what he liked . . . everything is equally interesting.[6]

Kirstein's strongest stance was the broad level of subject matter presented in the HSCA's exhibitions and in *Hound & Horn*, as well as his ability to synthesize and create a field or school by grouping works and bringing together various genres in one exhibition or in one edition of *Hound & Horn*. His "avid" curiosity drove him to search out the new during his undergraduate years at Harvard. While the HSCA was ostensibly founded to forward modern art, Kirstein later wrote:

For me this was rooted in what had been found viable in the last five hundred years. Similar siftings in my reading had launched Hound & Horn. . . . The Harvard Society was to prove a luxurious playpen laboratory in which I could make up my heated, but as yet still smouldering sense about the difference between "originality," "personality," and "quality," and whatever connected these in the present context.[7]

The Harvard Society for Contemporary Art

A dinner meeting at the house of Paul Sachs on December 12, 1928, led to the formal incorporation of the Harvard Society for Contemporary Art early in 1929.[8] Sachs was the linchpin of the HSCA. A Harvard graduate and assistant director of the Fogg since 1915, he taught the first museum course in America and through his family's major financial firm, Goldman Sachs in New York (in which he had been a partner), and their social connections, his students were able to visit many leading private collections. The director of the Fogg, Edward Waldo Forbes (a grandson of Ralph Waldo Emerson), gave the institution an aura of Brahmin New England. He established the conservation laboratory at the museum, and this structuralist approach, looking beneath the skin, did much to temper the museum's former compulsory aesthetic of Ruskinian and Paterian "appreciation."[9] Together, Sachs and Forbes dominated the Fogg and the museum world. The directors of the two important avant-garde museums were among their students; in fact, they were responsible for their appointments to these positions: A. Everett ("Chick") Austin to the Wadsworth Atheneum in 1928, and Alfred Barr to the Museum of Modern Art in 1929. Contemporary art has had a difficult history at Harvard, and was certainly not accepted into its curriculum of exhibitions in the 1920s, but Sachs and Forbes supported the HSCA as "an undergraduate effort toward an extension of art appreciation."[10]

In forming the society, Kirstein had two important collaborators: his classmates Edward M. Warburg, son of collector and banker Felix Warburg, who essentially provided the funding, and John Walker III, who later became director of the National Gallery in Washington. In Kirstein's words, Walker was "a rich boy from Pittsburgh. . . . He was welcome for the well-heeled social support he brought us."[11]

Although not officially involved, Agnes Mongan's contribution was considered by Kirstein to be equal to those of Warburg and Walker. A Bryn Mawr graduate only a few years older than the others, Mongan became cataloger of the prints and drawings collection belonging to Paul Sachs (with whom she studied at the Fogg) in the fall of 1928.[12] Her critical judgment was a significant factor, as was her ability to mediate between Sachs and Kirstein.

Kirstein has also described the role of two other collaborators:

Inconspicuous in the background were two young graduate students. Alfred Barr and Jere Abbott were my tutors junior- and senior-year. They shared an apartment . . . and were a mine of information about contemporary, modern and historic art. They had toured the Soviet Union, met Eisenstein, the great film innovator, considered cinema an art along with architecture and industrial design, as well as the new music, theatre, and dance. . . .

They reinforced our less-informed enthusiasms with pinpointed, wide-ranging data.

This implemented our program, suggesting prospective exhibitions. In return I think they learned something of the mechanics of obtaining loans and being polite to lenders. Within three years, they would jointly lead the new Museum of Modern Art. . . .[13]

Among supporters of the HSCA at the end of the first year were Philip Johnson, as well as Mrs. John D. Rockefeller Jr. and Lillie Bliss, both of whom were in the process of founding the Museum of Modern Art.[14] The purpose of the society, as announced, was "to hold exhibitions of contemporary painting, sculpture and decorative arts, which are frankly debatable."[15] Although its first exhibition was conservative, presenting the general tendencies of what Kirstein termed the older American "liberal tradition" (the school of Henri and Sloane), it was followed by "The School of Paris," "painters and sculptors who," they wrote, "have made the influence of 'Modern' art what it is today."[16] Along with the exhibitions American Cartoonists and *American Folk Painting*, the HSCA showed *International Photography*, *Contemporary Mexican Art*, *Contemporary German Art*, and Calder's Circus, as well as French, American, and other exhibitions (notably architecture—not yet in the realm of museums in America) that effectively set the precedent for the Museum of Modern Art.

The fourth show in May of 1929, titled "4D," was devoted to R. Buckminster Fuller's Dymaxion House,[17] an exhibition that brought Philip Johnson into Lincoln Kirstein's orbit.[18] The circle was beginning to be completed. About this time, Johnson met Alfred Barr through his sister, a student at Wellesley.[19] On Barr's recommendation, Johnson visited Dessau late in 1929, and was responsible for the Bauhaus exhibition, which he installed at the HSCA in December 1930. It continued through January 1931 and was a momentous event, marking the first time the Bauhaus was brought to

America. At the end of March 1931, the society held an exhibition of architecture and interiors, with models and photographs of works by Gropius, Howe and Lescaze, and Frank Lloyd Wright, among others.

Kirstein ran the HSCA alone for one year after graduation, leaving it in the hands of undergraduates until the enterprise ceased operation in 1934. Significantly, the network of collectors to whom Kirstein, Walker, and Warburg had access through Paul Sachs and their own family connections had made it relatively easy to schedule one good show after another. These collectors included Frank Crowninshield, Helen Frick, and the Samuel Lewisohns of New York, Frederick Clay Bartlett and the Art Institute of Chicago, the Carnegie Institute, and dealers such as Kurt Valentine and the Neumann and E. Wyhe Galleries.

Hound & Horn

Hound & Horn, founded in 1927 at the beginning of Kirstein's sophomore year, was his first initiative at Harvard. Devoted to arts and letters, the quarterly was to become a breeding ground for writers. Each issue contained important critical essays on literature, short stories, and poetry by those who were and would become leading figures. In fact, the list of authors reads like an index to a history of modern literature: James Agee, T. S. Eliot, Kay Boyle, William Carlos Williams, Marianne Moore, Ezra Pound, Erskine Caldwell, Katherine Anne Porter, e. e. cummings, Archibald MacLeish, Stephen Spender, Hart Crane, Sean O'Faolain, and Edmund Wilson, among others. Also included in each issue was a running commentary on advanced movements in music, architecture, art, drama, dance, and film. Lincoln Kirstein wrote recently, "perhaps there were not many other efforts of the epoch with as much gathered intelligence as our magazine."[20]

Hound & Horn continued publication for three years in Boston, and moved with Kirstein to New York for four more years. Its relatively long period of survival (in relation to the "little magazines" of the time) was due to its source of funding, Kirstein's father. Based on the British literary tradition,[21] T. S. Eliot's *Criterion* was its reference point,[22] but Kirstein also hoped to catch "the cachet of Marianne Moore's *The Dial*, then on its last legs."[23] The title of the journal came from Ezra Pound's poem, "The White Stag." Together with a quotation from an epitaph by Plato, the meaning of both was to be, according to the first issue:

> a valediction and a call to action. In the mood of Plato's distich it bids farewell to a land whose long familiar contours have ceased to stir creative thought: it bids farewell—and sounds the hunting horn.[24]

Pound and Eliot were early supporters and contributors, and according to Eliot, *Hound & Horn* had more vitality than any similar Oxbridge effort.[25] However, by 1930 they were distanced from the magazine.

Henry-Russell Hitchcock played an important role at *Hound & Horn*. His article "The Decline of Architecture," published in the first trial issue, encompassed many of its themes—the artist as individual, technics, and the importance of finding reference points from which to make value judgments. It was also a polemic against Surrealism: "We must accept all of technics; but we need not accept that technics are all."[26] Hitchcock argued that the choices to be made in designing buildings must be "entirely controlled by the consciousness of the designer . . . [so that the whole would be] intelligent and ordered."[27] Photographs of the Necco Factory in Cambridge, which Hitchcock called "the finest fragments of contemporary building," accompanied the article. They were by Jere Abbott, Kirstein's instructor in the fine arts department at Harvard, and Barr's roommate at Cambridge, who later became his associate at the Museum of Modern Art. In 1931, *Hound & Horn* published Abbott's diary of a trip to Russia with Barr.

Hitchcock was a continuing force at *Hound & Horn*. He wrote reviews of movie magazines, of Virginia Wolfe's *Orlando*, and among reviews of architecture presented a house designed by Peter van der Meulen Smith (another Harvardian), whom Hitchcock declared was "the first to develop an American version of what is . . . an international style."[28] Hitchcock would dedicate his 1929 publication, *Modern Architecture: Romanticism and Reintegration*, to Smith, who died in 1928; a year later Barr reviewed the book for *Hound & Horn*. In 1931 Hitchcock chronicled the Berlin Exposition of that year. When the magazine moved to New York in 1932, he wrote on Depression architecture, while another architectural critic, John Wheelright, reviewed Lewis Mumford's *Brown Decades*, and Harold Stern, a New York architect, reviewed Hitchcock and Johnson's International Style exhibition at the Museum of Modern Art.

Kirstein was the only continuous editor of the journal; nonetheless, its point of view was not constant: it changed as he progressed through his undergraduate years and with the succession of editors who joined him. Initially with Varian Fry, *Hound & Horn* was *A Harvard Miscellany*, "to provide, in a measure, a point of contact between Harvard and the contemporary outside world."[29]

For the third volume, published in 1929–30, Richard Blackmur, a Cambridge bookseller, and Bernard Bandler II, then a medical student, joined the editorial committee. In their commentary, they denied any special dogmas but took up the standard of technics announced in Hitchcock's earlier article, stating:

> A sound philosophy will not produce a great work of art and a great work of art is no guarantee that the ideas of the artist are sound. Consequently our standard for judging the arts is technical. We demand only that the work be well done.[30]

Dogma did appear. With the contribution of Eliot's essay "Second Thoughts About Humanism" in the spring of 1929, the magazine was obsessed with the subject for the next two years. In 1931 Kirstein became interested in Russia and communism, and subsequently in 1932–33 *Hound & Horn* was involved in a debate over class literature and communism. Sixty years later, Kirstein wrote that the magazine had been "completely taken over" by Blackmur upon the move to New York, and with the regional editors Alan Tate (in Kentucky), the Agrarians (in Nashville), and Yvor Winters (a neo-Classicist at Stanford) had become a "double-axis."[31] The year 1932–33 proved to be that of politics, of both the right and the left.[32] A statement of 1932 by editors Bandler, Kirstein, and A. Hyatt Mayor (later at the Metropolitan Museum of Art) reinforced the political:

> The early aestheticism is gone. More European writers of importance such as DuBos and Gilson are being introduced; more foreign books are being noticed in our reviews. The future will see an increase in our political scope.[33]

The end of 1933 saw a move away from politics. In April 1934 the great Henry James issue appeared. It was the penultimate issue of *Hound & Horn* to be published.

Chick Austin

Kirstein's circle rounds with Chick Austin, another Harvard classmate, whose watercolors were published by Kirstein in *Hound & Horn* and included in an exhibition mounted by the HSCA. In 1928, on the advice of Forbes and Sachs, Austin was appointed director of what was to be a renewed Wadsworth Atheneum.[34] Soon after his arrival at Hartford, Austin organized an exhibition of contemporary French and German furniture and decorative art. He reinstalled offices at the Atheneum with early Bauhaus-like walls of different colors and furniture and lighting fixtures by leading contemporary French and German designers. According to Hitchcock, these rooms were "among the very first modern work to be carried out with any thoroughness in America," together with Mies van der Rohe's New York apartment for Philip Johnson of 1930, and Richard Neutra's Lovell House of 1929 in Los Angeles.[35]

Chick Austin also made an important architectural contribution through his very active role in the design and construction of the Atheneum's Avery Memorial Wing in 1932–33, which "came precisely at the point in time generally accepted as representing the arrival of the European 'International Style'"[36] in the United States. Hitchcock claimed that this interior was one of the earliest modern museums, preceding by several years both the Boymans Museum in Rotterdam and the Museum of Modern Art in New York.

Austin was determined that the reputation of Hartford's artistic vitality would spread even to foreign cultural centers.[37] He achieved his goal through stylish panache—evident in the architecture of his house, which was modeled on a Palladian villa on the Brenta, with Piemontese and Bauhausian interiors,[38] in the museum balls with Venetian or Surrealist decor, and in notable productions in the new auditorium with sets he sponsored and helped to create, from Florine Stettheimer's sets for Virgil Thomson and Gertrude Stein's *Four Saints in Three Acts* to Calder's for *Socrate*. Austin made great acquisitions from all periods, from French eighteenth-century art to the Surrealists, mounting "Newer Super-Realism" in 1934, the first Surrealist exhibition in North America. He maintained active links with the Harvard group and with Kirstein through exhibitions he took from the HSCA, and it was he who brought Balanchine to America. He also remained close to Barr, Hitchcock, and Johnson at the Museum of Modern Art, bringing some of its exhibitions to Hartford.

The vitality of Kirstein's enterprise at Harvard represents a key moment in the history of the avant-garde in America. The various movements and events of the first quarter of the century, which had been engaged in revitalizing thought and art, found a consolidated center. This center was a major university, and without the intense concentration of intellectual inquiry, and without the network of students, graduates, and their families afforded by such an institution, as well as the extent of that network, tightly gridded in the Northeast but extending beyond, the Museum of Modern Art and the Hartford Atheneum would not have taken the form they did. Something would have happened, but something else.

JEFFREY KIPNIS

PHILIP JOHNSON

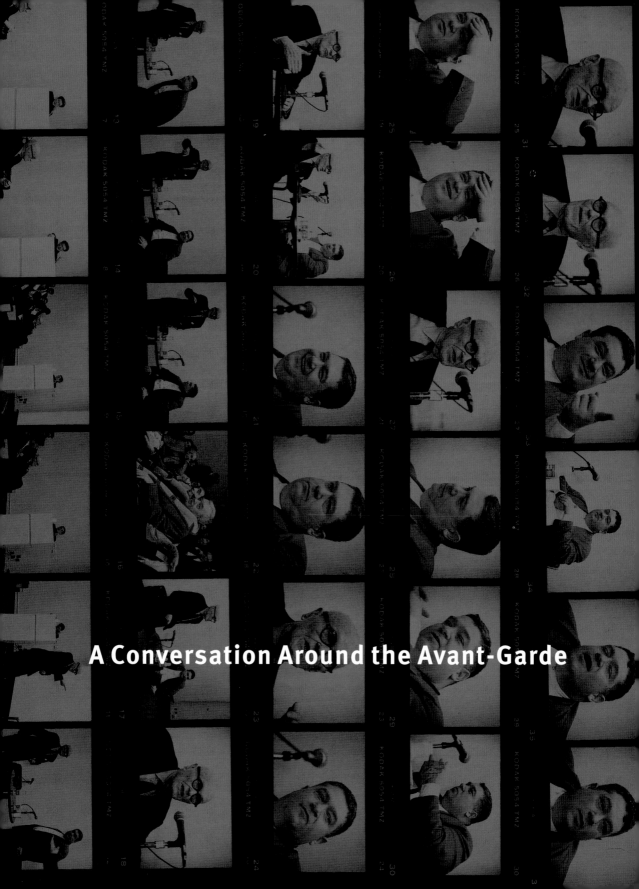

A Conversation Around the Avant-Garde

PHILIP JOHNSON   I must thank Phyllis Lambert for her kind introduction and congratulate her for her remarkable account of a major episode in the introduction of the avant-garde to the States. Of course, what stands as research material for Phyllis—all those names, dates, and locations—are, for me, memories. As I listened, her remarks felt to me like the teary-eyed beginning of an episode of *This is Your Life,* while to most in the audience, they must have seemed dry, obscure scholarship.

In any case, our subject tonight is the avant-garde. Now, I am not a scholar, not a historian, not an expert on the avant-garde as are many in the audience. Unlike them, I just happen to have been there when it happened, or at least when it got to the States. Now, that small advantage entitles me to a status that I have always yearned for, but that, until now, has eluded me. Because I was there, I can talk about things the experts do not know anything about, and they do not dare contradict me, whether I am right or wrong!

At one point, Phyllis mentioned the late Lincoln Kirstein, founder of the New York City Ballet and my lifelong friend. Lincoln once said that he thought the greatest catastrophe of twentieth-century culture was Alfred Barr, who, he believed, killed the authentic spirit of the culture by making it an emblem of money and society. Now, Barr, Jere Abbott, Chick Austin, myself, and a few others thought of ourselves as ardent enthusiasts, as sponsors of the avant-garde. We were proud to be avant-gardists; we wore our enthusiasm as a badge of honor that distinguished us as culturally superior to those around us.

In fact, we did not have the slightest idea what the avant-garde was. Nobody told us it was an intellectual and artistic movement devoted to revolution. I did not learn that it began with Baudelaire until the other night. At the Museum of Modern Art, we were ignorant of the political dimension of the art; for us it was revolutionary, but only aesthetically. Our job as we saw it was to advocate, to sell these new cultural innovations to the wealthy and powerful, to the Rockefellers and others. I must say that, if naive, our enthusiasm for the avant-garde was nevertheless real; we loved it, we never thought of ourselves as servants of the market system, the very system the work opposed. Though, of course, we were.

JEFFREY KIPNIS Today, as I mulled over this conference and our conversation, it hit me that what you and I have in common in this context is that both of us are profiteers on the avant-garde. Our friends and colleagues do experimental work, they tear their hair out and they sell their souls for it, then you and I package it and sell it. You to your corporate clients and I to my students and readers. Now, it seems you are saying that Alfred Barr was the same, that he and his friends from Harvard came to New York and commodified the avant-garde.

JOHNSON Yes, that is my point. We killed the avant-garde by making it a garde. The avant-garde cannot exist if it is a garde; it cannot exist apart from comedians and mountebanks and poets; it cannot thrive as a hobby of the bourgeoisie.

KIPNIS Why do you think it was such a popular product? I mean, why do you think it worked so well in the social and the intellectual circles of New York? Why did an idea of the avant-garde and certain samples of painting and architecture enable such an institution as the Museum of Modern Art? What was it that fascinated everyone about the avant-garde?

JOHNSON I hope you can answer your own questions, because I cannot. All of us were convinced that we were inventing a new world. For us, the term *avant-garde* was a blanket term for anything new and different. But why our efforts were so successful—I have no idea.

KIPNIS Was it possible that in your hands the avant-garde turned into fashion?

JOHNSON Yes, and in keeping with that idea, it is important to note that we tended toward safer work. I loved Klee, who at that time was not much appreciated, particularly at Harvard. But actually there was nothing very difficult about his work. So we were lucky. We could call our interests avant-garde and pride ourselves on our cutting-edge tastes and still play it safe. We knew damn well that established figures such as Cézanne and Degas were rather good painters, you see. But there was not such a gap between those established painters and the so-called radical work we admired.

43

Alfred Barr took great pride when none of the faculty at Harvard were able to comment on his thesis on Picasso. They simply did not know who Picasso was! Nevertheless, even at the time, Picasso was a fairly safe bet. And after all, these figures had already been introduced to the U.S. at the Armory show, at Stieglitz's gallery, and elsewhere. We just brought them to new circles, first to academia, then to New York society.

KIPNIS   Was it your idea to extend the search for the avant-garde to architecture?

JOHNSON   No, it was Alfred's. He included architecture, film, the theater, every facet of the unfolding of modernity. I knew nothing about architecture at all. He said to me, "That's all right, Philip, you will." And he was right.

KIPNIS   He sent you to Dessau?

JOHNSON   Yes. Barr was fascinated by the Bauhaus, which he considered the first avant-garde institution in the world.

KIPNIS   And upon arriving there did you detect a revolutionary sensibility?

JOHNSON   What a dumb question. When I arrived, I met amazing people, geniuses, and saw incredible work. I was intoxicated, overwhelmed. I did not "detect" anything. In fact, though I loved what I saw, I did not understand any of it, particularly in polemical terms. Sure, everyone at the Bauhaus, everyone everywhere at the time, the Germans, Corb, everyone argued that modern art and architecture would make the world a better place, that, so to speak, one would become a better person living in a glass house. I can testify it ain't true.

KIPNIS   Really? I thought you would testify that it was true.

JOHNSON   I wish. But it did not improve my temper, my thoughts and opinions, or my sense of social responsibility. All it did was make me more famous. Even if there were a social or political revolutionary zeal associated with the avant-garde at the Bauhaus,

I do not think I ever cared about it. Or let me put it this way: I always thought the visual revolution was more interesting and infinitely more important.

KIPNIS   It seems to me that there is an irresolvable conflict in the structure of any avant-garde. On the one hand, it must embrace in some sense the forces of disestablishment, mechanization, markets, etc., i.e., the forces that overturn traditional forms of authority. On the other hand, a true avant-garde must propose new forms of authority that resist those same forces.

JOHNSON   That's right.

KIPNIS   And therefore, an avant-gardist is trapped in the conflict of having to associate with disestablishment and resist it at the same time.

JOHNSON   I understand your point; that is why there is no longer any authentic avant-garde. But at the time, that conflict posed no difficulty for us. Alfred Barr firmly believed that virtue was on his side, and therefore that God was on his side. It helped to have God working with you. So that apparent contradiction was swept aside along with everything else in Barr's way.

By a stroke of luck, Alfred met the Rockefellers and started the Museum of Modern Art from nothing. I mean, talk about luck. To find somebody willing and able to finance such a wild idea as the Museum of Modern Art, to give it blue-ribbon authority, to turn it into a propaganda machine. It was opportunity given to very few and successfully carried out by fewer still. In some sense, the history of the avant-garde in the U.S. is a history of Barr's ego, his will.

It felt to all of us as if we had a calling. One must remember that Alfred was a preacher's son, and I was a Calvinist at heart. Such fervent devotion and commitment to improvement was in the American grain. For us, art was perfect. It was a virtue, just like religion. And we were the elect.

KIPNIS   How would you compare that sensibility to attitudes today?

JOHNSON Well, my answer is very simple. Today, there is no such thing as the avant-garde; it is not even a possibility. The Duchamps and the Kieslers ended a long line of sincere revolutionaries. Duchamp kept his last works secret, and Kiesler, today a mere footnote, spent much of his energy attacking us at the museum. These were the last true spirits of the avant-garde, the last true revolutionaries. But you see, the true avant-garde is never very good at selling things.

KIPNIS You are talking about a dialectical avant-garde, a revolutionary avant-garde that is seeking to overturn one authority and replace it with a new authority.

JOHNSON Yes, that is the only true avant-garde.

KIPNIS There are those who claim to represent a new, contemporary avant-garde. But these artists operate very differently. They do not seek to overturn dominant practices and institutions; rather, they seek to infiltrate and destabilize them. You have been implicated in such efforts in architecture, by organizing the deconstructivist show and by your patronage of certain kinds of architecture, even experimenting with their ideas in your own work.

JOHNSON I never was a member of the avant-garde. I was always a member of the upper class, a bourgeois if there ever was one, and content as such. No, I am just addicted to the new; it helps me fight the interminable boredom of bourgeois culture. Robert Hughes and Harold Rosenberg were right, the avant-garde gave way to the shock of the new, to the tradition of the new. Some critics call my fascination with new architecture flippant, lightweight. I get the point. But it just expresses my desire to be different, to see different things and yet to stay perfectly centered within the system. I am not out to change anything. I am just fighting off boredom.

For instance, I have just built that crazy building out in the country, the Gate House, you know the red one that goes waving in the breeze? The building is entirely rear-garde, harkening back to German expressionism. But to me it is something novel. What was the avant-garde has become a frantic search for novelty.

KIPNIS When we say the avant-garde is dead and all we have left is fashion, we imply that fashion is without substance, a trivial and destitute consequence of commodification lacking the depth of a true avant-garde. I think differently. I think we should revisit the question of fashion with the same respect that we pay the question of the avant-garde. To state it more forcefully, I think that the arts as a historicized cultural practice have never been anything other than fashions. The problem, therefore, is not the loss of the depth of the avant-garde, but the failure to recognize that that illusion of depth merely disguised the mechanisms of fashion. If it is true that the avant-garde is dead, then what provides the impetus for novelty, or for any resistance to dominant modes of practice?

JOHNSON A desire to be famous, and a hatred of boredom. Period.

A Conversation
Around the
Avant-Garde

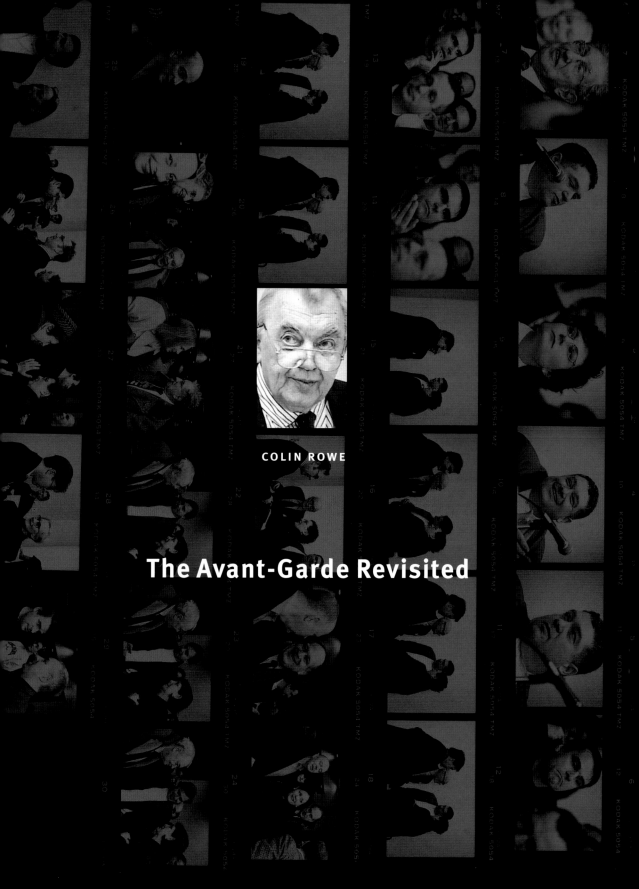

COLIN ROWE

The Avant-Garde Revisited

Precis of Approximate Intentions

The analysis of three crucial statements by Mies van der Rohe reveals a philosophical evolution that, in the end, is intrinsically critical of the topic of this colloquium. It discloses an ultimately Catholic and Thomistic mental formation that is, probably, incompatible with what *seems* to be the ethos of the avant-garde.

The notion of the avant-garde involves a conception of time and history that, to me, can only be problematic.

It, apparently, presumes the following: *that* the future course of time and history may be predicted; *that* the present is pregnant with the future—irrespective of human intervention; *that* this embryo already reveals sufficient genetic characteristics to permit identification of its future shape and growth; *that,* therefore, it must be the purpose of persons of intelligence, perception, and good will to assist in this impending delivery; *that,* as cultural obstetricians—and true professionals—these must then not become unduly fixated on the offspring recently admitted into the world; *that,* again and again, they must be prepared to repeat the process; *that,* only by their becoming so involved in the creative unrolling of time, can the ultimate stimulus, rapture, and happiness of humankind be assured. This, no doubt, is a case of the "modern marvelous."

This bundle of fantasies is so wholly extraordinary that it escapes general notice. It is so firmly established in the general consciousness, so much a convention of causal thought, that it has come to appear as no more than a normative emanation of collective wisdom. Yet at all points, it is disputable.

The essential problem that it presents was articulated with great distinctness by the Nobel Prize–winning biologist Peter Medawar. In his book, *The Art of the Soluble* (1967), he writes:

> What we want to know about the science of the future is the content and character of future scientific theories and ideas. Unfortunately, it is impossible to predict new ideas—the ideas people are going to have in ten years' time or in ten minutes' time—and we are caught in a logical paradox the moment we try to do so. For to predict an idea is to have an idea, and if we have an idea, it can no longer be the subject of a prediction. [1]

This would seem to be logically unfaultable; but such an impeccable logic need not, of course, have any practical effect.

Indeed our bundle of fantasies is strangely impenetrable by any logical critique.

No doubt the bias it ultimately discloses is naturalistic and materialist; *no doubt* the less conscious representatives of these sentiments prefer to think of knowledge as a *growth* rather than a succession of *interventions; no doubt* they tacitly subscribe to the notion that change—of mind—is to occur independent of any agency—of mind; *no doubt* one of their leading ideas is the idea that ideas, in themselves, can have no effect on the structure of the future; and critical of these positions is Medawar's laconic statement: "*It is impossible to predict new ideas. . . .*"

So very obviously, here one may be reminded of Bertrand Russell's "*What's mind? No matter. What's matter? Never mind.*"

But, to the naive and the impatient, what are all these distinctions about anyway? And really, *why* worry? For immediately ahead lies the romantic allure of intellectual heroics, of confidence in forming one of a select company, of a *corps d'elite* gifted beyond the norms of humanity and endowed with intuitions so dazzling that fame will not be able to refuse its salute.

Of French military origin, demilitarized during the after-events of 1789, the term *avant-garde* acquired valuable critical allies in the course of the nineteenth century. It became, most profitably, engaged with the suddenly powerful idea of *the spirit of the age;* and in this way, the marriage of an old French military term with the Hegelian concept of the zeitgeist (or was this a *liaison dangereuse*?) became, for the arts, the progenitor of a very noisy infant, born—perhaps—about 1890.

Apparently a healthy child, in its younger years, it was not uncreative.

But the infant was never an entirely innocent cultural playmate; and as time wore on, its talk scarcely came to serve as an eligible gambit of social chitchat. Nor, at more than a hundred years old, can this senile relic any longer be considered an item of intellectual *chic.*

Now my own pronounced distaste for this particular family of the mind (which has many outward charms) need not, I think, inhibit me from a cursory exploration of what I suppose to be its dubieties, or from gossip about its legitimacy. For if one is to desist from talk about *everything* one finds dis-

tasteful, dubious, or illegitimate, then conversation can only shrivel and its pleasures become *very* restricted indeed!

I

In Philip Johnson's book on Mies van der Rohe—still, I think, the best book on Mies (I possess it in the editions of 1947 and 1978)—Philip publishes three statements by Mies that, in themselves *and* as a sequence, for me, have been fraught with significance ever since my long-ago sojourn in Texas. These are statements of 1923, 1930, and 1938.

The first, 1923, is that famous definition of architecture as:

> the will of the epoch translated into space, living, changing, new.

This is a Hegelian definition. Present in the world there is an active zeitgeist or *Kunstwoll,* a "spirit of the age," an immanent spirit or "will" that breathes and must impose itself. An emanation of the historical process, this "spirit" acts to articulate important building that, therefore, is *necessarily* of *historical* significance.

The second, 1930, is not quite so famous; and it stipulates a more strenuous predicament for the architect:

> The new era is a fact: it exists, irrespective of our "yes" or "no." Yet it is neither better nor worse than any other era. It is pure datum, in itself without value content. Therefore I will not try to define it or clarify its basic structure. Let us not give undue importance to mechanization or standardization.

> Let us accept changed economic and social conditions as a fact.
> All these take their blind and fateful course.

One thing will be decisive: the way we assert ourselves in the face of circumstance. Here the problems of the spirit begin.

This is a distinctly different estimation of the architect's problem; and in the end, it is scarcely a Hegelian estimation. The "era" or the "epoch" or the "time" has been rendered neutral. It has become no more than a "fact," and it is now, in the architect's mode of reaction to "circumstance," that true "value" is presumed to reside. An apparent *determinism* has been set aside in favor of what would seem to be *free will*.

The third statement, 1938, while it admits that "we are dependent on the spirit of our time," further tends, I think, to diminish the influence of this "spirit." This statement is "concerned not only with practical goals but also with values":

> By our practical aims we are bound to the specific structure of our epoch. Our values, on the other hand, are rooted in the spiritual nature of men. . . .
> Human existence is predicated on the two spheres together. Our aims assure us of our material life, our values make possible our spiritual life.[2]

Decidedly there has been a development— since 1923 or even 1930; and the Hegelian influence seems to have languished. Nor has Hegel's progressive dialectic of "spirit" given way to a progressive Marxian dialectic of whatever-it-might-be. We are now presented with the opposition of "practical aims" (the "fact" of 1930) and "values . . . rooted in the

spiritual nature of men" (in 1930 "the way we assert ourselves in the face of circumstance"). Indeed we are, almost, confronted with the opposition between something that is ever mobile, always changing, and a something else that is ever static, always the same, immutable and inaccessible to change.

Almost but not quite . . .

Now this new condition that—again almost—predicates an argument between the "dynamic" and the "static" (with Mies as spokesman for the "static") was incipient in the pronouncement of 1930. In 1930 the "epoch" had been awarded a more-or-less neutral— though of course an active—status; and this continues to be the perception of 1938. But *in 1938,* the contrary assertion of "value"—one might say—has become more institutionalized and obtrusive. In 1930, its assertion was by way of being a "voluntary" act; but in 1938, it seems to have become much more of a duty.

Thus in 1938, with the *corsivo*—the ephemeral, the current, the contingent—now contrasted with, almost, a version of the eternally "valid," Mies had made public a momentous decision, perhaps the underpinning of his final position. Had he opted for something like *natural law* theory—with all its consequences? Was the "spirit" of the "law" now to be invoked as a checkmate to the "spirit" of the "age"?

It would seem so. And I believe that my friend Paolo Berdini, who nowadays teaches a seminar on Mies at Stanford, would be likely to say *something* like this. And since Paolo's family has been lawyers to the Holy See for longer than he cares to remember (himself is a godson of Pope Pacelli), I know that he would go on for quite a long time. I'd get a recitation about Plato, Aristotle, St. Thomas Aquinas, the entire juristic tradition, Grotius, Montesquieu, and what all; while

Paolo—always very skeptical and very perceptive—might feel able to add a few words about Mies's withdrawal from Hegel. He might suggest (I know he would) that the zeitgeist is not exclusively a liberal entity, that it is *without* ethical content, that it is unmanageable, that if the zeitgeist of 1923 could seem to sponsor the Weimar Republic and an architecture of modern sentiment, then, and not so much later, it could equally seem to sponsor the Third Reich and—ultimately—the architecture of Albert Speer.

So I would agree with Paolo's interpretation of *natural law* theory and its descent to us from Plato through St. Thomas, etc.; and Philip also tells us about Mies and St. Thomas: "In philosophy . . . he never digressed from Aquinas" (207). And if so much for the manifesto of 1938, then what about the free-will dilemma of 1930? Should we relate it to St. Augustine?

Of course, my own knowledge of St. Augustine is pretty dim (like Philip I am an intellectual lightweight); but what little I know derives from a very respectable source. In an attempt at my conversion (not very probable), the Catholic chaplain at the University of Cambridge, Monsignor Gilbey of Gilbey's gin, expounded the Augustinian philosophy; and thus it is that, when I buy gin (which is not very often), in spite of advertisements for alternatives I remain loyal to Monsignor and to his family outfit. But as for the rest of it, I don't remember very much. Monsignor was anti-Hegel. That was evident; and in this context, though I don't recall chapter and verse, I do recall some picture of Augustine's

ethical resistance to the idea of an implacable course of events: we cannot lament "bad" times, "corrupt" times, "evil" times because *we* are the times.

And then, again from Philip, from Mies in 1938, there are the concluding words of his address:

> We want no more; we can do no more.
> Nothing can express the aim and meaning of our work better than the profound words of St. Augustine:
> "Beauty is the splendour of Truth" (200).

It was clever of Philip to present all of these statements, and for this, we should be grateful, because I don't know that other expositors of Mies have made any big issue out of this *matériel*. But whether no more than a sophisticated apologia of the "Western" tradition, or whether the ensuing developments in building can be *claimed* to be avant-garde, there is no doubt *that* the bias of his 1938 position—*doctrines of natural law tend to associate themselves with doctrines of classicism*—was pretty crucial for quite a few architects in the United States.[3]

So doctrines of natural law may be among the props of a particular ecclesiastical hegemony; but I *can't* suppose that—whatever their condition of awareness—this was ever a particularly big deal with the average member of the A.I.A. I *can't* suppose that they ever *did* grab this sort of thing. And there *was* no reason why they should. For as long as this country is equipped with all the apparatus of what Mies called "*fact*" or "*circumstance*" with which "*practical aims*" are concerned, then in terms of simple pragmatics, there could be no resistance to his argument; and when Mies talked of "values . . . rooted in the spiritual nature of men," there was surely nobody in their right mind who could raise a flicker of objection.

So does it sound like "*family values*" and the frenzies of fundamentalist Christianity? Of course, the atemporal values of an almost Platonic idea may always be corrupted in the vulgar service of special interest. But neither in thought nor execution was Mies a *vulgarisateur;* and *his* "values . . . rooted in the spiritual nature of men" are very far away from the horrors of "the religious right." Catholic values of the Roman church though they are, they are also not remote from the secular and Enlightenment values of the American political settlement, and in this refined construction there is *vox populi,* quite properly the voice of "*contingency*" and what, in Italian terms, I have called the *corsivo;* and then, there is that countervailing power expressed and reexpressed in eighteenth-century manifesto and in the inspired statements of the juristic tradition.

For instance:
We believe these truths to be self evident . . . life, liberty, and the pursuit of happiness.
Inference: the empirical world may be subject to fluctuation, but beyond this flux, there *are* these principles. And a version of much the same:
this is a government of laws not men.
Inference: humanity *will* change its habits/predilections, but outside the casual "*accidents*" of everyday life, there exists "*the law*," subject to interpretation but, *in its essence,* impervious to *any* empirical exigency.

I am sorry to be inflicting upon you what might seem to be an elementary lesson in civics and only talking about buildings very remotely—in terms of their possible iconography. But ever since my time in Texas—*readin' Tocqueville in Texas*—Miesian statements as published by Philip have led me to interpret Mies in these terms. Something in Texas—I hate to call it *the genius of the place*—but something (perhaps close to Lampasas or New Braunfels) has conspired with something else (perhaps with the image of the Texas courthouse town) to deprive me of the modern architect's conventional belief in "the spirit of the age."[4] And this loss of primal innocence has been further abetted by subsequent exposure to the messages of Ernst Gombrich, to his friend and mentor, Karl Popper, to Isaiah Berlin, et al.

It is for this reason that I have long envisaged a multiplicity of spirits or *Geisten*—all of them active in the architect's fantasy life, and with comments, I will offer a little list.

- *The Zeitgeist, the spirit of the age,*
though damaged by the anxiety of libertarians this is proving surprisingly durable; as an object of devotion it is a direct ancestor of the "spirit" of the avantgarde; before the days of *Sturm und Drang* it was less active; it was known to Christopher Wren, for instance, as the "*the gust of the age*"—with *gust* enjoying the connotations of Italian *gusto* and French *gout;* in this less imperious phase of its life it enjoyed a useful though limited power, and as its present prestige *must* become attenuated, one may hope that it will continue to survive in this less elevated status.
- *The Genius Loci, the spirit of the place,*
experienced by myself in Texas and often encountered in Italy, workshop of this quasi divinity is, as of now, on the increase; it is practiced by ecologists and "contextualists"; while the *persona* of the zeitgeist is decidedly *macho,* the genius loci is of a more *feminine* disposition; proponents of the zeitgeist are apt to resent devotees of the genius loci; these are little concerned with "the creative unrolling of *time,*" they

are more preoccupied with a protracted elucidation of *space*.

- *The Volksgeist, the spirit of the folk, the people, and—at worst—the spirit of the race,*
a popular spirit with, often, pleasant vernacular manners; the *Volksgeist* may coexist with both the zeitgeist and the genius loci, and in both cases, the results of this cohabitation may be felicitous; however, the *Volksgeist,* unadulterated and alone, may indulge in activities of dubious reputation; unchecked by the zeitgeist, the spirit of the people may seek satisfactions in the most deplorable kitsch, and sometimes—*even associated with the zeitgeist*—the *Volksgeist* may indulge in sadistic atrocity; the *Volksgeist* is easily perverted—Disneyland *and* "ethnic cleansing" are both among its not quite legitimate offspring; the Volkswagen was a primitive attempt to propitiate this sometimes-affable, sometimes-incorrigible quasi divinity.

- *The Spirit of the Law—not quite the same as Montesquieu's Esprit des Lois* (1738?),
lawyers talk about it; they distinguish between this "spirit" and its *Doppelganger,* the "letter"; jurists worship it—and one may think of Mr. Justice Brandeis and his dictum "*the irresistible is often that which is not resisted*"; devotees of the zeitgeist avoid its presence—they consider it predisposed to casuistical performance; with the exception of Mies van der Rohe (who worshipped it in secret), architects of a modern formation find it tough to take and don't erect new temples to its cult; but as noticed, it is a very American semigoddess and it is a pity to see *her* (*blind* justice is always a *she*) so very largely neglected; more verbal and self-conscious than the other three spirits, her con-

versation is very often both instructive and entertaining; St. Paul (who didn't like women) gave her a backhanded compliment when he said "The law came in that the offense might abound"; Dominick La Capra, former colleague of mine at Cornell and former student of Levi-Strauss at the Ecole Supérieure, seems to be indulging a not-so-surreptitious flirtation with this *esprit* when he writes that modern culture and society have been preoccupied with the:

> relationship between the exception and the rule or, in other words, the relation between transgression and normative commitment;[5]

did Sebastiano Serlio, also concerned with norm and transgression, mean something like this when he wrote in the sixteenth century "*by a mistake, then, I mean to do contrary to the precepts of Vitruvius*"?
I think he did; and if the zeitgeist might be the presiding genius of expressionist excess, the "*spirit of the law*"—involving the opposition of the licit and the licentious—is at least something to think about. Is it the "structure" which seems to be invoked when Levi-Strauss speaks of "the precarious balance between structure and event"?[6]
For Le Corbusier, *l'esprit des lois*—the general that illuminates the particular (that validates it?)—was constituted by Maison Dom-ino, *les quatres compositions,* etc.; and unlike St. Paul, *he* got his kicks out of the abundance of "the offense." But like the mythical and law-abiding "good German," Mies van der Rohe was just not able to cope with vivacious disquisitions on one "sin" after another.

So these are my four "spirits" and of their intrinsic nature, *all* of them are *fictions*. And there may be others; but for the architect—and also for the years 1923 to 1949—these were surely the most active. From my conspectus of spirits I have excluded two candidates: the *Holy Spirit* of Christian apologetics, the *Heilige Geist* or the *Santo Spirito, not* because I am unprepared to "deconstruct" the *persona* of the Holy Ghost but because—right now—I don't think this would be a very opportune undertaking.

And, then, I have excluded the concept of any possible *spirit of science. This* because, though science is "*soft*" on "*the spirit of the law,*" true science has never been subservient to zeitgeist, genius loci, or *Volksgeist.* It has never been subverted by fantasies quite so provincial—in terms of time, space, *or* ethnicity. Nor—to science—can the term *avant-garde* be applied!

So Einstein was an *avant-garde* scientist? Forget it!

So Galileo and Newton were exponents of baroque science? If it seems ludicrous to accuse Descartes or Lord Shaftesbury of baroque metaphysics (*I'm living in the seventeenth century and there's no other way. I must perform according to the tenets of the Baroque*), then it can *only* seem intellectually depraved to tell the same story about Newton and Galileo.

Yes! The concepts of baroque, mannerism, romantic classicism, Biedermeier, and what-all, *may—up to a point*—be convenient equipment to have around, and one must be thankful to an art historical descent from Hegel for their existence. But when *abstract* concepts become *concrete* substance, when retrospective formulations become equipped with prospective capacity, when a posteriori analysis becomes the instrument of a priori speculation, when inevitable zeitgeist—ever renewing and always comprehensible—

becomes a means of ascertaining the shape of the future, when the metaphorical becomes the literal,[7] then *the cheerful exercise of engaging fantasy*—what is *innocent* in this mental condition—becomes *frightening*.

This is the route *Hegel-Marx-Marinetti-Mussolini*—the great *degringolade;* and as we *know,* it *might* take us to places *far* worse than Benito Mussolini could *ever* have thought about. For are we not aware of the story? The zeitgeist is endowed with predictive power; *The Decline of the West* (Oswald Spengler) is imminent; bourgeois society is a stinking mess; humanity is alienated. *But* with a little help from ourselves, the imperative zeitgeist will change *all* this. Therefore don't talk to us about constructive amelioration (*a liberal capitalist trap*) and *don't* talk to us about *any* rule of "law." That kind of talk is no more than the camouflage of special interests, and the zeitgeist—*in itself*—carries ethical content *quite* enough. So let's assume a heroic posture; let's ride the surf of the invincible; if what-is-to-be is to be, then let's get on with it quick.

At the beginning of this century, *this* was the ethical content of Italian futurism; and in societies less skeptical, more prone to excitement, less politically sophisticated, perhaps more intellectual than our own, we *do* know to what destinations this sort of talk has led. Take a quantity of zeitgeist, an equal quantity of *Volksgeist,* heat in a very hot oven, and—*as in that charming futurist cookbook*—meditate upon the achievement. But *get* away from Milan and all that *fa figura* stuff, and *what* sort of cooking is the *unmediated composite* of these ingredients going to lead to? *As in the Germanic lands, 1933 to 1945 (well within our period),* it is going to make that futurist cookbook look *awful* good.

Mr. Justice Brandeis—"the irresistible is often that which is not resisted"—*had* his forebodings.

II

But possibly, Mr. Justice Brandeis was too uptight. Perhaps he was too concerned about the potential coerciveness of what is alleged to be irresistible; and maybe there was no need to infer—as he seems to have done—that a principle of resistance might not be exercised. But in those parts of the world where the English language is the principal vehicle of communication, *should* this be necessary? For at least the English themselves have always shown a quite superb capacity to receive almost all ideas (no doubt including even the zeitgeist) with what Edmund Burke designated (and recommended) as "salutary neglect,"[8] and to consult Matthew Arnold:

> In truth, the English, profoundly as they
> have modified the old Middle-Age order,
> great as is the liberty which they have
> secured for themselves, have in all their
> changes proceeded, to use a familiar ex-
> pression, by the rule of thumb; what was
> intolerably inconvenient to them they have
> suppressed, and as they have suppressed
> it, not because it was irrational, but be-
> cause it was practically inconvenient, they
> have seldom in suppressing it, appealed
> to reason, but always, if possible, to some
> precedent, or form, or letter which served as
> a convenient instrument for their purpose,
> and which saved them from the necessity
> of recurring to general principles. They
> have thus become, in a certain sense, of all
> people the most inaccessible to ideas and
> the most impatient of them; inaccessible to
> them, because of their want of familiarity
> with them; and impatient of them because

> they have got on so well without them, that they
> despise those who, not having got on as well as
> themselves, still make a fuss for what themselves
> have done so well without.[9]

It was in such terms that Matthew Arnold (1822–86) enlivened critical discourse in England during the 1860s; and another specimen of this same style might just be permissible:

> Let us have a social movement, let us organize and
> combine a party to pursue truth and new thought,
> let us call it *the liberal party,* and let us all stick to
> each other, and back each other up. Let us have no
> nonsense about independent criticism, and intellec-
> tual delicacy, and the few and the many. Don't let us
> trouble ourselves about foreign thought; we shall
> invent the whole thing for ourselves as we go along.
> If one of us speaks well, applaud him; if one of us
> speaks ill, applaud him too; we are all in the same
> movement, we are all liberals, we are all in pursuit
> of truth. In this way the pursuit of truth becomes a
> social, practical, pleasurable affair, almost requiring
> a chairman, a secretary, and advertisements; with
> the excitement of an occasional scandal, with a little
> resistance to give the happy sense of difficulty
> overcome; but, in general, plenty of bustle and very
> little thought. To act is so easy, as Goethe says;
> to think is so hard!

And thus, in England, the fate of any idea, even the zeitgeist, will be neutralized; the zeitgeist will be disinfected of its possible virulence; it will become a tractable, ingratiating domestic pet; it will become the dear, sweet, funny, caressable, little old zeitgeist. In the end it will become an alibi for the architect's reluctance to be found talking in terms of *style* and *taste*. For if this kind of talk (about taste) is surrounded today by rigid taboos, the architect must still find *some* way of condemning what he doesn't like. But you don't have to be so alarmed by zeitgeist-ian probabilities as was Mr. Justice Brandeis. You just have to send the zeitgeist to London and *that* should be quite enough. Perhaps an enormous loss? Perhaps an enormous gain?

So Alexis de Tocqueville tells us that, in the United States, there is to be found a greater aptitude for general ideas than in the United Kingdom—a proposition that has almost become a platitude.[10] And of course, he was "right"; Tocqueville always was; and without any doubt, the reason for the prevalence, and the prominence, of—at least—*some* general ideas in the United States should not be too far to seek. It was the need to apologize for a revolution: a need that the English have not, as yet, experienced.

So what might be the mode of existence of an avant-garde in the United States? I can only think that, *when all the chips are down,* in spite of American partiality for ideas, it might be much the same as in England. Immediately though, in specific localities, an avant-garde might flourish as extravagant growth. Its existence might seem to concur with a populist and naively futurist interest in mobility and dynamic. Its style of life might acquire a somewhat science-fiction dimension; but as special interests are aroused, it might begin to find itself caught in a remorseless critical cross fire, with the terrain it seeks to occupy having become an enormous Bosnia-Herzegovina of the mind. Not able to assume a public role, with its private extravagance disclosed, its inherent imposture revealed, one

may easily imagine—for better or worse—the fate of any avant-garde in our society: its demolition would become the job of ever so many intelligent critical reviews—both academic and otherwise.

Privately, of course, as in England, a large residue of sentimentality will enjoy a favorite, self-styled avant-garde, that is, when reduced to the status of a pampered domestic animal—a good-quality, nice, little Siamese kitten; and thus, publicly, it will always be tolerated—another case of "salutary neglect." But all the same, as it becomes commercialized for the purpose of the market, for the excitement of its novelties, any avant-garde will become progressively debauched, simultaneously both spurious and impotent.

III

No! To talk about the *necessity* of an American avant-garde can scarcely be advisable, indeed can only be painful, can only hurt far too much. And to consider our present predicament, we are participating in a happily bizarre American anomaly. Without undue concern for the dilemma in which we find ourselves located, we are sitting at a *retro*spective, historicist colloquium on a "movement" or "movements" that, ostensibly, addressed itself or themselves to the "exigencies" of the future, to *pro*spective probabilities! But, apart from this diversionary aspect of the occasion and far more important to consider, is *that*—because of the constitution of our society—the life style of an avant-garde in the United States can only be as hopeful as the life style of a snowball in hell.

So do *try* to forget about the *necessity* of an American avant-garde. Talk rather about the *impossibility* of *any* avant-garde—either in the United States *or* in Western Europe. And also, do try *not* to lament this impossibility. Just allow your "hopes" to be blighted—it may not be, *altogether,* a bad thing. And instead, begin to talk—if you can bear it—about some *rappel à l' ordre,* about the possible constitution of some new context of valuation within which authentic novelty (perhaps subversive novelty) may, once more, become capable of insinuating itself into an always resistant social fabric.

Such, I suppose, is the condition that we all seek. And *such* is to posit our problem. Not, I think, to be solved by the antics of a romantic intellectuality; not to be solved by a historical anthology of the deeds (or to be avant-garde, should I say the *faits et gestes*?), however splendid, of particular persons, in particular places—and, all these, now more than fifty years ago. . . .

And, by a *rappel à l' ordre,* I don't imply an exercise of censorship and repression. I merely propose this *rappel* to be directed toward the possible establishment of some modest critical structure in which both the licit and the illicit alike may enjoy useful coexistence.

Too much to hope for? I rather fear it is. Like so many others, I found Ayn Rand's *The Fountainhead* to be a grotesque document. But though based upon a popular misconception of the mystique of Frank Lloyd Wright, I now begin to think that Rand surmised better than she knew. I seem to remember that (Republican politics apart) she implied a desirable situation of "total" freedom—no restrictions, no limitations, no holds barred; it was an illusory world without confines, without parameters, without social contract; and it is into this world that I am distressed to discover so many tem-

peraments related to architectural talent (secret Ayn Randians?) anxious to move—if not already *there* located.

Now, it is hard to comprehend such ambition—or such established residence. For if there are any lessons to be derived from the history of architecture (and I am perfectly willing to concede that—to protagonists of invincible ignorance—there may be none), it is the doctrine that *art languishes in freedom and flourishes in restriction.* This is, almost, a transcription of a statement by Leonardo; presumably it would have engaged Michelangelo's assent; and almost in our own time, though differently stipulated, it was a supposition of this kind that inspired the otherwise very different "genius" of Le Corbusier and Mies van der Rohe. And this is all that my *rappel à l' ordre* is about: how to affirm the checks that are as necessary to the balance of creativity as they are to the balance of the political process.

Very hard!—and not at all concerned with right-wing frenzy; I don't propose to push this how-to-do-it issue very much. I can't believe that technology is check enough: if, indeed, check at all. And then, what about those related groupings of ideas to be comprehended under the approximate titles: semiotics, structuralism, deconstruction? More hopeful are these, I think; but here, there is another problem to be noticed. For it is only too apparent that these groupings of ideas concerned with words are already beginning to serve as the cookbooks for a fashionable architectural *nouvelle cuisine à l' americaine*—appearance ever more mortified, exegesis ever more *recherché.*

But *all* those words! *All* that analysis become so hideously arcane! Is it not as though the word itself has detached itself from any physical reference to assume a quite appalling life of its own? Is it not become painfully detached from what it is alleged to be

59

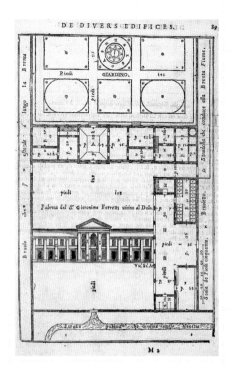

The Lord, in his infinite mercy, should remove the temptation from us; but in the face of so many American academics (those involved with the arts and the humanities), in the face of their continuing obsession with the words of Jacques Derrida (so different from the Word of St. John), I doubt whether even himself now enjoys the ability.

So the immediate prospect? Or *an* immediate prospect? As the current intellectualism *à la mode* begins to elicit disgust, as the separation between Word and flesh becomes institutionalized (and this seems to be threatened by the so *many* courses related to the "theory" of architecture that are said to be impending), shall we be compelled to witness, once again, the reemergence of an "architecture" in something like the style of Minoru Yamasaki?

Again, God forbid; but he's getting pretty feeble in his old age and I don't see how he can do much about it. . . .

IV
In the early spring of 1952 Henry-Russell Hitchcock took me on a little trip: he drove me up from New Haven to Hartford, Connecticut (he was a *very* erratic driver); and in what seemed to be a "good" residential neighborhood, we stopped in front of this house **(2)**. Apparently it was our first destination.

So having actually seen the original of this house **(1+3)**, having been inside it only a few months before—it is alongside the Brenta between Venice and Padua—I was surprised with its *nice, smart,* paint job:

about? Has it not arrogated preeminent significance to itself?

In the Gospel according to St. John (1.14) we are informed that:

> The Word was made flesh and dwelt
> amongst us . . . full of grace and truth.

And this is okay with me, an account of how things *have* been and *should* be; but when the Word (*logos*) has become fatally divorced from the flesh, in this arid and pedantic future, *what* then are we to hope for?

Do we *then* choose the oasis of the senses, or do we chose the Sahara, the fundamentalist Sahara, of the spirit?

the Hartford version was *ever*-so-much more pretty, and I could only gape and gasp—*Why! Vincenzo Scamozzi! The Villa Ferretti at Dolo! About 1596, I think.* And all this was news—even to Russell. He knew the house very well. That's why he had brought me there. But even he didn't know about its derivation.

And myself was quite astonished by this. I knew that Vincenzo Scamozzi is a pretty arcane kinda guy; but this was the sort of thing that Rudy Wittkower had rubbed my nose into: *Notice the combination of Palladio with the giant order from Michelangelo's flanking palaces on the Campidoglio.* But I'd had a mouthful of info like this; and knowing it myself, since I thought that everybody—but everybody else—must know it too, I was mildly disturbed by Russell's lack of knowledge. A major connoisseur of the arcane, was Russell already "misreading" the object to which he wanted me to be exposed?

Well, this was the house (on Scarborough Street) where we were expected for late-morning drinks; and this was the house—built for himself—by A. Everett ("Chick") Austin, director of the Wadsworth Atheneum from 1927 to 1945; and it was here that he had entertained Le Corbusier, Walter Gropius, Gertrude Stein, I believe Edith Sitwell; it had been a house frequented by Lincoln Kirstein, James Thrall Soby, Alfred Barr, by Russell himself, and by Marcel Duchamp and Pävel Tchelitceff, and by Philip. Chick Austin was now living down in Sarasota, Florida, director of the Ringling Museum; but inside, we'd be entertained by his wife, the former Helen Goodwin of Hartford, whose brother—

or cousin (I forgot which)—had been architect for the building of the Museum of Modern Art in New York City.

So I don't remember too much about the inside. There was another visitor—Alessandro—I think—Lamarmora, who was over from Lenox, Massachusetts—and this seemed to lead to a multiplicity of connections—a Risorgimento name and Piedmontese Lamarmoras, I believe, are some sort of connection with the Rucellai in Florence—and by this time it was getting to be rather thick Henry James—one had to recognize that Bernardo Rucellai (the representative Rucellai of 1952), who was second cousin to a friend of mine in Greenwich Village, was also the grandson of Katherine deKay Bronson of Providence, Rhode Island, long a resident of Venice and Asolo, sister-in-law of Richard Watson Gilder of the *Century* magazine, friend of Robert Browning, and—inevitably and big yawn—a friend of Henry James. Also one of the reasons, as Russell once said, why *there are so many bathrooms in Palazzo Rucellai.* [11]

So the Lamarmora guy almost seemed to be part of the furniture, like something that had been in the house for *generations;* and coming from *Piemonte,* he *must* have felt quite at home because the room in which we were received—to the left of the front door—just happened to be of Piedmontese origin—though Russell seemed to think it was just an eighteenth-century pastiche and so much for *that.* But myself, I thought it must be southern Piedmont—Mondovi? Alba?—and while Russell was snorting to Lamarmora, Helen Austin—without too much interest—concurred with my attribution.

So was it *all* a composite version of early-twentieth-century New England Italophilia that I had stepped into? But there was *rather* more. This *because,* among the replica rooms upstairs, there just happened to be a surprising repro of Walter Gropius's *own dressing*

'Odd' house a tribute to art
Renaissance man created reflection of his life

(1)
A. Everett Austin House, Hartford,
Connecticut, diagonal view

room from Dessau. And that's about all that I remember and something about which, from time to time, I have meditated. As I immediately recognized, the repro facade *is* rather more ingratiating than the Venetic original—and somehow, rather more stagey. It is obviously intended to serve as a provocative *mise-en-scène*—and I don't think that Gropius could have grabbed it *at all*—likewise Rudy Wittkower. But *how* is this house to be understood?

Chick Austin, for installation in the Ringling Museum, later went on to buy a small horseshoe theater from Asolo, Mrs. Bronson's *villeggiatura* town in the Veneto, and I don't think that *she* would have approved the *transaction.* And then just *why* such an affluent little town as Asolo—Albergo Cipriani, etc.—could allow its little horseshoe theater to be shipped abroad . . . well this may be proof of Chick Austin's genius; but all the same, it doesn't help interpretation of his pseudo-Scamozzi job.

A specimen of bourgeois decadence? Too easy, too biased, not helpful.
A specimen of dada? Maybe. But not quite.
A specimen of surrealist culture? Could be. And this is a better question to propose.

Evelyn Waugh said of his contemporary Cyril Connolly that he was the representative man of his generation: "*he had the authentic lack of scholarship,*" which is a pleasantly malicious tribute to the English tradition of *belles lettres.* But *does* this apply to members of the same generation in the United States?; I think, not entirely. But it *may* assist a certain recognition and it *will* permit a caricature of Austin as both scholar and *poseur,* which, I have the impression, he might have enjoyed.

A theater for: a surrealist avant-garde? an apolitical avant-garde? an avant-garde *à rebours*—with the meaning of in reversed action? All of these questions assist a tentative definition of the iconography of this—otherwise—eclectic house, which is *very far* from deadpan. Is a *genuinely* advanced position represented here? In any case *much* more of a foyer of fashionable intellect (and important influence)—and I try to use these words with neutrality—than *any* location to be found within the orbits of Richard Neutra, Lewis Mumford—virtuous persons—and ever so many more? But surely.

So it is a house in which Cecil Beaton (and many of the very *chic* of this world) might have felt happy; and as we leave it, we might just take a look at the diagonal view (4).

So is this side elevation a case of incompetence? It gives you to think. *Not* a confrontation of side elevation and facade of the brilliancy of that advertised by Corbu at the Villa Stein–De Monzie? Scarcely a case of Levi-Strauss with his "structure" and "event"? This exposure *may* be self-conscious; but, *very likely*, it is *not*.

But, we will now drive over from drinks in Hartford to lunch in Farmington, to the house of James Thrall Soby, which I remember as a sort of Federal-style affair with a door in the middle. There is an extension at the back, a biggish living room about which I remember nothing of the interior except a ravishing cocktail shaker—simple, pure, exquisite, cut and ground glass—which *consumed* my admiration. And this living room was Russell's very own addition to the house (published, inside and out, in *The Architectural Review*), a creation about which he was, very demonstratively, proud.

But now to the dining room where, between two long windows, I can remember (impossible *not* to) a big bird cage. It was a *chinoiserie* item with, maybe, Gothic diversions attached; but it was memorable for the sake of its contents. Inside, there were *no* birds—in the sense of chirping, a bit smelly, *live* birds—instead, the inside was furnished with *artificial* birds, a bit abstracted, and these were the production of Alexander Calder. If you pressed *one* switch they would flap their wings; if you pressed *another* you could activate the sound: the birds would squeak and squawk.

Then to the left of the front door, I remember a small sitting room; and inside it was to be found that very poignant Picasso, oil and charcoal, 1923: *The Sigh* (5). And to make it more so, it didn't hang upon the walls of the room. Instead, it was propped up against the back of a chair—more or less the same chair in which its subject is sitting: a double illusion-allusion.

This was the presentation of Hartford-Farmington that Russell made for me—an opulent and aestheticized society (such as a social realist will *still* deplore) and a circle intimately connected with the early days of the Museum of Modern Art. And myself makes no judgment about it. Instead, I think of a comparable circle in London, perhaps of half-American Harold Acton, perhaps Nancy Mitford, and certainly, the much older Lady Cunard, born Maude Burke in San Francisco (by the more depressing considered to be frivolous). And particularly, I think about Lady Cunard's most superethical and socially outrageous intervention. Among her other dinner guests, she is entertaining Joachim von Ribbentrop and, with an affectation of innocence, down the table she calls: "But TELL me, my DEAR ambassador, because we ALL so much LONG to know, but WHY does Herr Hitler SO much dislike *the Jews*?"

A politically neutral question? But I am able to suppose that its style may not have been entirely remote from the surrealist consciousness of Hartford-Farmington—frivolous to the depressing though this may still appear to be.

And now, to transfer attention to a different world—though still connected with Russell.

Russell dedicated his first book, *Modern Architecture: Romanticism and Re-Integration* (1929), to "the memory of Peter van der Meulen Smith," who had died in 1928 in Berlin); and he illuminates this memory with two studies for a house on the Massachusetts North Shore of 1927 (6). Remarkable drawings in themselves, there are three lines of text related to influences upon them—Lurcat, Le Corbusier, and Oud—and that is all. But the further story is like this.

Russell had arrived in Paris, probably in 1926, with a fellowship from Harvard—this must have been the influence of Kingsley Porter—to study Merovingian architecture; and *this* was his purpose and obligation. But whatever Merovingian architecture may have meant at Harvard in the early 1920s (and one is compelled to wonder), it suddenly came to mean very little in Paris. For in Paris and perhaps just around the corner, there was Peter Smith working for André Lurcat; and evidently, Russell became completely bowled over—I think as much by the man as by what he was doing.

So there ensued some incandescent, maybe life-transforming, relationship; and by now, it is perhaps only these perspectives for a house on the North Shore that remain to speak about it. But when, in a different context, Russell used to speak of Friedrich Gilly as the Giorgione to the Titian of Karl Friedrich Schinkel, there was something in his tone of voice that might have indicated his more private meaning. He

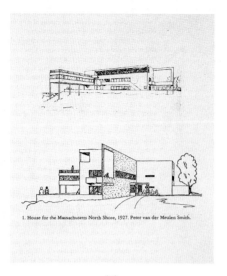

1. House for the Massachusetts North Shore, 1927. Peter van der Meulen Smith.

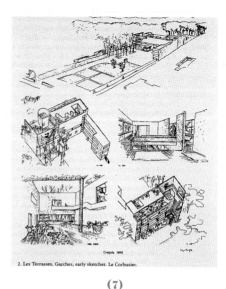

2. Les Terrasses, Garches, early sketches. Le Corbusier.

(6)

Peter van der Meulen Smith, project for a house on the
Massachusetts North Shore, 1927
(from Henry-Russell Hitchcock, *Modern Architecture:
Romanticism and Re-Integration*)

(7)

Le Corbusier, Les Terrasses, Garches, early sketches,
1926 (from *Le Corbusier, Oeuvre Complète*)

had understood Peter Smith as a Giorgione-Mozart of modern architecture, as the genius who died young; and it must have been with this conviction that he traveled to Berlin on the occasion of the tragically early death.

Whether, in any technical sense, the two were "lovers" I haven't a clue; but from his drawings, the impact of Smith's personality must be easy to understand. He had knowledge of the most significant new material from at least three countries; his talent was animated; he obviously knew the Steins, Sarah and Michael, and had enjoyed access to the preparatory drawings of *that* house at Garches before it was built (7). By the most enlightened and international standards his accomplishment was the most highly precocious.

Then, though I don't imagine that you can have an *American* avant-garde of just one man—traditionally the avant-garde was apt to be too gregarious—if Peter Smith, now dead for almost seventy years, with this project for a house on the North Shore, published by Russell so very long ago, is *not* to be regarded as a representative of, at least, a Parisian avant-garde, then words can have no meaning. So Parisianized American architecture ain't nothing new; and *why* this failure to recognize? By listening to incredibly dreary criticism we close our eyes—and minds—far too tight; and myself would most emphatically nominate Peter van der Meulen Smith, this neglected individual, as American avant-gardist Number 1.

And meanwhile, what about Mies, who didn't want to be "interesting" but wanted to be "good"? And what about the corner of the Library and Administration Building at IIT, 1944 (8)? An exhaustive analysis *of* and a laconic solution *to* the problem of the outer angle and of how to turn the corner, this achievement can easily be trivialized by cheap mockery; but wherever there is generosity of sentiment it *must* remain a classic state-

(8)
Mies van der Rohe, Library and Administration Building,
Illinois Institute of Technology, Chicago, 1944

ment. It should be compared with the corner of Alumni Memorial Hall, 1945–46; and it is, perhaps, all the more poignant than this because it is all the more ambivalent. Probably it exudes a certain disquiet—who knows? And probably, canonical though it may be—indeed precisely because it is *so* canonical—it is not to be located within the category of the avant-garde. For one would think that because of the nature toward which an avant-garde pretends—addiction to speed and to novelty, to a continuous supersession of itself—for any of its products it will be unable to claim exemplary status.

A problem with all futurisms? But if a very "liberal" interpretation of terminology *might* permit Mies's entry into the avant-garde category, a moderately strict interpretation will never permit it. And could he even be seen as a representative of an avant-garde *à re-*

bours, an avant-garde with a retrospective inclination? It is to be imagined that the designation would have given *him* no pleasure. For as already emphasized, with Mies it is *technology* that *moves* and *values* that remain *static;* and this is a dialectic—between *becoming* and *being*—that, of its nature, an avant-garde is not prone to accommodate.

Better, I can't help thinking, to recall that involvement with the positions of St. Augustine and St. Thomas that Mies found so important; and as exposure to such texts as Jacques Maritain, *Art and Scholasticism,* and Erwin Panofsky, *Gothic Architecture and Scholasticism*—particularly to Maritain—might serve to explain his position. But this is not to attribute any *necessary* or *absolute* validity to the critical messages of *either* St. Thomas or St. Augustine. No way! It is merely to infer their possible cogency—for Mies.

The product of a scholastic argument between *technology* and *value*—this is a probably reading of the corner of the Library and Administration Building; and as such, this is to make it a difficult candidate for any election to the company of the avant-garde.

So Mies van der Rohe? No! And Peter van der Meulen Smith? During his day, and in Paris, the term "avant-garde" enjoyed an undebased currency. So let him in! Along with Le Corbusier and certain individuals in Moscow/St. Petersburg and Milan, he is the protagonist of the genuine avant-garde—with a capital A and a capital G.

But please, please, do not apply the term for any unexpected and emergent tendency in the visual arts; and as though anyone questioning it were, ipso facto, a fascist hyena pig. An architecture of elegance and rigor requires—at least—*some* elegance and rigor of thought.

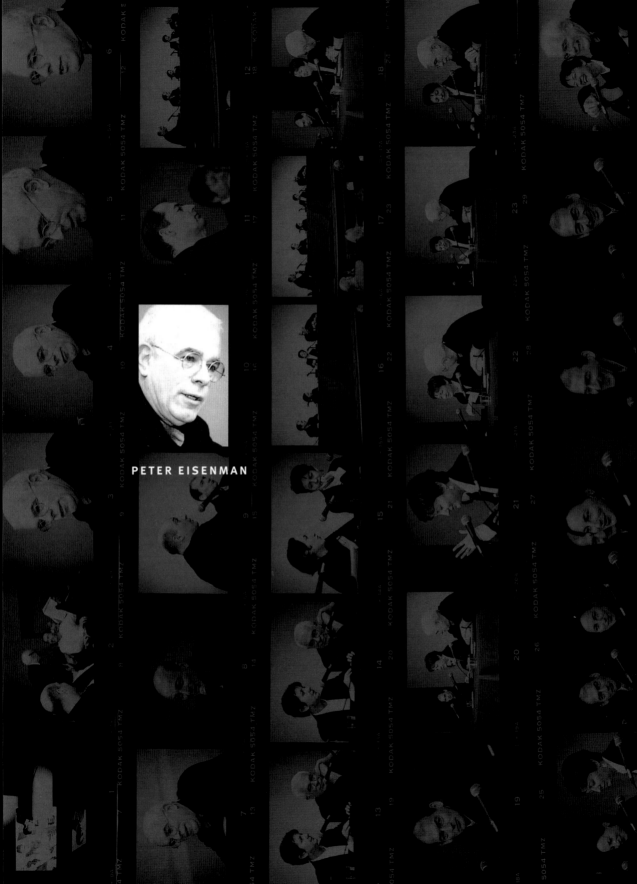

PETER EISENMAN

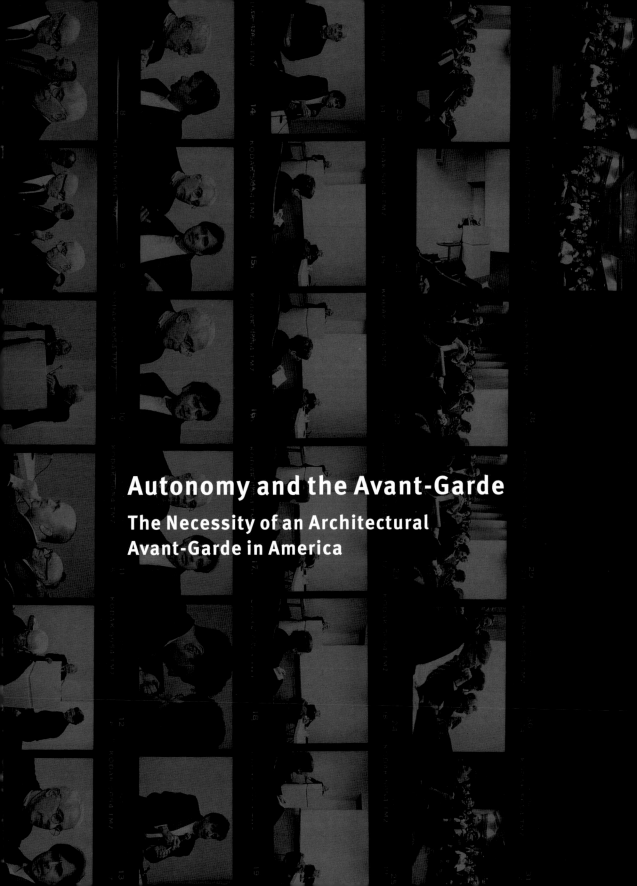

Autonomy and the Avant-Garde
The Necessity of an Architectural Avant-Garde in America

Corsivo I: Going Last. *The problem with going last at any conference is that what one wants to say seems always to have already been said by everyone else. In turn, one then feels the compulsion to reply to everything that has been said. This latter feeling overcame me last night at about three in the morning after hearing Colin Rowe talk about our Stuttgart trip. I remembered the occasion and I also remembered where I had heard the term* corsivo *for the first time. It was in a search that I led Colin on to find magazines of Italian origin of the prewar period. One of those magazines we uncovered was a special issue on the Casa del Fascio published sixty years ago in a magazine called* Quadrante, *edited by Massimo Bontempelli and Pier Maria Bardi. What is interesting about this magazine is that there are no essays, there are merely* corsivi, *that is, a series of points,* uno, due, tre, *etc. Colin reminded me of this in his mention of the term last night, so I thought I would structure my talk today as a series of* corsivi *because I could not allow Colin the last word on the zeitgeist.*

Corsivo II: Obiter Dictum. *On February 3, 1959, in Clear Lake, Iowa, an anniversary to this day, Buddy Holly, the Big Bopper, and Ritchie Valens died in an airplane crash while they were taking off in a snowstorm in a small plane:* the Geist of the Zeit.

Corsivo III: Obiter Dictum. *I remember flying to Seville not many years ago. I had arrived at the Madrid airport. I used to worry, when I needed to make a connection, that there would be some kind of weather problem. On this day, however, the Madrid airport was brilliantly lit by a blue sky, not a cloud to be seen. Since I had a confirmed first-class ticket from Madrid to Seville, there would be no problem in flying. I arrived at the check-in counter, speaking little Spanish, but enough to communicate to the person of authority who was to check me in for my continuing flight. This person was both less and more of an authority, since she referred herself to a computer in front of her. She said, "Well, I am afraid, Mr. Eisenman, that your name does not appear on this computer. You have no ticket." And I said, "But you don't have to worry about the computer, here is a ticket and it has my name on it, and it says OK, it is even in first class." And she said, "I am sorry, the computer says that you are not going." So despite the beautiful weather and despite the fact that I had a confirmed ticket, I did not get on the flight:* the Geist of the Zeit.

Corsivo IV: Mad Dogs and Englishmen. *Eighteen months after Buddy Holly's plane went down, and after a series of strange coincidences, I met Colin Rowe. From that moment* on, some thirty-six years ago, he has been in one way or another railing against the zeit-geist. What I always find strange about this continuing antagonism toward the zeitgeist is that if, as he says, it doesn't exist, why has he been going on so long about it? How is it that architectural historians can speak of the color and texture of a place, such as a city, or even the style of an architecture, in abstract terms, but they are not able to discern the same abstraction about time? Clearly, therefore, the idea represents some concern for him and for me. Because if Rowe was so passionate against the zeitgeist, in my oedipal condition, I should inquire as to what it was that stirred up such passion. If there is no zeitgeist, or if there is, how does one act to change things, and what determines the value of our actions?

Corsivo V: Taste and Temperament. *I remember Colin introducing me to a book with* *this title that I believe was written by a Joan Evans. It was in 1961 when he suggested that an alternative to the zeitgeist might be a condition of a psychological imperative. Evans' book is a bastardization of the Jungian typology of sensation, intuition and feeling and thinking. In it she says that there are artistic temperaments, which deal with things not according to taste but according to psychological makeup. She categorizes these types as quick and slow, introvert and extrovert; here, then, is another* Geist: *that of the psychological.*

Corsivo VI: The Two Tents. *Colin mentioned yesterday that there were two tents in his Southern apocalyptic fantasy, one circular and the other oblong. He mentioned that I was clearly expounding in the circular tent but he never told us that he was the person, the Episcopalian priest manqué, in the oblong tent. Was it for Colin merely a question of taste, or was it also a question of temperament?*

Corsivo VII: The Dream Before. *I was reminded as I listened to Colin Rowe last night of a Laurie Anderson tape called* Strange Angels. *On it there was a song called "The Dream Before" dedicated to Walter Benjamin. Now I am not about to sing this little verse to you. Although Colin is always wanting to sing little songs, my voice is not up to it. What I find so interesting is that it begins with words to the effect Hansel and Gretel are alive and well and living in Berlin. While Colin mentions Stuttgart, he does not tell us much about his role in Berlin. Hansel, for me, is the recently deposed Hans Stimann, and Gretel could be the* Geist *of Colin Rowe. And it is very interesting how much the current planning in Berlin resembles the Hansel and Gretel story. The end of the verse goes, "And she said, what is his story? And he*

said his story is an angel being blown backwards into the future. And he said, and, there is a storm blowing from paradise and that storm keeps blowing the angel backwards into the future and the storm, that storm, is called progress." That is also dedicated to Colin Rowe.

Corsivo VIII: Stasis as Movement. *A remembered quote from Colin Rowe: "There is nothing worth talking about in architecture since 1965."*

Corsivo IX: Esprit Nouveau, Towards a New Architecture, City of Tomorrow, 1965. *These correspond with the death of Le Corbusier and, in a sense, the death of Colin's fascination with the avant-garde architect. Like his fascination with the zeitgeist, his preoccupation with Le Corbusier is quite remarkable. It is no coincidence that nothing happens for Colin after 1965.*

Corsivo X. In the context of this conference, this *corsivo* may seem somewhat heretical. This is because in the terms of the definition of the avant-garde that is being proposed, the architectural avant-garde in America did not exist until 1966. While there have been various modern or modernist tendencies that from time to time may have appeared in the 1920s and even the 1930s, these tendencies, it can be argued, should not be confused with the avant-garde. To propose such figures as Frank Lloyd Wright, Louis Kahn, or perhaps even a Bruce Goff as the avant-garde is to misread the essential differences between an avant-garde, modernism, and individual expressionisms.

The argument that there was no avant-garde in American architecture until 1966 coincides with the date of the publication of two books by architects, which in their essence, and unlike anything these architects were to write or do after that moment, contain the seeds for such an American architectural avant-garde. These two books, Aldo Rossi's *The Architecture of the City* and Robert Venturi's *Complexity and Contradiction in Architecture,* each in their own way propose an idea of an autonomy of architecture. It is this idea of autonomy that I suggest will begin to distinguish modernism from the avant-garde, and the architectural avant-gardes from those of other disciplines.

While both books seem at first glance to be returns to a former historicizing mode of speculation about architecture, upon closer inspection this turns out not to be the case. For Rossi, the issue of autonomy is very clearly spelled out; in Venturi's book, the idea of autonomy is implicit. Basically, both say that in the restoration of the hegemony of Western capital after the war, and in the return to the possibility of architecture as a social instrument, one aspect of modernism that had been lacking from its social contract was the idea of history, the history of the language and discipline of architecture, and thus the historical conditions for meaning. What both books argue, in one way or another, is that in order to understand the city, architecture must be placed back into its historical discourse, that is, onto its own historical language. The idea of architecture and its own historical language in both Venturi's and Rossi's cases becomes a condition for autonomy.

This is not the first time that the idea of a historical language of architecture as a condition of its autonomy had been debated in architecture. For example, in the Italian Renaissance the difference between the work of Serlio and Michelangelo rests on this issue. For Serlio, autonomy was to be found in the historical language, and his speculative work was always rooted in variations of that language. For Michelangelo, autonomy lay in the invention of new forms of language, and not in variations. Clearly the idea of invention also involves the idea of the constantly new, the original, and originality, terms that have underpinned the more recent discussions of the avant-garde. So in a sense, from the beginning autonomy has been linked to either invention or variation in architecture. Yet in Rossi and Venturi it is the first time that the idea of a specific linguistic concept of architecture, as both autonomous and outside the classical idea of an architectural language, is introduced in the American context. This is not merely the idea of language as an abstract concept but rather the idea of a continuing language of architecture, which in a sense exists outside of and thus autonomously of any style, whether that style be classicism or modernism. What Rossi and Venturi are arguing is that the historical language, which had been lost in the modernist impulse, was in fact constituted against the propelling vector of the zeitgeist, and thus stood outside of both narrative time and the zeitgeist. It is this standing outside of linear time that becomes part of the idea of an autonomous language, autonomous to the history of architecture, and becomes an autonomy in itself. Here for the first time, autonomy is no longer linked to either invention or variation. It is also the first time that such an idea enters into an American architectural discourse. And because of this, another idea of the avant-garde is proposed, one not linked to time or, in the particular case of the present, to a modernist notion in twentieth-century architecture.

It was the separation of the idea of modernism from that of the avant-garde—a link that had previously conditioned all twentieth-century avant-gardes up until that moment—that would forever change the assumption that avant-gardes in general would now be modernist in their disposition. What Rossi and Venturi did simultaneously was to break this linkage. It is this break that is important in this context. For in doing so, both Rossi and Venturi introduce, each in his own way, the idea of autonomy into the idea of the avant-garde. This in turn begins to separate the idea of an architectural avant-garde from those of other disciplines.

This idea of an autonomy linked with the avant-garde is a departure and perhaps even an inversion of these terms as they are commonly understood today, wherein modernism is usually associated with autonomy and the avant-garde with a social project. To link modernism with a social project and the avant-garde with autonomy has the following consequences.

First, autonomy must be separated from an idea of originality, and from the value of origins. Second, autonomy must be understood as a singularity that for its preservation requires it to be cut from its previous modes of legitimation. For this idea to make any sense it is necessary to go back to the supposed origin of the avant-garde in the late eighteenth century and the early nineteenth century.

According to most definitions, there are two factors that animate the idea of an avant-garde. First, that there is a consciousness of a bourgeoisie and, second, that this consciousness carries with it the idea of a zeitgeist. This produces two different forms of the avant-garde, one hostile to the mechanisms of bourgeois society and the other complicit with it. In the former, which is evident in the first avant-gardes in the 1820s and 1830s, the avant-garde was seen as a form of aestheticism, as a withdrawal from the consumptive and instrumental mechanisms of a modernizing society. This withdrawal occurred at the same time as the formation of aesthetics as a separate discourse in philosophy. Both of these conditions led to the idea of art as an autonomous discipline, distinct not only from philosophy but also from the practices of bourgeois society. So from the earliest beginnings of the avant-garde, the detachment of art from a means-ends society—that is, the autonomy of art—was the precondition for the possibility of an avant-garde.

Thus in one sense, the European avant-garde movements of the 1830s can be defined as attacks on the changing status of art in a bourgeois society, that is, the art of the new marketplace. What Peter Bürger says is "What we negated was not an earlier form of art as style but art as an institution that is unassociated with the life praxis of man." He says that the avant-garde did not negate previous art as style, but challenged the autonomous institution of art. It negated artistic institutions that allowed art to be separated from social praxis. Bürger in this context is defending the historical avant-garde's attack on autonomy.

However, what develops in the avant-garde of the 1920s is almost diametrically opposite the conditions proposed in the nineteenth century. Ironically, instead of disassociation, and thus an autonomy from social practice, the avant-garde of the 1920s demanded that art be practical once again, that it should become socially significant. Another commentator on the avant-garde, Manfredo Tafuri, has a different view of the phenomenon. For Tafuri, this meant that art was a model for action, a coming to terms with the new laws of production as part of the universe of conventions. Here the implication remained that the autonomy of art was important. It was, as Tafuri says, a recognition that art and life were antithetical and that some mediation had to be found even if it meant the realization of the Hegelian prediction of the death of art.

It is here that Tafuri makes the necessary distinction between avant-garde art and architecture. He says that while art attempted to represent the chaos of the modern condition through an irony and thus a new frontier of visual communication, through the forms of assemblage, through a control of formlessness and chaos, it was architecture that offered the possibility of dealing with the real place of the improbable, and that was the city. It was at this point that architecture could enter, according to Tafuri, absorbing and going beyond the avant-gardes. The result, he says, was that the aesthetic experience of the city was revolutionized by formal dissolution through the processes of assemblage from the standardized cell to the city.

Unlike other arts, specifically painting, what constitutes the autonomy of architecture is always conditioned by a certain form of social practice. This gives to architecture a specific condition of autonomy unrelated to that of painting. For example, while painting is a form of social practice, no one has any trouble distinguishing conditions of its autonomy from its social practice. The idea of the materiality of the canvas, the saturation of paint on a surface, the edge stress and the frame, are never confused with the social practice of art. When similar formal characteristics are found in architecture, they have always been inextricably linked to its social function: shelter, accommodation, symbolism, etc. The problem for architecture has always been to define its autonomy by attempting to remove it from precisely the social practice that supposedly defines it. This removal or displacement has various functions. For one, it defines the autonomy of architecture as transgressive of its time and place, thus counter to any idea of the zeitgeist. This idea of autonomy as transgression of architecture's social practice—cutting it off from its previous modes of legitimation—already defines a condition of its avant-garde nature.

It is in this sense that my linking of autonomy and the avant-garde disagrees with Tafuri. Tafuri makes a distinction between what he calls the constructive or experimental and the absolutist or totalitarian aspects of the avant-garde. The absolutist, he says, claims to build a brand-new context, while the experimental is constantly taking apart what exists, moving toward an unknown from within the known. He says that while the absolutist subverts, the experimental decomposes and recomposes linguistic material, the infringement of codes. For Tafuri, this experimental attitude is called the critical, and he opposes it to the avant-garde use of irony or, as he says, the disenchanted game. Tafuri's distinction between the avant-garde and the critical suggests that the avant-garde is always wrapped up with the new and therefore with a zeitgeist and the constant notion of change, while the critical always involves a measure of experimental work. In my discussion the avant-garde is by nature critical of the zeitgeist, rather than an apparatus of it.

Tafuri is caught up with the separation of the critical, or creative, work from the new in its reaction to time or, more specifically, the zeitgeist. Tafuri seems to imply that the avant-gardist, in dealing with the perpetual new, is always bound up with the zeitgeist. For me, critical work exists in some form of an internal time, or what will be called here an autonomous time, that is embedded within the history of architectural discourse.

It is Tafuri's division of the experimental from the avant-garde that is problematic for this argument. For me, the critical or experimental work and the subversive absolutist must both be seen as avant-gardists. The latter is involved with manifestations of the zeitgeist, while the former is concerned with a denial of the zeitgeist and the question of the autonomy of time. It is this autonomy, introduced by both Venturi and Rossi, as a historical time internal to architecture, that is outside any consideration of the zeitgeist. In both the idea of autonomy is no longer concerned with originality.

(1)
Piranesi,
Nolli Map of Rome, 1754

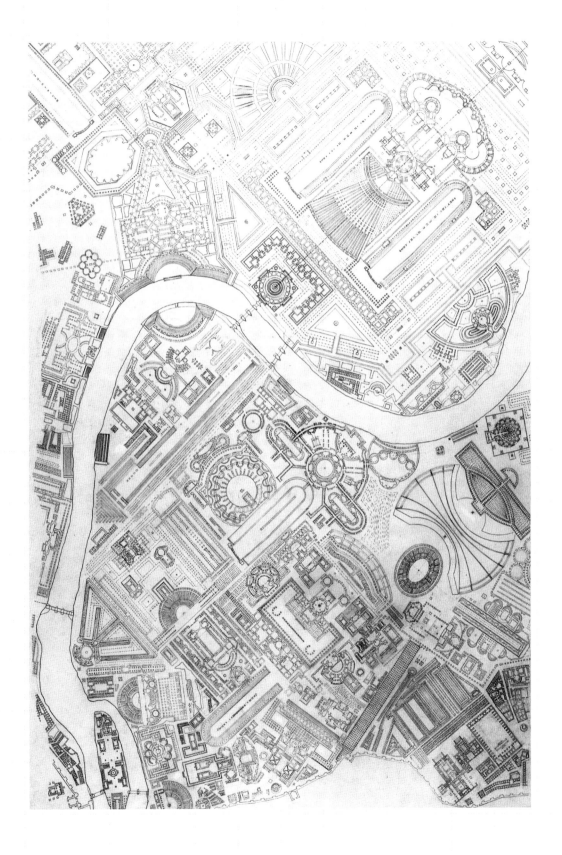

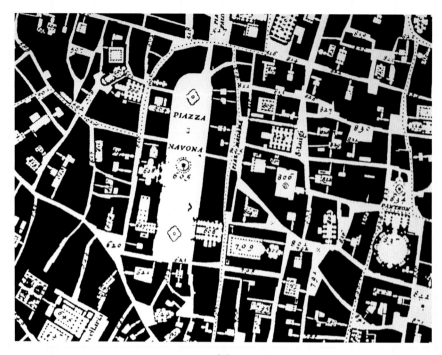

(2)
Piranesi, Campo Marzio, 1762

What must be understood in this context is that my definition is not autonomy as a neo-avant-garde (as some of the other papers have suggested) but rather autonomy as the idea of a singular difference. And it is this idea of autonomy in its many guises—from time to language to space itself—that ultimately answers Jeffrey Kipnis's diagnosis as to the possibility of an avant-garde today. Neither the autonomy of architecture nor the idea that this autonomy, in particular with respect to architecture, constitutes a permanent condition of the avant-garde can be merely willed away. To attempt to do this, as both Rowe and Tafuri have done, despite their apparently opposing interests, is to demonstrate the continuing power of such an idea. It remains for us today to continue to explore and expand the possibilities for such an autonomy in the face of the hegemony of world capital.

Corsivo XI: Piranesi. *Figure (1) is what is known as the Nolli Map of Rome of 1754. Figure (2) is the Piranesi drawing of the Campo Marzio of 1762. It is interesting that they are both drawn by Piranesi, but more important is the change in the eight years between 1754 and 1762. The Nolli Map is one way of looking at what exists. It has become an enormous source of fascination for Colin Rowe, and for his ideas of Collage City and of the contextual. Why Colin assumes that such a figuration, which had a significance at that time and at that place, which relied, as it were, on a* Geist, *can assume that same power in a new time and a new place, can assume the transference of not only a zeitgeist but also the genius loci, which he prefers, has always been, for me, problematic in his argument. What is interesting is that while Colin focuses on figure (1), he owns figure (2) and looks at it every day. In some way he manages not to engage that drawing. For me, figure (2) possesses a notion of criticality and autonomy in its notion of autonomous time, in its movement of buildings, in its invention of buildings, in its denial of the hierarchy of the baroque city. In all of these it transgresses the established norms of the time to establish an autonomous discourse of architectural time.*

Corsivo XII: The Gust of the Zeit. *I tried to make it in eleven but I will settle for twelve—the twelve apostles, the twelve tribes of Israel, etc.—and go on from there. Yesterday, Colin Rowe mentioned the idea of "the Gust of the Zeit" as spoken by Christopher Wren in 1728. Christopher Wren started his architectural practice, as we are reminded by Sir Bannister Fletcher, in 1662. He had no work until 1666 when the Gust of the Zeit, the great wind that fanned the fire of London blew London, away, and created an instant practice for him. Now really, Colin, of course Christopher Wren had an investment in the Gust of the Zeit: he made his practice out of it. And of course Peter Eisenman has an investment in the Gust of the Zeit: he has made his practice out of it as well.*

JOAN OCKMAN

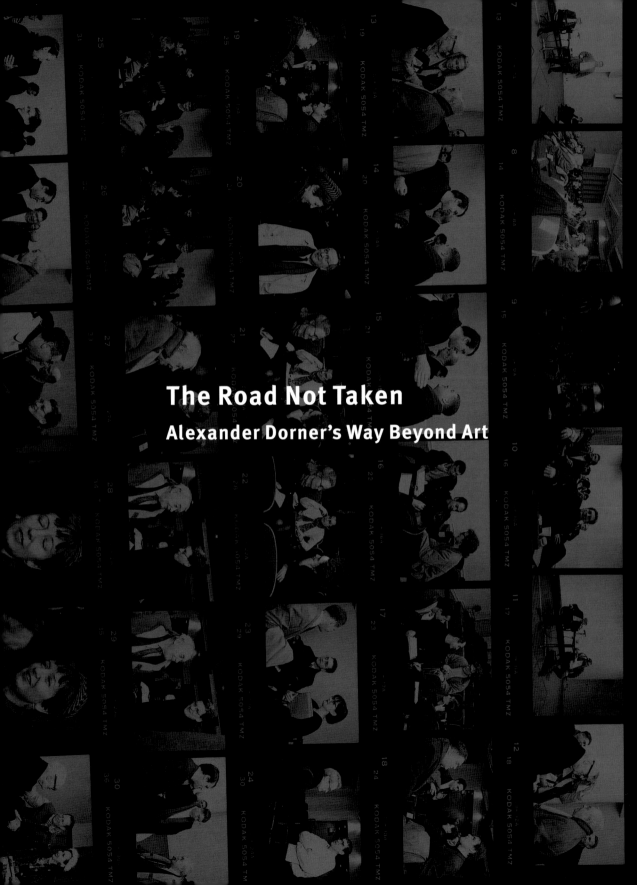

The Road Not Taken
Alexander Dorner's Way Beyond Art

A museum can either be modern or it can be
a museum, but it cannot be both.

—ATTRIBUTED TO GERTRUDE STEIN
WITH REFERENCE TO THE MUSEUM OF MODERN ART [1]

Vicissitudes of Art and Life

Among the animating ideas behind the most socially radical European art and architecture movements of the 1920s was the desire to reintegrate aesthetic practices with everyday life. This essay traces some of the migrations and mutations of that idea by way of a polemical personality, Alexander Dorner. A museum director and art historian, Dorner pursued his critique of aestheticism first in Weimar Germany and then in post–World War II America. Although in certain ways naive, his "way beyond art" nonetheless represents an alternative route through the familiar history of the twentieth-century avant-garde.

According to Peter Bürger's influential theory, now more than twenty years old, the shift from aestheticism to avant-gardism took place at a moment when progressive artists and critics began to comprehend the contradictions of an autonomous practice of art in modern society. With the perception that modernity had altered the traditional relationship between the producer and the means of production in all other spheres of activity, these artists and critics sought to bring the bourgeois institution of art in line with other social practices. But since, in Bürger's view, such a realignment or "sublation" could take place only if bourgeois society itself were superseded—a utopian hope—the avant-garde's efforts were historically doomed to failure, and not just to failure but to distortion, which Bürger calls "false sublation." In the context of late capitalism, art could only return to life as a commodity or as propaganda. Bürger therefore raises the question, following Theodor Adorno, of "whether a sublation of the autonomy status can be desirable

at all, whether the distance between art and the praxis of life is not requisite for that free space within which alternatives to what exists become conceivable." [2]

In the face of Bürger's pessimism and the various autonomy arguments advanced since the 1920s by theorists like Adorno and Clement Greenberg, the ideas of Alexander Dorner offer a somewhat different perspective on the institutionalization of the avant-garde. Dorner's intention was, paradoxically, to be an *avant-garde museum director*. Believing the task of the new museum to be the same as that of the new art—to educate and condition the mass public for life in a modern industrial society—he set out to challenge the institution of the museum from within. His views having been formed before the various early twentieth-century aesthetic tendencies had been codified as *modernism,* before the relationship between the museum, the public, and modern art was a foregone conclusion, it was his idealistic assumption that the institution would itself have to transform to accommodate the new art rather than vice versa. To perpetuate the museum as a sanctuary for fetishized art objects, whether historical or contemporary, was anathema to him.

Dorner represents a unique instance: a figure centrally associated with the German avant-garde who would come to the United States in the late 1930s as an émigré from Nazism and discover in American Pragmatism—specifically the thought of John Dewey and William James—a philosophical support for his own theory of the museum as a radically democratic, self-transforming institution and an arena of engaged artistic praxis. Best known in this country for a book published in 1947 entitled *The Way Beyond "Art,"*[3] which is dedicated to Dewey and contains a short introduction by him, Dorner's critique of aestheticism emerged out of his criticism of his own classical training as an art historian.

Dorner would later describe his discovery of Pragmatist thought upon his arrival in the United States in 1938 as follows:

> I felt as though a helping hand had been proffered me when, in America, I became acquainted with the philosophy of American Pragmatism through the writings of James and Dewey and, last but not least, through personal contact with Joseph Ratner, who has interpreted Pragmatism. . . . The pragmatic liberation of art history from Kantian and Hegelian absolutistic vestiges seems to be an evolutionary act of the highest importance, since our art philosophy, despite its increase in inner flexibility, is still largely indebted to the Kantian and Hegelian tradition and is hence anxious to preserve the unity of history statically, i.e. through eternal mental faculties (categories). I have reached conclusions similar to those of Pragmatism through long practical experience, and I am convinced that here lies the only road toward a reintegration of art history, esthetics and the art museum with actual life.[4]

Avant-Garde Genealogy

Dorner summarized his intellectual genealogy in the following diagram:[5]

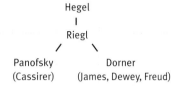

Born in 1893, Dorner was descended from six generations of Lutheran theologians. His grandfather was a professor of theology at the University of Berlin who had taught at Harvard and Columbia in the 1870s. His father, a philosopher and theologian at the University of Königsberg, was an academic whose neo-Kantian conceptions of beauty and harmony Dorner, coming to maturity in the turbulent years before World War I, found stifling. Rejecting his paternal background, he became increasingly critical of the German idealist tradition.

Taking up art history, Dorner completed his studies at the University of Berlin under Adolf Goldschmidt, an empiricist who had little use for the cyclical categories of art history propounded by his own predecessor in Berlin, Heinrich Wölfflin. Dorner appreciated Goldschmidt's suspicion of generalization and his methodological rigor, but found himself in search of some larger philosophical construct that could go beyond detailed stylistic description.[6] His colleague in Goldschmidt's seminar was Erwin Panofsky. Together Dorner and Panofsky discovered such a construct in Alois Riegl's *Kunstwollen.* Unlike previous historians, Riegl had interpreted art

83

(1)

Alexander Dorner (seated, center) and Kurt Schwitters (standing, right)
casting votes on the jury of the Hanover Art Association

history as a concrete and dialectical sequence of types of vision. The *Kunstwollen,* first articulated by Riegl in his book *Late Roman Art Industry* (1901), was a given epoch's "way of seeing." Closely related to the larger *Wollen* or *Weltanschauung* of that period, it comprised the visual principles at work in its artistic phenomena. For both Dorner and Panofsky, Riegl's *Kunstwollen* had the force of a revelation, although, as we shall see, with divergent results.

After receiving his doctorate in 1919 for a dissertation on ornament in Romanesque architecture, Dorner obtained a post at the state museum in Hanover. He became director of its collections in 1923 at the age of twenty-nine, also taking charge of twenty-five smaller art museums in the northwest region of Germany. In the heyday of the Weimar Republic, Hanover was a cosmopolitan town with a brilliant cultural life. As described by Dorner's biographer, Samuel Cauman,

> Hanover belonged to the world of scientific advances, artistic experiment, fast motors, night clubs, and dozens of informed and eager minds discussing the latest developments in a hundred fields of human activity. In this atmosphere neo-Hegelian myths were beginning to appear quaint and outmoded.[7]

Among the artists, architects, and modernists who lived in Hanover during the 1920s were the dadaist Kurt Schwitters; the abstract artists Carl Buchheister and Friedrich Vordemberge-Gildewart and the architect–furniture designer Hans Nitzschke (the latter two of whom were instrumental in founding *Gruppe K,* an organization of Hanover constructivists along the lines of the *G* group in Berlin); the expressionist painter Otto Gleichmann; and the modern dancer Mary Wigman. There were also the collector Herbert von Garvens and the Kestner Society impresario Paul Küppers, whose wife, Sophie, would marry El Lissitzky after Küppers' death. The pioneering exhibitions of the Kestner Society (an international society for the promotion of art and literature), the Hanover Secession, and Schwitters' *Merz* activities, which brought Theo van Doesburg and Lissitzky into Hanover circles, gave the town an avant-garde reputation.

Dorner plunged into Hanover's art world, where he quickly became an ardent champion of contemporary art, especially the abstract and constructivist tendencies that were overtaking expressionism in Germany and throughout Europe by 1922–23 (**1**). Upon seeing Schwitters' *Merzbau* taking shape in the artist's house, Dorner's first reaction was repulsion at its "free expression of the socially uncontrolled self . . . a sick and sickening relapse into the social irresponsibility of the infant who plays with trash and filth." Admiring Schwitters' collages, however, he soon became the artist's friend and supporter.[8] After assuming the presidency of the Kestner Society, Dorner was responsible for bringing to Hanover exhibitions and lecture programs on Bauhaus, de Stijl, and Russian art, on modern architecture and design, and on the new film and dance. He was close to Gropius, and invited him to Hanover in 1923 to lecture on the unity of art and technology, a theme that marked the changing orientation of the Bauhaus at this time. Later in the decade

and in the early 1930s, Dorner staged a series of exhibitions at the Kestner Society on the design of the mass-produced object. Exhibitions like "Good Design in Mass-Produced Home Furnishings" and "Pure Form in Household Equipment" propagated the new aesthetics of functionalism. These exhibitions, like similar shows sponsored by the German Werkbund, were the precursors for the "Good Design" series to be staged by the Museum of Modern Art in New York a quarter century later.[9]

Dorner also taught architectural history at Hanover's university and served as a commissioner for the maintenance of monuments in northwest Germany. Obliged to put Riegl's ideas on the modern cult of monuments to the test of practical experience, he found himself often on the side of development rather than that of preservation. Only those monuments that promoted "evolutionary forces" were worthy of being preserved, in his view:

> I had time and again to make up my mind as to which historical buildings and monuments were to be preserved; i.e., had continually to focus my thought on the role of the historical art work in the context of our present-day life and on its value and legitimacy as a life-improving factor. Which of the two was more important: the better functioning of a street, bringing about an elimination of accidents, or the preservation of a medieval building? Was it not a sign of our clinging to a rather primitive cult of relics allegedly containing timeless values that we were still basing our culture on the concrete maintenance

of a maximum of historical buildings, while everything around us furnished mounting proof that the value of life consisted in the act of transformation? . . . The humanistic eternity cult was indeed about to become an obsolete clog on life instead of a directional force. [10]

Meanwhile, his major energies went into reorganizing the holdings of the Hanover museum according to his emerging conception of the twentieth-century museum. Built in 1901, the Landesmuseum in Hanover was a neo-baroque edifice housing crowded suites of galleries arranged according to the ownership of the various collections, with objects spanning from antiquity to late-nineteenth-century German romanticism. [11] Searching for a way to reorder this heterogeneous material, Dorner turned again to Riegl's developmental history, and again found himself forced to come to grips more critically with the latter's approach. Riegl had offered a narrative of Western art that extended from the "haptic" to the "optic," from the self-contained image of the figure in Egyptian relief sculpture to the relational, perspectival space of the Renaissance and baroque. Now, forced to account for the break with perspectivalism initiated by romanticism, and seeking to encompass in the sequence at Hanover art from prehistory to his own time, Dorner found it necessary to go beyond the Rieglian telos. Riegl's theory of the emergence of optical vision began to appear too linear, orderly, and vestigially rooted in the mind-body dualism of traditional metaphysics.

This critique of Riegl led Dorner in an opposite direction from the one Panofsky was taking at the time. Having come under Ernst Cassirer's influence in Hamburg, Panofsky clung to the Kantian vestiges in Riegl's art history, postulating a coherent internal unity between the subjective (perceptual) and objective (conceptual) aspects of works of art in a given period and, in Dorner's view, regressively imputing to the *Kunstwollen*

the status of an immanent category. For Dorner, on the other hand, what was revolutionary in Riegl's art history was its open-endedness, acceptance of contingency, and psychological insight into visual perception. The dispute between the two former members of Goldschmidt's seminar was vented in the *Zeitschrift für Aesthetik und Allgemeine Kunstwissenschaft*, where Dorner attacked Panofsky in 1922 for grounding his art history in a priori concepts and thereby insufficiently crediting history's potential for innovation. [12] Panofsky replied at length in an excursus to his article of 1925 "On the Relationship between Art History and Art Theory." Stating that he had never intended to imply that his "fundamental concepts" had the "character of reality," he contended that they were "meta-empirical" constructions necessary for interpreting empirical facts. He further argued that his view of art-historical development was based not on a determinist notion of historical necessity, as Dorner had suggested, but rather on principles of logical consistency (*Folgerichtigkeit, Sinngemäßigkeit*). [13]

In the applied context of the museum, Dorner's practical rereading of Riegl's art history led him to transform the Hanover museum's haphazard collection into an evolutionary sequence with a strongly didactic bent. He put major emphasis on the provision of explanatory texts, captions, and guidebooks and, prophetically enough, made efforts to bring audio commentary into the galleries. Most innovative was his concept of the atmosphere room. Instead of presenting artworks as isolated objects or, on the other hand, as stylistic manifestations accompanied by associated decor—as in the traditional period room, with its simulated interior—Dorner attempted to re-create the "way of seeing," or *Kunstwollen,* specific to each epoch. He thus distinguished the suites of galleries representing the respective periods by perceptual cues like color. The medieval rooms were rendered dark, causing the luminosity of the works to emerge; the Renaissance rooms were painted gray and white; and the artworks in the baroque galleries were framed in gold and hung on red velvet backgrounds. With this approach, Dorner sought to emphasize the newness of each context, giving art history a sense of both specificity and dynamic development.

Dorner's synaesthetic concept of the atmosphere room—implemented by the mid-1920s, and to culminate in 1927 in the Hanover museum's most famous room, the Abstract Cabinet—ran counter to conventional museum practice. An attempt to reproduce not just the conditions of seeing but the full sensorium of aesthetic experience of a particular period, including its architecture and music, the atmosphere room had something of the *Gesamtkunstwerk* about it, even if Dorner's intent was manifestly more pedagogical than theatrical. In an exchange with Dorner in the Frankfurt newspapers in 1931, the medievalist Georg Swarzenski, then director of the museum in Frankfurt, criticized Dorner's approach as an intrusive interpretive apparatus that impeded rather than promoted the appreciation of art, compromising the directness of the relationship between the art object and viewer. Swarzenski felt it was the curator's role not to offer a particular reading of past periods but rather to expose art's timeless qualities. Dorner argued that works of art took on meaning only when their history could be related to the present, insisting on the museum's educational and "life-improving" responsibilities.[14]

Space-Time and Giedion

By the late 1920s Dorner had worked his way from Riegl's theory of art history, which culminated with perspectivalism, to a tendentious account of twentieth-century abstraction. Riegl's telos, in Dorner's view, had been supplanted by a pulsating, all-sided spatiality that no longer relied on the "window view" and "picture frame" optics of traditional painting. Dorner compactly formulated this "new concept of space in the plastic arts" in two articles published in 1931, one in German in the journal *Museum der Gegenwart,* the other in French in *Cahiers d' art* **(2)**.[15] Although not the first to revise the narrative of art history in the direction of non-representational art, Dorner offered more than a synthesis of the most advanced aesthetic thought of his day, especially inasmuch as he would also use the Hanover museum as a laboratory to test his ideas. Following is a synopsis of his argument, which was to have a significant influence on another theorist of the new space, Sigfried Giedion. It is paraphrased from the French text.

Space, according to Dorner, had been conceived from a fixed point of view and seen as absolute and uniform during the preceding four centuries. Three-dimensional volumes, whether solid or transparent, were discrete and clearly defined. In this conception of spatial reality, systematized in perspectival representation, the painting was analogous to the scene viewed through a window frame. This conception persisted from its development in the Renaissance and the baroque through impressionism and pointillism. But with modernity a new conception

(2)

Plate from article by Alexander Dorner, "Considérations sur
la signification de l'art abstrait," *Cahiers d'art,* 1931

of space emerged. The first impulse made itself felt in early-nineteenth-century romanticism. Its culmination, a hybrid state in which the fundamentals of the traditional image were still present but shaken deeply by the elements of a new vision of space, was expressionism.

The breakthrough of abstract art followed. "The decisive novelty of cubism" was "the substitution of a relative point of view for an absolute one." Replacing the perspectival system was "supraspatial contact." Near and far objects were now delineated in the same way, and background and foreground entered into a perpetual oscillation. "The factor of time" thus became an element of the representation of space, and as a corollary all points of view came to be understood as relative. Abstract forms lent themselves most naturally to the representation of this new vision. With the abandonment of the traditional concept of space, the framed view no longer needed to prevail. Another consequence was that matter ceased to be understood as opaque mass. The viewer now envisaged different aspects of space simultaneously, inside and outside, convex and concave at once. Matter was decomposed into simple surfaces and lines (as in Mondrian) or became transparent and interpenetrating (as in Lissitzky). With these developments, space came to be understood as "a crossing of movements and energies." Initially, in cubist painting, this supraspatial contact produced a passive sliding from front to back and back to front. With constructivism, it generated an active push, moving toward back and front at once.

Dorner then compared the architecture of Versailles to that of the Bauhaus building at Dessau in order to show that this transformation in visuality was not limited to painting. The perspectivalism at Versailles was rigorously frontal. Building and park together constituted a spatial unity, and both mass and space remained tangible in their infinite perspectival recession. The Bauhaus, by contrast, was an ensemble freed from mass, composed of planes and lines radiating in all directions spatially, with no principal view. "To understand its character you have to walk around it." Modern architecture revealed its predilection for glass and for effects of light, which produced intangible forms in space.

Dorner considered the Neue Sachlichkeit in painting a return to romanticism and the optical conception of space. He saw surrealism, on the other hand, as more heterogeneous and fertile: in Picasso's 1926 painting *Head* and in Arp's compositions, new representations of objects and new psychic content were combined with many-sided space and a relative point of view. But it was film, with its absolute union of space and time, that in Dorner's view corresponded "better than anything else to our representation of reality." Its critical potential was especially evident in the work of filmmakers like Viking Eggeling, László Moholy-Nagy, and the cubists. Yet the movie screen still partook of the frontality and perspectivalism of traditional theater. "That is why painting and film are developing side by side for the moment, each with its advantage, each with its disadvantage relative to the ideal representation of the desired reality."

Concluding by suggesting that architecture and abstract painting were instinctively moving in the same direction as the natural sciences, art and science constituting "parallel phenomena" reflecting "a new conception of the world," Dorner offered three analogies. First, just as the plastic arts had recently moved away from the representation of opaque masses in favor of interpenetrating, massless energies, so the natural sciences had done so some time ago, as exemplified by X-rays. Second, just as painting was now abandoning an absolute, immobile, and perspectival point of view for a mobile and relative one, so science had relinquished belief in an absolute system of relationships, embracing the theory of relativity. Third, just as the "fourth dimension" of time was now entering into the three-dimensional representation of space, so the continuity of space and time had become the basis for the new physics. Dorner finished by affirming that although the present style of abstract painting was in its superficial aspects only one manifestation of the new spatial conception, it was in its essence a historically necessary phenomenon of greatest consequence.

From this line of argument it is clear that Dorner, like Riegl, had not entirely abandoned Hegelian dialectics. His new system of space configuration implicitly overcame and negated the previous one; space-time superseded optical space (even if he emphasized that the new *Kunstwollen* was likely to have various and unpredictable manifesta-

89

tions). Yet what was not Hegelian about Dorner's view, as already anticipated in his argument with Panofsky, was his interpretation of history as a human construction rather than a manifestation of immanent principles. Repudiating the idea of an "eternal truth behind all change," he would later describe his view of history as "biogenetic." Although condemned to "complete irreversibility," history in its forward movement was "an open growth freed from immutability."[16]

It is also clear that Dorner's theory of modern space as set out in his writings of the late 1920s and early 1930s bears comparison to Sigfried Giedion's central thesis in *Space, Time and Architecture* (1941), written in the mid-1930s. In the section of Giedion's book, entitled "The New Space Conception: Space-Time," the resemblances to Dorner's argument are more than coincidental. Giedion acknowledges as much in an article of 1932 that anticipates his subsequent argument concerning the seminal role of cubist painting in modern architecture's development:

> At the last International Congress for Aesthetics (Hamburg, 1930), Alexander Dorner (Hanover) showed how Cubism had achieved a new understanding of space—for the first time since the Renaissance. Instead of the Renaissance perspective with its unidimensional depth of field, we now see space as being multidimensional. We have added a fourth dimension, time, to the previous three (length, breadth, depth). Independently of this, modern physics has arrived at similar concepts and results.[17]

In *Space, Time and Architecture,* however, Giedion would omit any reference to Dorner. Dorner was to write to Wilhelm Valentiner in 1943, "I must say I am ashamed for Giedion at the way he ... has used ... my various essays."[18]

Even more significant than the similarities between their theories were the differences, however, as Dorner himself realized. In a long footnote in *The Way Beyond "Art,"* he would express his dismay not so much that Giedion had borrowed his ideas but that he had recast them into a "semi-static philosophy of art and history." Rather than accepting Dorner's biogenetic "world of change," Giedion sought to discover "timeless elements." "What else can modern art and architecture become under these circumstances," asked Dorner, "but a new arrangement of basic elements, i.e., a 'new style'?"[19]

The Abstract Cabinet

Giedion had in fact been acquainted with Dorner's ideas since at least 1929, when he wrote a review for the journal *Der Cicerone* of the latter's most celebrated achievement at the Hanover museum. This was the Abstract Cabinet, a gallery on which Dorner collaborated with El Lissitzky. "This gallery proves that museums need not be mausoleums; it all depends on the hand whose touch gives life to the material," stated Giedion in his review, entitled "Living Museum."[20]

Dorner intended the Abstract Cabinet, designed and completed by Lissitzky in 1927, to be the culmination of the Hanover museum's art historical sequence and a didactic representation of his theory of the new spatiality. Dedicated to art from cubism on, it was described some thirty years later by Alfred Barr Jr. as "probably the most famous single room of twentieth-century art in the world,"[21] and seen by visitors from all over, including American museum people like

(3)
Abstract Cabinet, 1927; three photographs of Lissitzky's painting *Floating Volume* (1919) from different standpoints, showing change in coloration of metal wall slats from white to gray to black

Barr, Katherine Dreier, Albert Barnes, and Philip Johnson. Johnson apparently visited the gallery in 1930 while scouting in Germany for the Museum of Modern Art's International Style exhibition.[22]

For Lissitzky, one of the principal creators and disseminators of constructivist aesthetics and the chief emissary between Soviet and German avant-garde circles, the gallery at Hanover was his most fully elaborated scheme in a trio of "demonstration rooms" that he designed in the mid-1920s for display of the new art. In the first, a room sponsored by the November Group at the Great Berlin Art Exhibition of 1923, he constructed a total environment using his *Prouns*—painted reliefs intended as "the interchange station from painting to architecture"—engaging not only the walls but also the ceiling and floor. "We are destroying the wall as a resting-place for [traditional painters'] pictures," he declared.[23] Lissitzky's second exhibition space for contemporary art was the Room of Constructive Art, installed in 1926 at the International Exposition in Dresden. This room, which included artwork not just by himself but by other major exponents of the new tendency, was the immediate precursor for the Abstract Cabinet.

Dorner had initially entrusted the commission for the Abstract Cabinet to Theo van Doesburg, but he rejected van Doesburg's scheme, which consisted of a transparent mural on the room's window wall, as too decorative.

Lissitzky's scheme, in contrast, aimed to produce a total transformation in the viewer's experience of the room and its objects:

> The great international picture-reviews resemble a zoo, where the visitors are roared at by a thousand different beasts at the same time. In my room the objects should not all suddenly attack the viewer. If on previous occasions in his march-past in front of the picture-walls, he was lulled by the painting into a certain *passivity*, now our design should make the man *active*. This should be the purpose of the room.[24]

Located in the Hanover museum just to the left of the main staircase bringing visitors up from the entry hall to the second floor, the Abstract Cabinet measured 5.32 by 4.40 meters. Lissitzky lined the walls of this small space with over five hundred slats of metal set perpendicularly to the wall plane. Framed by horizontal molding strips at floor and ceiling and spaced two centimeters apart, the slats were enameled white on one side and black on the other. They projected three centimeters from the back wall plane, which was painted gray. A refinement of the scheme at Dresden, which employed deeper and more widely spaced wooden slats, they cast strong vertical shadows, making the wall planes look pleated. Lissitzky varied the color sequence along the length of the walls, flipping the groupings of slats from light-dark to dark-light and vice versa **(3)**. The effect of this "irrational surface," as Giedion described it in his article, was that as the viewer moved around the room the walls shimmered and dissolved into "total intangibility," destabilizing the visitor's sense of space.[25]

91

On three of the walls Lissitzky interrupted the slats to introduce a flexible system for displaying artworks. This consisted of an arrangement of panels with components that slid on either vertical or horizontal tracks, permitting alternate paintings to be shown while ensuring that only an optimal number would be seen in the gallery at one time. As at Dresden, where Lissitzky had used a similar display system, visitors could move the panels themselves. The canvases, some unframed, were mounted on the panels and gallery walls without primary reference to eye level. Their placement was instead orchestrated to produce specific juxtapositions and create an abstract three-dimensional composition. On the room's fourth wall, which had a large window, louvers and a soffit covered with white fabric diffused natural light above two canted vitrines on either side of a radiator. The contents of the vitrines rotated horizontally on drums, also operable by the visitor. Next to the left-hand vitrine was a corner alcove containing a shelf with a torso by the sculptor Archipenko. Behind it a mirror reflected both the sculpture's back and the slats, now seen in reverse coloration.

Among the paintings and drawings displayed in the Abstract Cabinet were works by Pablo Picasso, Fernand Léger, Juan Gris, Louis Marcoussis, and Gino Severini; by Schwitters, Wassily Kandinsky, and Oskar Schlemmer; and by Mondrian (the first of Mondrian's paintings to be purchased in Germany, and the first to be acquired by a public museum), Lissitzky, Moholy-Nagy, Friedrich Vordemberge-Gildewart, Willi Baumeister, Carl Buchheister, and Walter Dexel. In one of the most widely reproduced views of the gallery, two lithographs from Lissitzky's series *Victory over the Sun* appear counterposed to two geometric paintings by Mondrian. Works by van Doesburg, Hans Arp, Herbert Bayer, Max Burckhartz, Hans Richter, and others were also exhibited at different times. Besides

the Archipenko, the three-dimensional objects included one or more pieces by Naum Gabo (whose work was also first acquired for a museum by Dorner) and pieces from the glass and metal workshops at the Bauhaus. The rotating vitrines contained works on paper as well as examples of "the effects of abstract art on the features of everyday life"—wallpaper, fashion design, printing and advertising, and photographs of modern architecture. The lines between art object and object of use would seem to have been decisively blurred by the placement in the Abstract Cabinet of a piece of modern furniture—in a photograph of the gallery taken in the 1930s it remains ambiguous whether a chair designed by Mies van der Rohe was to be looked at or sat in.

Through the participatory nature of the gallery and especially the kinetic, or kinematic, invention of the varicolored slats, Lissitzky produced an unprecedented kind of environment within the Hanover gallery. His installation defamiliarized the "private drawing room style" of the traditional museum, subverting habitual modes of perception (even if his "optical dynamic" would soon be reappropriated and institutionalized, eventually passing down to Op and environmental art in the 1960s).[26] Yet despite the success of Abstract Cabinet, Lissitzky was to abandon this approach to the exhibition gallery almost immediately afterward. In the Soviet Pavilion for the "Pressa" exhibition (Cologne, 1928), the "International Hygiene" exhibition (Dresden, 1930), and other designs of the late 1920s, he created more monumentally scaled settings, mobilizing the

(4)
El Lissitzky, drawing of Abstract Cabinet
for Landesmuseum, Hanover, 1927

effects of large-scale photomontage and photofresco. Only such heroic expression, he now believed, was adequate to the task of reorganizing the consciousness of the proletariat for the socialist state. But the intimate space of the Abstract Cabinet created within the institution of the bourgeois art museum remains a vivid episode in the history of twentieth-century exhibition design. In its quality of "radical reversibility," likewise captured by Lissitzky in an axonometric drawing of the gallery meant to be read both right side up and upside down (1), it achieves the same transformation of spatial values that marks his most utopian work of the mid-1920s.[27]

Dorner, for his part, never ceased to believe that the Abstract Cabinet was a seminal step in overcoming the static and bourgeois concept of the individual object. "This room was, as far as we know, the first attempt to overcome the fixity of the gallery and the semistasis of the period room, and to introduce modern dynamism into the museum," he would write in *The Way Beyond "Art."* Notwithstanding the gallery's small scale, the subordination of the individual artwork to the overall environment of the room and to a relativistic concept of space had all-important psychosocial implications. "Mobility shattered the room, as it were"—he states in a passage reminiscent of Walter Benjamin's description of the impact of film on twentieth-century perception— releasing the pent-up energies in abstract art, which are "close to the dynamism of modern life." "Once set to work in the practical context of life," these energies "might well influence life on a tremendous scale."[28]

Original and Facsimile

In 1929 Dorner was responsible for another installation that caused a stir in the German art establishment. This was an exhibition at the Kestner Society called *Original and Facsimile*. Three months earlier he had contributed an article to the Lübeck *Blätter* entitled "The End of Art?" He wrote:

I consider it certain that the *possibilities of painting*, which represents the traditional aspect of reality, *are exhausted.*
Photography takes over its heritage and is able to transfer it into the new modern vision of a supra-spatial reality. *The film is the ideal bridge from the old to the new aspect of what is real*, because it merges both the old static surface-aspect of three-dimensional solids inside of the traditional "real space" and their interpenetration, and this can only be given by all-sided movement. . . .
After Abstract art has found its goal in modern, massless architecture we have no other means of representing our new reality, which gives us the new actuality we see. It seems very doubtful to me whether to our modern mind which conceives only moved realities as "real," traditional sculpture and painting will ever be able to give us the intensified rational and emotional relations we have learned to consider real. . . .
That the means of photography are technical does by no means speak against them. The means of all art in the past have been technical within the technical abilities of its different ages. [29]

For almost a decade many avant-garde artists had been advocating an art based on the new means of technical reproduction. At the Berlin dada fair of 1920, George Grosz and John Heartfield proclaimed the death of easel painting, celebrating Vladimir Tatlin's "machine art." In the Soviet Union, Alexander Rodchenko and the Lef group made a further move by 1924, as Benjamin Buchloh has traced, from the compositional approach of *faktura* to the "iconic" or documentary mode of factography, a use of photographic techniques aimed at "rendering aspects of reality visible without interference or mediation."[30] Meanwhile, in Germany Moholy-Nagy, proselytizer of a "new vision" of art and life consonant with industrial modernity, remained a primary exponent of the technoaesthetic position, continuing to experiment with the photogram, a technique he was instrumental in developing, through the 1920s and beyond. More interested in a creative use of mechanical apparatus than an unmediated presentation of reality—even if as a provocation he once produced five paintings by ordering them from a sign factory by telephone—Moholy-Nagy believed that the processes of technical reproduction, thus far used only to replicate existing relationships of production, had untapped artistic potential. In an article entitled "Production Reproduction" first published in *De Stijl* in 1922 and again in his 1925 Bauhaus book *Painting/Photography/Film,* he stated that the purpose of art was "to establish far-reaching new relationships between the known and the as yet unknown optical, acoustical, and other functional phenomena." He continued, "We must endeavor to expand the apparatus (means) which has so far been used solely for purposes of reproduction for productive purposes."[31]

Despite the circulation of such ideas among the more technically oriented wing of the avant-garde, however, the end of art position was still an extreme one for a museum director with a collection based on a patrimony of European painting. Even more heretical in this regard was the exhibition "Original and Facsimile," in which Dorner pushed the aesthetic debate on reproductive technology in a new direction. At this exhibition Dorner installed ink drawings, pastels, and watercolors by old and recent masters—Paul Cézanne, Käthe Kollwitz, Claude Lorrain, Pierre Auguste Renoir, Giovanni Battista Tiepolo, and Hans von Marées—alongside high-quality facsimile reproductions of the same. The

originals and facsimiles (or in some cases just facsimiles) were framed alike and placed behind glass. He then challenged the public to detect which were which, with prizes going to the winners. One hundred forty people, from laymen to specialists, entered the contest, some examining the work with loupes and microscopes. The result was that no one appraised all the work correctly; astonishingly, according to Dorner, better scores came from students at a local *Gymnasium* than from many of the experts.[32]

In dramatizing that the differences between an original and a high-quality reproduction were often imperceptible, Dorner's intent was to challenge the mythos of the original artwork with its purportedly inimitable signature and aura of rarity. He also sought to demonstrate the sophistication of the new reproduction technology, which by the 1920s had reached a high level among many printers in Germany. This led him to the iconoclastic proposal that facsimiles might be exhibited by museums as a way of filling gaps in their collections, an idea he would elaborate further later on.[33] Meanwhile, "the effect of the show was a bombshell."[34] Dorner's gambit resulted in a move, led by the Hamburg museum director Max Sauerlandt, to bar him from the International Association of Museum Officials. Six years before Walter Benjamin wrote "The Work of Art in the Age of Mechanical Reproduction," the exhibition also spawned a heated debate among museum authorities, art critics, and university professors around Germany. Authorities in Berlin called for facsimile reproductions to be legally banned as "hostile to art." A six-month exchange of opinions in the Hamburg periodical *Kreis* elicited a carefully argued response by Panofsky, who again took a considerably more moderate position than Dorner. Panofsky allowed that the production of more and better facsimiles was desirable insofar as it served to heighten appreciation of the originals, but maintained that once the machine overtook the hand, art would be finished.[35]

In an article entitled "What Can Art Exhibitions Do Now?" published in 1930 in *Das neue Frankfurt,* Dorner wrote:

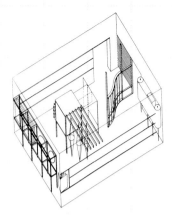

László Moholy-Nagy, project for the Room of Our Time, Landesmuseum, Hanover, 1930; drawing by Luderer

The immeasurable increase in the number of exhibitions only gives us a kaleidoscopic, passive empathy with the psyche of individual artists of past or present. This kind of cultural enrichment no longer serves the real demands of our time.

Our present is in real need of exhibitions which have a deeper and more active connection with our own problems. Therefore, we should replace "specialist exhibitions" by "surveys" and the "collecting of blossoms" by "road signs."

This does not mean that exhibitions of old masters should be discontinued, but it means that they should be transferred into the new soil of an activating philosophy.

Even exhibitions of facsimiles when executed in the new spirit could be of great help—particularly because they can be shown at the same time in different places and in the smallest communities.

Most important of all, I think, is that the public should always be given a feeling and understanding of what is still part of our present and what has already been part. Exhibitions should help to explain our present position in the course of historical growth. They should help to explain the meaning of our present controversies. Thus exhibitions could be turned into liberating incentives and productive energies for our public life.[36]

The same year, Dorner visited the German Werkbund installation at the exhibition of the Society of Decorative Artists in Paris, designed by Moholy-Nagy, Marcel Breuer, and Herbert Bayer under the direction of Gropius. Immediately afterward he approached Moholy-Nagy about creating a second gallery of contemporary work at the Hanover museum. This was to be called the Room of Our Time, and its purpose would be to show the latest developments in Western visual culture. It was to include many of the exhibits from the Paris exhibition, to be acquired by Dorner from their lenders or manufacturers. Unlike the Abstract Cabinet, the Room of Abstract Art would deemphasize artwork as traditionally defined, giving a privileged place at the end of the museum's evolutionary sequence to the new reproductive arts—photography, film, and the print media—as well as to architecture and industrial design, from automobiles and airplanes to machines and engineering structures.

Assisted by the engineer Luderer in Gropius's office and in close consultation with Dorner, Moholy-Nagy projected a multimedia gallery for the Hanover museum. As may be approximately reconstructed from Luderer's preliminary axonometric sketch (5), the ensuing correspondence between Dorner and Moholy-Nagy, and the retrospective description in Cauman's book, it would have been closely related in concept and content to the space Moholy-Nagy had designed in Paris.[37] A section of the curved glass wall he had used there to define the circulation route was to be reinstalled at Hanover to usher visitors into the gallery. The two long walls of the room would document the development of industrial design and architecture— one wall, as at Paris, treating "Darmstadt through Dessau" (the Werkbund through the Bauhaus), the other tracing the evolution of modern architecture from Louis Sullivan, Frank Lloyd Wright, and the Vienna Secession through Gropius, Mies van der Rohe,

Eliel Saarinen, Otto Haesler, and Breuer. A third wall was to contain two glass screens showing short films, one documentary (e.g., Sergei Eisenstein), the other abstract (Eggeling, Richter). On the fourth wall was to be a screen scrolling a continuous loop of images. The various film projections in the room were to be activated by pushbuttons controlled by the visitor. In the middle of the room another screen was to be hung, possibly featuring work for the contemporary stage like Schlemmer's *Triadic Ballet* and Gropius's designs for Erwin Piscator's *Total Theater*. The centerpiece of the gallery, housed within a booth, was to be Moholy-Nagy's own *Light-Space Modulator,* a device on which he had worked since 1922 and which had had its first showing at the Paris exposition (6). Initially conceived as a prop for an electric stage and built with the help of technicians at the AEG electrical company, the mechanized sculpture was designed to revolve slowly while a ring of colored lights on a timer flashed at it, causing constantly changing shadows to be cast on surrounding surfaces.

Tectonically, the Room of Our Time would have been an ethereal ambiance of lightweight metal, glass, and projected light. But Dorner was only able to carry out part of the scheme. He had purchased an expensive fourteenth-century Westphalian altarpiece the same year, exhausting his budget. Concurrently, Weimar liberalism was under attack, and Dorner began to meet increasing resistance from his museum committee.

97

The Road Not Taken

(6)
László Moholy-Nagy, *Light-Space Modulator*, 1922–30

Modernism and Fascism

By the summer of 1933 the effects of National Socialism were felt in the Hanover museum. An anonymous article appeared in the Hanover *Tageblatt* noting that the museum was deemphasizing the Abstract Cabinet, which it had previously treated as an "idol," and according expressionist painting a less important role. One historian has surmised that this article was written by Dorner himself in an effort to make the museum's holdings of contemporary work less of a target for the Nazis.[38] A letter written in March 1934 by the painter Buchheister suggests that Dorner's too earnest efforts to reason with the current regime—to convince them of modern art's relevance to contemporary life—were becoming embarrassments.[39] In a photograph of the Abstract Cabinet taken in 1934 one of the horizontal panels may be seen to contain a poster for *Das Dritte Reich*, a book written in 1923 by the right-wing aesthete Arthur Moeller van den Bruck, whose synthesis of modern classicism and German nationalism had strong mythic appeal for the Nazis **(7)**. Significantly, the poster is turned ninety degrees, emphasizing its formal resemblances to an abstract geometric painting by Vordemberge-Gildewart on the left. (The chair by Mies mentioned earlier may also be seen in this photograph.)

During these years Alfred Barr made a return visit to the Hanover museum. He later recalled his experience:

> I last visited the Hanover Museum in 1935, two years after the Nazis seized power. The first thing I asked to see after being welcomed by Dr. Dorner was the gallery of abstract art. Elsewhere in Germany modern painting had disappeared from museum walls, so I half expected to find the famous room dismantled. Yet it was still there and accessible to the public, though to visit it may have been risky for a German, since here were spies even in the museums. Dr. Dorner showed me the abstract gallery proudly. But it was the last redoubt. Within a year or so it was closed, its works of art dispersed, destroyed, or sold abroad, its director a voluntary "cultural" refugee in the United States.[40]

On this visit Dorner showed Barr a large cache of paintings and drawings by Kasimir Malevich that he had stowed in the basement of the Hanover museum. He had obtained custody of these works when the Soviet artist left them in Germany following

(7)

Abstract Cabinet; 1934; above the chair by Mies van der Rohe is a poster for Arthur Moeller van den Bruck's book
Das Dritte Reich (turned ninety degrees)

an exhibition of his work in Berlin in 1927. Dorner helped Barr to smuggle two Malevich canvases out of the museum rolled around his umbrella; Barr also carried out two drawings in his briefcase. Dorner succeeded in shipping another group to Barr via Holland concealed under some engineering drawings. These appeared in the exhibition "Cubism and Abstract Art" at the Museum of Modern Art in 1936, where their provenance was listed as "lent anonymously." It is thus that a number of suprematist works, including the canonic *White on White,* entered the museum's collection, to remain there permanently.[41]

In late 1936 Dorner returned from a trip to London where he had curated an exhibition of the work of the painter Edvard Munch to find the Abstract Cabinet dismantled and its contents removed. In all, 270 works from the museum's collection were confiscated. Of these many ended up in the "Degenerate Art" show in Munich in 1937, and many found their way to auction in Lucerne where they were purchased by Western collectors. Dorner resigned from his post at the museum in February 1937, fleeing first to Berlin, then to Paris, where he and his wife boarded the *Normandie* for New York. Among the passengers on his voyage of emigration were Henry-Russell Hitchcock and Herbert Bayer.

The Diaspora of the Avant-Garde

Elaborating upon Peter Bürger's thesis, Andreas Huyssen has argued for a more specific analysis of the relationship between art and politics in the context of the various avant-garde movements of the 1920s:

> The failure of the avantgarde to reorganize a new life praxis through art and politics resulted in precisely those historical phenomena which make any revival of the avantgarde's project today highly problematic, if not impossible: namely the false sublations of the art/life dichotomy in fascism with its aestheticization of

politics, in Western mass culture with its fictionalization of reality, and in socialist realism with its claims of reality status for its fictions.

If we agree with the thesis that the avantgarde's revolt was directed against the totality of bourgeois culture and its psycho-social mechanisms of domination and control, and if we then make it our task to salvage the historical avantgarde from the conformism which has obscured its political thrust, then it becomes crucial to answer a number of questions which go beyond Bürger's concern with the "institution art" and the formal structure of the avantgarde art work. How precisely did the dadaists, surrealists, futurists, constructivists, and productivists attempt to overcome the art/life dichotomy? How did they conceptualize and put into practice the radical transformation of the conditions of producing, distributing, and consuming art? What exactly was their place within the political spectrum of those decades and what concrete political possibilities were open to them in specific countries?[42]

These questions are unavoidable with respect to Alexander Dorner's career, especially in light of his experience in the aftermath of the Weimar years. The three artists with whom Dorner had, at successive points in his career, his most consequential contacts, each central in the development of modernist aesthetics—first Lissitzky, then Moholy-Nagy, and finally Herbert Bayer—may be seen in retrospect as delimiting a paradigmatic spectrum. Geographically as well as historically, the overlapping but ultimately divergent careers of these three artists represent alternative destinies of the European artistic culture of the 1920s, inflected by both historical circumstance and personal temperament. This is not to suggest that Dorner himself saw it this way; in carrying the banner of art-into-life from Europe to the United States, he remained fully confident about its future within the new context.

With the completion of the Abstract Cabinet, Lissitzky, as already described, relinquished the abstract constructivism of his *Proun* period and reoriented his work to the rigors of Stalin's first Five-Year Plan and the new socialist realism mandated of cultural production. To what extent his shift was voluntary, founded on a belief that the representational image was a more efficacious instrument of mass education, remains a subject of debate.[43] Through the 1930s, he continued to be a faithful adherent of the Stalinist state occupied in producing propaganda graphics for the Red Army and Soviet industry. He died of tuberculosis in 1941.

Moholy-Nagy resigned from the Bauhaus for ideological reasons in 1928, the year Gropius left, denouncing Gropius's successor, Hannes Meyer, for trying to transform the school's humanistic pedagogy into a vocational training program. He remained in Berlin through the early 1930s. In addition to collaborating on the 1930 Werkbund exposition in Paris, he worked (again with Gropius and Bayer as well as another Bauhaus colleague, Xanti Schawinsky) on the Building Workers Unions exhibition in Berlin the following year. He also did theater and graphic design and continued to experiment with photograms and filmmaking. In 1934, the year after Hitler's accession to power, he left Germany, moving first to Amsterdam and then to London. In 1937, on the recommendation of Gropius, he was invited by the Association of Arts and Industries in Chicago, a business organization, to found a design school in that city modeled on the Bauhaus. (Gropius

had turned down the job, as he was shortly to become chairman of the architecture department at Harvard.) Moholy-Nagy's "New Bauhaus: American School of Design" was inaugurated in November 1937.

Over the next seven years Moholy-Nagy overcame a series of financial difficulties as well as crises of confidence among his backers. He successively reorganized the school as the School of Design and then the Institute of Design, all the while striving to implement a design education based on an integrated curriculum of artistic training, scientific-technical knowledge, and humanistic development. Support came from Pragmatist circles, Chicago being a prime base for that philosophy in America. Moholy-Nagy also borrowed humanities faculty from the Pragmatist-oriented philosophy department at the University of Chicago, Charles Morris, exponent of the Unity of Science movement there, becoming a dedicated contributor to his program. Dewey (then in New York) lent his name to the school's list of sponsors.[44] But it was the friendship and patronage of Walter Paepcke, an enlightened Chicago industrialist and president of the Container Corporation of America, that was instrumental in keeping Moholy-Nagy's program solvent during these years. A pioneer in grasping the potential of modern art and design as tools of corporate advertising and public relations, Paepcke had become a convert to modernist aesthetics in the 1930s and had high personal ambitions as a cultural impresario. He was ultimately more a pragmatic businessman than a Pragmatist of the philosophical sort, however, and his generous support for Moholy-Nagy's program

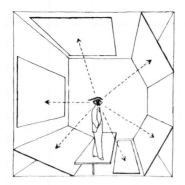

(8)
Herbert Bayer, diagram of
extended field of vision, 1935;
from *The Way Beyond "Art"*

came at the price of the latter's successive pedagogical concessions to the realities of an increasingly corporatized and efficiency-conscious American design profession.[45] By the time Moholy-Nagy, stricken with leukemia, died in 1946 at the age of fifty-one, the school was well on its way to realigning itself with the new managerialism of the ascendant American business culture. Moholy-Nagy would leave a less compromised version of his philosophy in his book *Vision in Motion,* a summary of his holistic educational-artistic outlook published posthumously in 1947, the same year as Dorner's *Way Beyond "Art."*

From this it should already be clear that of the three artists constituting our spectrum, it was Moholy-Nagy who had the closest philosophical, if not personal, affinities with Dorner. The two maintained contact in the United States, Moholy-Nagy bringing Dorner to lecture at the Institute of Design, and after Moholy-Nagy's death, Dorner giving a eulogy for him at a memorial service at the Art Institute in Chicago. But as it turned out, it was not Moholy-Nagy whom Dorner chose as the exemplary subject of the monographic essay that constitutes the second half of *The Way Beyond "Art."* Perhaps Dorner considered that Moholy-Nagy, already ill, could no longer represent the future of modern design in America; perhaps it was clear that Moholy-Nagy had adequately constructed his own theoretical position and did not need someone else to do it for him. In any case, Dorner chose Bayer.

Dorner had first met Bayer in 1927 when he visited the Bauhaus in Dessau, where Bayer, previously a student at the school in Weimar, was a master in the visual communication and typography workshops. Dorner acquired a work by Bayer at this time for the Hanover museum, Bayer's first purchase by a public art institution. Like Moholy-Nagy, Bayer left the school when Gropius's tenure ended and moved to Berlin. There he became art director of the Dorland Studio, a branch of an international advertising agency with important clients in Germany like Blendax, Blaupunkt, Olympia typewriters, and the magazine *Die neue Linie*. Also increasingly involved in exhibition work, Bayer designed a small typography display at the 1928 "Pressa" exhibition in Cologne, where he had a firsthand opportunity to study Lissitzky's installation for the same show. Lissitzky's dynamic approach to exhibition design had a powerful influence on Bayer, inspiring his "field of vision" concept, a technique he would use from this date on for extending the viewer's experience by activating areas of space other than the conventional wall planes (8). Bayer's first diagram of this concept appears in the catalog for the 1930 German Werkbund exhibition in Paris.

Bayer's graphics and painting of the early and mid-1930s remain polemically modernist. At the same time, they also partake of the new classicism infusing German culture, even if he often undercuts the ambient nostalgia for a heroic past with surrealist wit or de Chiricoesque irony. A photomontage series done in 1930 for the popular magazine *Uhu* gives a newly literal meaning to the idea of transforming art into life (9). Illustrations for a story entitled "Undress and You Are Greek," the series consists of classical Greek statues sporting modern undergarments, accessories, and peasant costumes, a conceit Bayer was later to explain as follows: "Our traditional reverence for man of classic antiquity is shattered by an experiment. Photos of sculptures, retouched to appear dressed in contemporary clothing in banal situations of everyday life, reveal that modern man is as classic as Greek man when undressed."[46]

superimposed on a photograph of a vast crowd with a text that reads in four languages, "The Führer speaks and millions listen to him. The working people, the peasantry, and the regained right of self-defense are the supports of National-Socialist Germany." A somewhat more innocuous-looking work bearing the Nazi insignia and the slogan "Arbeitsfreude durch grüne Werkhöfe/Fort

(9)
Herbert Bayer, *Undress and You Are Greek*,
from *Uhu* magazine, 1930

Bayer remained in Germany until 1938. During this period he also undertook commissions for the Nazis. A 1935 catalog for the exhibition "Das Wunder des Lebens" (The Wonder of Life) includes a photomontage depicting Hitler in the role of charismatic orator exhorting the unemployed to participate in the task of building the autobahn **(10)**—an image that makes ironic Dorner's claim in *The Way Beyond "Art"* that "Bayer managed to brave the fascist authorities in Berlin with his utterly anti-absolutistic, visual speeches."[47] Likewise does a contribution by Bayer to the 1936 "Deutschland Ausstellung," an exhibition staged to coincide with the Berlin Olympics. A double-spread in the brochure he designed for this event depicts the heroic heads of a soldier, factory worker, and farmer

mit dem Schmutz" (Joy in work through green factory yards/ Away with dirt) is signed "Herbert Bayer–Kranz" (11). An undated color plate, the upper half illustrates a modern white factory building set in cheerful greenery dominated by a large sunflower; this image is exposed (in the construct of the montage) by a fist entering from the bottom right and peeling away an antiquated brick factory in a litter-strewn landscape, rendered in gritty black and white.[48]

In 1937 an exhibition of Bayer's paintings took place in London, and Dorner wrote the introduction for the catalog. The same year at least one of Bayer's abstract paintings ended up in the "Degenerate Art" show. By this time Bayer realized he no longer had a viable future in Germany. In addition to his aesthetic offenses, his wife (an American who had been a fellow Bauhaus member, from whom he was separated but not yet divorced at the time) and daughter were Jewish. Bayer sailed to the United States to explore the possibility of starting a new life; it was on this voyage that he traveled with Dorner, who was emigrating. He succeeded in getting his own exit visa the following year. In the United States, Bayer would enjoy a long and prolific career as a commercial designer. Successor to Moholy-Nagy in Walter Paepcke's patronage, he eventually became chairman of the Department of Design at the Container Corporation of America and a founding member of Paepcke's cultural institute in Aspen, Colorado.[49] He died at the age of ninety in 1985.

As for Dorner himself, he enthusiastically embraced his new homeland. Within several months of arriving in the United States, largely through the efforts of Barr, but aided as well by his fellow émigrés Panofsky and Gropius, he became director of the art museum of the Rhode Island School of Design. There, starting in 1938, he began implementing ideas he had developed in Hanover, refining his concept of the atmosphere room in his reinstallation of five historical galleries. A new Renaissance gallery was projected for which Dorner had Bayer, with whom he had discussed ideas about the museum on their transatlantic voyage, make drawings. Dorner also expanded the museum's pedagogical role through an intensive program of publications, didactic exhibitions, and the formation of an educational department that reached beyond the design school to the local community. Children and teachers from public schools throughout Rhode Island were bused to Providence for museum tours, lectures, and concerts.[50] Hitchcock, whom Dorner commissioned to write the catalog *Rhode Island Architecture* for an exhibition on that subject in 1939, noted the natural affinity between Dorner's point of view and the original mission of American museums, which unlike their European counterparts, were founded more to provide practical art education for the public than as "treasure houses." This orientation still persisted at the Rhode Island School of Design museum, originally established as an adjunct to the art school.[51] It also found new favor in the 1930s when United States government support of public art was at its height through agencies like the WPA.

Dorner's tenure at the Rhode Island School of Design was to be brief, however. In 1941 internal politics at the museum brought about his resignation. He also found himself suspected by the F.B.I. that year of being a German spy,[52] although an investigation of this came to nothing. From the Rhode Island School of Design, Dorner went to teach art history for several years at Brown University.

(10)
Herbert Bayer, *German Workers Begin!*, from exhibition catalog *Das Wunder des Lebens*, 1935

(11)
Herbert Bayer–[Kurt] Kranz, *Joy in Work through Green Factory Yards*, n.d.

Then, in 1948, he joined the faculty of Bennington College, where he spent the rest of his life in the congenial environment of a small women's liberal arts school founded on John Dewey's principles. But he would remain centrally preoccupied with the problem of the contemporary museum, returning to it in *The Way Beyond "Art"* as well as in a number of essays and unfinished writings.

Highways and "Buy-Ways"

Before following Dorner's developing conception of the twentieth-century museum to its conclusion, it is necessary to consider the monographic portion of his book dealing with Herbert Bayer in more detail. Dorner's relationship to Bayer poses a thorny interpretive problem: namely, how to reconcile Dorner's Pragmatist commitment to cultural reform with Bayer's "pragmatic" professionalism?

A simple answer is that Dorner was politically naive. In the early 1930s he seems to have believed he could win over the Nazi censors to the cause of modern art simply by educating them. Likewise, his subsequent gratitude to the United States for taking him in inclined him to see the future of modern culture in the context of American capitalist democracy with the same rosy optimism, newly influenced by Deweyan Pragmatism, through which he viewed American organizational methods and technology. Thus, continuing to believe, like others who had been associated with the Werkbund and Bauhaus in Germany, in the possibility of an enlightened alliance between art and big business, he identified the objectives of a progressive culture with those of a progress-oriented economic system:

> There has developed within capitalism a new and
> more efficient species of mind to replace the old
> autonomous "I," and that species sees deeper and

plans farther ahead. The final ground is
no longer the autonomous individual but an
interpenetrative collaboration of all individuals to dissolve autonomy. . . . Already, with
Henry Ford, we could see this thrust into a
new economic reality.[53]

That the refugee from Hitler's Germany should be so uncritical as to cite an avowedly anti-Semitic American captain of industry—Ford was, of course, the only American to be mentioned with admiration in *Mein Kampf*—is telling. But there is more than naïveté or irony to Dorner's utopia of the farsighted capitalist. Like many of his compatriots, including Gropius and Mies van der Rohe, Dorner believed that aesthetic culture had the option to remain "apolitical," that it could exist untainted by political ideology. As these émigré intellectuals rationalized, the "idea" of modern art transcended national boundaries and political differences. In this context, the fact that Bayer was now working for American patrons, especially an enlightened industrialist like Paepcke, appeared to Dorner—at least initially, as we shall see—perfectly consistent with his own project, "the liberated and life transforming power of Abstract art . . . transferred into practical use."[54] As such, when Dorner was asked in 1945 by the president of Brown University to prepare an exhibition and book about "an artist exemplifying successful integration of scientific and artistic activity," Bayer appeared a natural, if not inevitable, choice, especially given their closely intertwined experiences in Germany and the United States over the past two decades.[55]

Dorner's admiration for Bayer was reinforced by the series of exhibition designs that Bayer began to execute shortly after his arrival in the United States. The latter's outwardly seamless professional transition from Europe to America had in fact commenced even before he left Germany for good, when, on his preliminary trip to the United States in the summer of 1937, he was drawn, along with Dorner, into the planning of a major exhibition at the Museum of Modern Art. This was the exhibition "Bauhaus 1919–1928." Mounted in December 1938, nine months before the Nazi invasion of Poland, it was a tribute to the Gropius years in Weimar and Dessau—the subsequent periods of Hannes Meyer and Mies being excluded—and a first major presentation to the American public of the school's work. It was also intended as a direct response to Hitler, who had closed the Bauhaus in 1933 and persecuted many of its members. The names of artists still living in Germany whose work was included in the show had to be omitted for fear of reprisals to them. John McAndrew, then curator of architecture and design at the museum, was in charge of the exhibition, working together with Barr and Walter and Ise Gropius. Upon visiting Gropius—who had himself arrived in the United States only a few months earlier and was summering on Cape Cod—Bayer was not only commissioned to design the installation and catalog but, during his return to Germany in 1937–38, to do the dangerous job of collecting work from Bauhaus members still living there. Dorner, also among those assembled at Gropius's "summer Bauhaus" in 1937 (along with other Bauhäusler like Breuer, Schawinsky, and Josef Albers), was asked to write the introductory essay for the catalog. Beginning by describing the hostility that surrounded the Bauhaus when it was in Weimar, Dorner's essay was an implicit condemnation of the Nazi suppression of artistic freedom. Dorner concluded by stating, "We believe that we have only glimpsed the great potentialities of this technical age, and that the Bauhaus idea has only begun to make its way."[56]

The exhibition was held in the museum's temporary quarters in the concourse of Rockefeller Center, the last of its shows there before the museum moved into its permanent building on West 53rd Street. Bayer, employing his field of vision concept, used lightweight and suspensional supports to mount many of the displays, minimizing the presence of structure and pitching photographs and objects at confrontational angles (12). Directional shapes, footprints, and arrows painted on the floor guided the circuitous circulation path through a sequence of small galleries. The reaction to the exhibition by both the professional critics and the public at large was mostly negative. It was so badly received, in fact, that Barr and McAndrew had to take steps to mollify the museum's trustees. Comments ranged from bewilderment at the "agglomeration of abstracts . . . and distorted forms" to criticisms of the exhibition as "clumsily installed," "gadgety," and "chaotic."[57]

This reception, however, did not dissuade the Museum of Modern Art from hiring the talented Bayer a few years later to design two propagandistic exhibitions mounted in the midst of World War II, "Road to Victory" (1942) and "Airways to Peace" (1943). In "Road to Victory," Bayer, working with the museum's photography director, Edward Steichen, elaborated his previous spatial strategies. Circulation was tightly channeled to reinforce the compelling visual narrative of large-scale angled photographs and patriotic text panels. In "Airways to Peace" (13), Bayer again exploited the devices of suspensional display and ramped viewing to create,

(12)
"Bauhaus 1919–1928,"
Museum of Modern Art, New York, 1938;
Herbert Bayer, designer

in Dorner's words, "an atmosphere of lightness, bodilessness, and hence spacelessness."[58] Networks of ropes, screens of poles, and map patterns of contour lines created dynamic optical vectors, while the focus of the exhibition was a cable-suspended walk-in globe. Another major exhibition held two years later at the Chicago Art Institute, entitled "Modern Art in Advertising," designed in collaboration with Stamo Papadaki and showcasing the advertising designs of forty-four modern artists commissioned by Paepcke for the Container Corporation of America, restated the concepts Bayer had been honing for nearly two decades **(14)**.

In an article published in 1939 but written as early as 1936, entitled "Fundamentals of Exhibition Design," Bayer stated:

[In an exhibition] paintings, photography, etc., make only part . . . of a new and complex means of communication. A theme exhibited . . . should not retain its distance from the spectator, it should be brought close to him, penetrate and leave an impression on him, should explain, demonstrate, and even persuade and lead him to a planned and direct reaction. Therefore we may say that exhibition design runs parallel with the psychology of advertising. And here lies an essential cause of the intensification of the exhibition. . . . The organism of a successfully designed exhibition includes . . . mobility . . . forcefulness . . . interpenetration and intersection . . . the movements of the individual. As a result of the dynamic quality in man, a dynamic and purposeful construction is reached. . . . Not only artistic views produce the new, open and seemingly variable groundplan. . . . The groundplan is built up from a motif or theme, which is to be displayed. . . . It takes shape from the solution of the direction problem. . . . Groundplan and direction of the visitor must become one.[59]

Bayer's concept of dynamism and interpenetration reflects his proximity to the aesthetics of Lissitzky and Moholy-Nagy. Yet his explicit analogy between exhibition design and ad-

(13)
"Airways to Peace," Museum of Modern Art, New York, 1943; Herbert Bayer, designer

vertising already indicates a basic difference between his work and theirs. While Lissitzky and Moholy-Nagy both undertook commercial work, they remained committed to the idea that their work could effect a liberatory transformation of everyday life— Lissitzky with his concept of an engaged, collective spectatorship, Moholy-Nagy with his creed of organic integration. Bayer's psychology of advertising, in contrast, blurred the distinction between education and manipulation. It reduced the avant-garde's social critique to a technical instrumentality, making modern art equally available for propaganda and consumerism. The production of a sense of dynamism and mobility in the exhibition gallery no longer had to be couched in the language of revolutionary cognition or linked to the humanistic discourse of holistic vision. It was rather a matter of professional mastery, a psychological technique of spectatorial control and persuasion.

The same instrumentalism characterizing Bayer's approach to exhibition design also characterizes his American graphic work, which is at once inventive and repetitious. Formal motifs and design strategies continually get recycled, hinting that the messages Bayer is conveying are interchangeable. Thus the same hand that symbolizes the "Bauhaus synthesis" in a panel at the entry to the 1938 Bauhaus exhibition **(15)** could also itemize *4 Easy Buy-Ways*—ways of buying on credit—in a poster produced a year later **(16)**.[60] A more cynical example of the reuse of imagery is that of the highway that vectors toward infinity, first used by Bayer in his photomontage of Hitler and the autobahn in the catalog *Das Wunder des Lebens*. Six years later the same motif reappears on Bayer's book jacket for Giedion's *Space, Time and Architecture*.

Yet in *The Way Beyond "Art"* Dorner insists on presenting Bayer as exemplary of an evolutionary new type of artist, "the designer of the future." To Dorner,

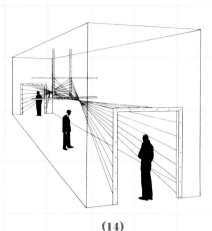

(14)
"Modern Art in Advertising," Art Institute, Chicago, 1945; Herbert Bayer with Stamo Papadaki, designers

111

Bayer's instrumentalism represents nothing more—or less—than a healthily antiromantic and rigorously functional approach to artistic problems; his repetitions are a function of the universality of his new visual language. Dorner locates Bayer's aesthetic style between abstraction and surrealism, labeling it "Modern Realism," a form language that draws on "simple and universally comprehensible symbols" understandable "by everybody." [61] In a comment relegated to a footnote, Dorner insists that advertising can be an ethical pursuit, distinguishing between the "retrogressive surrealism" typical of conventional commercial imagery and the more constructive impulses he finds in Bayer's work:

> Retrogressive surrealism plays a curiously asocial role and imparts this tone to the business. It makes of the offer of merchandise a frivolous, almost undignified display of stagnant superfluity, as if production were something very different from that necessary energy in the nexus of creative growth it actually is. Doesn't the public need the producer just as much as the latter needs the public? Why should the artist's self-expression step between public and producer; why should it divert the spectator's attention from the vital life-process underneath? Why shouldn't it rather inform that process with individual energies and show the production and consumption of goods as part of the higher functionalism of growing life in universally recognizable signs? Why shouldn't we leave behind that confusing hothouse atmosphere in which business, artist and public are still isolated, that chaotic autonomy of the world of the "free individual"? Wouldn't it be better to take the straight road of stimulating information instead of the bypath of confusing by surprise? Why do we prefer diversion to construction? And what do we wish to divert people from? When Bayer says: "In the field of visual communication I have always been more for INFORMATION than for ADVERTISING" he states in unmistakable terms the new spirit. [62]

In the new capitalist spirit of undistorted communication and collective symbolism, advertising art will exist as much to further consumer education and mass information as to sell products for profit. Dorner's argument recalls the distinction between commerce and commercialism that John Dewey made earlier in an article entitled "Pragmatic America":

> Commerce itself, let us dare to say it, is a noble thing. It is intercourse, exchange, communication, distribution, sharing of what is otherwise secluded and private. Commercialism like all isms is evil. [63]

Yet Bayer was the wrong exemplar of Dewey's pragmatic America. If, like Paepcke, he could be characterized as "pragmatic" in his no-nonsense approach to problem-solving and his consummate professionalism, he was hardly a Pragmatist in the Deweyan sense. [64] Ironically, as a painter who continued throughout his life to value the practice of fine art at least as much as applied art (even if his reputation rested on the latter), Bayer found Dorner's critique of aestheticism in *The Way Beyond "Art"* inimical. Although flattered by Dorner's attention, he would later express his discomfort with the role in which the latter had cast him:

> alexander dorner in his book "the way beyond art, the work of herbert bayer" has projected interesting ideas of the function of the artist in our industrial society, taking my work as an example to illustrate his philosophy. although i am not in accord with all of his ideas, this book was an audacious

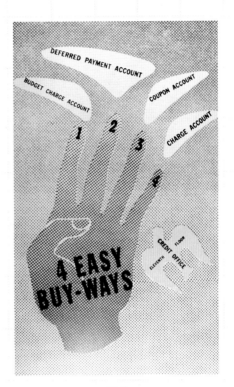

(15)
Herbert Bayer, *The Bauhaus Synthesis*,
entry panel for "Bauhaus 1919–1928,"
Museum of Modern Art, 1938

(16)
Herbert Bayer, *4 Easy Buy-Ways*,
advertisement for Bamberger's
department store, 1939

statement in view of the re-emergence of a romantic, unrealistic outlook on the function of the artist.[65]

In hindsight, Dorner's choice of Bayer as the exponent of his own philosophy of art into life can only be viewed as a judgment error. In postwar America, art would enter life more powerfully than the avant-gardes of the 1920s had ever imagined. A critic for *Art News* magazine commenting on the reception of the exhibition "Modern Art in Advertising" noted, "The painter has proved his economic worth in the world of industry. Art has come out of the studio and entered the lives of 131,000,000 people."[66] But it would do so as packaging and image rather than as the culturally regenerative force envisioned by Dorner.

Did Dorner retrospectively recognize Bayer's contribution to this destiny? Did he grasp the contradictions for the artist of functioning within the mainstream of capitalist practice? The original edition of his book gives no indication of this, and he may have died too early to achieve much perspective on the forces sealing the commodification of modern culture. At the same time, we may perhaps infer Dorner's subsequent disaffection with Bayer from the fact that the monographic section on Bayer is dropped from the revised edition of *The Way Beyond "Art,"* published in 1958. Nor does Bayer figure significantly in Cauman's intellectual biography of Dorner. Curiously, especially given Dorner's views on studio art, Charles Kuhn's introduction to the 1958 edition of *The Way Beyond "Art"* connects Dorner's thought less to developments in applied design than to the rise of abstract expressionism in painting, by the 1950s "the dominant style of the Western world . . . a reflection of the untrammeled political freedom in the democratic West."[67]

From Avant-Gardism to Pragmatism

I have characterized Alexander Dorner as an avant-gardist. It would probably be better to call him a futurist. (Not surprisingly, Reyner Banham was among his admirers.) Going through the clippings, notes, letters, lectures, and finished and unfinished writings left to the Busch-Reisinger museum by Dorner's widow, one gets the impression that Dorner cut out anything he came across that said "tomorrow's": tomorrow's house, tomorrow's skyscraper, tomorrow's city plan. He was interested in new technical systems, in new materials like cellophane and aluminum, in inflatables, in new uses of rubber, plastics, and glass, in prefabrication, in radiant heating and air conditioning. He had a passion for floating buildings, suspended lightweight structures, and space frames. He was excited by the schemes of Buckminster Fuller. He had no use, on the other hand, for what he called *Ego-Kult-Künstler*. Between two "houses of tomorrow" exhibited at the Museum of Modern Art in 1952, one by Frederick Kiesler and one by Fuller, Dorner unequivocally preferred Fuller's. What he hated was anything static, monumental, or self-consciously formalistic. A 1949 article clipped from the *New York Times Magazine* about Philip Johnson's Glass House, in which the writer suggested that "the real significance of the house" lay in its "emphasis on the permanent," bears Dorner's inscription "photo best-seller" in purple ink.[68] In *The Way Beyond "Art"* he had this to say about architecture, however unprophetic:

The mind of the new architect has developed a greater and more effectual depth than the three-dimensional mind of the architect who started thinking first in intellectual "forms" and later in terms of "movement in space." If we look for a specific house to illustrate this evolution tellingly we may find it in Gropius' and Wachsmann's "growing and shrinking house" of 1943. It seems almost certain that the progressive energization of architectural thinking will do away with what has been called the "international style" in modern building. That style still betrayed vestiges of the autonomy of "form" which architecture had taken over from Abstract painting. Form and function were still running parallel without real integration, creating the false impression that modern architecture was concerned with a perpetuation of "absolute basic elements."[69]

In his ongoing pursuit of corroboration for his antiabsolutist view of the world, Dorner also took lively interest in contemporary developments in science, especially the behavioral sciences—psychology, physiology, and visual perception. In the mid-1940s he engaged in discussions with Dewey, then in his eighties, and Hadley Cantril, of the psychology department at Princeton, concerning experiments in visual perception being carried out by the physiologist Adelbert Ames Jr. at the Hanover Institute (formerly the Dartmouth Eye Institute) in Hanover, New Hampshire. Ames's research purported to give empirical verification to Dewey's transactional theory of experience, proving the relativity and contingency of human vision. Ames's best-known demonstration offered a reinterpretation of the axiomatic relationship between seeing and believing: a viewer peering through a monocular peephole at three different arrangements of sticks and shapes in space tended in each case to constellate the elements into the familiar form of a chair by applying the laws of optical perspective. From this trompe l'oeil exercise Ames derived the conclusion that sensory perception did not correlate with objective truth, but rather "establish[ed] between the evolving organism and the ever-changing environment a relationship on the basis of which the organism may effectively carry out its purpose," a finding in line with basic Pragmatist tenets.[70]

When, in 1947, Dorner sent Ames a copy of *The Way Beyond "Art,"* Ames pronounced it "epochal," suggesting that his own conclusions supplemented Dorner's "to an extraordinary degree."[71] Dewey, who entertained the idea of "some sort of combined scientific and educational activity" involving Ames, Dorner, and himself,[72] was hardly less effusive in his praise for Dorner's book:

> I have had time to read [*The Way Beyond "Art"*] with more care than before. I am even more impressed with it in consequence. The chapters on the magic, classic and romantic periods have thrown more light for me upon the general cultural historical developments than anything I have ever read, philosophy, science, politics as well as art. You have held the latter up as a search light on the whole affair—and I am confident you are right as to what is going on now. You have a profound sense of the scientific revolution and its implications for the future.[73]

For his own part, Dorner seems to have found in Pragmatism a potential alternative to the impasse of the avant-garde—and ultimately a way beyond "art" that did not necessarily lead in the direction taken by

Herbert Bayer. From a contemporary perspective, we might characterize this impasse as the problematic of Benjamin versus Adorno, or optimistic engagement versus pessimistic withdrawal and autonomy. Deweyan Pragmatism, also presenting itself as a critical theory of cultural praxis, potentially offered a third way. Avant-garde ideology tended to be revolutionary, schismatic, utopian. Pragmatism, no less committed to social and cultural transformation, was evolutionary, organic, democratic. What Dewey's philosophy implied was that the avant-garde idea of transforming art into life might possibly be sustained by translating it into the Pragmatist philosophy of art as education and experience.

Dewey's conception of art as "consummatory experience" was not only an assault on the idea of art as the production and conservation of fetishized objects, but also an emancipatory conception of aesthetic activity in the context of a democratic society. Even though Dewey's taste in modern art was hardly advanced by Dorner's standards—formed, as it was, by Albert Barnes, for whom the history of modern painting ended more or less with Cézanne and Matisse—Dewey saw the function of art as that of being a "liberating event," as he states in his introduction to *The Way Beyond "Art,"* not just for the artist who produced it, but also for the viewer who perceived it intelligently, "without pre-formed routine."[74] Dewey had opened his book *Art as Experience* (1934) with a paean to the organic integration of art and public life in ancient cultures and a brief but incisive critique of the "museum conception of art" as this emerged in the context first of European imperialism and then under American capitalism. Dewey would almost seem to anticipate Michel Foucault in suggesting, "An instructive history of modern art could be written in terms of the distinctively modern institutions of museum and exhibition gallery."[75]

The Museum of the Future

It was to the question of what architectural form the new museum should take if it was no longer to "propagate 'art' in the old sense," no longer to be a "temple

wise unleashed powerful energies in its time. With this image in mind, Dorner asserted that the museum "would not require any gorgeous palaces of absolutistic ideal art but would be constructed functionally and flexibly of light modern materials."[77]

At least this was Dorner's thinking around 1947–48 when he was invited to set the program for two studios given in consecutive years at the Harvard Graduate School of Design. His 1947 brief, for a "living museum"

116

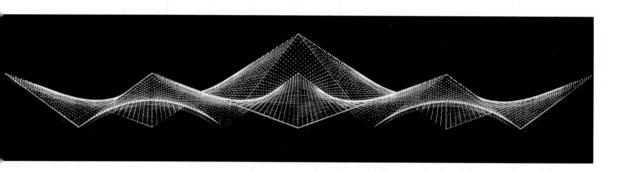

of humanistic relics," that Dorner devoted the concluding pages of *The Way Beyond "Art."*[76] Declaring that the future museum must dramatize "the forces behind the various historical realities, using all possible sensory and intellectual sources of representation," he went on to posit that the museum building itself should be flexible, in both overall architecture and interior planning. Rather than presenting itself as a shrine or, on the other hand, "a loose arrangement of diverse styles," the new type of museum should be "a powerhouse, a producer of energies," analogous to the most dynamic new art of every period, which like-

in the city of Cambridge, called for a building that would house both permanent and changing exhibitions as well as a lecture hall, tearoom, offices, workshops, and ancillary spaces. With respect to the permanent exhibition space, Dorner stipulated that each of the galleries be "completely different in shape, light, and treatment of its boundaries" and that they "should have no 'architecture,' that is, they should have no fixed walls." He added:

(17)
Eduardo Catalano, roof design, 1956,
from Samuel Cauman, *The Living Museum*

We would like to emphasize again that this Permanent Exhibition has no static permanence whatsoever. It should remain entirely flexible (a) for external extension toward the future and for additional branches; (b) for the improvement of the representation of the past by increase in knowledge, understanding, and technical means of conveying both.[78]

Cauman's book, in which the full text of this program is published, provides further elaboration on Dorner's thinking with regard to the architecture of the living museum. In Dorner's view Le Corbusier's Mundaneum was misguided not only because its ziggurat form positivistically represented "the ascent of man" as a telos based on metaphysical speculation rather than "evolutionary realities," but also because Le Corbusier had amputated the "head" of this "picture of progress" by relegating modern art and industry to a separate building. Nor was Frank Lloyd Wright's Guggenheim a more viable solution: "The uniform dictatorship of academic dogma is replaced by the chaotic dictatorship of the freely inspired neo-romantic artist."[79]

Instead, Dorner preferred the lightweight structures and space frames of a Pier Luigi Nervi, a Felix Candela, an Eduardo Catalano (17), a Fuller. In 1950 he and Fuller engaged in conversations at Bennington (where Fuller's daughter was a student) about the museum of the future, and Fuller produced a sketch and calculations (18). In the end, though, Dorner found even Fuller's geodesic dome too traditional a model. He sought an expression more consonant with his concept of the new spatiality, a container for the history of art that would be nothing more than a weightless and interpenetrative field of forces: "complete inner flexibility, a cobweb of massless interacting members so thin, so light, that it is less a closed permanent form than an action, a process."[80]

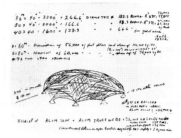

But Dorner's conception of the museum of the future went beyond metaphors. By this time he also found the programmatic contradictions of the "permanent living museum" unreconcilable. Even if no longer monumental in form, such an institution was still geared to the display and status of unique originals and accessible only to a limited public. Dorner's Pragmatist views on art education thus led him to a radically democratic solution. What he proposed was a chain of facsimile museums:

> Turn the living museum into a museum of facsimiles.... Mass-produce it. Set up two, three, half a dozen, twenty museums of facsimiles in different parts of the country, in sizes to match conditions of attendance and financial support.[81]

This, Dorner now believed, was the only way to justify museums as public institutions, to make them widely available and financially viable. The collection of the facsimile museum would combine whatever originals the local museum had with a supplemental program of reproductions—an idea he had already anticipated in 1929 with his "Original and Facsimile" exhibition—as well as educational materials like books and slides. The supplemental materials would be coordinated by a central "museum institute." The decentralized chain of facsimile museums would not replace the Louvres and Metropolitans of the world, but instead function on a regional and community scale, somewhat like the public library system, displaying local works alongside representations of those deemed more universal.

From a contemporary perspective, the idea of the community-based facsimile museum appears provincial both literally and figuratively, while that of a central institute disseminating reproductions of "great works" seems tantamount to establishing a new canon, directly contradicting Dorner's own objectives. Moreover, the notion of a chain of art institutions set up to exhibit reproductions of masterpieces would seem to have the propensity to devolve into a theater of simulation. Yet Dorner's effort to break down the elitist boundaries of the museum and to put the new technology of reproduction in the service of the mass public bears comparison to André Malraux's *musée imaginaire,* an idea published at nearly the same time. [82] "A 'Museum without Walls' is coming into being," declared Malraux, "and now that the plastic arts have invented their own printing-press, it will carry infinitely farther that revelation of the world of art which the 'real' museums, limited perforce, offer us within their walls." [83] While Malraux's prophecy of the "museum without walls"—a twentieth-century version of Victor Hugo's "this will kill that"—has little of Dorner's reformist intentions about it, Dorner would undoubtedly have endorsed Malraux's conviction that the universality of the book of color reproductions would make the temple of auratic objects obsolete.

Dorner's facsimile museum may have an even closer correlate today, however, in the virtual museum that is now becoming available on the computer screen. In this evolving "public space" of art reception and education, Dorner's vision of a "cobweb of massless interacting members" is, for better or worse, quite literally being realized.

Conclusion

The relationship between the museum and the mausoleum is more than merely phonetic, as Adorno once pointed out **(19)**. [84] Indeed, virtually from its inception as a public institution the museum was associated with death. Julien Guadet writes in *Eléments et théorie de l' Architecture* (1890):

> In all epochs really creative artistically, museums have been unknown: least of all would those times have comprehended an artist's producing a work for immediate interment in such a domain of death. . . . a museum is a kingdom of the past, a place for the preservation of that which is no longer living. [85]

In the same vein, the American Benjamin Ives Gilman, a museum man, could write in 1918:

> If we love art, we must rejoice in proportion as museums are unnecessary; and look upon [art's] conservation therein as the Greeks looked upon existence in the underworld, all of whose years were not in their minds worth a single day of warm and breathing life. [86]

It was Dorner's lifelong desire to revitalize the relationship between art and everyday life by bringing about a total transformation

(19)
Marcel Duchamp, installation for exhibition "First Papers of Surrealism," New York City, 1942

of the museum as an institution. Art objects were not idols to be worshiped, but points of departure for public discourse, catalysts to new ways of seeing and experiencing the world. Needless to say, his iconoclastic vision has had little impact on the course taken in this century by most museums. Even in a postmodern intellectual climate, few in the art establishment would risk acting on his view that artistic masterpieces are as much products of the history and culture of interpretation as individual acts of genius. For the museum to do so would be to gamble recklessly on its investments, aesthetic and financial. Nor, contrary to Walter Benjamin's prediction, has the original artwork relinquished much of its aura despite accelerating stylistic cycles and the ubiquity of technical reproduction.

Yet the controversies over public art that have arisen in the last decade, challenging not only the art establishment but the public at large, suggest that a more democratic conception of art is still alive. In this context, and as a counter to Adorno's tragic critique of the relationship between art and life in late capitalist society, Dorner's powerhouse remains at least a provocative futurist image:

> The new type of art museum must be not only not an "art" museum in the traditional, static sense, but, strictly speaking, not a "museum" at all. A museum conserves supposedly eternal values and truths. But the new type would be a kind of powerhouse, a producer of new energies.[87]

In 1955, in a letter to Dorner, Philip Johnson recalled the impact that the Abstract Cabinet had made on him a quarter century earlier:

> The Abstract Cabinet at the Hanover Museum was one of the most vivid memories and most exciting parts of the Weimar Republic.

It was this kind of experience that first aroused my interest in the Bauhaus Movement and indeed in Modern Architecture in general. I do not believe anything since that period of the late twenties has been quite as exciting for me.
My belated congratulations.[88]

Johnson's tribute was more than belated. There is a transatlantic irony in the fact that the classically trained German art historian Dorner was on his way to embracing the "growth and change" philosophy of American Pragmatism at precisely the time when the American Johnson was engaged in recasting the work of the European architectural avant-gardes as a "classic" aesthetic style. The evolution of the Museum of Modern Art, in whose exhibitions, acquisitions, and spatial determination Johnson played an instrumental role, typifies this development. In 1953 the museum reversed its original policy of deaccessioning works more than fifty years old in favor of amassing a permanent collection of modern masterpieces. Thus was realized Gertrude Stein's oxymoron of the modern museum:

> So long as the museum remains content to preserve old truths and to collect relics that house the timeless spirit of QUALITY it acts as an escape from life. Despite its air of restless activity it . . . is like a dead hand reaching forward into our lives and stopping them.[89]

MARK LINDER

Wild Kingdom

Frederick Kiesler's Display of the Avant-Garde

Frederick Kiesler's career spans the entire history of modern architecture. An original member of the De Stijl group in Central Europe, he is the greatest non-building architect of our time.
—PHILIP JOHNSON, *Art in America*, March, 1960

The basic fallacy is that Mr. Kiesler's concept of architecture is not really architectural. He . . . camouflages abstract sculpture as a kind of building. Sculpture becomes structure, by a slick, expertly rationalized, unpardonable reversal of legitimate architectural procedures.
—ADA LOUISE HUXTABLE, *New York Times*, March 27, 1960

To the Art Editor: In an article on Sunday, March 27, you quote Mr. Philip Johnson's double-edged compliment naming me as the "greatest non-building architect of our time." . . . It is true that I have continuously rejected purely commercial orders. I still feel that it is better to concentrate on a few honest possibilities to build and otherwise wait, unconcerned at being named "the greatest non-building architect of our time," than to be, as is sometimes the case, a most-building non-architect.
—FREDERICK KIESLER, *New York Times*, April 21, 1960

I

At 11:30 in the morning on March 20, 1960, the announcer of the CBS television show *Camera III* introduced Frederick Kiesler to the viewing audience as the designer of the Endless House and, quoting Philip Johnson, as "the greatest non-building architect of our time." One week later in a review of the show in the *New York Times*, Ada Louise Huxtable not only reiterated Johnson's barb, her editors used it in the title of her article: "Architecture on TV: 'Greatest Non-Building Architect of Our Time' Expounds His Ideas."[1]

Today, Huxtable's and Johnson's characterizations remain largely intact, and even after several recent exhibitions in Europe and the United States, Kiesler's reputation as an architect is still tied to just two projects: the Art of this Century Gallery, which was built in 1942 to exhibit Peggy Guggenheim's growing collection of modern art, and the Endless House, which was exhibited numerous times in various versions but was never built. The 1989 Kiesler retrospective at the Whitney Museum of American Art presented Kiesler not as an architect but as a curiously prolific, innovative, and idiosyncratic designer who, in the words of the curator, Lisa Phillips:

resists the signature style that has long been regarded as the signpost of artistic achievement and identity. Neither stylistically consistent nor bound by the limitations of single
medium or discipline, Kiesler has always been difficult to categorize. He has therefore
remained an enigmatic, elusive figure despite the fact that during his lifetime he was well
known in artistic circles. . . . [H]e operated in so many areas at once that his work has seemed
fragmentary and diffuse, known to particular groups—artists, architects, theater designers,
for example—only for the work done in their respective fields. In our Postmodern era,
it is precisely this interdisciplinary quality and multidimensionality that make Kiesler so
intriguing, and somehow sympathetic. [2]

Three years before the Whitney show, Robert Pincus-Witten had also described Kiesler as a
misfit modernist, arguing that "it is in the fray of postmodern debate that he is more easily
understood." [3]

Kiesler certainly would resist his postmodern rehabilitation. In a 1961 interview in *Progressive Architecture*, he insisted that his entire career records the "continuity and the multiplicity *of an idea*," even though he declined to give that idea a name: [4] "But one can learn to
recognize it by corollary happenings; . . . [in] projects, some only planned, some executed,
quite different in function and form, yet all in the same vein and of the same spirit." [5]

Each project, Kiesler maintained, represents one instance of a persistent and continuous
investigation, from his interest in avant-garde theater and stage design in the early 1920s to
his "galaxies," his "environmental sculpture," and the many revisions of the Endless House
in the 1950s and 1960s. In response to the question "When did you first conceive the Endless House?," Kiesler replied: "The three years 1922, 1923, 1924 were the most fruitful in my
life. What I am doing today are follow-ups of these ideas and I'm still looking, as I was 40
years ago, for a chance to build them." [6] However unrealized or inadequate its final versions,
the various precursors and permutations of "the Endless"—with their changing programs,
rhetorical purposes, materials, and technologies—are consistent reformulations of the
same conceptual issues that compelled his futurist, multimedia stage set for Karl Capek's
1923 play *R.U.R.* and his constructivist Space-Stage—a scaffoldlike theater-in-the-round
erected as part of the 1924 International Exhibition of Theater Techniques in Vienna, which
Kiesler directed and for which he adapted and applied the principles of de Stijl not only

to the exhibit, but also to the catalog, tickets, and posters.[7] According to Kiesler, he was drafted into de Stijl in 1923 based on the success of his set for *R.U.R.* Over the next two years, his design for the Vienna exhibition and his "City in Space" at the 1925 Paris exposition would be acclaimed as among the finest examples of de Stijl in architecture.

It was the success of the Vienna exhibition that brought Kiesler to America. Jane Heap, the editor of the *Little Review*, invited Kiesler to restage the exhibition in New York in 1926, a decade or more before the arrival of émigrés such as Kaufmann, Giedion, Gropius, and Mies.[8] Kiesler presented himself as an enthusiastic, but atypical, member of the de Stijl group, an awkward and opportunistic affiliation that would be his only formal relationship with the avant-garde. In fact, Kiesler had begun to challenge the principles of de Stijl even before he arrived in New York.[9] As it turned out, his eccentric posture served him well in a context that, while less than supportive, was almost entirely defenseless against his extravagant imagination. Like his friend Marcel Duchamp, who first came to the United States a decade earlier, Kiesler's migration to America granted him a propitious independence of practice and approach—one that depended, however, on both his distance from and close attachments to the European avant-garde. Constantly referring to work produced during his brief membership in de Stijl—most notably, his "City in Space" and its manifesto, "Vitalbau—Raumstadt—Funktionelle Architektur"—Kiesler conferred a kind of legitimacy, at that time rare in America, upon his artistic ambitions.[10] His constant awareness of events in Europe, combined with his ability aptly to revise them for a skeptical American audience, allowed him to operate between and across disciplines and cultures as an independent, displaced, and tireless advocate for advanced architecture and art. Shrewdly evading the twin authorities of autonomy and ideology, he exploited and amplified his hybrid identity as artist, architect, set designer, and visionary, as well as his ambivalent cultural position (as a radical European antagonistic to American versions of "modern decoration" and an iconoclast in regard to the European avant-garde).[11]

Although Kiesler's restaging of the Vienna show in New York left its de Stijl design intact, he could not transport or rebuild the Space-Stage. Instead, he exhibited a model of a revised, more visionary project that he called the Endless Theater—an elliptical volume of "welded glass" containing a multimedia theater, comprised of a complex of spiral ramps, screens, and platforms.[12] Over the next forty years, the aims of that project resurfaced in the many versions of the Endless House. Thus, while his association with de Stijl brought him international notoriety and established him among the European avant-garde, the Endless Theater effectively announced the beginning of his career in America. That project both reinterpreted the aims of de Stijl and extended important aspects of his prior experimental work in the theater.[13] Like the Space-Stage, the Endless Theater asserted interests—display, dynamic staging, fluid shape, monolithic form—that persistently reemerged in his subsequent work, even as he doggedly reinvented his thinking and readily realigned his associations.

II

The story of Kiesler's calculated ingenuity is not only an index of his evolving attitudes toward the discipline of architecture and his shifting alliances with avant-garde groups; it also provides a unique and important case study of the relocation and reinvention of the European avant-garde in the United States before World War II and before Peggy Guggenheim's Art of this Century Gallery announced the wartime reorganization of the Paris avant-garde in New York. Kiesler's diverse work and evolving identity were constructed and reconstructed from a series of specific and calculated responses to contemporary trends, opportunities, and conventions, from the pseudo-scientific aims of his theory of "design correlation," to his friendship with Duchamp and his involvement with surrealism. Never lacking for techniques or tactics, Kiesler adopted the role of translator—continually reconstructing and revising various modernist idioms and restaging them theatrically as what might be called "the display of the avant-garde."[14] Like Borges's parable of "a certain Chinese encyclopaedia," the catalog of Kiesler's work seems incoherent only because his world is so strange. His seemingly disparate work hangs together as a matrix of interrelated artifacts or species—a wild kingdom of elusive, hybrid creatures whose taxonomy remains undeciphered, in part because their appearances are so fitful and so fleeting.

Kiesler's fascination with the techniques and problems of display pervades almost all of his projects. His work in the European and American theater (he was director of scenic design at Juilliard from 1933 to 1957), his architectural commissions, his installations (of his own and others' work), and his published criticism all exploit display as a specific kind of endlessness or continuity—interactive and temporary, a substitute and a provocation—that unfolds as a staged "event." As George Nelson acknowledges in his otherwise straightforward book, *Display* (1953), the intensely practical problems of display combined with its diverse sources and aspects creates a peculiarly modern discipline:

The word "display" comes from a Latin root which means to unfold or to spread out. As used by us, in a variety of situations, it always conveys the idea of calling someone's attention to something by showing it in a conspicuous way. . . . The plumage of a male bird and the antics of the fighting fish are "display." So are the illuminated letters in a medieval manuscript. . . . The object of display may be to attract a member of the opposite sex; to establish identity (as in the heraldic symbols blazoned on the shields of the knight, or the markings in the undersides of airplanes); to indicate social position (whether actual or desired) by means of school ties, crowns and tiaras, the amount of land around a house, the uplift in the rear fender of a Cadillac; to convey information, as in road signs, traveling exhibits, posters, billboards. And to attract customers. The great bulk of display, in this unromantic age of ours, is designed to persuade someone to buy something he may or may not need or want.[15]

Nelson's capacious definition of display as "virtually any three-dimensional design activity in which the main purpose is to show something" is a surprisingly apt description of the various aspects of Kiesler's approach, which began with futurist and constructivist concepts of dynamism, then explored concepts of pure vision and spatial continuity derived from de Stijl, and ultimately led him to devise modes of display that combine a heterogeneous, intersubjective concept of space with notions of visuality derived from surrealism and psychoanalysis.[16]

The conceptual sophistication of Kiesler's displays has been obscured by most accounts of his career, including his own.[17] By the 1950s Kiesler had become something of a media star and a darling of institutions and gallery owners. He began to exhibit his artwork—"galaxies" and sculptures—and articles appeared not only in the art and architectural press, but in popular magazines like *Time, Life*, *Vogue,* and *Harper's Bazaar.*

His notoriety was largely a result of Philip Johnson and Arthur Drexler's enthusiasm for his Endless House, which Drexler (doubtless aware of its publicity value) had hoped and promised to construct in the courtyard of the Museum of Modern Art.[18] The media portrayed Kiesler's most famous project as an idiosyncratic exercise of personal defiance against the strictures of high modernism and an assault on the boundaries of architecture. For example, Huxtable ridiculed the Endless House as "a slick, expertly rationalized, unpardonable reversal of legitimate architectural procedures." She found his television performance Barnumesque: "Mr. Kiesler has a singular talent. He is a master of intellectual persuasion, an esthetic salesman on an almost evangelical level."[19]

But Huxtable's critique essentially dismisses Kiesler's involvement with contemporary issues in art and his persistent evasion of conventional disciplines.[20] Kiesler exhibited a singular ability to exploit his awkward position as a hinge figure between and among disciplines, producing work that is not merely iconoclastic, enigmatic, or evasive; he operated as an inhabitant of an "art world" long before 1964, when Arthur Danto popularized the term. As Virgil Thompson remarked in his eulogy at Kiesler's spectacular funeral, "being with Kiesler was like touching an electric wire that bore the current of contemporary history."[21] Thompson's phrase "contemporary history" aptly describes a key art-world attitude of the mid-1960s. Kiesler died at the onset of a protean moment in the course of American art and architecture, one that presents itself as a historical "knot" or "navel," a concept borrowed from psychoanalysis.[22] At once a coherent historical convergence, as well as a time of confusion and hidden potential, the very density of this moment—the complex of trends, influences, events, and individuals—establishes an opening up of practical possibilities while, at the same time, covering its criss-crossing tracks. Properly speaking, it is an unconscious time.[23] As Jacques Lacan writes, such a knot marks "something always missed" because it "closes up again as soon as it has opened."[24]

III

Thus it is understandable that most histories of modernism treat Kiesler as an enigmatic figure and lead us to believe—like Huxtable—that his work amounts to a loosely related series of innovative, though largely undeveloped, explorations of the boundaries of architecture. But Kiesler is better characterized not as a misfit modernist but as an inadvertent precursor of the neo-avant-garde artists of the 1960s: his restless experimentation with hybrid media appears to anticipate their disillusionment with the received strategies of the avant-garde. It is not primarily his built works, sculptures, or paintings (almost all of which were produced in the last twenty years of his life) but his early architectural projects and other work prior to 1950—exhibitions, theater sets, furniture, store windows, and criticism—that are most allied with the events, tactics, and works of the neo-avant-garde.

Wild Kingdom

Looking back from the sixties, Kiesler's varied affiliations constitute a remarkable matrix: more than any architect who was involved with the 1920s avant-garde, Kiesler's rejection of conventional disciplines and his association with Duchamp, Katherine Dreier, Peggy Guggenheim, surrealism, film, theater, and experimental exhibitions combine many of the specific traits that would converge in the neo-avant-garde.[25] Those interests align him with his friend Duchamp; both concentrate upon what Peter Bürger calls "the social effect (function) of a work."[26] But Kiesler's historical role is different from Duchamp's; unlike the neo-dada "revival of Marcel Duchamp as godfather" in the late 1950s and early 1960s, Kiesler's work is not exemplary but emblematic of the concerns of the 1960s.[27] Kiesler's "display of the avant-garde" shares many traits with the self-consciously subversive, site-specific practices of the minimalist neo-avant-garde and its "institutional critique" of late modernism. Thus Kiesler seems to anticipate what Hal Foster has described as the "second moment" of the neo-avant-garde. Foster explains that the "first moment" is exemplified in neo-dada's

> reprise of the historical avant-garde attempt "to reconnect art and life," . . . in which it is
> not the institution of art that is transformed, but the avant-garde—into an institution.
> (Thus one could speak, as early as Johns, of a Duchampian "tradition.") . . . In the second
> neo-avant-garde moment—that of minimalism and pop art—the aim is not naively to
> reconnect art and life but, on the one hand to reflect on the perceptual conditions of art
> (minimalism), and on the other to exploit the conventionality of the avant-garde . . . [pop].[28]

The notion of Kiesler as a precursor of the neo-avant-garde can be traced in his concerted exploration of display. Not simply the presentation or promotion of avant-garde strategies, Kiesler's approach to display persistently mediates and configures the relationship between artifacts and their situations as a condition of mimicry—a showing for subjective consummation. What Kiesler would as early as 1937 call "correalism" might thus be understood as a first effort toward an aesthetics of mimicry, offering work that spans the intervals between display and disguise, or action and observation, by staging the complicity of various disciplines.[29] Using techniques adapted from surrealist collage and photography, Kiesler's displays deploy a sophisticated visual rhetoric designed to lure the observer into an alien world of incessant and evasive images where appearances are fundamental and substantial, not a cloaking of things or functions.

One version of such a world was described by the Swiss zoologist Adolf Portmann, whose book *Zoologie und das neue Bild des Menschen* was in Kiesler's library.[30] Swerving from the behaviorist trend (and following German existentialism), Portmann suggested that the psychic dimension, or "inwardness," of living beings is bound to visible form and the processes of identity, individuation, and identification. He argued that what we call "life" can be traced in the socializing aspects of animal morphology and the intersubjective realm those gestures and markings constitute:

> The surface's display is a part of the presentation of self [*Selbstdarstellung*] of a living
> being. . . . That opaque surface also implies the power to establish relationships. We should
> not depreciate what appears on this surface by thinking of it as a "front," an incidental extra
> which is plastered over a far more genuine and authentic "inside." No greater allotment of
> reality or honor can be ascribed to what is hidden than to this appearance we derive from
> an opaque, patterned and designed outermost surface. Indeed, the inwardness of the living
> thing is a non-dimensional reality which is spatially located neither inside nor in a center.[31]

Portmann often drew analogies between aesthetic and zoological forms, implying that deer's tails or birds' feathers—like human works of art—play a role in forming the social life of the species. In one essay, he cited a statement of Wölfflin's (which itself draws a parallel to the "life sciences"): "Every 'form' is life-enhancing."[32] He also explained his ideas in terms of architecture and functionalist aesthetics. Referring to Louis Sullivan in a 1965 lecture, Portmann challenged the orthodox notions of "form follows function" and suggested that science itself had encouraged certain excesses of interpretation:

> Today we must realize how the one-sidedness of this principle misinterprets natural forms
> and how widely it threatens to divert us from a real understanding of living form. If the vision
> of architects and the conception of life given us by the influence of biological work have
> been compelled—specially in physiology—to move toward a heightened stress on function,
> it is presently all the more incumbent upon the life sciences to examine their own proper
> object again, to ponder, that is, whether the mode of investigation which biology itself pro-
> duced during an earlier phase is really the most important, or whether, as a consequence
> of that mode, meaningful aspects of living appearance have not wrongly been forgotten.[33]

Portmann's explicit critique of neo-Darwinian functionalism presumed that functions sustain forms—that physiology serves morphological appearances. In other words, "life" is manifested in acts of "self-display" for others: an organism's vital signs are not numerical indexes—heart rate, temperature, or growth—but visual symbols—gestures, coloration, shape, and patterns.

Kiesler shared Portmann's desire to reverse, or at least equalize, the hierarchy that places form in the service of function.[34] His 1949 essay, "Pseudo-Functionalism in Modern Architecture" parallels Portmann's approach and, like his earlier theory of "design correlation," was clearly inspired by biology and zoology.[35] Portmann's critique of functionalism helps to explain Kiesler's otherwise cryptic (and seemingly heroic) aphorism: "Form does not follow function. Function follows vision. Vision follows reality."[36] For both Kiesler and Portmann, vision is not merely a matter of perceiving, but is the active correlation of images according to their social significance. Beginning in the early 1940s, Portmann had applied that ethic in his writings on zoology:

> The morphological features have a special form value which cannot be understood either as a function of preservation or as structures for manifesting changes in mood. . . . I have designated it the "presentation value" . . . to draw attention to an essential meaning of the outward form which has only too often been overlooked as we sought for immediate vital functions.[37]

> The more closely we look at those phenomenal aspects of life whose sole purpose is to serve self-expression and not self-preservation, the more evident it becomes that those forms on which technical thought prefers to fasten are merely the most obvious. We begin to realize that the vast majority of living forms cannot be explained in terms of technical or preservation effects alone, but that they must be evaluated first and foremost in terms of self-expression.[38]

The sources of Portmann's theory lie in phenomenology and gestalt psychology, but it is now well-known that a psychoanalytic variation of the theory of self-display emerged somewhat earlier in the writings of Roger Caillois and in Jacques Lacan's theory of the "mirror stage."[39] Lacan implicitly accepts the assertion that animal morphology constitutes a quasi-symbolic visual system, but refuses Portmann's phenomenological description of a "realm of images" that constitutes an all-encompassing life-world. Instead, Lacan proposes that that realm or system (what he calls the "imaginary") undergoes a traumatic reconfiguration in the early development of the human subject.[40] In his theory of the mirror stage, the ego develops out of the recognition of one's own body in or as another—a recognition that escapes animals. The subject first enters—is lured into—a *spatial* world during this "stage" of corporeal iden-tification; the human subject is "reborn" in this imaginary movement from the closed circle of the *Innenwelt* to an unstable, unending interplay of both *Innen-* and *Um-welt*. Lacan's mirror stage is, in effect, an entrance into a veritable hall of mirrors, at once giving and taking away a coherent or stable identity for the subject, which becomes implicated in a disturbing process of "spatial identification" and, as a consequence, is ever unable to resolve the perceived split between self and image or to assuage the impossible anticipation of attaining the complete, "orthopedic" image of others. The very possibility of recognition of oneself in the mirror—that is, to identify a self—entails the consequence of a fundamen-tal loss; identity is not found to be a substantive characteristic of the subject but rather is conveyed relative to the reflection of another.[41] This striving to supplement an insufficient self through identification destabilizes the phenomenal distinction between inner and outer worlds; rather than accepting the phenomenological notion of an all-encompassing outside, Lacan's schema of the subject involves a puzzling intertwining of *Innenwelt* and *Umwelt*—a confusion that is addressed, deferred and reproduced in acts of display and vision.

133

IV

Both Portmann's and Lacan's theories can be used to elaborate Kiesler's peculiar approach to design. His display of the avant-garde not only inhabits a strange realm between major avant-garde movements and the conventional disciplines but exploits the effects of the mirror stage and operates as a kind of mimicry, presenting a dual "subject"—a disciplining of both artifact and observer—in a situation that promotes both identification and dissembling.

Kiesler's displays build upon two historically established but loosely defined aesthetic prac-tices. Both involve intersubjective relationships: first, his numerous *collaborations* with artists—including architectural projects, exhibition designs, stage sets, and "multimedia" presentations; second, his few, astute essays in *criticism,* which apply criteria from diver-gent disciplines "improperly" or comparatively to produce a heterogeneous representation of others' work.

Wild Kingdom

While Kiesler's collaborations are effective demonstrations, his criticism offers the more explicit presentations of the issues of display. The most obvious example is his 1930 book, *Contemporary Art Applied to the Store and Its Display*. As one reviewer wryly remarked, Kiesler's explanation, early in the book, of a painting by de Chirico also describes his own mode of criticism, which leaves the reader to identify and reassemble the materials on display: "It brings together all kinds of objects in a naturally illogical way, but he orders these things into a logical pictorial harmony."[42] Kiesler refined that strategy during his brief employment at *Architectural Record* in 1937. Under the heading "Design Correlation," he produced six installments of what the magazine's editors called "a new approach to art and architectural criticism." Unlike anything previously published in that magazine, Kiesler's graphic design abandons the de Stijl techniques that he first used in his Vienna catalog and that remained basically intact in his 1930 book. Kiesler's six "displays" in *Architectural Record* are not only his most explicit attempts to demonstrate the "correlation" of the arts, but the seemingly unrelated subjects he treats—from mural painting (February) to "Architecture and Animals" (April) to Duchamp's *Large Glass* (May) to theatrical staging (June) to the history of "photo-graphy" (July and August)—present the techniques and concerns he combined in his display of the avant-garde.

Thus Kiesler's criticism for *Architectural Record* represents his most intensive and innovative effort—technically, graphically, and rhetorically—to translate avant-garde concerns into an American idiom and to offer an alternative to institutional events and books such as Hitchcock and Johnson's *The International Style* (1932) or Alfred Barr's *Cubism and Abstract Art* (1936). Until at least 1950, when Johnson purchased an early model of the Endless House for the Museum of Modern Art, Kiesler was constantly at odds with the major American modernists.[43] In a 1939 article, and ten years later in "Pseudo-Functionalism in Modern Architecture," Kiesler pointed to the same four pages in *Cubism and Abstract Art* where Barr compares the architecture of Le Corbusier and Mies to contemporary painting (by Le Corbusier and van Doesburg). Kiesler praised Barr for recognizing that functionalism and formalism are interdependent, but argued that while "modern functionalism in architecture has it roots . . . in contemporary abstract painting," a superficial understanding of that connection has cheapened their relationship: architects "have confused geometric forms with abstraction, have taken simplicity (or planimetry) for functionalism."[44] In pointing out what he saw as the fallacies of functionalism and formalism and their ultimate stylistic complicity in the classic works of modernism, Kiesler was presenting one of the most basic tenets of his approach to display and, in a sense, was teaching the very lessons he had learned during his own reeducation in America.

V

During Kiesler's first twenty years in the United States, many of those lessons arrived in one way or another through Marcel Duchamp. The two probably first met at the 1925 Paris exposition, and their working relationship began in New York late in 1926 with Kiesler's "telemuseum" for Katherine Dreier and the Société Anonyme. Ten years later, Kiesler's piece on Duchamp in *Architectural Record* was the most accomplished and intriguing of his contributions to that magazine. Kiesler's article (which was the first American publication to present the recently reconstructed *Large Glass*) pleased Duchamp enough that he sent a letter of thanks and praise to Kiesler, along with a copy of his *Green Box*.[45] From that time until at least the late 1940s, Duchamp's influence punctuated Kiesler's American experiences, and the *Large Glass* continued to inspire Kiesler's approach to display as well as his increasingly adamant critique of competing versions of the architectural avant-garde. More important, Duchamp was directly involved in Kiesler's two most didactic displays of the avant-garde: they collaborated closely in 1947 on the design of the Salle de Superstitions for the Exposition Internationale du Surréalisme in Paris, and in 1942, during the construction of the Art of this Century Gallery, Duchamp lived with Kiesler and his wife, Steffi.[46] Both projects took extreme measures to mediate the reception of the exhibition by installing the collections in what amounts to a habitat, yet this ambition to create a total work of (environmental) art had been part of Kiesler's approach since his work in the theater in the early 1920s.

His breakthrough in terms of display had come in a series of store windows for Saks Fifth Avenue that were installed between 1928 and 1930. Kiesler characterized those commissions, which allowed him to combine his theatrical and architectural backgrounds with his increasing interest in surrealism, as the initiation of a new art movement in America. In his *Contemporary Art Applied to the Store and Its Display*—a direct outgrowth of his work for Saks—he congratulated himself and his client with the audacious claim that "in 1928 a new era began in American retail and manufacturing life."[47] Clearly, Kiesler was referring to his own store windows, which had prompted a subsequent series of exhibitions sponsored by Macy's and Lord & Taylor. Those events, Kiesler claimed,

Wild Kingdom

brought the contemporary industrial art of Europe to the knowledge of the general public. Not only New Yorkers, but hundreds of thousands from all parts of the country viewed the expositions. Newspapers carried reports. Controversies arose. Wherever a newspaper opened, in the remotest villages, the syndicated reports of the sensational novelty brought a knowledge of the coming revolution in taste.[48]

While Kiesler continued to pursue more conventional architectural work, he argued that commercial display held the greatest potential for the avant-garde in America: by his own account, modern art would be accepted in America not through museums and art galleries but through "show windows, institutional propaganda and advertising."[49]

Here was an art gaining acceptance not through slow fostering of its theories and principles in academies and art schools, but simply by planting its creations down in the commercial marts. In Europe the process was reversed. . . . First came an artist and his theory, then a slow evolution and a general acceptance. . . . Unprecedented though it may be in the annals of art, a main channel through which the new style will approach popularization is the store. Here is where a new art can come into closest contact with the stream of the mass, by employing the quickest working faculty: the eye.[50]

Every one of Kiesler's subsequent projects, despite their programmatic, stylistic, or technical variation, explicitly explores and exploits the visual problematics of display, and none aspires to less than a thoroughly avant-garde effect. An early example is his Space-House, constructed in 1933 inside the Modernage furniture gallery in New York. It was as much a model home as a home for modern art. Art objects such as Brancusi's *Bird in Space* were displayed inside, while the house was itself the major display within the gallery. Kiesler's Mobile Home Library (fabricated between 1937 and 1939 in the Design Laboratory he directed at Columbia University) was, as its name implies, as much a piece of furniture as a house itself, and each of his gallery designs—Art of this Century (1942), Salle de Superstitions (1947), Bloodflames (1947), New World Gallery (1957)—fostered an approach to the display of art that manipulates the boundaries and correspondences between object and room— neither content nor occupant is neutral.[51]

Kiesler's conception of display was most elaborately realized in the Art of this Century Gallery. At once an art store (an inhabitable show window) and a didactic display of the avant-garde, its architecture "functions" as an extraordinarily malleable environment—an apparatus for display that organizes and enacts a staged event. The gallery consisted of three permanent spaces: a surrealist room with concave walls and lighting timed to illuminate different paintings at two-minute intervals (separated by three-and-one-half-second intervals of darkness announced by "a roar of an approaching train" just before the lights go out);[52] an abstract and cubist room with an undulating canvas partition and a system of taut ropes to suspend the works; and a kinetic gallery housing mechanical devices that structured the interaction between the visitor and works by Duchamp and Klee. Looking through peepholes, visitors to the kinetic gallery turned a large spiraling wheel to reveal the individual contents of Duchamp's *Boîte en Valise,* or used a push-button to view several reproductions of paintings by Klee mounted on a conveyor belt.

Kiesler's elaborate and often cumbersome modes of display not only demonstrate his critique of functionalist architecture, but also undermine the formalist notion of the avant-garde that was beginning to dominate American discourse on modern art. Kiesler's devious incisiveness is clear in Clement Greenberg's review of his design.[53] While he clearly admired Kiesler's understanding of contemporary conflicts in painting, Greenberg offered different evaluations of the display techniques in each of the three major spaces. He was pleased with the surrealist room because it so effectively demonstrated what he believed to be the deficiencies of that movement.[54] Greenberg maintained that the surrealists were not truly advanced artists because they continued to accept easel painting's "traditional discontinuity between the spectator and the space within the picture." Thus he was pleased that "the surrealist paintings seem . . . to hang in indefinite space" (as did those of Klee, who "was almost alone among the more abstract artists to maintain the fictive nature of the world within the picture frame"). But Greenberg was disturbed by the display of the abstract and cubist paintings, not because Kiesler misunderstood them, but because his system of ropes "overdid the functionalism." That is, on the one hand, they carried "to an ultimate conclusion" a "tendency dominant in painting since cubism . . . which, by means of abstraction, collage, construction, and the use of extraneous elements such as paper, cloth, sand, cement, wood, string, metal, and so forth, tries almost literally to disembowel the painting." But on the other hand, to Greenberg's eye, the result of Kiesler's efforts was "a little crowded and scrappy," an evaluation that was not simply a matter of taste: by so *literally* implicating the paintings in their context, Kiesler polluted their pure visuality. More important, Kiesler muddled Greenberg's distinction between easel and mural painting, a distinction that supports both his conception of the spatial implications of cubism and his claim that only abstract paintings are appropriate for contemporary murals.[55] For Greenberg, the cubist evisceration of painting allows a kind of mural in which "the physical fact of the canvas itself . . . enter[s] the actual presence of the spectator on the same terms, and as completely, as do walls, the furniture, and people. What takes place within the borders of the picture has the same immediate status as the borders themselves." That "status" is abstraction: murals should strive to make the total environment seem abstract (in the manner of de Stijl or Mondrian).

But Kiesler's treatment of the abstract and cubist paintings did not produce a proper mural:

> The ropes should have been covered in dark cloth and the walls toned more darkly to set off the high-keyed colors and pale tints of the abstract and cubist paintings. As it is, the eye is unable to isolate them easily.

But, of course, for Kiesler the eye's task is not to isolate but to correlate. Not surprisingly, Duchamp was crucial to Kiesler's divergent understanding of the issues.[56]

Kiesler and Duchamp's "encounter" in the pages of *Architectural Record* was directly related to Kiesler's participation in the debates surrounding mural painting and modernism in the 1930s. In fact, his display of the avant-garde evolves in part out of a critical discussion of mural painting and a negative assessment of exhibitions such as the Museum of Modern Art's 1932 show "Murals by American Painters and Photographers." Kiesler's first contribution to *Architectural Record* was an elaboration of an article he had published just two months earlier on Gorky's WPA murals at Newark Airport. In that article, "Murals without Walls," Kiesler first advocated his notion of "heterogeneous unity," which he would elaborate in his presentation of Duchamp's *Large Glass*, a work that, Kiesler believed, offered a solution to interdisciplinary problems raised by the installation of murals in modern architecture.

Kiesler had used his articles on Gorky's murals to protest against the Federal Art Project of the WPA. He questioned the use of "modern murals within a framework of classical or semiclassical architecture. *They cannot integrate.*"[57] Launching into a technical discussion of fresco painting, and sounding a bit like Greenberg, Kiesler argues that an "easel painter has the control of the unity and finality of his work in his own mind and hand, not so the mural painter." But unlike Greenberg's advocacy of pure abstraction, Kiesler emphasizes technical integration:

> The architect of today is again, after a pause of twenty-five years, at work to coordinate such strange parts as painting, sculpture, industrial furnishings, and building structure into a heterogeneous unity, called Architecture.[58]

Kiesler blasted the Federal Art Project for its decision to commission paintings on canvas and affix them to the wall. His more ambitious agenda proposed that modern building methods require equally innovative mural techniques that could be integrated with the architecture.

Kiesler's own use of murals extends back at least to his Space-House of 1933 and culminates in a 1950 exhibition at the Kootz Gallery, "The Muralist and Modern Architecture." For that show Kiesler collaborated with the sculptor David Hare and exhibited the version of the Endless House that Philip Johnson purchased for the Museum of Modern Art.[59] In an article on the Space-House, published in *Hound & Horn*, Kiesler insisted upon the adequacy of displays as an experimental approach to architecture. The article begins with what seems to be an apology, but turns out to be a statement of principle and a moment of critical positioning:

> The actual realization of my Space-House at the Modernage Company is a proportionate substitute indicating the actual possibilities of the original plan. But the Principle it advocates is demonstrated. That is all that can be expected at present.[60]

While the entire "building" is a display, inside the "house" is a more allegorical, condensed display: a photomural titled "Work and Play," which might be read as both a constructivist composition and a parody of social realism. But most of the published photographs of the photomural crop the peculiar images on the left-hand portion of the wall. Astonishingly abstract and cryptic, the images suggest an industrial-age rebus or a graphic account of the economies and technologies of modern construction. They also indicate (and initiate) Kiesler's unusual understanding (and exploitation) of the potential of photography.

In September 1936—two months before he published his article on Gorky and four months before his first piece of criticism appeared in Architectural Record—Kiesler happened upon a one-page article in the same magazine under the heading "Technical News and Research" that described a new technology of photomural production. (The same issue also included illustrations of the mural in the Space-House—a differently cropped photo had been published in the January 1934 issue—and his stage sets for Joseph and his Brethren at Juilliard.) Kiesler would reference this article in his first contribution to Architectural Record in his capacity as a "critic." Titled "Walls are Made into Pictures," it described "a new photo mural process" in which walls were treated with a photo-sensitive emulsion. Images were then projected onto it to produce

> a photographic enlargement of any selected size, printed directly onto the wall, or any other surface, at a comparatively low cost and in a comparatively short time.... Jointless photographs with a hard washable surface can be produced not only on a flat wall but also on any bas-relief, curved, corrugated or fluted surface. [61]

More important, the inventor of the new, projected photomural technique seemed to share Kiesler's belief that such new technologies promised a new correlation of the mural and architectural space—a step toward the ideal of heterogeneous unity and what Kiesler described as "an entirely new spirit energy in conjunction with new social and technological intensities." [62] Architectural Record reported that:

> In the inventor's own opinion, the reproduction of original snapshots or naturalistic photographs is hardly correct, for this would constitute a tour de force in decoration. He has found that reproducing microscopic designs, or photographs of plants, enlarged to about 200 times their real size, is more suitable.... He believes, in short, as a new technique in pictorial reproduction, the process calls for the development of new designs impossible to achieve otherwise.

The influence of the new technique is evident in Kiesler's piece on the Large Glass, where an enlarged X-ray of an insect's wing and a life-size X-ray of a mouse were juxtaposed with carefully cropped and, in some cases inverted, details of Duchamp's "X-ray painting of space" (1). But Kiesler's previous work already had shown this tendency, using mechanically reproduced images as an integral part of his displays and interiors. This is the case not only in the

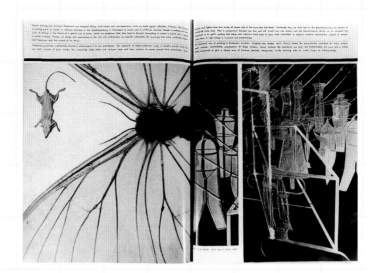

(1)
Frederick Kiesler, spread from
"Design Correlation: [From Brush-Painted
Glass Pictures of the Middle Ages to 1920s],"
Architectural Record, May 1937

Space-House but in his use of immense projected images of leaves showing in detail their structure and veins in 1935 for the sets for John Seymour's opera *In the Pasha's Garden*, in his use of photomurals in the unbuilt 1934 design for the WGN studios, and in his 1929 Film Guild Cinema, where he imagined that its multiple screens would be used not only to project simultaneous films but to create a thematically appropriate, simulated environment.

VI

In the 1930s and 1940s photography proved to be the medium that promised the most for Kiesler's display of the avant-garde. His last contribution to *Architectural Record* was a two-part schematic history of "photo-graphy" titled "Certain Data Pertaining to the Genesis of Design by Light." That ambitious, if selective, chronicle of technical innovation in the mechanical (re)production of images cleverly positions his own interests in the vanguard of photographic art. For Kiesler, photography began with the camera obscura and, he predicted, would reach its most advanced development in television, which he hyperbolized as the "eye of infinite vision":

When television will be technically and economically ready to be released for service, it will then reach the profession of architects and industrial designers. They in turn will incorporate in their design for individual and group shelters control of the most efficient and phonetical factors of telecasting. Photography will then constitute an integral part of the architectural scheme and not be a mere wall ornament as has been the framed Daguerreotype photo and its up-to-date successors. [63]

Kiesler's desire to use television as an integral part of his work began in 1923, long before it was technologically feasible. In his set for *R.U.R.* he devised two methods to simulate closed-circuit television. The set was an elaborate backdrop conceived as

> a huge montage, compiled from the most diverse apparatuses and machine parts (mega-phone, seismograph, tanagra device, iris diaphragm, light bulb) — some real, some painted. According to their functions, the devices could send light signals or sounds, as well as project films or perform optical illusions, with mirrors.[64]

According to R. L. Held, *R.U.R.* was the first stage design to use motion pictures as part of the illusion of theatrical scenery (rather than as an interlude or an extension of a scene).[65] But the most fantastic of the technical illusions was the tanagra device, a mechanism developed around the turn of the century in the puppet theater. Comprised of mirrors, the device acted as a sort of periscope that allowed the audience a view of activities backstage, but reduced in size. Kiesler's imaginative use of television would reemerge three years later in his "tele-museum." In his 1930 book, Kiesler explained that he designed the telemuseum for an expo-sition of modern paintings to be held at the Brooklyn Museum:

> The purpose was to show the relationship between painting, sculpture and interior archi-tecture. My sketch showed the two ways in which painting and sculpture will contribute to the decoration of the future interior: 1. With sensitized panels which will act as receiving-surfaces for broadcasted pictures. 2. With built-in "shrines" for original masterpieces that will be concealed behind walls and revealed only occasionally. The use of pictures as a permanent wall decoration will be a discarded practice.[66]

Following his explanation of the telemuseum, Kiesler suggested possible uses for television in store displays, and then predicted that it would provoke new forms of art and decoration for American culture:

> Television will bring fashion news into the show window, creating a "Window Daily" to be read with ears and eyes. To the retail store Television offers a promotional medium of tremendous potentialities. Apart from the fact that it will greatly enlarge trading areas and permit the presentation of merchandise to an audience over a wide radius, its application to the store window will introduce a number of entirely new effects.

Television will be a final solution to your decorative problems. Its scope will be vast. It will be the quintessence of efficiency in decoration. It will be (a) Quick. (b) Inexpensive. (c) Highly individual; or standardized. (d) Novel, giving variations at a moment's notice. (e) It will relate the whole outer world with your store and your store with the outer world.[67]

Kiesler's interest in television—or "photo-graphy" as he broadly conceived it—also inspired his outlandish project to design a "vision machine." That project, beginning in 1937 and extending into the 1940s, explicitly records his increasing involvement with surrealism and psychoanalysis, and suggests that Kiesler's displays may be some of the most complex ventures into the architectural implications of those two movements.[68] His use of mechanical devices in his displays to produce and organize an integration of images, figures, and space constitutes a simulated "vision machine," in which photographic modes of representation produce what could be called a "stain of the real." As Rosalind Krauss has written:

> Photography is an imprint or transfer of the real; it is a photochemically processed trace causally connected to that thing in the world to which it refers in a way parallel to that of fingerprints or footprints or the rings of water that cold glasses leave on tables. The photograph is thus genetically distinct from painting or sculpture or drawing. . . . Technically and semiologically speaking, drawings and paintings are icons, while photographs are indexes.[69]

While the images in "Work and Play," the WGN project, or the Film Guild Cinema are certainly legible as indexes and thus as what Krauss calls a "transfer of the real," the notion of a stain of the real suggests a different condition in which the photomural acts as a rupture in the facticity of the architecture and a "real" disturbance of the surface of the wall. Stains do not register a specific event or object; they display a synchronic, alternative reality and recall the "spacings and doublings" (as in double exposure) of subjective "reality":

> photography, with its technical basis in an instantaneous recording of an event, captures what we could call the simultaneity of real space, the fact that space does not present itself as successive in nature, like time, but as pure presence, present-all-at-once.[70]

Thus stains advance a kind of transparency—more like a mirror than a window—that exploits the spatial effects described in the writings of Lacan and Caillois. A connection between

Kiesler's work and the writings of Caillois and Lacan is entirely probable. Both published early essays in the journal *Minotaure*, through which Kiesler was aware of the surrealists' uses of literature, science, and especially photography. Kiesler owned a copy of *Minotaure* 7—published in June 1935—which included Caillois's now-famous essay, "Mimicry and Legendary Psychasthenia," an essay that is known to have influenced Lacan's concept of the mirror stage (which was first presented as a paper one year later, in 1936).[71] Caillois's "Psychasthenia" essay, as well as his earlier essay in *Minotaure* 5 on the praying mantis, presents a concept of animal mimicry that, in a more extreme manner than Portmann, revises Darwinian theory. According to Caillois, psychasthenia is the self-effacing desire motivating animal camouflage: the tendency of an organism to surrender its own "distinction" by blurring the visual boundary between itself and its context. Thus the animal becomes dispossessed, even derealized, as though yielding to "a real *temptation by space*," a temptation to "renunciation." Caillois's language is startlingly sympathetic with Kiesler's own concept of "integration," his understanding of "photo-graphy," and their application in his display of the avant-garde:

> Morphological mimicry could then be, after the fashion of chromatic mimicry, an actual photography, but of the form and the relief, a photography on the level of the object and not on that of the image, a reproduction in three-dimensional space with solids and voids: sculpture-photography or better teleplasty, if one strips the word of any metapsychical content.[72]

Kiesler shared Caillois's and Lacan's complex attitudes toward the complicity of visuality and identity, yet his display of the avant-garde operates as the inverse of psychasthenia, striving to retain a degree of "distinction" through the manipulation of space.[73] Rather than a loss of self-possession in space—what Krauss calls "the inscription of space on the body of an organism"[74]—the display of the avant-garde inscribes the subject in a realized space. As practiced by Kiesler, display is a resistance of the crowd, the mass, pure visuality, or the uniformity of the International Style. This is the subtext of Kiesler's 1930 statement regarding the relationship between mass culture and the machine age:

> The expression of America is the mass, and the expression of the masses, the machine. The machine is our greatest aid. The machine, not as Europe has understood it, but as America understands it today. Not as a means of reproduction, but as a power for creative production.[75]

As Kiesler would later make clear in his article on Duchamp, the *Large Glass* exemplifies this attitude toward the machine, not only in terms of its iconography (which he declines to discuss) but in terms of its techniques and function:

> We look at it not to interpret its bio-plastic exposition of the upper half of the picture or of the mechanomanic lower part; such physio and psychoanalysis will readily be found here and there, now and later—but I bring to the technicians of design-realization the teaching of its techniques. Translucent material such as glass being used more and more in contemporary building finds its manufacturing not for commercial but spiritual reasons. . . . Glass is the only material in the building industry which expresses surface-and-space at the same time. . . . It satisfies what we need as contemporary designers and builders: an inclosure that is space in itself, an inclosure that divides and at the same time links.[76]

When Kiesler commissioned Berenice Abbott to photograph the *Large Glass* at Katherine Dreier's home, he was thinking of it in terms that parallel Caillois's remarks on distinction and space:

> The structural way of painting is Duchamp's invention. Anybody who designs space (forms) knows the pre-conscious command for sharp contour, exact contour, unmistakable accentuation of shape horizons. Areas between boundaries are here, not brush-stroked, but once and a million times tamponed to give a vibrant mass of luminous densities, transparent, lucidly shivering with its tender layers of color coverings.[77]

But Kiesler also warns:

> A contour is the illusion of a spatial joint of forms. Joints are dangerous links; they tend to dis-joint (everything in nature is joined and a group of joints is form). Hence, all design and construction in the arts and architecture are specific calculation for re-joining into unity, artificially assembled materiae, and the control of its decay.[78]

Thus, contrary to Ada Louise Huxtable's characterization of Kiesler's work as "camouflaged sculpture," he would more likely think of architecture as supporting a camouflaged form of life—that is, as a habitat that engenders both display and dissembling in a heterogeneous unity of architecture, sculpture, painting, and people.

Lacan's and Caillois's writings suggest a similar role for architecture. Lacan argues that the subject, emerging out of the mirror stage, discerns a fundamental imaginary distinction between contained (contents) and container. While the subject never escapes containment, Lacan also insists that content is available only because it is imaged in complicity with the container (portrayed as something like a concave apparatus of projection or reflection), a condition he explains figuratively in terms of optics.[79] The very concavity of the container creates a visual field where the real and the virtual are easily confused, combined, or exchanged, and the subject's grasp of any object is always prone to mistaking, or misrecognition (*méconnaissance*). Unlike the anamorphic displacement and distortion engendered by a flat picture plane or the logic of perspective, a container will produce crossings, splits, and inversions that are entirely coherent and direct, but nonetheless unrecognizable as images of "the world."

Further, because the subject comes into being, developmentally and existentially, through the persistent anticipation and pursuit of the real through others, seeing (vision) is ever corrupted by being seen (the gaze). The subject is caught between two tangled, diametric aspects of seeing, which force an irresolution and manifest a lack. The split between the gaze and vision displaces the phenomenological premise that perception is sustained by eidetic apprehension of phenomena as well as by phenomenology's claim that an already immanent world (a reality prior to the subject and in which the subject dwells) is entirely continuous with the subject. Phenomenological experience and perception are the effects of a seamless encounter with the real, not the chance, fleeting encounter—the *tuché*—of Lacan.[80] The notion of the *tychic*—the repeated encounter with the real, which is in effect always a *missed* encounter—is yet another way to bring attention to the difficulty presented by any simple differentiation between an inside and an outside of the subject. The *tychic* encounter with the resistance of real phenomena is not simply a question of the interpenetration of inside and outside, but an enfolded continuity that provides moments of contact and separation, what Lacan calls "sutures."

Lacan argues that subjects do not share a "common certitude" with others; rather, subjects share *a common lack of certainty regarding the real.*[81] The subject is diagrammed by Lacan as an involuted topology invading the body of the individual *and* pervading the realms of images, signs, and "being"—the imaginary, the symbolic, and the real. In such a scheme of the subject, the unconscious is not structurally contained or veiled under, behind, within, or even outside of individual consciousness. Rather, it is beyond the individual's mental grasp and "structured" by the linguistic and visual fields. Objects are not simply outside of the subject or of consciousness.

> It is a question of something inside that is also outside. This is why such considerations [of "topological configurations"] are particularly necessary when it is a question of the unconscious, which I represent to you as that which is inside the subject, but which can be realized only outside, that is to say, in the locus of the Other in which alone it may assume its status.[82]

Superficially, the topological scheme of the subject resembles the Endless House: it can be configured as "a perimeter involuted upon itself."[83] Architecture appears as both contents and container: the subject identifies with both aspects. According to Lacan's notion of the subject, architecture cannot simply construct the subject, nor can subjects simply construct architecture. Architecture is reconfigured as neither an analog of the whole body nor a determinate structure that defines, constructs, or envelops the subject. Rather, architecture is understood as an anticipatory act that strives to recognize the role of the subject as container, to manifest an appearance of the real, and to structure the relations of intersubjectivity.

Lacan's schematization of the subject provokes a series of seemingly fantastic questions regarding the conceptualization of space as well as of the role of the unconscious in architecture: How does the subject become involved in architecture? Is the relation between buildings and individuals better described as one between buildings and subjects? Is architecture—as a spatialized mirroring apparatus—more like a subject than the body-image that precipitates the development of the ego? How can architecture act like a subject?

Lacan's discussion of visual stains offers one suggestion of how the subject becomes implicated in a world of images. Referring to Caillois's essays in *Minotaure* as well as to his strange and provocative book, *Meduse et Compagnie* (1960), Lacan's concept of the stain derives from Caillois's consideration of the role of eyespots, or ocelli, on numerous insects. Normally explained in functionalist terms as an imitation of the organs of sight, the eyespots are supposed to operate as illusions. That is, a predator mistakes the ocelli for the eyes of a larger animal and is stunned or frightened away. Yet in Lacan's terms the resemblance may be real as well as imaginary, or in the vocabulary of science, the eyespot may be an "organ" as well as a deceptive and effectively—if not "actually"—functional appearance. In other words, drawing upon Caillois, Lacan takes an interest in mimicry because it is not what it seems to *appear* to be; mimicry is not simply an improper identification between two apparently related forms, but a real identification of two interdependent sights: the functions of the eye and of the gaze. In effect, ocelli are seen, seeing, and seeming.

Against functionalism, Caillois suggests that the ocelli are effective not because they appear to be eyes; they do not intimidate because of an inauthentic appearance. Rather, the ocelli might be called uncanny eyes: traps for vision. They fascinate in the manner of eyes, but of course they do not see. More importantly, they are *not quite seen either*. Phenomenologically speaking, they are not an immanence, but a remanence. Like an eye they are neither contained nor a container; they are an identification and collusion of virtual and real images. [84]

Ocelli disturb the reality of the visual field in a peculiar way. They are not expressive, yet they emerge distinctly from the visual field. In this sense they are like what Lacan calls a stain, a concept that accounts for the inadequacy of vision by attending to the effects of visual distortion and distraction. The stain's evident distortion of vision is a tychic encounter with the gaze; it shows—abstrusely—what escapes vision yet provokes the eye. The stain's peculiar distortion of the continuity of the visual field (neither elusive of nor reducible to vision) appears to dissolve the distinction between passive and aggressive mimicry, between showing and exhibiting.

Thus Lacan is able to argue, in a discussion of painting, that mimicry involves situating oneself in a picture as a stain, a definition he develops out of Caillois's outrageous explanation of butterfly wings as a phenomenon with affinities to representational painting. [85] The butterfly's wings, like a picture, give something peculiar to be seen; both a painting and a butterfly invite the vision of others and engender an elision of the gaze. Both are disarming. But unlike the effect of the eyespots on animals, a person is not "taken" by a painting; rather, the viewer "takes a look." While animals are effectively victimized by mimicry, the human subject "is not . . . entirely caught up in this imaginary capture. He maps himself in it." [86]

VII

Kiesler's display of the avant-garde exploits this subjective capacity by pushing it to the point of crisis. At the same time that the displays manipulate space and construct an enticing world, they also—like all architecture—thwart vision. Kiesler's displays seem to pose the question, what would it mean for a person to be situated as a stain in architecture? Distinct from Lacan's notion of a representational picture as a "trap for the gaze," the subject is able to enter into architecture without arresting the function of the gaze: in other words, architecture is a significant and remanent spatialized picture in which both subject and object appear as stains. Such a definition of architecture is encouraged by Lacan's well-known comment, following Sartre, on the capacity of a window to provoke an awareness of the gaze:

> I can feel myself under the gaze of someone whose eyes I do not even see, not even discern. All that is necessary is for something to signify to me that there may be others there. This window, if it gets a bit dark, and if I have reasons for thinking that there is someone behind it, is straightaway a gaze.[87]

In that case, the window is symbolic (a sign of the gaze), while the dark light behind it is a stained form; Sartre's window is but one of the most obvious instances of the collusion of real and virtual images in architecture, and Kiesler seems to have believed that every aspect of architecture might play a similar role. This can be demonstrated in three of Kiesler's displays, each of which involves Duchamp and each of which spatially integrates three conventionally distinct architectural elements—window, wall, and mural: his store windows (1928–30), his article on the *Large Glass* (1937), and an ingenious, folding "triptych" photomontage published in a special issue of the magazine *View* (March 1945) dedicated to Duchamp.

Kiesler explained his store windows as a kind of surrealist "painting" or stage set framed by "metal border."[88] Their purpose was to mediate the differing demands of public and commercial space—to "stimulate desire" on the outside for the other world of products on the inside.[89] This "Coordination of Street and Store" occurs in "two steps": "First step: the relation between the passerby and store. Second step: the coordination between the show window and the store interior."[90] Particularly at the ground level, Kiesler advocated specific solutions and hybrid architectural elements. In the most advanced store fronts, "windows and doors . . . in fact become one."[91] Ideally, the entire facade would become glass (in 1928 he designed a glass department store), and the building itself would operate as a colossal display inside and out,

Wild Kingdom

with store windows at street level and transparent walls above giving views of the interior or of projected images. "The metamorphosis is complete. Show window and interior are one."[92]

For his store windows, Kiesler collected, imagined, and tested new techniques and mechanical devices like those he would later install at the Art of this Century Gallery, from perspectival illusions derived from theatrical staging to etched and illuminated translucent "murals," to television as a means to transform the facade from a distinct membrane into a spatial device.[93] From picture windows to television, Kiesler wrote, "Selling through glass is becoming more and more important."[94]

150

Like many artists at the time, Duchamp had also been captivated by shop windows. In 1913, as part of his preparation for the *Large Glass*, he composed a note on that subject that he chose not to include in the *Green Box* and would not publish until 1966.[95] In it he describes the dissolution of desire that occurs when, after "examining" and "choosing" some merchandise in a shop window, one enters a store and obtains the object that had been so effectively and provocatively displayed behind glass. The glass poses a paradox, both stimulating and delaying desire. This delay is what Duchamp called "The shop window proof of the existence of the outside world":

> The question of shop windows∴
> To undergo the interrogation of shop windows∴
> The exigency of the shop window∴
> The shop window proof of the existence of the outside world∴
> When one undergoes the examination of shop windows, one also pronounces one's own sentence. In fact, one's choice is "round trip." From the demand of shop windows, from the inevitable response to shop windows, the fixation of choice is determined. No obstinacy, ad absurdum, of hiding the coition through a glass pane with one or many objects of the shop window. The penalty consists in cutting the pane and regretting it bitterly [*s' en mordre les pouces*] as soon as possession is consummated. Q.E.D.[96]

Duchamp's explicit diagram of the shop window's manipulation of desire begins to establish connections between Kiesler's fascination with the *Large Glass* and his architecture of display. The *Large Glass*, like Kiesler's displays, strives to delay "consummation" and what

13

(2)
Frederick Kiesler and Percy Rainford,
photograph of Duchamp in his studio,
January 1945, for "Les Larves d'Imagie
d'Henri Robert Marcel Duchamp"
for *View* 5, no. 1 (March 1945)

151

must be described as the psychasthenic moment of "coition" when the barriers are removed between a person and the object of desire. In fact, Kiesler's descriptions of the *Large Glass* could also be descriptions of his store windows: "Glass . . . expresses surface-and-space at the same time . . . : an inclosure that is space in itself, an inclosure that divides and at the same time links." For Kiesler, "Duchamp's painting's outstanding (tectonic) achievement is its new joint-design. . . . It is architecture, sculpture, and painting in ONE."[97]

Those quotations give new meaning to Kiesler's phrase "Murals without Walls." While Kiesler first intended it to refer to the inappropriateness of modern murals painted on canvas (which could be removed from the wall and reinstalled elsewhere), it also begins to explain the epigraph to his 1937 essay on Duchamp: "Architecture is the control of space. An Easel-painting is illusion of Space-Reality. Duchamp's Glass is the first x-ray-painting of space."[98] In other words, the *Large Glass* is a mural, a window and a wall.

Kiesler's original interpretation of the *Large Glass* initiates a relationship of mimicry between him and Duchamp. Looking into the *Large Glass* Kiesler sees the display of the avant-garde. As the bride is above and the bachelors below, so the *Large Glass* joins and separates Kiesler and Duchamp. The genius of the *Large Glass*, as Kiesler says, "is its new joint design": constructed, broken, and reconstructed, it is, so to speak, the best of both worlds. The pane was "cut" but reconstituted: there are no regrets.

For the next decade, Kiesler remained close to Duchamp. When Duchamp left the Kieslers' apartment in 1942, he moved nearby to the studio at 210 West 14th Street that he would occupy until his death and that would inspire Kiesler's most compelling display: the complex "triptych" photomontage, inscribed in the lower right hand corner as "Poeme Espace dédié à H(ieronymus) Duchamp. Kiesler."[99] On January 1 and 11, 1945, Kiesler and Percy Rainford photographed Duchamp in his studio (2). With those images and others of Duchamp's work, Kiesler constructed the triptych that is his exemplary display. He implanted into the photo of Duchamp in his working space (through montage, cutouts, and visual puns) elements of the *Large Glass* and other works (3). The result, as described by Kiesler, "when unfolded represents three walls of Duchamp's studio on 14th street in New York. The cut-out flaps, left and right, when bent toward the center, transform the interior wall into a vision of the 'Mariée mise à nu'"[100] (4). Those flaps, whether folded or unfolded, form the contour of one of the bachelors, which is revealed to have been held in the palm print of Duchamp (5). Of his motives, Kiesler writes: "There seems to be a definite although unintentional correlation between the daily utilities of the artist's environment and the inner structure common to all his work."

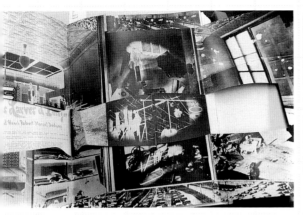

(3–5)
Frederick Kiesler, "Les Larves d'Imagie
d'Henri Robert Marcel Duchamp," *View* 5, no. 1 (March 1945)

In terms of display the *Large Glass* appears as a stain in the representation of the studio; the triptych displays Duchamp's imaginary in the real space of the studio—or, conversely, Duchamp's work is a stain of the real in an image of the studio. On the obverse of the photomontage (the outside of the studio), Kiesler printed characterizations of Duchamp and Raymond Roussel that mirror one another. Each is an "artist inventor of illusion" thus implying not only that Duchamp's work mimics Roussel's, but also that Kiesler's display is no less than a mirroring of himself in Duchamp's world. Kiesler situates himself in Duchamp's studio as a stain viewed through the absent "fourth wall" of the room. The mirroring is thus a complex set of permutations that appear as stains in the triptych, from Roussel's presence as the "chessboard with large rectangle" to the juxtaposition of Duchamp's *Fresh Window* with an actual window to the identification of Kiesler's choices and sutures in the construction of the photomontage, including above all the cutout of the malic mold—which, not by chance, is the "department store delivery boy" (perhaps it is Kiesler), which when unfolded, obscures Duchamp with a ghostly image of the *Large Glass*. In fact, Kiesler hints: "Many more integrations can readily be found in the Triptych; others might be evoked between the lines." With those joints, or distinctions, Kiesler construes Duchamp's studio as a "habitat," and implicates him, his environment, his work, and his affiliations in an intricate matrix of mimicry and display. A rare and elusive creature is on display—merging, building, and enticing the viewer to map him- or herself in Frederick Kiesler's wild kingdom: the display of the avant-garde.

PAULETTE SINGLEY

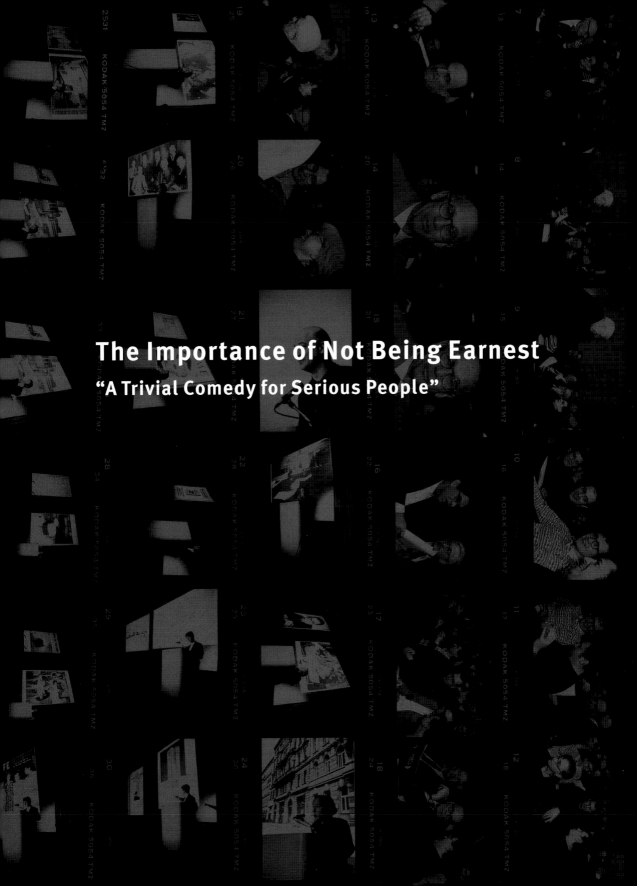

The Importance of Not Being Earnest
"A Trivial Comedy for Serious People"

In the opening scene of Oscar Wilde's play *The Importance of Being Earnest* (1895), Algernon Moncrieff asks his manservant, Lane, "Why is it that at a bachelor's establishment the servants invariably drink the champagne?" Lane responds: "I attribute it to the superior quality of the wine, sir. I have often observed that in married households the champagne is rarely of a first-rate brand." This observation provokes Algernon to exclaim, "Good heavens! Is marriage so demoralizing as that?"[1] In addition of such repartee concerning the impoverishment of living standards sanctioned by the institution of marriage, this play contains several of Wilde's more famous aphorisms, which reveal the aesthete's sensibility toward matters of taste, elegance, and especially domesticity. Thus Wilde writes: "In married life three is company and two is none"; "If I am occasionally a little over-dressed, I make up for it by being always immensely over-educated"; and of particular interest to this discussion on Philip Johnson's specter across modern architecture in North America, "In matters of grave importance, style, not sincerity, is the vital thing."[2]

Between the first and last scenes of Wilde's three-act play (originally written in four acts, with one later omitted), the set shifts from Algernon's flat on Half-moon Street in London to the drawing room of John, or rather Ernest, Worthing's manor house in Woolton, Hertfordshire, while, coincidentally, the action moves from the predatory maneuverings of a confirmed bachelor to his eventual marriage proposal. In this staged progression from town to country and bachelorhood to matrimony, Wilde outlines a spatial imperative for the modern male that encompasses the urban flat, the private club, and the manor house, invoking a topos of domesticity divided between an individual's debased, urban haunts and a couple's fecund, country estate. Although Wilde establishes the rather pedestrian dichotomies of earnestness and frivolity, truth and deception, and family and bachelorhood, he also challenges these oppositions with the more ambiguous and less dichotomized coupling of style and sincerity. This later opposition suggests the more insidious antinomies of earnestness and artfulness, naïveté and subtlety, frankness and flair, truth and creativity, nature and artifice, and so on. As the play's conclusion reveals, the entire stability of these oppositions has been predicated upon deceit: John discovers his true identity to be Ernest and the long-lost bachelor-brothers find each other, as well as their prospective brides, only through pretending to be what they are not, and that is a man named Ernest Worthing. In Wilde's perfect world, where style eclipses sincerity, the pun embedded in the title of the play — *The Importance of Being Earnest* — also means that it is important not to be so. It follows that this literal play on words collapses space into situations where the previously identified polarities of town and country or marriage and bachelorhood no longer hold—where morality, matrimony, celibacy, fertility, and sterility mutually adulterate each other on a stage that critiques the assumptions of middle-class values.

One continent away and some fifty-five years later at the Museum of Modern Art in 1949, the McAndrew-Barr sculpture garden featured a similar transvaluation of normative spatial distinctions when Philip Johnson curated Marcel Breuer's prototypical house for a single family of middle income. If viewed retrospectively from a bachelor apartment on the eleventh floor of Cesar Pelli's Museum Tower, possibly from the window of Johnson's own apartment, an afterimage of the Breuer House in the garden stains the Abby Aldrich Rockefeller Sculpture Garden that Johnson designed in 1953.[3] Such an airy perspective suggests superimposing not only the Breuer House, but also Johnson's 1943 bachelor salon in Cambridge, Massachusetts, upon the space of the museum courtyard. To approach the residence as a site for displaying art and, conversely, the art museum as a site for displaying residences (Gregory Ain also designed a house for the Museum of Modern Art garden in 1950) portrays the sculpture garden in terms of Johnson's description of it as a series of roofless rooms, as a private house within the museum, or as the nervous superimposition of two purportedly opposed value systems: American domesticity and the privileged apparatus of museum connoisseurship. Wilde's play demonstrates that the siting of Breuer's house in the museum garden collapses the urban flat, country house, and private club upon one anther in a stratified archaeology. Furthermore, given that Breuer's museum-built house follows a tradition of modern architecture that exploited the artist's atelier as a vehicle for residential reform, the House in the Garden also locates the single-family residence in a museological domain that is uniquely indebted to the *maison d' artiste*. The Breuer House demarcates the domestic interior as a space for screening the anxiety of exhibition while it simultaneously transforms the art museum into a residential attic that domesticates avant-garde impulses. The uneasy relationship between the worlds of architecture and art provoked *Architectural Forum* to comment on the Breuer residence with the disclaimer that it "will be acclaimed by many for its fine design, but criticized by the unthinking as arty."[4] Although such innocuous criticism as "arty" may not be a sophisticated enough label to provoke much damage to modern architecture in North America, its resonance within the artist's atelier and the pedigree of such residences in the European avant-

garde might well have. My objective is to disclose the facile distinction between the single family dwelling and the bachelor atelier, between sincere and stylized architectures as, instead, describing domains that rely upon each other as insincere adversaries in order to delimit domesticity through a reciprocity of public exhibitions and private curtains. To counterpose the space of the bachelor, specifically the solitary artist, with bourgeois morality describes the domain of the single inhabitant as something to be mistrusted, as an immoral realm where art seduces and seduction is an art.

Act I: An Urban Flat

Wilde's brief instructions for setting the first scene of his play, the morning room of Algernon's bachelor flat, states only that it is a "luxuriously and artistically furnished" room

where "the sound of a piano is heard."[5] His terse description supplies scant information for orchestrating the surroundings of a character understood by virtue of his banter and breeding to possess impeccable taste, and it introduces a series of still-life sets that Los Angeles architect Christine Magar has directed through Wilde's drama and into the architecture of this paper. As illustrations for what Wilde refers to as a "trivial comedy for serious people," Johnson's Cambridge house substitutes for the London flat of Act I; his Glass House substitutes for the country house of Acts II–III; and his sculpture garden at the Museum of Museum Art thematizes the displacement of the country house onto the urban stage of London's St. James's theater, where the play was first performed.

ALGERNON. *Why is it that at a bachelor's establishment the servants invariably drink t̶ champagne?*

Wilde's stage directions also introduce the following queries: What indeed was an artistically furnished house in 1895, and how, by 1949, did this appellation degenerate to the approbation of "artsy"?[6] We know from Mario Praz that "the drawing room at the end of the century was meant, above all, to look 'artistic.'" Likewise, Edmond Goncourt fashioned such a pervasive aesthetic sensibility with the publication of his *La Maison d' un artiste* (begun in 1878) that, according to Philippe Jullian, "the fin-de-siècle has made us disgusted with the word artistic."[7] Finally, Russell Lynes writes that the "artistic" trappings of ornamental tiles, precious teapots, Japanese fans, and peacock feathers were very much the same in America as in England, "from which the craze came."[8]

In one notable artistic interior that can be found in Wilde's *The Picture of Dorian Gray* (1890), the music heard from the piano might be Richard Wagner's *Tannhäuser* and the adjoining room is finished "with a vermillion-and-gold ceiling and walls of olive green laquer."[9] An alternate abode for Algernon might be James McNeill Whistler's Peacock Room, an interior Wilde celebrates in his essay "The House Beautiful," describing it as a space that "when lighted up, seems like a great peacock tail spread out."[10] Chances are, though, even with the peacock serving as a symbol of narcissism par excellence, this room might not be suitable for an *arbiter elegantiarum;* overloaded as it is with design, it may not be the kind of space for an urbane person with artistic sensibilities who requires room for more idiosyncratic expression than this highly prescriptive interior allows. These rooms do, however, begin to identify a source of prejudice against living artistically that is predicated upon an ad hominem critique of the eccentric and scandalous personalities who animated such spaces. As Martin Fido writes, during the nineteenth century "artistic sensibility could be regarded as a mark of effeminacy. Wit and elegance, articulacy and open charm, became suspect among men who wished to be noted for their virility."[11] And even more blatantly, "Perhaps the most important myth to arise from the public exposure of Oscar Wilde was the belief that his personal style itself derived from his homosexuality."[12]

In Wilde's denouement of *Dorian Gray,* a character whose good looks promoted suffering and whose convictions lead to living outside convention, he almost justifies the anxiety of an artistic lifestyle by delineating a figure who symbolized the "triumph of mind over morals."[13] The plot could not be more simple or, given MGM's film adaptation in 1945, more familiar: the portrait of a handsome young man grows old and depraved while the subject's countenance remains youthful and virtuous. Within this story, where art is the alchemical medium for indulging the narcissism of youth, the portrait—in other words, the artifice— must be hidden up in an attic, behind a locked door, and under a curtain. Meanwhile, the artist himself—not exactly the sorcerer but merely the vehicle through which Dorian's desire to remain young passes onto canvas—ends up murdered by his handsome model. The real catalyst for Dorian's transubstantiation from flesh into paint is the artist's cultured friend, Lord Henry Wotton, who advocates a "new hedonism" for the century, arguing that "sin is the only real colour-element left in modern life," and perhaps most compellingly, claims that "pleasure is the only thing worth having a theory about."[14]

Motivated by a powerful aversion to matrimony and forced by the portrait's presence to live only in the company of his servants, Dorian remains a bachelor in a house free of the mirrors and reflective surfaces that betray his Faustian pact. In this solitary yet elegant domain, he finds solace in the arts, exploring the particularly effete subjects of perfume, jewelry, tapestry, and ecclesiastical vestments. In addition to the murder of the artist who painted the ill-fated portrait, in Dorian's metamorphosis from impressionable youth to depraved and paranoid homicidal monster, he also provokes the suicide of a young actress, the death of her brother, and the ruin of several young men whom he astounds with the "wanton luxury" and "gorgeous splendor of his life."[15] Such ruination emphasizes a structural contradiction in the novel regarding decay that transforms this simple story into a nuanced critique of appearances; as the protagonist's morals progressively decline, his body remains immutable. Hence, decadence is based upon its near opposite, preservation, while the actual degeneration takes place within art itself.

The Decadent movement in Europe became a near synonym for "the artificial" and for a style of writing that valorized psychological ills. Along with Nietzsche's indictment of Wagner, Baudelaire's "rhetoric of sickness," the unconventional lives of many artists, and nascent racial theories professed by figures such as Max Nordau and Cesare Lombroso, the creative personality came to be categorized as a physiognomic type that necessarily exhibited signs of decay based upon an inherent deviancy.[16] Among the more onerous responses to this body of sick literature, besides the "Degenerate Art" exhibition of 1937, was that modern architecture and other fascist regimes responded to the fear of eviration and feminization with the cult of virility and normative physiognomic paradigms that ranged from advocating either a national regionalism or an international modernism. In the context of a larger cultural anxiety regarding the decline of civilization at the end of the millennium, the Decadent was, by definition, degenerate. Insofar as the pseudoscience of degeneration legitimized Lombroso's publishing the portraits of Baudelaire and Wagner and drawings of the skulls of Kant and

Foscolo in the same book as illustrations of the criminally insane, artists and philosophers were catalogued alongside sociopaths. Thus Lombroso writes of sterility, "Many great men have remained bachelors; others, although married, have no children. 'The noblest works and foundations,' said Bacon, 'have preceeded from childless men, which sought to express the images of their minds, where those of their bodies have failed.'"[17] Within these "pre-freudian theories of degeneration," as Barbara Spackman observes, it was understood not only that "sick bodies produced sick thought," but also that such an understanding could describe "social classes, political positions, genders, and even literary texts."[18] Spackman concludes that nineteenth-century writing focused on a "rhétorique obsédante," or excessive rhetoric, of "sickness and health, decay and degeneration, pathology and normalcy."[19] In a world where "epilepsy and 'moral' madness were metonymies for genius," precise craniometric and physiognomic analyses demonstrated that artists and intellectuals inherently displayed the atrophy of one organ, and consequently a behavioral pattern, as requisite for the hypertrophy of their ability.[20] Rather than retreat from these systems of classification, Decadent authors embraced the rhetoric of their critics, adopting the hysteric, convalescent, or androgyne as privileged figures of deviance and abnormality and constructing spaces around these aberrant bodies. As Debora Silverman argues:

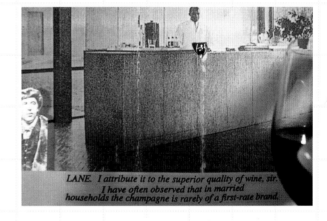

LANE. *I attribute it to the superior quality of wine, sir. I have often observed that in married households the champagne is rarely of a first-rate brand.*

> We can trace the development of the unity of the interior and the inner world of the self from the architectural writings of Edmond de Goncourt, to the Baudelairian "double room," to the neurotic interior of Huysmans' Des Esseintes, to the Proustian sealed chamber, where the boundaries between inner and outer realities ultimately dissolve in a dynamic flow.[21]

By generating a discourse of psychophysical pathology, Decadent authors also engendered space with a language that produced, to borrow a phrase from Nietzsche, the "psychologically picturesque" interior.[22]

From *The Birth of Tragedy* (1872) to *The Case of Wagner* (1888), Nietzsche emerged from the saturated polychromy of *Tannhäuser* only to change his position and proclaim: "Wagner's art is sick."[23] Nietzsche identifies the composer's "Protean character of degeneration" and by extension, located Wagner's villa at Bayreuth as central to Decadent discourse.[24] The Villa Wahnfried was a pilgrimage site for aspiring artists, composers, and writers, rivaled only by the palace and adventures of Wagner's patron, Ludwig II of Bavaria—a notorious decorator who furnished his Moorish kiosk at Linderhof with a peacock throne.[25] Moreover, the villa's name is rooted in the etymologies of *Wähnen* and *Wahn,* fantasy and madness, with the composer confessing, "Here where my fantasies found peace for their madness, let this house with this name resound."[26] From Wagner's madness to modernism's "alliance of beauty and sickness," Nietzsche refers to Decadence as "a world that is always five steps from the hospital," fingering a normative aspect of modern architecture that aligned aesthetics with anesthetics.[27] Susan Buck-Morss identifies a reciprocity between these two terms, explaining that *aesthetics* derives from the Greek *Aisthitikos,* a term meaning "perception by feeling," which initiated a discourse concerning the body.[28] She argues that modernity is characterized by a need to anesthetize the body from the trauma of overstimulated senses, leading the discussion toward a gendered distinction between the onanistic modern and the contextually aroused Decadent. Buck-Morss writes:

> Nietzsche's ideal of the artist-philosopher, the embodiment of the Will to Power, manifests the elitist values of the warrior. . . . This combination of autoerotic sexuality and wielding power over others is what Heidegger calls Nietzsche's *"Mannesaesthetik."* It is to replace what Nietzsche himself calls *"Weibesaesthetik"*—"female aesthetics" of receptivity to sensations from the outside.[29]

Nietzsche's critique of Wagner reveals a paradox within the hospital paradigm endemic to modern architecture: as a curative mechanism for the social ills of Decadence, it nonetheless ingests the illness, sterility, and hence bachelorhood of the Decadent project. Indeed, Nietzsche specifically writes, "Wagner's heroines never have children. Siegfried 'emancipates woman'—but without any hope of progeny."[30] Likewise, regarding the polarities of fecund country and sterile city, Nietzsche understands Decadence as occupying a world that is filled with "entirely metropolitan problems," a world and word—outlined by the Goncourt brothers—that is symptomatically French.[31]

Act II: A Country Home

According to Praz, the *Picture of Dorian Gray* represents "the classic of decadence in England"; it is a story where the hero is "depraved by the reading of French books [and] professes the principles of pagan hedonism . . . refined by more recent recipes of des Esseintes."[32] The reference to des Esseintes invokes the notorious protagonist of J. K. Huysmans' novel, *A Rebours* (1884), a book that influenced countless narratives and artists' spaces.[33] Translated variously as *Against Nature, Against the Grain,* or *Down Stream, A Rebours* is the secret book hidden in Dorian Gray's townhouse that offered febrile inspiration for his studied decline. After reading this book "there were moments when [Dorian] looked on evil simply as a mode through which he could realise his conception of the beautiful."[34] In addition to Wilde's description of the novel at his Queensbury trial as "the strangest book he ever read," his summary in *The Picture of Dorian Gray* offers a compelling analysis:

> The style in which it was written was that curious jewelled style, vivid and obscure at once, full of argot and archaisms, of technical expressions and of elaborate paraphrases, that characterizes the work of some of the finest artists of the French school of Symbolistes. There were in it metaphors as monstrous as orchids, and as subtle in colour. The life of the senses was described in terms of mystical philosophy. One hardly knew at times whether one was reading the spiritual ecstasies of some mediaeval saint or the morbid confessions of a modern sinner. It was a poisonous book. The heavy odour of incense seemed to cling about its pages and to trouble the brain.[35]

The only action in this novel concerns the neurasthenic and agoraphobic Duc Jean des Esseintes, who retires to his bachelor château above Fontenay-aux-Roses, just outside of Paris, proceeds to decorate his hermitage in a manner that will comfort an acute compulsion for solitude, falls ill, fails to recover, and is compelled by his physician to return to the city. In this case, neither the city nor the country serves as a curative site; both are equally stylized in Huysmans' novel.

Huysmans portrays des Esseintes—a frail, anemic, and high-strung bachelor—as suffering from the "degeneration of an ancient house" that had taken up to intermarry among itself only to produce heirs who became "progressively less manly."[36] While still living in his Paris apartment, des Esseintes draped his dining room in black fabric as the backdrop for a funeral

banquet held in memory of his temporarily deceased virility. He employed family servants who were familiar with his mother's sickroom routine, "inured to the absolute silence of cloistered monks, confined to rooms where the doors and windows were always shut."[37] As the last of his line, des Esseintes was, nonetheless, vehemently opposed to reproduction, exclaiming, "Ah! if in the name of pity the futile business of procreation was ever to be abolished, the time had surely come to do it."[38] Besides his aversion to children, Silverman explains, des Esseintes exhibited "medical states of nervous excitation and exhaustion" that Huysmans had "absorbed from a careful reading of Doctor Alexander Axenfeld's 1883 text *Traité des névroses*."[39] Silverman's specific research on the nineteenth-century interior suggests that there was a reciprocity between neuropsychiatrics and Decadent literature in deciding the psychology of the picturesque interior. Not only was Huysmans

interested in modern neurology, Dr. Jean-Martin Charcot, who founded the field, knew Edmond de Goncourt personally. This attraction between the cognitive and decorative arts may be understood as a mutual fascination with reading the interior as an expressive physiognomy of psychological disorders.

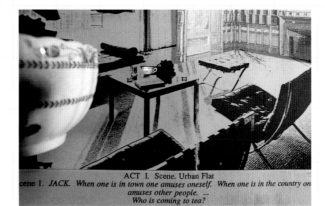

ACT I. Scene. Urban Flat
cene I. JACK. *When one is in town one amuses oneself. When one is in the country on amuses other people. ... Who is coming to tea?*

An adroit connoisseur and amateur designer, des Esseintes decorated the rooms of his château thematically, covering the walls of his library with bindings of Moroccan leather, embellishing his dining room like a ship's cabin, inventing an organ to administer liqueurs in synchrony with musical notes, hanging paintings such as Gustave Moreau's *Salome* that suggested an aura of corruption, ordering rare and exotic flowers, and going so far as to encrust the shell of a living tortoise with gilt and jewels. In comparison with Walter Benjamin's anecdote of the flâneur, who would stroll the Paris arcades at the pace of a leashed tortoise, des Esseintes' pet expired from its heavy burden, offering further evidence for the paralysis of overornamentation. These various episodes from *A Rebours*, understood as a primer for the Decadent interior, distill into a single space the combined precedents of the seraglio, the monastery, and the sickroom.

The actual existence of the jewel-encrusted tortoise upon which Huysmans based his improbable story provides a clue to a clandestine figure lurking within Dorian Gray's secret French novel. The Comte Robert de Montesquiou-Fezensac—who once referred to Wilde as "the Antinous of the Horrible," was himself known as the Parisian Dorian Gray, and was termed the "professor of beauty" by Marcel Proust—was a living model not only for Gray and des Esseintes, but also for the Baron Palamède de Charlus, who appeared in the volumes comprising Proust's *A la recherche du temps perdu*.[40] Each of these works captures various aspects of Montesquiou's captivating appearance, flamboyant life, and witty conversation, disseminating his lifestyle directly into bourgeois culture through what might be understood as sophisticated instruction manuals disguised in the form of novels. Likewise, Montesquiou promoted himself and his aesthetic in poetry and interior design, with a family inheritance, which he quickly consumed, that allowed him to indulge in writing and decorating as expressions of his consummate narcissism. He furnished his attic apartment on

Scene 2. *ALGERNON. You don't seem to realize, that in married life three is company and two is none.*

the quai d'Orsay, the one that Huysmans caricatured in *A Rebours,* with a jumble of incongruous objects that provided an elegant setting for his influential salon.[41] With his debonair appearance immortalized in portraits by Whistler, Giovanni Boldini, and Lucien Doucet and through the costumed fetes and other gatherings held at his several city and country residences, Montesquiou established himself as a reigning luminary of Parisian culture during the decades leading up to World War I. He promoted the painters Gustave Moreau and Odilon Redon, and he refined the artistry of idiosyncratic expression that aroused the interest of Apollinaire, the Goncourt brothers, Gabriele d'Annunzio, and Sarah Bernhardt.

Montesquiou followed a distinguished tradition of interior design that culminated earlier in the eighteenth century with J.-F. Bastide's *La Petite Maison,* a novella that portrayed a house as the central protagonist in the progress of a seduction.[42] A subtext within these overwrought interiors was to orchestrate corporeal delight in rooms where each of the senses would be marshaled toward sensual gratification through an elaborate exhibition of objects and furnishings. Given that many of the individuals who lived in these houses cultivated an artistic existence, the *maison d' artiste* approached the seductive connotations of the *petite maison.* Likewise, as a domain for the creative individual who required isolated room for thoughtful reflection, the atelier also approached the *garçonnière* as a site for liaisons and other illicit activity not always sanctioned in more traditional surroundings. Bernhardt, for example, recognized as an artist not only through her stage performances but also through her work in the fine arts,

ene 3. *GWENDOLEN. ...the name Earnest. There is something in that name that inspires absolute confidence.*

slept in a coffin, and her last home, to quote Robin Middleton, was an "effulgent, richly textured and scented" setting for her "own glorious persona."[43] While not all artist interiors were so morbidly furnished with necrophilic objects, regardless of the decor, they were associated with the personality and sexuality of their inhabitants, who were understood as bachelors regardless of their marital status, gender, or sexual orientation.

Perhaps the most recent and convenient equivalent to Montesquiou's cynosure would be Charles de Beistegui, patron and partial author of two significant residences that forcefully propel this discussion from turn-of-the-century aesthetics into the empire of modern architecture. Beistegui, a known amorist, was a "cosmopolitan and fashionable cultural attaché from the Spanish embassy" who symbolized "a golden age of novelty, of elegance, and of interior decoration."[44] Besides the more famous penthouse that Le Corbusier designed for him in 1929, seven years later—with the assistance of architect Emilio Terry—Beistegui also decorated and enlarged a château of Groussay at Montfort-l'Amaury, near Versailles. While distinguished scholars, most notably Beatriz Colomina, have studied the nuances of Beistegui's pied-à-terre in Paris, his château further explicates the penthouse's noted formal ambiguity.[45] Insofar as Beistegui's collection appears to be less of an oxymoron in the country house than it does when situated in the Paris apartment, the existing neoclassical chateau provides a more hospitable, if less piquant, context. The centerpiece of the château is a library that Aslet describes with sparkling detail as a

> strongly masculine room, owing more to Empire than any other historical mood. Busts of Roman emperors flank the fireplace, the convex mirror bears a military trophy, the pietra dura table has griffin feet, a model of the Place Vendôme column stands on one of the tables, there are columns and obelisks on the desk. It is a room in which every surface seems to support a drawing, a bronze piece of biscuit de Sèvres. But it is also a working room, and the books—except those on the top shelves, which were bought for their backs—reflect Beistegui's passion. For they are almost exclusively on houses, architecture and decoration.[46]

Likewise, the contents of the penthouse complement the collection at the château, with the former suggesting a "surreal" combination of Beistegui's baroque and modern sensibilities, replete with, as Mauriès describes,

> a cinema screen masked behind a wall of Venetian mirrors, a crystal chandelier disappearing automatically, like shrubs into their cement beds, a spiral staircase . . . twisting around a glass column, a display of arabesques, pouffes decorated with cabochons and glass beads, and finally the legendary open-air room—the turf-covered terrace featured a mirror, a mantelpiece and various items of furniture. All without electric light, which was spurned by the master of the house.[47]

The apparent antimony between Le Corbusier's modern architecture and the objects it contains augments a dialogue between the private exhibition, the *garçonnière*, and the penthouse, where the mixing of historical styles contaminates modern architecture's purported aesthetic sincerity. Beistegui rebelled against modernist aestheticism with rooms where "no inch of space was left bare," where "a faint glimmer of gold enlivened the sombre mahogany surfaces," and where "the general impression was a weird combination of retreat, intimacy and pomp."[48] This was a glittering world in which the melange of Beistegui's fabulous

167

furnishings and his extravagant fetes construed a model of domesticity that was directed at "a very special society indifferent to conformism and the rules hallowed by etiquette."[49]

When approached in concert, the château misconstrues the penthouse's urban detachment, including it as part of Beistegui's larger collection of artifacts, which stretches from the country to the city. In this respect, the château includes the penthouse among the several follies that range from a Ledoux pyramid, a Palladian bridge, a triumphal column, a Kew pagoda, and a Tartar tent. In the 1950s Beistegui added pavilions to the existing house and finally completed the theater that he had originally intended to construct in the form of a pyramid in the middle of a lake. Modeled on the eighteenth-century Margravine's Theater at Bayreuth, as Clive Aslet explains, Beistegui's theater may owe something to his "admiration for a later member of the Bavarian royal house, King Ludwig II—a madman but a passionate decorator."[50] The diverse historical precedents of these pavilions, particularly the reference to Ledoux, invites comparison with an article Philip Johnson published in *Architectural Review* in 1950 in which he outlines the precedents for his own house at New Canaan, including among his collection of references Le Corbusier, Mies van der Rohe, van Doesburg, Choisy, Schinkel, Ledoux, and Malevich.[51]

The most compelling affinity between Le Corbusier's modernism and Beistegui's irreverent eclecticism is the spiral staircases that wrap around columns, occupying the library of the château and penetrating the penthouse's roof garden. The spiral stair also winds its way into a definitive example of the *maison d' artiste,* represented by Le Corbusier's studio for Amédée Ozenfant, a house-atelier that anticipated Museum of Modern Art's display of the Breuer House as another such habitable model delineating domesticity through the lens of modern art. The ground floor of Ozenfant's house contained a wine cellar, servants' quarters, and a garage for either his Citröen 5CV or his Bugatti two-liter racing car. The piano nobile, reached from either a stair in the garage or an exterior spiral stair, consisted of a gallery containing Ozenfant's Louis XVI furniture, a kitchen adjacent to a *musée* that doubled as a dining room, and a sleeping area with bathroom and wardrobe. The third-level atelier was reserved exclusively for work, with only the darkroom and the stairs—leading to the lower gallery, library, cockpit, and balcony-loft—disrupting the open plan.

With no less than four separate stairs connecting the different floors, such obsessive articulation of vertical circulation propels the machine aesthetic of ships' ladders and cockpits into the domain of Huysmans' ship's cabin and Whistler's peacock. The freestanding stair attached to the balcony-loft hovering within a two-story volume culminated here as a requisite element for artistic spaces. The garret with an angled skylight that Puccini romanticized in *La Bohème* (1896) becomes the factory aesthetic of modern architecture. After the Maison Citrohan and the Ozenfant studio, as Reyner Banham writes, Le Corbusier developed a standard studio-house section that was "deep in plan," with "windows across the narrow ends," and a "high living-room with bedroom at the back" that persists as a leitmotif in the Pavillon de l'Esprit Nouveau, the Weissenhof, and Marseilles.[52] With only one bedroom in this house and the suspended library suggesting a monk's cell, the apartment fits the role of a bachelor *atelier* or *garçonnière,* replete with its function of exhibiting art and seducing patrons.

The *musée*/dining room and kitchen sequence associates visual and corporeal consumption, where the appetite whet when viewing art adheres to the culinary demands of the art museum's pervasive *café*. Indeed, when discussing the Museum of Modern Art, Johnson argues that visitors who suffer from "museum fatigue" should be able to "stop and have a Campari."[53] In contradistinction to this comment, Ozenfant explains purism with

ACT II. Scene. Country Home
Scene I.   *ALGERNON.* *If I am occasionally a little over-dressed, I make up for it by being always immensely over-educated.*

the declaration, "Après les cocktails, l'eau fraîche," likewise recalling Mies van der Rohe's adage that architecture is not a cocktail.[54] Transparent and salubrious water describes purism as a stainless experiment that corresponds to Ozenfant's barren studio. The myth of modernism personified the artist as a chemist-painter, mixing philters in clear glass beakers, in an atelier maintained with hospital standards of hygiene. As Ozenfant writes, "We want our walls white; and empty; that is free, pure."[55] The disarray, mess, and clutter that characterize the artist's atelier formed a paradoxical adversary to those modern architects who were preoccupied with vacuum cleaners, but who, nonetheless, developed their architectural vocabulary upon a messier tradition of painting.

Banham describes the *maison d' artiste,* in one of his more or less erudite moments, with the statement "Even if we can't all become artists, Le Corbusier has helped a lot of people to live like them."[56] This observation, however sanguine, exemplifies the dilemma of modern domestic architecture as indebted to the experiments of studio spaces and the "artistic" interior. Similarly, Johann Gfeller argues that "It is possible to formulate the hypostesis that the 'house-atelier' represents a *model* of house rather than a variant of this."[57] Agreeing that the artist's atelier formed a dominant paradigm for domestic space, this history might account for a basic incompatibility between the architect's aspiration to design a new way of living and a middle-class conception of domesticity sacred in North America. The implicit silhouette of the bachelor-artist within the studio, and by extension, avant-garde residential programs, threatened the structure of the nuclear family with the presence of an avuncular guest who stayed too long and drank too much. Despite the fact that there may not be a strict typology for the artist's house-studio, even given the dicta of flexible work-spaces and natural light, artist houses at the turn of the century do, nonetheless, uncover the irony of modern architecture dormant in Wilde's play: that an elite society sincerely imbibed styles of living developed by artists and architects who critiqued their lack of sincerity.

And yet, when modern artists banished the live and often unclothed model from their work, they also eliminated this figure from the studio—an accessory that invoked the topos of lascivious activity draped under the aegis of art. When inhabited by the model, the *maison d' artiste* becomes the *garçonnière,* a space where creative and sexual production are difficult to distinguish. If not the actual model, then the painting and sculpture exhibited in artistic rooms often would refer to this absent presence as a catalyst for corporeal imagery based upon the naked body or upon iconographical references to libertine activities. While this argument concerning the carnal allusions of art may appear facile or spurious, it is not beyond the scope of American imaginations. Lynes, for example, discusses the public titillation surrounding the display of Hiram Powers' nude sculpture "The Greek Slave." Lynes compares P. T. Barnum's selling of tickets to view art, displayed next to sideshow oddities, with the statue's 1847 exhibition, explaining:

> When she was put on display thousands of men and women paid admission to see her, and such was her reputation as a piece of high art that even children were permitted to view her blameless nakedness. It didn't take the sharpers long to realize that here was a good thing.

A man who called himself Dr. Collyer introduced at Palmo's Opera House in New York what he described as "a new moment in the fine arts." Here he attracted the public in droves, from the most fashionable to the least refined, with a *tableau vivante* which he advertised as "living men and women in almost the same state in which Gabriel saw them in the Garden of Eden on the first morning of creation." In no time at all there were "taverns, hotels, saloons, and other drinking houses, where young men and women were exhibited as *tableaux vivants*, in every form and shape, and for every price from six pence up to fifty cents."[58]

Both the worlds of art and of sex could be viewed for a nominal fee. As Lyne's narrative indicates, at one level the artwork that was displayed in studios and drawing rooms either served as artistic inspiration or cultural legitimacy; at another, it alluded to the seductive appeal of maiden slaves bound in chains. The prevalence of classical statues and plaster casts in artistic spaces—just as often an Antinous or, in Wilde's case, the Hermes of Praxiteles—would serve as part of a larger mise-en-scène that welcomed high culture into the house along with base desire.

Closer still to the hallowed domain of architecture in North America, Stanford White's scandalous lifestyle and eventual murder on the roof of Madison Square Garden introduces a wealth of innuendo regarding the bachelor lurking even within the American architect-artist. In his biography of White, Paul Baker writes, "Stan and a very few close companions, as 'bachelors for the evening,' for years carried on a secret life of sexual adventures, which were hidden from their families."[59] In fact, White characterized *The Memoirs of Casanova* as the most thumbed book in the Century Club library. White's death in 1906 at the hands of Harry K. Thaw resulted from his liaisons with an enchanting young model who had become popular as a Gibson girl. The story was made famous in a film adaptation titled *The Girl in the Red Velvet Swing* (1955); its title derives from the famous seduction scene where White, played by Ray Milland, enthralls the sixteen-year-old Evelyn Nesbit, played by Joan Collins, with glasses of champagne and a rapturous flight on an indoor swing hung from the ceiling of his New York apartment. White transformed this apartment into a machine of seduction employing art and architecture—statues, etchings, paintings, mirrors, etc.—as vehicles for conveying culture and connotation. His two-story-high studio featured a "swing hanging from the ceiling on red velvet ropes, with green smilax wrapping around the ropes and trailing down from its red velvet seat."[60] He attended to every detail of this *garçonnière*, from the kimonos his mistresses would wear to the bed in which they slept: "The headboard of the bed, and the dome of its canopy, and the wall next to the bed, were all mirrors. Hidden around the top of the bed, upon its canopy, were tiny electric bulbs that could be regulated by pushing different buttons for different effects."[61] With news of Thaw's murder trial and subsequent insanity plea offering daily tabloid headlines, even an architect as staid and respectable as White could be exposed as a bachelor-artist.

Scene 2. *JACK. It is very painful for me to be forced to speak the truth . . . and I am really quite inexperienced in doing anything of the kind.*

Act III: House in the Garden

This protracted introduction to Marcel Breuer's exhibition house in the museum garden suggests that the artist's atelier formed an ambiguous prototype for modern domestic architecture in North America, one that threatened simultaneously to erode and to reify the moral and cultural values it purported to reform. This is a simple enough argument to proffer, but one more difficult to defend when directed at the subdued and normative House in the Garden that reproduced forms already well digested by North American architects through its most obvious prototype, Le Corbusier's Errazuriz House (1930). As Klaus Herdeg writes:

A comparison with a much earlier house by Le Corbusier suggests itself almost naturally because the latter also has a "butterfly" roof and is a residence of similar dimensions. . . . These houses, comparable in the ways just mentioned and in the use of rustic materials like flagstone and fieldstone, are utterly different in the attitudes they display toward architecture. While the first strains to accommodate an American middle-income family with the most efficient "zoning" of functions possible and then shower the resulting diagram with (by 1949) safely modern references, thus giving the occupants the feeling of living in harmony with the *Zeitgeist*, the second displays an intention not only of accommodating the occupants' immediate needs but of creating a basic confrontation between architecture as an abstract idea and architecture as a craft and tradition.[62]

Herdeg offers a provocative analysis of the Breuer House, one that defends his position that modern architecture in North America offered nothing more than an avant-garde suntan. He also identifies the butterfly roof as an archetypal moment in domestic architecture. The butterfly: Whistler's personal symbol flutters out from a world that Lynes had characterized through the trappings of ornamental tiles, precious teapots, and Japanese fans and into the Museum of Modern Art sculpture garden as an *objet décoratif*.

As much as modern architecture with an avant-garde edge, on sale here were art, furniture, dishes, and finishes. At a moment when modern art was produced specifically to hang on gallery walls—supplanting the period room and its thematic exhibition with a supposedly neutral background—the Breuer House in the Garden displayed art in an architectural context of furniture and functional objects that had been eschewed by the museum's great white apparatus. Having previously introduced the Breuer House as a lamination of domestic and museological ideologies, its official press describes it more simply as "a moderately priced house for a man who works in a large city and commutes to a so-called dormitory town."[63] The house efficiently accommodates a growing family of middle income that could not afford servants but, instead, could purchase a home costing, after the completion of phase two, no more than $25,000 (this price does not include the costs of land, architect, landscaping, and connections to public utilities). The ground floor of phase one contains living and sleeping areas, separated at opposite ends of the house, with rooms looking out through large plate-glass windows into outdoor spaces described by terraces, fieldstone walls, and louvered partitions.

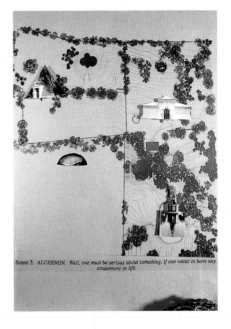

Scene 3. *ALGERNON. Well, one must be serious about something, if one wants to have any amusement in life.*

Breuer most clearly articulates his concept of the binuclear plan in phase two, with the name of this typology proposing to bifurcate the nuclear family. In this model of domestic reform, he isolates the parents' and the children's sleeping areas on opposite ends of the house. In so doing, he adds a garage and a master bedroom to the west wall of the existing living room, providing access to a new second floor with one set of stairs leading from the garage to an exterior balcony and a second set connecting the living room to an open balcony that forms part of the parents' bedroom. The balcony-bedroom, or rather, bedroom-loft, remains open to the living area unless enclosed by privacy curtains—drapery delineates a space where activities may occur *ob scena*. Despite the differences of program and cultural context, the house nonetheless adopts what it dilutes: modifying the formal criteria of the avant-garde "cocktail" into a less intoxicating and hence less explosive beverage. In this watered-down form, the domestic exhibition, loft section, expansive glass, and walled garden may be understood either as paradigmatic expressions of modern architecture or as elements that directly refer to the *maison d' artiste*.

While the Breuer House may have been marketed as the home for a family of middle income that lived in the suburbs, its actual siting within the museum garden and the prestigious collection of art it exhibited distinguishes it from popular culture and locates it in the center of the Museum of Modern Art's social elite. Within this domestic exhibition, the living room displays a Hans Arp relief specially designed for the house, the master bedroom contains Juan Gris' *Fruit Dish, Glass and Newspaper,* and the guest bedroom features Fernand Léger's *Woman Combing Her Hair* (both from the museum's collection). There is a metal stabile by Alexander Calder on the west wall of the building, a Paul Klee (also from the museum's collection), and finally, the windows frame views of different pieces of sculpture standing in the museum garden. As a counterpoint to the language of architectural journals, the list of furniture reads like a Museum of Modern Art exhibition catalog, with galleries containing an assortment of tables and chairs by Breuer, Eero Saarinen, and Charles Eames. Recalling in abatement the artistic rooms of the fin de siècle, sumptuous fabrics—imported, screenprinted, and handwoven—cover the windows and furniture, while rugs finish the floors. Of particular interest to theorists of architecture and television, the living room centers on Breuer's design for a coffee table with a set of dials that could be adjusted without getting up from the couch and a separate unit containing a record player, radio, and television. Breuer envisioned domestic remote control, a total entertainment system signifying the American banalization of Wagner's *Gesamtkunstwerk*.

Approximately 70,000 visitors walked into this domestic exhibition of furniture, art, and quotidian objects and through spaces where the windows from the museum and the house would mutually reflect the residence and the gallery as reciprocal, yet necessarily circumspect, viewing apparatuses. This was a peep show between two diverse, but nonetheless engaged domains: the provinces of suburban domesticity and the private club. The Breuer House exhibits a collection of "clean" or iconographically neutral abstract art. But, as I have argued, if the puritan revolution that characterizes modern art and architecture may have attenuated the human figure in its horizon, it could not entirely eliminate the memory of the lecherous bachelor from its studio; this was dirt in another sense of the word. A vestige of artistic exhibitionism filters through the curtain that circumscribes the *frons scaena* in front of the parents' bedroom, transforming the living room into a domestic theater. As with Wilde's play, which transports provincial domesticity to a London stage, displacing the country house into the city, the context of the Museum of Modern Art's sculpture garden presents the entire house as a theater of daily life where visitors enjoy the pleasure of peering into a private diorama located in the most public forum. Not only does the House in the Garden enjoy a tension between display and concealment, it also endorses a split between work and daily life, country and city. The father commutes to work from the suburbs—most likely in a Ford or an Oldsmobile—where he might adopt White's role of "bachelor for an evening," while his wife, it is assumed, remains at home and supervises the house from her command post in the kitchen, arranging each room as per the published photographs. With the Breuer House sited between the museum and the 54th Street mansions, the neighboring residences that peer down into the garden heighten the pleasure of domesticity on display that would have been less thrilling if the house had been built on the suburban site it was planned for.

As a *hortus conclusus,* or secret enclave locked off from unpaying guests, the sculpture garden offered the serenity and calmness suitable for contemplating art. The allusion to contemplative spaces, of course, alludes to the bachelor monk meditating in a private cloister, also recalling des Esseintes' persona of the solitary monk who, in this case, adopts modernism's religious asceticism. And it is no accident that the monk's robe is a form of dress that allegorizes both Decadents and moderns, with one group profaning and the other idealizing the secluded life of solitude. The Breuer House, inserted as it was within the courtyard of the Museum of Modern Art, shared in the museum's postlapsarian mission, with the typical family atavistically framed as a biblical clan set adrift in the suburbs in their little wooden ark.

Modernism's preoccupation with healthy domesticity inhabits the rhetoric surrounding the Breuer House, with *Architectural Forum* writing "The location of the playroom next to the child's bedroom is another excellent arrangement. In case of measles or mumps, one bed can be moved into the playroom and quarantine easily established."[64] Quarantine indeed. The walls of the museum garden segregated the house from direct contact with suburban America and, likewise, protected suburbia from avant-garde influenzas. Des Esseintes already understood, between cloister and clinic or sacristy and sanitarium, that spiritual and physical healing often maintained similar requirements for seclusion and privacy.

ACT III. Scene. House in Garden
Scene 1. *GWENDOLEN.*
s of grave importance, style, not sincerity, is the vital thing.

Sited in the sculpture garden designed by McAndrew and Alfred Barr, the Breuer House marks a transitional moment in the Museum of Modern Art's history, between experimental exhibitions and its reification of modernism into the commercially viable entity that Johnson's polished renovation would announce. In other words, after the completion of Johnson's courtyard, the museum lost a valuable piece of inchoate space that could be used for the installation of large outdoor displays, such as those by Breuer, Ain, and even Kiesler, while in turn, its collection acquired a sophisticated piece of landscape architecture. While the original sculpture garden consisted of a series of random fences wrapping around and serving as a background to the featured pieces, Johnson's garden transformed the space into a court-house. In a published interview, where asked if the museum courtyard is an urban version of his Ash Street house in Boston—distinguished by a garden enclosed on the street side by a wall and on the house side by sixty-five feet of glass—Johnson responds: "It's a court-house. I took it from a Catholic institution of some kind located on 70-something street here in New York that has an even higher wall. So I said to Nelson, 'We have this wall as in any institution that's private, any monastery.'"[65] The presence of St. Thomas's Episcopal Church directly in the garden formed an ecclesiastical background for the McAndrew-Barr site where the Breuer House was displayed. Although the house was sited in a different section of the museum garden, which is now hidden behind the café, the exterior walls and court spaces of the Breuer House presage the domestic character of Johnson's courtyard.

Scene 2. *JACK. I've now realized for the first time in my life the vital Importance of Being Earnest.*

Once the residential plan underlying the sculpture garden is uncovered, the previous inventory of concerns regarding domesticity and the space of the artist — the seraglio, the clinic, and the cloister — inhabits the museum, which itself emerged from a slow institutionalization of private-domestic art collections. While Breuer was still teaching at Harvard, in 1942 Johnson developed his own house for a master's thesis. Regarding this enterprise, Schulze informs us that, with the help of a servant and his own accomplished social skills:

9 Ash Street became a conversation piece among the local architectural community as well as the neighborhood. . . . One of the first dinner guests was . . . I. M. Pei. . . . The new American Society of Architectural Historians . . . convened at least once at the house — to hear the critic and historian Emil Kaufmann discuss his book *Von Ledoux bis Le Corbusier: Ursprung und Enwicklung der Autonomen-Architektus*. . . . Henry-Russell Hitchcock . . . made his way to the Ash Street place. Even Gropius accepted an invitation. So did old friends Alfred Barr and George Howe. The house became a bachelor's salon.[66]

177

In comparison to his own "bachelor atelier," Johnson responded to American domesticity in the Wiley House (1953) with a version of Breuer's binuclear living, separating living and representational requirements on separate floors. He explains this solution as an "attempt to reconcile the (perhaps) irreconcilable. Modern architectural purity and the requirements of living American families."[67] He asks, "Why can't people learn to live in the windowless spheres of Ledoux or the pure glass prisms of Mies van der Rohe? No, they need a place for Junior to practice the piano while Mother plays bridge with her neighbors."[68] Revisiting rooms tainted by the sound of a piano, Johnson's quip suggests a certain amount of disdain when it comes to the standards of living in North America that he critiques with this transvaluation of normative spatial distinctions. Between Baudelaire's double room—a mental ward of psychological disorders—and middle-class double standards—closets of repressed desire—Johnson tilts the scales of daily life from truth toward artifice.

In this respect, and by way of a conclusion, I propose responding to Robin Middleton's provocative question to Johnson, left unanswered in *Architectural Design* (1967). Middleton writes, "A busy, eclectic architect, a master of techniques, a detail-at-a-time genius, a scholarly romantic, a demolisher of all over-earnest beliefs, a scandal-monger, you raise a delicious question—are you in fact earnest?"[69]

When earnestness is equated with sincerity, then its antipode, according to Wilde's system, is style, leading to the precarious dichotomies of naïveté and subtlety, frankness and flair, truth and artifice, or more provocatively, American and European. Such a corollary invites comparison to Colin Rowe's similar assessment of the differences in Europe's and America's approaches to the structural frame, where he argues:

> In Chicago it might be said that the frame was convincing as a *fact* rather than as an *idea*, whereas in considering the European innovators of the twenties one cannot suppress the supposition that the frame to them was much more often an essential *idea* before it was an altogether reasonable *fact* (emphasis added).[70]

In a continent where facts resemble truth and sincerity, it is possible to approach Rowe's "ideas" in terms of Wilde's "style." To recover style as a viable approach to design rather than as a loose term of approbation acknowledges the value of ideas, creativity, wit, and humor that are not inherently predicated upon facts and figures. This is neither to rehearse nor to debunk clichés regarding the "continental" as lacking sincerity or the "colonial" as lacking style but rather to indulge, for one moment, Johnson's ability to play the field. Furthermore, the recovery of style in opposition to sincerity challenges the critique launched at

North American architecture as having reduced the earnest explorations of the European avant-garde to a set of stylistic formulas. Seen in an alternative light, Americans embraced modern architecture with serious and enthusiastic vigor, translating European style into American sincerity. In response to this interpretation, Johnson has taken artifice from out of the attic and behind the curtain in order to display it, dangers and all, in spaces where mirrors and reflective surfaces enhance the pleasures of vanity and intrigue. Thus, "the importance of being earnest," is also to master, as Johnson's polymorphism has succeeded in doing, the style of sincerity, sometimes Wilde, sometimes sober.

179

SYLVIA LAVIN

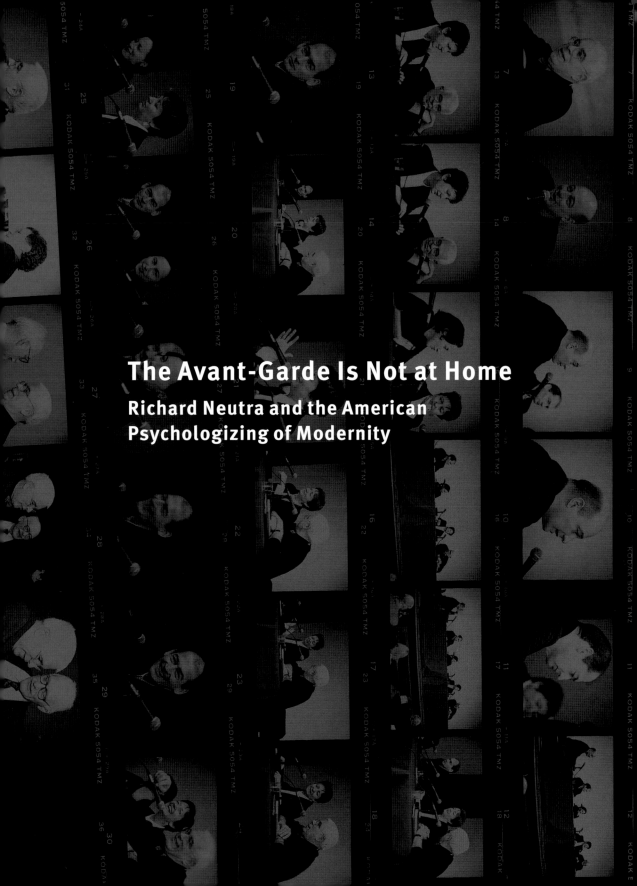

The Avant-Garde Is Not at Home

Richard Neutra and the American
Psychologizing of Modernity

In his essay "A Home Is Not a House," Reyner Banham claimed that a "mechanical invasion" had intruded upon the domain of modern architecture, threatening the cultural position of the architect and of the American architect in particular. The consequence of this invasion was conceptually to render the American house a nostalgic token of sentimentality and misplaced European-style monumentality. Banham offered the *unhouse* as an anti-monumental and pragmatically technological counter-model, and used Philip Johnson's Glass House as an example. Because the Glass House is comprised of just a heated floor slab and a standing bathroom unit, Banham claimed it best articulated "the threat or the promise of the unhouse." The only improvement Banham suggested was that "the house would have been better off without its glass walls."[1]

Without its glass walls, however, the building in New Canaan could not be the Glass House or even the glass unhouse, and the desire to eliminate the plate glass reveals Banham's rather exclusive and almost obsessive attention to bathrooms and mechanical systems. Although glass does not register its "mechanics" in the visual field the same way plumbing pipes do, the material and its effects were technologically important to the avant-garde invasion of the house. Simply wishing away the glass walls does not undo Johnson's house or propel it into a more authentically avant-garde position. Equal in significance to this rejection of glass as too architectural was Banham's elision of the concept of home, mentioned once in the essay's title and never referred to again. By shifting attention away from the difference between house and home and toward the opposition between house and unhouse, Banham attempted to distance and protect the latter from the sentimentality that he maintained was malignantly deforming the modern American home.

Ironically, the twentieth-century American house may not have required much protection against sentimentality. In 1953, an infamous New York madam published her autobiography, *A House Is Not a Home*, brandishing the phrase that Banham and others would erroneously associate with sentimental notions of the domestic. Polly Adler was instead interested in the fact that "to the uninitiated it might seem that there can hardly be much difference in houses, and of course in the bedroom the procedure is fairly well standardized, varying only with the customer's whim. (This last item . . . is a subject I will leave to Kinsey and Freud.)"[2] According to this modern courtesan there was more at stake in the various relationships between homes and unhouses, whorehouses and unhomes, than Banham had suggested. Is the Glass House, with its peek-a-boo walls, the home of a prostitute?[3] Although Johnson would answer yes, the question more significantly suggests that rather than turning on matters of sentiment or plumbing, the house/home dyad, so energetically debated during the postwar era, revolved around sex.[4]

Not just sex but the whole panoply of psychosexual dynamics, and it was in this context that by the end of World War II the concepts of home and house had become sites of intense technical investigation. Banham considered all elements other than pure mechanical pragmatics unnecessary to the production of architecture and as mere "psychological gestures." Gestures, such as glass walls, however, were techniques through which psychoanalysis and psychology joined architecture in constructing a new type of subject. Like the visitor to Polly

Adler's house, this subject would expect to receive, and would ultimately demand, nothing short of psycho-sexual resolution from his environment. Banham's beloved mechanical invasion—when domestic appliances, heating and cooling systems, TV sets, and cars came rolling home—was accompanied if not enabled by a psychological invasion, a development that might be called the "psych-ops" of the postwar architectural environment.

The joining of forces by psychoanalysis and modern architecture in the United States was perhaps historically overdetermined.[5] Both fields began what is understood as their avant-garde phase in Europe, and in Vienna in particular, but were ultimately codified, disciplined, and popularized most intensely in this country. The medicalization of psychoanalysis, for example, structurally parallels the trend toward systematization seen in the International Style. The most powerful agents bringing together architecture and psychoanalysis, however, were the two world wars. As they generated and then proliferated a wide array of techniques and technologies, these conflagrations guaranteed the success of both psychology and modern architecture in the civilian culture of the United States.[6]

The hearty welcome that psychoanalysis received in the United States began with its success in treating the victims of shell shock during World War I.[7] This first accomplishment, which focused on the treatment of individuals, earned the nascent profession the ear of government, and by World War II psychoanalytic principles had become an important military weapon. The effort to develop forms of psychological warfare, or "psych-ops," produced an unprecedented number of psychotherapists of various kinds who would ultimately need to work during peacetime. One result of this invasion of clinicians into the civilian world was the development of concepts such as national morale, an object that could now require treatment, and the

subsequent pathologizing of everyday life. A second and related result was a shift in attention from the individual psyche to collective mental health. Legislation like the National Mental Health Act of 1946, in turn, established the basis for what would become generalized social engineering and human management. By the 1960s, thinking of society and its environment in broadly psychological terms was accepted without question or note. New disciplines, such as environmental psychology, were founded, psychologists came to play major roles in almost every aspect of public policy from education to foreign affairs, and psychotherapy became a generally available and widely sought commodity.[8]

In order to explore how modern architecture became a transference object in the ever more psychologically saturated landscape of the American middle class, I will consider the example of Richard Neutra and Otto Rank. These Austrian immigrants were important yet illegitimate sons of psychoanalysis and significant contributors to postwar American culture. Both were secularized Jews of the same generation raised in Vienna who immigrated to the United States, bringing with them aspects of European avant-garde practice. Although Neutra's early architecture has certainly been linked to the avant-garde, his connections with Viennese psychoanalytic culture have yet to be systematically explored. Neutra was in fact a close friend of Freud's son, Ernst, and frequently visited and traveled with the Freud family group. In a properly Oedipal play of sons and brothers, Ernst was to become an

183

(1)
Otto Rank and Sigmund Freud,
Time, June 23, 1958

DISCIPLE RANK, MASTER FREUD
Sick, sick, sick.

architect just as Neutra's brother would become a psychiatrist. Moreover, when Neutra and his wife realized that their elder son was retarded, it was Freud to whom they turned for consultation.[9]

Neutra was himself psychoanalyzed more than once for depression. The following unpublished text of 1942, entitled "Inferiority-Nightmare," would suggest that Neutra's treatment was not entirely successful:

Modesty, humbleness are far from describing my dejection. . . . But in my desperation I sometimes miraculously have succeeded in concealing it. So I survive from trick to trick. But how long can I keep it up? One day, no doubt, I will be exposed and thrown into the "abyss" of ridicule and bankruptcy. . . .[10]

Even a brief perusal of the full length of this document reveals that Neutra structured his own self-analysis according to standard psychoanalytic concepts such as ego, projection, repression, and sublimation.

Yet Neutra was far from a pure Freudian and had many reservations about Freud in relation to architecture.

After having been invited to return to Vienna for the filming of a documentary on his work, Neutra revisited Freud's apartment at Berggasse 19, and wrote:

Despite my admiration for the great doctor, I had wondered about this place. The building was one of those pseudo-Renaissance piles of the 1880s, and the dark study in which he worked . . . seems to contradict the impassioned scrutiny he was according to other psychological influences . . . we have more to learn from Freud than his famous "depth psychology." . . . He did not recognize that the sensory assaults to which our systems and psyches are subjected have a surreptitious, often delayed effect . . . he remained oblivious to environmental deficiencies out of trained disregard.[11]

Neutra's criticism of Freud as a holdover of an outdated mode of architectural perception could be leveled at Neutra himself. The emphasis in this passage on sensory experience and its relationship to psychological states is one of Neutra's own apparently retardataire fascinations. Neutra was an avid admirer of Wilhelm Wundt, one of the leading experimental psychologists of the nineteenth century, who was widely influential in popularizing the notion of physiological psychology.[12] Much of Neutra's work, and especially his theory of biological realism, which concentrated on the deterministic influence of environment on human physiology and therefore psyche, derives from this tradition.[13] By the time of Freud's depth psychology it was precisely this determinist and somatic view of the psyche that was to be overturned.

An important contributor to the dissemination of this Freudian thought in which Neutra was ensnared, despite himself, was Otto Rank, for a time Freud's most devoted follower and almost adoptive son.[14] Rank, who ultimately settled in the United States after an ugly break with Freud, began as a true believer. Having been encouraged to study psychoanalysis by Freud himself, Rank became the secretary of the Psychoanalytic Society and member of the Committee.[15] In 1923 Rank presented Freud, on Freud's birthday, with a copy of his recently completed text, *The Trauma of Birth*.[16] What was originally thought of as a contribution to psychoanalysis, by both Rank and Freud, was soon thereafter seen as a heretical departure from its teaching. Rank was ultimately expelled from Freud's circle and not only labeled a deviant thinker but accused by some of being downright insane (1).[17]

Although many factors contributed to this schism within the psychoanalytic ranks, the basic controversy derived from ideas first developed by Rank in his book on the birth trauma. Concerned with the etiology of anxiety, Rank developed an idea, previously noted in passing by Freud, that the source of anxiety, and hence of neurosis, could be found in the moment of birth. This original and universal experience, for Rank, generated and was related to all subsequent human experiences of anxiety. While it was primarily Rank's shift away from the primacy of the Oedipal complex and Freud's theory of drives that led to the parting of their ways, this same shift has led to a recent renewal of interest in Rank's work. Rank's theory gave new priority to the role of the mother in infantile psychological development, established foundations for what would subsequently be called object theory, and led to significant shifts in therapeutic technique.[18]

In theorizing that separation from the mother's womb, and ultimately from the mother more generally, was the basic cause of neurosis, Rank assigned a new function to therapy: enabling the patient to *master* in the present the trauma of birth.[19] Thus Rank became interested in short-term analysis and in emphasizing the termination date of analysis, so that separation from the analyst could repeat, in a more productive manner, the original separation from the mother.[20] A major component of Rank's focus on individuation included a consideration of the arts and their role in this process. He wrote, for example, that "the house is, for all its corporeal symbolism, much more than a mere copy from nature of maternal protection: it . . . has become the symbol of the creative ego that has freed itself from the maternal protective covering and risen to an independence of its own."[21] Rank's psychoanalytic approach to works of art engaged an important strain in Germanic psychologically oriented art theory and history.[22] Elaborating this tradition, Rank's work would lead to investigations not only of the separating subject, but of the individuated object and its relation to space.

On the occasion of Richard Neutra's sixtieth birthday, just as Rank had done for Freud, Mrs. George Rourke, the owner of a Neutra house in Beverly Hills (2+3), completed in 1949, presented the architect with a testimonial:

> Since you are to celebrate a birthday soon, this seems an appropriate time for me to tell you . . . of the delight I, my husband, and Michael [their son] have experienced living . . . in the house you designed for us. . . . [N]o aesthetic aspect of our house has

(2)
Richard Neutra, Rourke House,
Beverly Hills, 1949, exterior view

palled on me, or bored me or grown obvious. . . . [I]t has remained a continually fresh experience, adapting itself, so to speak, to the hour of the day, the mood of the weather, or the change of seasons.[23]

Mrs. Rourke later argued that what Neutra provided to his clients was "a new living experience," and when *Time* featured Neutra on the cover the same year the Rourke House was completed, the author of the story wrote, "When they had sold their antiques and moved in, Mrs. Rourke could think of only one word to describe the way she felt about it: 'Liberation.'"[24]

The language used by Mrs. Rourke to describe her experience of the Neutra house, emphasizing its role in getting rid of past encumbrances and in providing new life and liberation, recalls the vocabulary that had first led Otto Rank to become interested in the birth trauma. He found that after successful analysis patients often used metaphors of rebirth to describe their experience.[25] This led him to extrapolate that to the original separation at birth could be traced all subsequent acts of separation and the entire process of individuation. Moreover, all cultural production is, according to Rank, "only a human creation of the world on the pattern of one's own individual creation. Whether it is the primitive hut covered with foliage . . . or whether it is the

(3)
Richard Neutra, Rourke House,
living room

American skyscraper with its flat, outer surface and the elevator shafts within; everywhere it is creative shaping . . . approximating in form to the substitution of the primal situation."[26]

Given the parallels Rank draws between the physical fact of birth, the individuation of the psyche, and cultural production, it is no surprise that when describing his own intellectual evolution and making a case for biological realism, Neutra wrote:

> Survival starts before birth. There, in the womb, it is best insured. After the "birth trauma," the shock to get into our outer unassorted scene . . . we all slip right into the hands of the architect.[27]

While the drawing of a connection between architecture and the space of the womb is both ancient and frequent, rarely has it attained this level of explicit detail. Moreover, Neutra's image is one that associates not only the space of the womb with the space of the world, but the body of the mother with that of the architect, as we are led to imagine the birth canal metamorphosing into the architect's outstretched hands.

Neutra found in this moment of transformation the generation both of life and of trauma. But above all, he found in this moment the function of architecture:

In life, and especially in the artificial surroundings designed by the architect . . . there are millions of occasions to make us sink back into vague and fuzzy indeterminacy. . . . These are the psychological "dis-satisfactions" of design . . . which we who are responsible for it must learn to avoid.[28]

The traumatized infant, who slips from the womb into the hands of the architect, requires, according to Neutra, protection from regressing into indeterminacy. Claiming that it is the architect who will offer this protection, Neutra assigns to architecture an expressly psychoanalytic function.

Architecture, for Neutra, is a technique and an instrument that engages the processes of individuation and intra-subjective experience. The articulation of spatiality plays an important role in this function for, according to Rank, space evokes the terror of being outside the mother but also recalls the womb as protective vessel: space is prerequisite to separation and individuation and is simultaneously the place of dependent nondefinition.[29] Neutra's response to this link between space as both generator and master of the birth trauma was the representation of neither regressive fantasies of returning to the womb nor of what Rank called masculinist fantasies of autonomy.[30] Indeed, Neutra's response was not representational but rather operated in the visible register to disarrange traditional distinctions between space and object.

One of the most noted features of Neutra's work, particularly as it developed during the 1950s, was an intense concentration on dismantling conventional barriers between inside and out **(4+5)**. Although Neutra's interest in the landscape has been normally understood as a regional adaptation to the mild climate of southern California and as part of a general concern to use landscape as foil to the austerity of architecture, it is rather the psychological smoothing of both the difference between spaces and objects as well as the transition between spaces that is the organizing principle in his work. Using abstraction as a means of establishing continuity between landscape and architecture, deploying the free plan less as a formal and spatial creed than as a therapeutic technique, Neutra's designs operate on the trauma of being an autonomous object in infinite space. With walls that recede toward invisibility, attenuated threshold zones, and promiscuously mobile landscapes, these houses suggest indeterminately bordered material intensities within an oceanically spatial environment.

189

(5)
Richard Neutra, Singleton House,
Los Angeles, 1959

(4)
Richard Neutra, Perkins House,
Pasadena, 1955

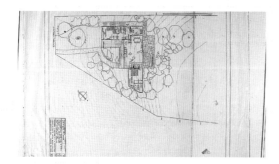

(6)
Richard Neutra,
Rourke House, plan

190

(9)
Richard Neutra,
Rourke House, patio

(7+8)
Richard Neutra, Rourke House,
perspectives

In the Rourke House, one side of the building floats above the ground while the other side is coterminous with it, simultaneously providing escape from and connection with the natural matrix **(6)**. In the central living space, the outside world intrudes within through large glass panels. These are not primarily picture windows that frame views or glass walls, as Banham would have it, but doors that move and permit movement **(9)**.[31] The wide overhang of the roof creates a zone of shadow attenuating and extending the boundary of the interior. The indeterminate simultaneity of enclosure and exposure is further reinforced by the overhangs, which all but eliminate reflection. The glass becomes not transparent but invisible.[32]

While the design **(7)** permits a liquid movement between interior and exterior—indeed, Neutra drew the Rourke House as though it

(10)
Richard Neutra, Kaufmann House,
Palm Springs, 1947

were just a roof, collapsing any material distinction between space as vessel and space as extension—bedrooms remain clearly defined, as protectors from primal scenes and preservers of individuation. As Neutra wrote, "The break in the natural individual to group relation occurred when children . . . were relegated into segregated rooms for privacy . . . [and] to early unnatural fears of loneliness. . . . Not the 'first watching' . . . is the original trauma. The original trauma seems rather that . . . the family group is much too early interrupted by the mystery-of-individual producing separation."[33] Attempting to balance the various needs of human attachment and disconnection, particularly in the Rourke House, which was designed for a family with an adult child, Neutra directs a complex choreography of psychologically resonant continuity and disjunction.

The Kaufmann House in Palm Springs (10), built just a few years before the Rourke House, was designed perhaps more dramatically in relation to this Rankian psychotherapeutic function. Every architectural feature that normally would articulate the distinction between one spatial enclosure and another is minimized in some way. Walls and windows become large expanses of glass that conflate landscape and architecture into a single environment with no sudden changes. The mechanization of these glass plates enabled even the material opening of the space to be done automatically—as in birth, changes in physical conditions lead to an opening up of the spatial enclosure. The most remarkable aspect of this insistence on continuity lay in Neutra's never properly functioning temperature control. The same heating and cooling devices within the interior's floor extend to the exterior terrace and lounge area surrounding the pool. Thus thermal conditions are used to create interior and exterior environments that are as stable and coherent as the womb itself but of psychologically unlimited extension.

Neutra was particularly concerned with emphasizing this aspect of the house's design and used the photograph for this purpose. The Kaufmann House was to be photographed by Julius Shulman, who was by this time, after having been initiated into architectural photography by Neutra himself, a competent and successful architectural photographer. Neutra nevertheless wrote Shulman giving what he called a "few rules."[34] Neutra specifically dictated that Shulman produce spatially continuous images—"evening shots from the exterior into the illuminated interior," for example. Even more insistent were photo captions Neutra wrote: "Exterior enclosure ceases to exist when frontal partitions slide back: the exterior pavings, cooled and heated, like the inner floors—as changing wheather [sic] itself directs the thermostatic controlls [sic],—have successfully eliminated any demarcation line between interior and exterior use of space."[35]

Neutra's interest in conflating the normally primary architectural distinction between exteriority and interiority was most symptomatically developed in relation to what he called "spider leg" outrigging (4+5+8). In this typically Neutra-esque element, beams and fascia are continued beyond the edge of the roof and turned down to reach the ground. By displacing the corners of rooms, and in some cases the very structure of the house, such normally stabilizing architectural elements are indeterminately inside and outside at the same time.[36] In addition, the spider legs create what might be called an intermediary zone, a kind of birth canal that

193

mediates the passage from inside to outside. Given Rank's interest in the fear created by bugs and insects in small children, Neutra's spider legs might be considered counter-phobic aids. Rank theorized that the insect's ability to crawl into the ground reminded children of their incapacity to return to the womb.[37] Neutra's spider legs would strive to minimize this anxiety by functioning as architectural umbilical cords. They both aggregate all fears of indeterminacy to themselves and enable the architect to catch the traumatized and slipping infant at the moment of birth.

Even before the war, Neutra had begun to develop these themes both programmatically and formally. In his widely imitated designs for schools, for example, he was particularly insistent on allowing classroom activities to spill outdoors. For children then, where the temporal proximity to the birth trauma is greatest, so is the need to demonstrate how to complete the mastery of moving from inside to outside. During the postwar period, moreover, Neutra began to maintain that birth, traumatic inherently, had become even more catastrophic through increases in technological mediation. As births took place ever more frequently in hospitals—full of metal instruments, strange sounds, and harsh light, according to Neutra—his domestic architecture began to insist on an increasing organicity, more abundant spider legs, and greater continuity of interior and exterior materials, especially the archetypally uterine material of water (4).

While all these devices together suggest Neutra's faith in the potentially therapeutic effect of architecture, they indicate equally that Neutra assigned to the architect and hence to himself the role of therapist (11). Neutra developed a rather distinctive way of relating to his clients, particularly those for residential projects. They were asked to complete highly detailed questionnaires as part of the design process. Sometimes he even asked clients to write diaries over the course of several weeks, recounting every aspect of their daily activities. These documents, which articulated private concerns about lifestyle and various other idiosyncrasies, were understood as deeply personal by the clients and have been referred to as "self-analyses."[38]

NEUTRA LISTENS TO A CLIENT

Murray Garrett—Graphic House

(11)

Richard Neutra, *Time*, August 15, 1949

Neutra was deliberate in his use of the therapeutic situation as a model for relating to clients. Describing what he called a "diagnostic procedure," Neutra maintained that the architect must first elicit and then connect subjective material provided by the client with the objective conditions determined by the project. He was especially interested in "shock of a favorable type, or trauma, as Professor Freud called it. These effects are extremely important to an architect for he is primarily working for emotionally loaded reception." Neutra even compared the client's production of information to "lying on a couch, figuratively speaking, and talking with a psychoanalyst."[39] Not only was Neutra imitating the techniques of the analyst in seeking to discover hidden experiences in the life of the analysand, he imagined this strategy as having effects that long outlast the period of analysis. Neutra wrote, "The architect can't stay with [the client] for twenty years . . . straightening out matrimonial friction and imbalance caused by environmental design. His job is simply beyond words—a silent long range job."[40]

Silence, on the part of the analyst, is of course an important technique used in psychoanalysis to induce transference. The deliberate neutrality of Neutra's architecture reflects a desire to engage this analytic condition by making the buildings themselves function as transference objects—objects that do not produce images for the viewer but blank screens waiting for images to be produced by the viewer.[41] While he went to great lengths to elicit highly personal information from his clients, the buildings that emerged were not portraits but rather expressly and abstractly neutral containers.[42] This sense of depersonalization may recall Le Corbusier's famous dictum that a house is a machine for living, but Neutra argued the contrary stating that a "home is . . . not a machine for living. Architecture is a stage for living" and a substitute for the environment that first influenced "the plastic purposeless, passively receptive mind of the infant."[43] By restaging the "emotionally loaded" experience of the viewers' first environment, an architectural transference object is produced that does not interrupt but indeed invites projection. The architecture is only complete, the house only becomes a home, when the viewer fills in the psychologically missing pieces.[44] At this moment, a drama of spatial substitution and transference unfolds wherein architecture and psychoanalysis cooperate to transform the generic house into the ideal home from which perfect psychological satisfaction can be demanded.

Transference, however, does not form a one-way loop, and Neutra was subject to the forces of counter-transference. In 1953 he wrote:

How am I, that I can subjectively feel so endowed with empathy. . . . I am liked by many; by all my clients. More than that they became extremely fond of me and I of them. It is almost like a love affair that ends happily in, by far, the most cases. But in spite of being most informal, not leonine, not monumental at all, I grow to heroic dimensions particularly to women. I make no bid for this, it happens unknowingly, but analytically and critically trying to remember: This is what happens. There is a tragic touch to the heroism I assume.[45]

Although Neutra has traditionally been considered an unrepentant egomaniac, this sense of identification with his clients, particularly his female residential clients, might rather be seen in relation to the fact that Neutra considered the home "primarily a place to rear children. . . . Next to the diet our mothers feed us . . . it is the . . . architectural environment . . . which imprints itself most forcibly on our . . . mental habits."[46] Neutra then imagines himself in the role not only of architect/therapist but of architect/mother. It was precisely underscoring not only the great psychological importance of the mother that was one of Rank's most influential hypotheses but specifically the parallel between therapist and mother. Separating from the analyst, according to Rank, is exactly what enables the completion of the originally ill-mastered birth trauma. Hence it is the therapist-mother, and in the case of Neutra, the architect-mother, who gives birth to a healthy child.

Neutra seems to have added one caveat to his desire to act as mother to architecture, namely that the various births involved be painless. In 1957 he attended a convention of obstetricians in Rome and was fascinated by their new techniques. He wrote with excitement about the "tremendous statistics piled up of very successful painless childbirths. . . . By training the expectant mother . . . to control her muscles . . . and influencing her to produce a certain frame of mind . . . pain is minimized. . . . It reminds me of . . . how one gives birth to a planning project."[47] Neutra's ultimate fantasy, it would seem, was to convert the trauma of birth into the imagined painless birth of architecture.

Neutra's fantasy seems to affirm Rank's theory that art was always created in response to the birth trauma, produced by the processes of idealization, repression, and sublimation required to convert trauma into beauty. For Rank this was a universal principle, yet he identified the avant-gardes in particular as "the last projections of the 'psychologizing' art school which consciously represents the 'interior' of man, namely his unconscious."[48] This was an unfortunately premature assertion, for the European avant-gardes were neither the last nor the most intense instances of "psychologizing" art. The thematics of birth and the womb, in relation to both the unconscious and the physical body, generated a great many architectures that fall outside classical definitions of the European avant-garde. In such works as Paul Nelson's ovoid operating rooms of the 1930s and 1940s and Frederick Kiesler's Endless House of the 1950s, a new type of architecture sought to meld object and space and to merge the responding subject into this protective environment.[49] Perhaps the most explicit example is Eero Saarinen's womb chair, which he argued "attempts to achieve a psychological comfort by providing a great big cup-like shell into which you can curl up and pull up your legs."[50]

Neutra's houses, although not conventionally avant-garde, were certainly "psychologizing" as they operated upon the external world according to presumed psychological need — perhaps especially his own, since his extraordinary and prolonged interest in birth and his assigning to himself all maternal functions might well provide fodder for an analyst. But in the context of postwar America, psychologizing no longer meant representing or revealing the structures and topographies of the Freudian unconscious, as it had for the historical avant-gardes according to Rank. Rather, psychologizing architecture had become a micro-technology of the self. Like most such apparatuses, from the movie camera to the transference object, this architecture was understood to function best when not seen. Many of Neutra's houses of this period remain relatively unknown and unseen, perhaps because their modernity too successfully merged with the middle-class suburban landscape.[51] Rather then stem from neglect or disinterest, this oversight suggests that the naturalizing and camouflage materials of these houses, their dematerializing structures and glass walls, speak of a desire not for transparency but for invisibility. Evading the gaze and disappearing into the landscape had become part of the psychic technology used to redirect the architect's function from professional taste-making to personal counseling: the "psych-ops" of the transference object would transform houses into homes.[52]

Using infinite space to set off the clarity and autonomy of objects in the visual field is a hallmark both of Enlightenment thought generally and of modern architecture in particular. The improperly bounded subject construed by Neutra's later work participates in the collapse of this modern epistemology and paradigm of visuality. By the postwar period, a new schema began to emerge in the work of a wide array of architects that considered not the opposition between objects and space but their fusion into a dense psychological environment. When Neutra made architecture into a mother and Saarinen made chairs into wombs, the separateness of subjects and objects, houses and homes, began to diminish. "Holding environments" were created instead, architectures modeled after the space produced between mother and infant.[53]

Neutra's fantasy that birth could be without pain and that architecture could be as nurturing as an idealized breast, however, set up expectations that architecture could only fail to meet. Created by an invasion as technological as that described by Banham, the American dream had become one of fusing the incommensurable architectural house with the mother as psychological home.[54] On the one hand, this fusion created a perpetually dissatisfied architectural subject demanding full psycho-sexual resolution from its environment-mother. As a result of this impossible goal, and just like the bad mother who emerged after the war as the cause of all psychic distress, modern architecture easily became demonized as the root of an ever proliferating number of social evils.[55] On the other hand, this same fusion and the new more fluid relation between objects and space it permitted fulfilled many of the goals of integration and psychic resonance sought by the historical avant-gardes. The new house/mother was, in other words, simultaneously a good and a bad object, striated by the many conflicts inherent in postwar American life. The micro-technologies of self that invaded the house produced a new subject both seeing and blind, attached and separated, seeking the perfect "holding environment" and finding instead just the architecture of house and home.

FRANCESCO DAL CO

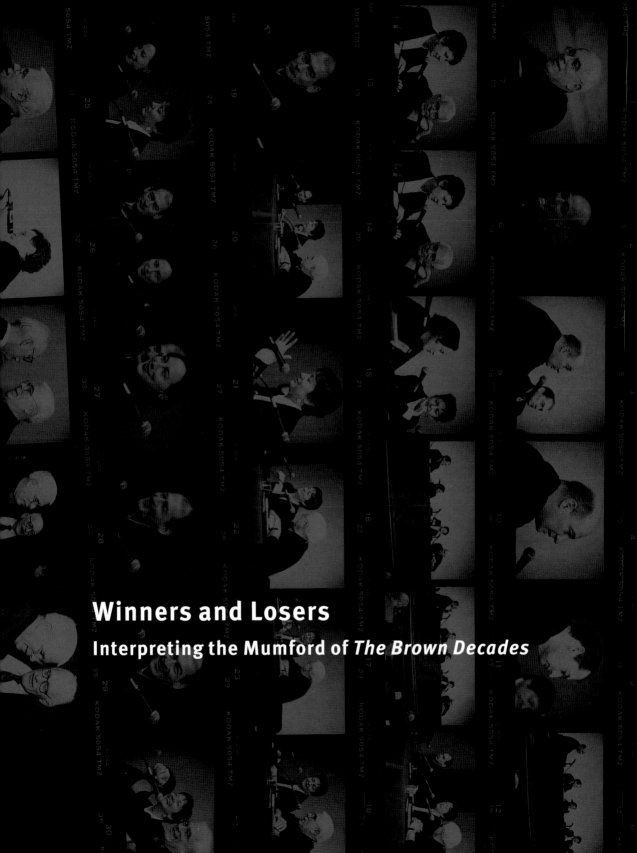

Winners and Losers

Interpreting the Mumford of *The Brown Decades*

What the people are within, the buildings express without; and inversely, what the buildings are objectively is a sure index of what the people are subjectively. In the light of this dictum, the unhappy, irrational, heedless, pessimistic, unlovely, distracted, and decadent structures which make up the great bulk of our contemporaneous architecture point with infallible accuracy to qualities in the heart and mind and soul of the American people that are unhappy, irrational.

This passage, taken from *Kindergarten Chats*, is at the center of one of the densest paragraphs of *The Brown Decades*: it is devoted to Sullivan, and the fact is significant. Not by accident, the "brown decades" are the years between 1865 and 1895; but the issues taken up by Mumford do not fit readily into that period—a strange lack of coherence and a significant forcing, as we shall see—and it is completely in character that the gray decades end with a word of hope, with a beautiful literary essay describing the "rising sun" on the portal of the Transportation Building, the only discordant note, according to Mumford, in that festival of irrational kitsch that was the World's Colombian Exposition of 1893.

In Mumford's pages, Sullivan unexpectedly takes on a special dimension: the work of the Chicago master is the keystone that sustains the arch of contradictions and potentials that unite the "good" and the "bad" of the dark years the American Dream has passed through. Mumford's treatment of Sullivan's role and work explains much of the former's theses and critical assumptions. These are aimed at proving that, appearances to the contrary, social decay and disintegration preserve "bright flowers" at their core; the heroic, perverse, contradictory battles of Sullivan are the equivalent of the extraordinary, introverted creations of Emily Dickinson. If Dickinson's poetry speaks to us of a closed world (a hedge is its limits, Mumford assures us) flooded, however, by a "highly vital" interior light, in the same way the great Sullivan buildings sing a positive note and morally redeem the contradictions and the chaos, the miseries and the riches of a Chicago resurgent after the Great Fire.

The work of the Mumfordian heroes is always described as a reflex image: a faithful expression of the contradictions of the environment, but also a promise of renewal and of transformations that even the dark moments society passes through cannot erase. This explains the choice of the passage of Sullivan quoted at the outset. In intellectual creation lives the possibility of expressing what is in danger of being suffocated in social development; from it can emerge teachings capable of re-creating conditions of innocence, "natural" models, new modes of social organization. But above all, there is the distance that separates "heroes and prophets" from the surrounding grayness, a distance that is the guarantee of a value that cannot be forsaken: that of a creative relationship with tradition, the key to all *continuity*.

To confront the roots of this continuity in the native terrain of that tradition: the premises of Mumford's Americanism are all contained in a passage in *The Brown Decades* that exalts this *positive* condition. Thomas Eakins and Albert Pinkham Ryder, then: the flight from America is the false alternative to an insecurity that has identifiable historic origins. It is not the Europe of runaways, of "indecisive men," of those who seek in the great European culture a way of assuaging their sorrow. Eakins and Ryder: the epic of America, of the *surrender to America*, if you like, is reflected in their work and finds its confirmation in the Chicago of the 1890s, while it possesses its own unexplored monuments in a past to be rediscovered and relived. The ships of the prairie carried its seeds; the first shoots point out the "land" to which we must return to dissipate the mists of the dark decades. *The Brown Decades*, from this point of view, is one of Mumford's key works. Certainly, though the quality of its judgments shows considerable unevenness, a great part of the text is dedicated substantially to the problem of the birth of modern American architecture—but we shall return to this point. For there is another characteristic of this book that will repay our dwelling on it. In this small volume, Mumford undertakes the rehabilitation of some mythical figures of American culture; the pages on George Perkins Marsh and Frederick Law Olmsted are particularly significant. From them emerges a kind of nostalgia for the values that inspired the work of these founders. But this nostalgia is kept from revolution by a lack of clarity about the contemporary implications of this position. More generally still, *The Brown Decades* reveals a contradiction that is characteristic of Mumford's thought: in, for instance, the pages that deal with the design and construction of the Brooklyn Bridge or the "scientific" paintings of Eakins, whose experiences in the field of photography would merit a discussion in themselves. The contradiction consists in the impossibility of finding a correct synthesis between the consequences of technical and scientific conquests and the values of tradition. How far can such a spirit survive in the new technical age? Or better, up to what point are the original values able to function once more as rails for the development of new technology?

On closer inspection, beyond the sometimes irremediably old-fashioned pages that occur throughout the book, this is the nucleus of Mumford's attempt. This, then, is how all history is, in the end, the history of heroes and prophets: a synthesis like this can appear only in the subjectively conceived work, only in isolated cultural products. Moreover, the concept of *equilibrium*, which conditions both the style and narrative of Mumford's work, is decisive for any such historiographic approach. Think of the descriptive technique he uses: to each character are dedicated brief biographical remarks, usually with an insistence on that person's isolation, and where the least piece of evidence is used to stress the role that the subjective experience of the discovery of the surrounding world has for each protagonist. The peregrinations of Olmsted, the solitude of Winslow Homer as an old man, the wanderings of Whitman: in opposition to the systems of neotechnical cultural education, Mumford exalted the subjective experience, the discovery of America through a taste for the *land*, the exaltation produced by the ability to "savor" the gifts of nature. The rustlings that became thunders disturbing the delicate soul of Dickinson, the long walks of Thoreau and Emerson, Olmsted's discovery of the South, and even the "urban realism" of the later Philadelphia school: such are the ways the Mumfordian hero arrives at subjective equilibrium; such, finally, are the antidote to the divisions, contradictions, and moral lacerations produced by the age of the machine, Mumford seems to be admitting. But such a destiny will be all the more tragic in the degree that it is not guaranteed by the equilibrium of experience, the continuity of those values, the tradition of the relation with the land and with nature that forms the truer and more original basis of American culture.

Out of this comes a glorification of the concept of the environment. This is not the place to go more deeply into its sources, but there is certainly a profound sense of the influence of Geddes and Comte, of German authors whose discussion might carry us very far. The ideology of an American *Volk*? Description of the unity that ties the Young American to the American Land? There is no doubt that elements such as these lie at the basis of Mumford's work, even though in *The Brown Decades* we can gather only the premises of an argument that will extend over much wider horizons. But to sketch this plan, comparison with the gray decades was necessary. Mumford's *The Golden Day* had already discussed the foundations of the American renaissance. But how to tie up the threads of tradition, apparently broken but in reality only entangled, without having to strain to grasp their ends, despite the dark shadows of the Civil War? Mumford's design takes its cue exactly from that necessity; in parallel, Van Wyck Brooks was facing, literarily, exactly the same problem. The letters exchanged between Mumford and Brooks from the times of *The Freeman* or *The Dial* are essential to the

202

understanding of this parallelism, a window open on many important moments of American cultural life. Generally, the cultural ambiance in which Mumford moved traces its way through his design. One way we can get some notion of what that ambiance is to analyze the bibliographical suggestions with which Mumford himself accompanies his book.

After the first literary experiments and after Melville, then, the basic problem is further clarified: what is the basis of the continuity of tradition that leads to Sullivan's Golden Door, to the explosion of the early Wright? American culture, Mumford affirms, survives as a legacy of the great figures of the 1850s: *Democratic Vistas*, the most important work of literary and social criticism produced by American culture, and the legacies of Emerson, Thoreau, and Melville are the matrices of whatever vital and new things are germinating under the mud of the Brown Decades. Despite the fogs of the industrial city and the horrors of metropolitan America, their teachings make clear the premises of an alternative. Such an alternative, which must hold true today, can be given concrete form using collateral but equally fundamental guidelines. Henry George and Edward Bellamy, for instance, are expressions of them. Henry George: Mumford, not all that cryptically, speaks of the "shingle tax" as a project aiming at the nationalization of the soil. Much more limitedly, all it was really about was a return to physiocratic conceptions that George further complicated in opposing the theory of wages, as Schumpeter, among others, has noted. But there is no doubt that Mumford sympathizes somatically with these ideas, and the reader can find, in *The Brown Decades* itself, a heated defense of these views. What is interesting is the way in which Mumford takes over George's theories, which, to tell the truth, intrigued not only Mumford but many progressives and socialists in the American political tradition. The abolition of ownership of land means to cut off at the roots the causes that distort the relationship between humanity and the environment: the hunger for land, the systematic plunder of resources, the organized violence against nature are not only the products of the thirst for property that has been made gigantic by the advent of industry and the organized conquest of the frontier, no longer left to the organic penetration of the pioneers. If we think about it, the relationship with Bellamy's utopia is the same: in this case, too, we find ourselves faced with a subjectively brilliant critical synthesis, but the ideological scheme does not change. If the "shingle tax" could cut the legs out from under the indiscriminate conquest of what remained of the wilderness, the organization Bellamy contemplates for the industrialized universe—the great army of labor?—is a promise that the metropolitan chaos will be reduced to order and, more than that, represents a neotechnical solution to the antagonism between the two great "paleo-technical" systems personified by the models of social organization supplied by the Soviet Union and the United States. This is a significant step: the *true American utopia* is expressed by Mumford, once again, as a project of historically "superior" equilibrium.

This conception throws light on the controversy over Mumford's relationship to the currents of Marxist thought and of his political position. This is too wide a subject to be broached at this time, with manifold implications for American cultural and political life in the 1920s and 1930s. Still, the passages of *The Brown Decades* that examine the prospects for such "syntheses," and that scorn Engels' criticism of a prescientific utopia, are especially significant. For accuracy, it ought to be said that the attitude that now predominates in relation to the Soviet Union is in itself indicative of a particular way of dealing with a theme that would turn out to be basic and critical for American cultural history following World War I.

The "brown decades" themselves produced, then, the antibodies against their own dominant characteristics. On the institutional level, Henry George represents the point of suture between "the organic basis of life" and the dark world of politics; Mumfordian evolutionism identifies in him an example of organic equilibrium. The institutions in which politics live and in which customs are reflected are being reclaimed by science and by the ideal: both terms express an unconditionally positive fundamental value, justifying the expectation of a better future that can take concrete shape in the creations of humankind. Bellamy's *Looking Backward* is an exact example of this. The study of history seems to teach a fundamental pessimism that contrasts with the optimism of the "origins": such is the message that can be found in the tradition; here is its energy, despite the fact that "no abstract ideal can take concrete form in a real situation or in an institution, without its undergoing a negative conditioning." In this way, another recurrent aspect of Mumford's thought is delineated: the force of tradition does not reside in the institutional forms in which American democracy is expressed but, quite the contrary, in all those cultural experiences that have fought against such formalization. Mumford moves on a terrain geographically antipodal to that covered by the great bourgeois reformist assumptions: anti-institutional criticism has its own roots sunk deeply in the American renaissance and, still deeper, in the "first American cultural revolution," and finds its outlet in a high level of "antibureaucratic" polemic. But from another point of view, the preconditions for the exaltation of the archetypal figure of the American scene, the pioneer, could not have been otherwise. The pioneer, the "hero" isolated from the city, nature as a program for living, the rejection of politics, etc.—we have met all of them before. This means that the relation with European culture comes to be understood in fairly specific terms that find an unexpected but inevitable confirmation in Spengler.

If the presentation of the work of Marsh implicitly leaves some things out—what better confirmation of Spenglerian pessimism than the planet-wide analysis made by Marsh of the decay of natural resources as "sources of life," or of the examples of "socio-moral" decomposition supplied by the collapse of the classical Mediterranean civilizations?—it leads Mumford to hand down some partial judgments on some cardinal figures in his story. A good example of this is one of the most important parts of *The Brown Decades*, devoted to a reconstruction of the "parks movement" tradition.

This is an indisputably original contribution. Mumford has thrown light not only on the role and the weight of important but forgotten figures who are not easy to understand, but also on the internal linkages of this important element of American culture. It would be reductive and superficial to analyze the history of the parks movement and the conservation movement from a narrowly disciplinary point of view. Certainly, both terms are synonyms for a process that leads to technical maturation in architectonic and urban-planning actions on the territorial scale. To put it another way, when the whole range of experience of the park and conservation movements is considered, they show how fractures and divisions have taken place in the heart of the architectonic/urban-planning movement, fractures and divisions that are the result of specialization and renewal and that, taken as a whole, are irreversible. What Mumford brings into relief—though we may have reservations about the standpoint he operates from—are not so much the peculiarities of the disciplines but the whole range of implications that this "renewal" involves from a generically cultural point of view. The description of the work that begins with the construction of Central Park, work that proceeds with an extraordinary continuity and coherence from the 1850s right up to the first decade of our own century, a work punctuated by the presence of pivotal figures in American culture, such as Olmsted, remains one of the most useful pages of Mumford's book. But in fact, it is a description that might form part of a study of more complex problems but that, though it does not lack value, still ends inconclusively. But this is indeed coherent with Mumford's assumptions: Olmsted must appear to the reader as a figure in full relief, almost

Winners and Losers

the symbol of a particular moral attitude, hero of a tradition that lives perennially through its "prophets" despite "civilization's" continuing efforts to cut it off at its roots.

What is missing, then, is the structural datum of the questions. To speak only of Olmsted: we can share everything that Mumford says about his work, but that doesn't exhaust the questions that Olmsted's work raises. First of all, Olmsted's cultural background is colored by idealist influences (just think of Fourier and his importance for many of the experiences Mumford cites or refers to). This background enriches the universe of the American tradition that Mumford reduces, without really saying so, to the problem of the relationship with the "land," nature, the conquest. Again, Olmsted's battles are not the product of the moral coherence of an individual subjective sensitivity to the importance of natural values so much as the fruit of a lengthy and recurring meditation on the destiny of American civilization as put into the concrete terms of urban reform. So if Olmsted's work is the result of a profound process of modification of the ways in which we act on the landscape, it is also a sign of the affirmation of a new discipline, a new specialization, indeed, of a new division of intellectual work. This division is the product not only of theoretical and ideological trends, but also of the assertion of new social and productive relationships. That in turn means that the institutional terms of the question, which Mumford leaves out of discussion, deserve much more careful consideration. To put the argument into more general terms, Olmsted looks ahead not only to a new type of technician and a different kind of intellectual, but also to a new designer of the urban cityscape in its widest sense. Olmsted's limitations and strengths are all there in that passage: the moment of reform saw the last glimmers of hope for an idealist utopia flicker and die. What inevitably escapes Mumford is the impossibility of dissolving the dialectical knot that ties this "continuity" to similar fractures.

It is no accident that Olmsted's work finds its conclusion in Boston in the plan of Charles Eliot Jr., and it is equally suggestive that Olmsted was to be the planner for the World's Columbian Exposition in Chicago. The 1893 plan was welcomed by one of Mumford's favorite critics, Montgomery Schuyler, as the only positive result of the whole massive enterprise put together by Daniel Burnham. But both Schuyler and Mumford inevitably miss the deep significance of this unexpected alliance between the great master of landscape planning and the dynamic, cynical manager placed at the head of the fair: the collaboration between Olmsted and Burnham (John Root's early death would not affect it) concludes what had already been implicit from the days of Central Park. Now there was a clear and definitive division in the sacred body of architecture: on one side, planning; on the other, the design of manufactured goods. The synthesis between these still exists, but it no longer finds expression in *form*. That is a value with other purposes.

The Chicago exposition proves that the synthesis produced by the collaboration of "different" disciplines does not come from the disciplines themselves. For Mumford, it looks like a storm or a menacing cloud that in a tempest of bad taste overwhelms the new seed that had sprouted in Chicago over the previous two decades. The only one who triumphed at the 1893 fair is Sullivan, but in reality, his defeat had already begun. The fair, though, is valuable for other purposes and other programs. Between the two cultural alternatives that Mumford offers to American anxieties, the flight to an unknown Eden such as Europe or the return to the original spirit of the land, a third hypothesis makes its appearance. With the Chicago exposition we see an America that can face the world confident of its own unity, clearly possessing the power to make its own way, capable of bringing to life stupendous and extraordinary enterprises, of treating the multiplicity of people who make up the nation as a unity, as homogenous *public*, as universal and potential consumers of the very myth of American progress.

Faced with this synthesis, which cannot be divorced from the subtle original qualities that Mumford hopes to salvage from every work of art that is American in origin, the judgment of *The Brown Decades* is entirely negative. And the book begins a long line of historiographical interpretations that have enjoyed great fortune: although Mumford shows himself to be a good deal more perceptive than later critics in his judgment of Sullivan's *Autobiography of an Idea*, there is no doubt that the contrast between his highly positive assessment of the Chicago school and his equally negative one of the World's Colombian Exposition (and by reflection, of Burnham) supplies an example that would be authoritative for those who followed him.

But this judgment of Sullivan is important for the functioning of Mumford's argument, not only for the reasons cited above, but also for another substantial one. And it is at this point that an examination of Mumford's ideology takes an unforeseen turn. On closer view, Mumford's analysis, which reaches the drastic conclusions previously noted on the cultural implications of the 1893 exposition, ends by revealing unexpected coincidences with the very meaning of that enterprise. Elsewhere I have remarked on the "liberating" nature that the exposition eventually assumed, and not only for architectural culture. As a mirror of the "nation," the 1893 fair was the ideal location to nurture and symbolize that *renewal* that was implied by the "passing of the frontier" that Frederick Turner had postulated the very same year. But isn't Mumford's goal to demonstrate how the potential of America is not only independent of, but even superior to, what Europe can offer, even in the field of culture? If the very scale of the fair does away with any timidity about comparison with European models—and not long afterward, Daniel Burnham's plan for Chicago would demonstrate just how mature that process of liberation had become—at the same time that scale also reveals how style was now playing a supporting role in the program, how form was subordinated to plan. Isn't that pretty much what Mumford is arguing when he looks to the American renewal for highly suggestive and original assumptions, when he exalts the new industrial aesthetic that has Roebling as its morally dominant figure, an aesthetic that will be simplified still more by the anonymous works that have become typical of the American landscape, and last, when he claims Chicago as the place where modern architecture began? And in more general terms, isn't he saying much the same thing in his analysis of the work of Ryder, Homer, and Eakins, or when he claims for Stieglitz the merit of having put the machine and the reproducibility of the image at the service of a poetic realism that had been obscured by the fashionable conventions and falseness of the dark decades? What other purpose, if not that continuing attempt to demonstrate the absolute maturity and autonomy of the culture of the New World in opposition to the false myths of escape, of the rediscovery of "foreign civilizations," can explain the ideological construction that is expressed in linking Melville and Whitman, and Emily Dickinson to somebody like Georgia O'Keeffe, so unlike Dickinson but discussed in exactly the same terms?

The road that Mumford is following along the windings of the history of American architecture and culture now becomes clear: the main highway runs from the redemption by Henry Hobson Richardson—an act of liberation whose implications are no less important than those performed by the masters of the American renaissance or by Olmsted—through the work of Root and of Sullivan, to arrive at Frank Lloyd Wright, who takes the whole literary heritage upon himself. Certainly, the new quality that American architecture is pursuing changes destination and emigrates to other territories. The works of Richardson are monuments consciously elevated to the victories of great entrepreneurs—and we may note how Mumford insists on the positive function that business magnates had in spurring on and underwriting the efforts of the masters of the Chicago school. Richardson's works may sing, but the chaotic development of the city would finally drown out that song, despite the contribution made to it by Sullivan and Root, a contribution whose development would be broken off prematurely. This new quality, the announcement of a new season and a new maturity in American society, of a *morality* that the metropolis would either ignore or try to suppress, does not however disappear, despite the 1993 fair, despite the weaknesses of Sullivan, despite the death of Root. It revives in Wright; it is recovered by his suburban residences, which stand outside and against the metropolis. It revives in the lost qualities of an organic relation with nature, the fascination for past lifestyles, for that aristocratic spirit of conquest and independence that in the meantime animated the pioneer community of New England, the true homeland of tradition, and the solitary epic of the discovery of the land. Land, but in almost biblical terms; source of culture as in Thoreau, supreme wealth, decisive experience—that is the meaning the term "land" takes on in the pages of *The Brown Decades*. The plundering and aggression that the land undergoes are only the product of the degeneration of instincts, of a "moral decline," themes that Mumford touches upon with the ardor of someone who sees a faith, a doctrine, a church betrayed. But all this only explains the importance that the concept of *tradition* has in Mumford: where it ceases to be epic, all value disappears. Tradition, then, holds the secret, now being rediscovered, that binds architecture from Richardson to Wright: one interprets a heroic age of capitalist development, while the other, aristocratic prophet, is the interpreter of the flight from the decadence produced by capitalism, of the rebirth of the spirit of *community*.

This clarifies for us a typical passage of Mumford's ideology that has generated not a few misunderstandings. The logical structure of *The Brown Decades* is based on demonstrating the correspondence between the human-artist and the environment; the second term cannot be explained without the aid of the first, given that a biological relationship exists between them.

The keys to and the origins of this position are many and various, and certainly Mumford's long familiarity with Geddes is not enough to explain every implication. But what interests us here is this unusual dialectic. There are two very meaningful examples in *The Brown Decades*: the pages on Eakins and those, already addressed, devoted to Sullivan. Eakins is the interpreter of the America of the Scientific Revolution, master of a new realism, unexposed to other cultural experiences but with deep roots in the ongoing transformation of the "nation." He is the poet of a subjective, individual energy, of the human tension that marks every stage of the general conquest of consciousness. But if the work of Eakins might not be explainable without its ties to an unusual sensitivity for that component of American life, in the same way Sullivan would never have existed without Chicago. The peremptory way in which Mumford dismisses Sullivan's last works is symptomatic, and just as meaningful is the correspondence that Mumford suggests between Sullivan's achievements and the potentialities of Chicago, where Richardson's promises would find their definitive fulfillment. That relationship also clarifies the implicit concept of progress that Mumford is tracing for us: in the light of the pages that describe the Brooklyn Bridge, we can see how wide of the mark are those critics who have tried to associate Mumford's ideology with regressive, that is, purely reactionary, positions. On the other hand, his sincere exaltation of Chicago, and his naive praise for the work of Irving Gill, for example, as compared to the achievements of the European avant-garde, make it clear how his anti-urban ideology is sometimes equivocal, rife with contradictions and conflicting facets. This is confirmed by his convincing assessment of the urban realism of the painters of the Philadelphia school, to whom we owe some of the more suggestive documentation of metropolitan America at the turn of the century.

Finally, to bring together, even if only approximately, the two aspects of Mumford's ideology, we should not forget the judgment that we find in *The Brown Decades* on the monthly magazine *The Masses*, one of the more lively voices of American radical and Marxist culture in the 1910s. Mumford's positive judgment of this publication—in which some members of the Philadelphia school collaborated, along with famous personalities like John Reed and Max Eastman—brings up the question of where he stood in the political spectrum. This is an argument that needs to be examined in greater detail; its complexity cannot be fully appreciated here. However, it is symptomatic that Mumford, in the years preceding the publication of *The Brown Decades*, was very close to the more radical positions of American culture, while at the same time retaining an aristocratic and critical detachment from them. We can better appreciate the breadth of that detachment if we keep in mind the lacerating experiences that shattered and dispersed the ranks of progressives during the 1930s. Mumford's political positions—and one example of these is the various and repeated judgments he makes on Marxist concepts and on the meaning of the Soviet experience, which run through all his works and are the subject of some of his lesser arguments—are positions of openness toward radical tendencies, but must be read in a very special way: even the most advanced experiences are accepted only in the degree to which they show themselves to be consonant with the restoration of the most authentic values of the American tradition. If there is a distinctive trait in Mumford's political position, it is very much what is found in his judgment on Richardson's "monuments to trade"; that is, there is a rooted anticapitalist ideology, which if it exalts the epic era of commerce, does so because it finds in the age of laissez-faire the survival of that individualism that industrial capitalism wipes out by photographing its own silent face in the indifference of the masses and in the apparent chaos of the metropolis. The metropolis, as collective chaos, is the outcome of this phase of capitalist development: the architecture, as social event and as the moral warning advocated by Sullivan, no longer has space in the metropolis. It should not be surprising, then, that all the sociological observations of *The Brown Decades* are imprinted with a profound anticonsumption pessimism. The unbridled consumption of industrial civilization, advertising, the collective vices, are read by Mumford as the revelation, in the dark decades, of a moral decay, a biblical curse. To this decay, to the euphoria of consumption, he opposes the old values, nostalgia for the community reappears, New England glows in the light of a utopian natural equilibrium. Behind these pages is the shadow of Veblen, while we can see more clearly the road that is carrying Mumford into the area of "collectivist" conceptions, of which Bellamy's provide an example. But the synthesis he is dreaming of is not between the America described by the Philadelphia school and the models of the socialist tradition, the synthesis will be between an arcadian America and an anticapitalist moralization taken selectively, for example, from the Soviet revolution. Such a synthesis opens unfathomable prospects for regressions that will no longer fit into any system. The Mumford dilemma becomes a general problem for many aspects, even the most forgotten and secondary, of contemporary culture.

211

DETLEF MERTINS

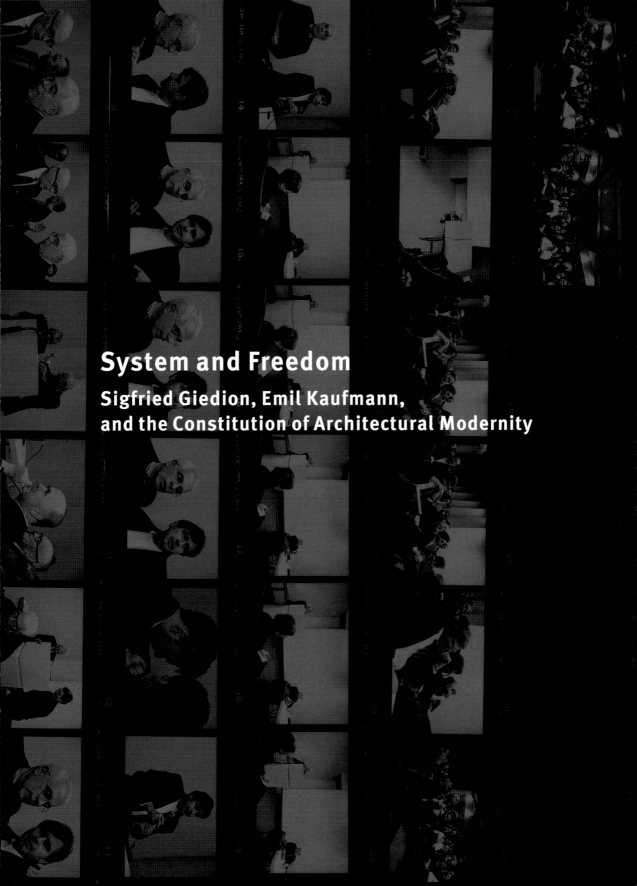

System and Freedom

Sigfried Giedion, Emil Kaufmann, and the Constitution of Architectural Modernity

In his letter to Walter Gropius of October 25, 1937, Sigfried Giedion—the Swiss architectural historian, critic, and secretary of CIAM—explained that he had been working for the past several years on a history of the development of the modern era in terms of the various fields of knowledge and the relationship between life, architecture, and art, hoping to "make a contribution to the self-consciousness of the age."[1] Hoping as well for an invitation to lecture in the United States, where Gropius had recently assumed the chair of architecture at Harvard University, Giedion's letter was explicit in articulating his view of the challenge that still faced America, in terms that echo Gropius's early admiration of American engineering and his simultaneous disdain for America's historicist architecture. "Let us hope," wrote the historian, invoking the hierarchic distinction between a materialist *Zivilisation* and a redemptive *Kultur* so powerful in so many German intellectual traditions,[2] "that something half-way similar [to America's advances in technology] will be possible in the cultural sphere in the future." And more specifically, "Surely little depends on whether the people [in America] already have correct judgement. What seems to me important for today's culture is that today's ideas are not taken up as fashion, but rather organically so that later they may gain new potentials for development through American forces and strengths."

That Giedion's conception of the challenge in America accorded with Gropius's own is clear from the latter's reply, written only two months later to inform Giedion that he and Marcel Breuer had convinced their dean, the

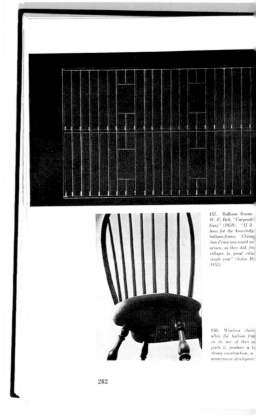

(1)
Spread from Sigfried Giedion's *Space, Time and Architecture* (1941) showing a balloon frame, a Windsor chair, and a balloon-frame house designed by Richard J. Neutra

influential modernizer of architectural education Joseph Hudnut,[3] to make the case for Giedion in the Norton Committee and that Hudnut, in turn, had succeeded in getting the committee to nominate Giedion as its first choice, over the author Thomas Mann. Gropius urged Giedion to accept, "because it is really important and will not only give you much publicity but will, at a single stroke, bring your ideas to a wide audience." In agreeing to the internationally prestigious series of eight lectures, a semester at Harvard, an honorarium of ten thousand dollars (the equivalent of Gropius's annual salary), and publication by Harvard University Press, Giedion

...ry, ridicule, and abuse of all who have seen fit to attack ... Its name was given in contempt by those old fogy ...anics who had been brought up to rob a stick of timber of ... strength and durability, by cutting it full of mortices, ...s and auger holds, and then supposing it to be stronger ... a far lighter stick differently applied, and with all its ...bilities unimpaired. . . . The name of ' Basket Frame ' ...d convey a better impression, but the name ' Balloon ' has ...ago outlived the derision which suggested it."

...alloon frame marks the point at which industrialization ... to penetrate housing. Just as the trades of the watch- ...r, the butcher, the baker, the tailor were transformed ...industries, so too the balloon frame led to the replacement ...e skilled carpenter by the unskilled laborer.

...man and a boy can now (1865) attain the same results, ...ease, that twenty men could on an old-fashioned frame.

283

also accepted Gropius's charge to him: "Since my coming and Hudnut's being here has now put the whole question of architecture in everyone's mind in a real sense, I thought that there could be no one better than you to widen the gap and give truly fundamental explanations of our movement."[4]

As a textbook for modern architects, the success of Giedion's *Space, Time and Architecture* is legendary.[5] After it was first published in 1941 (following two frustrating years at the press), Walter Gropius called it "undoubtedly the best book of its kind." The historian Kenneth John Conant, also of Har-

vard, hailed the book as "wonderful . . . an adventure in international scholarship" that "reads like a detective story. . . . Architectural students . . . say that once started on it, they have read it the night through."[6] Elizabeth Coit, writing for *Architectural Record,* commended it for incorporating the social institutions of daily life and recognizing American developments such as the balloon frame (1), steel skeleton, and elevator—concluding that "rarely has our life been so vividly presented."[7] John A. Hartell, in *ARTnews,* appreciated that Giedion's treatment of new developments as a "new tradition" allowed the confusion over the issue of "style" to subside—"the aim of reassuring us by establishing 'that, in spite of apparent confusion, there is . . . unity in our present civilization' may or may not have been accomplished in this volume. But one and all should now be convinced that architecture since 1800, for all of its fluttering, has not been *quite* a headless chicken."[8] Henry-Russell Hitchcock told readers of *Parnassus* that "every scholar and student of architecture in America should own and master [the book] in detail," its insights into the American story "pregnant" for further research and its understanding of Frank Lloyd Wright more "penetrating" than that of any previous foreigner.[9] And Philip Johnson, in his article "Architecture in 1941," singled out the book by the "eminent Swiss critic" as "the most important work on general architecture to appear" that year —"an ambitious history of the background of modern architecture written as a morphology" that included the "especially

215

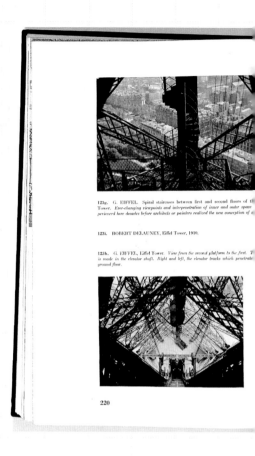

(2)
Spread from Sigfried Giedion's *Space,
Time and Architecture* (1941) showing two views of the
Eiffel Tower and Robert Delauney's painting of it

(2)
Spread from Sigfried Giedion's *Space,
Time and Architecture* (1941) showing two views of the
Eiffel Tower and Robert Delauney's painting of it

noteworthy" stories of "the effect of engineering on aesthetics" and "the effect of social patterns on architecture."[10]

In the book, Giedion argued that a new "space-conception" defined the modern era, structuring art and science, buildings and cities, production and reception, just as perspective had during the Renaissance. Having found affinities between the spatial effects of engineering structures, post-cubist art, modern mathematics, and the new architecture, Giedion called the new post-perspectival space conception "space-time." Elaborating on the use of the term in both art and science, he distinguished space-time by its openness to relativity, incompleteness, dynamism, and the constitutive ambiguity of the mutual mediation of subject and object.[11] In contrast to the graphic rules of perspective, he presented space-time as a phenomenology of spatial perception in the unrepresentable, yet equally scientific, fourth dimension, in which inside and outside, subject and object, were considered interwoven. Informed by theories of *Raumgestaltung* (space-creation) proffered by the art historian August Schmarsow in the 1890s and reiterated by the artists Theo van Doesburg and László Moholy-Nagy in the mid-1920s,[12] Giedion's notion of space-time

focused on the cognitive status of buildings as contingent on the partial and shifting perceptions of observers moving through and around them. He conflated this with theories of image-formation coming from the discourse of "new optics" in the late 1920s — in which new worlds were seen to appear through the expansion of vision made possible by scientific instruments, airplanes, photography, and film. Rather than presuming to comprehend buildings definitively from a single viewpoint, Giedion deferred cognitive closure indefinitely and kept the process — like Le Corbusier's concrete Dom-ino skeleton — "eternally open," the subject forming and perceiving space while being formed by and for it. In order to grasp the true nature of space, Giedion suggested that "the observer must project

himself through it" and cited the dizzying stairway of the upper levels of the Eiffel Tower as one of the first opportunities for this (2). Le Corbusier's Dom-ino represented, for Giedion, the means for making that experience structural to mass society in the form of housing.

Giedion's enthusiasm for such space-time experiences erupts at key moments in his text to invoke the ideal of hovering excitedly above the ground, dissolving the boundary between artifice and nature into the dynamic infinite beyond representation—in likening Borromini's dome at Sant Ivo to Picasso's

Head and Tatlin's tower; Valadier's terracing Piazza del Popolo to van Doesburg's open assemblage of transparent hovering planes; the dematerialization of Paxton's Crystal Palace to the atmospheric effects of Turner's paintings; the pin-joint of the Palais des Machine to Degas' pirouetting ballerina; the opened volumes and suspended planes of the Bauhaus to Picasso's first double-faced portrait; and above all, the simultaneous assertion and denial of volumes in Le Corbusier's Pessac housing and the hovering transparency of his purist still lifes.[13] The importance assigned by Giedion to these effects is revealed most clearly in the almost ecstatic, and hardly believable, prose of his earlier, more youthful book—*Building in France. Building in Iron. Building in Ferro-Concrete* of 1928. There he defended the paper-thinness of the buildings at Pessac— their solid volumes eaten away with cubes of air, rows of windows passing suddenly into the sky, corners merging into one another, collapsing into two-dimensionality only to spring back into depth a few steps later. For him they "create—as in a landscape of snow under certain light—that dematerialization of fixed borders, within which it is no longer possible to distinguish between rising and falling, and walking feels like being in the clouds."[14]

Notwithstanding the sales success and general endorsement of *Space, Time and Architecture*, most reviewers did express serious reservations, which focused on three interrelated issues: Giedion's Europeanness, the architects that he chose to emphasize, and what they called his aesthetic or philosophical approach to the rich historical material that he assembled. From the *Art Bulletin* to the *Nation*,[15] the reviews reveal an overarching suspicion (not surprising for those historians largely uninfluenced by German aesthetics and art history) of Giedion's neo-Kantian structural categories and his neo-Romantic notion of art as the making of symbols capable of mediating the antinomies of modernity—especially what he called the tragic split between reason and emotion—and working productively and performatively toward a future system already inscribed within it. Taking his examples to be arbitrary and his history incomplete, his critics also failed to register that in approaching the past from the perspective of contemporary "questions"[16]—criticized by John Summerson as "philosophical," and by Nikolaus Pevsner as "topical" and "creative"[17]—Giedion did not intend to codify the present but rather to open up the potentiality of the future within the existing system of mediation. He also opened himself to charges of vagueness, favoritism, and dogmatism by basing his selection of works and his critical judgment of them on a distinction whose purpose was rarely understood—on the extent to which they manifested what he called "constituent facts" structuring the modern epoch, in distinction from "transitory facts" or surface symptoms of the unreliable manifold of appearances within the flow of historical change.[18] His immanent critique of the system of modern production and consumption, his ideal of open constructions and expanded vision in space-time, and his ethical pursuit of self-overcoming through a purifying, essentializing, and rationalizing self-discipline of means were largely dismissed as obscure aestheticism.[19]

In his review, Hitchcock had hinted that Giedion's lectures were "none too well received," and indeed one of the students at Harvard, H. Seymour Howard Jr., reviewing the book in the student journal *Task*, recalled that:

> A large proportion of the students from the Harvard School of Design went regularly and were stimulated by his aesthetic sense, which he was able to share with his audience. But they were also puzzled and bewildered by his theory and by his historical approach. An unmistakably metaphysical air permeated his thought.
> The wealth of factual material which Dr. Giedion presented so overwhelmed his listeners, however, that many felt that further study on their part would clarify his ideas for them. The publication of this book has permitted this study. Unfortunately, the bewilderment remains; the metaphysical worm still eats out the heart of the apple.[20]

Howard's strident and positivist critique turned on two points: a disappointment that Giedion simply asserted vague parallels between architecture, industry, theory, and social needs without explaining their relationship in specific historical terms and without "a few examples of laboratory and drafting-board techniques" that might serve to guide students; and a concern that Giedion's insistence on creative intuition emerging from the unknown precluded him from clearly stating "the fundamental problems of today" and "the methods by which they can and will be solved." In the context of America restructuring and modernizing in the wake of the Great Depression and Roosevelt's New Deal, evident, for instance, in the editorial focus of *Task* on social responsibility, public housing programs, new techniques, and economical solutions, Howard was eager to "analyze, study and solve these problems, not as superior people who will produce great solutions from the clouds, but in close day-to-day collaborative work with other architects, and with the people as a whole."

Giedion replied to Howard's "purely materialistic attitude" by amplifying his case that "the influence of feeling is often regarded as unimportant, but inevitably permeates the decisions of men." While he acknowledged an affinity between Howard's views and the "pure functionalism" of the late 1920s in Europe, he warned against this for risking "a belated imitation of certain European formulas" that had ignored the emotional demands of the people just when in Europe "questions far beyond the purely materialistic have become decisive." Giedion suggested that, in the final instance, it was the irrational that governed:

> It is not so easy to find an expression today for things which cannot be explained by materialistic reasons only.
> There is something that appears suddenly in the logical analysis! The irrational. It cannot be explained exactly and governs, nevertheless, the decision whether a building will be accepted or not by public opinion. . . . It may be that an architectonic conception which is moved only by the help of an all too circumscribed materialistic comprehension of the world leads just to solutions from the clouds. [21]

* * *

What are we to make of this combination of success and failure in the reception of Giedion's book, of the fact that its "higher" philosophical and artistic aspirations were either ignored or dismissed; that his call for self-discipline to transmute technology into the means of ineffable poetics—into *"construction spirituelle"*—failed to win an audience; and that his historical portrait of industrialization may have served, instead, to simply legitimate the rush of modernization that he hoped would transcend itself in a new architecture of unity and harmony? In asking these questions, it is not my purpose to either defend Giedion against reductive interpretations and critiques or to side with these critics. Rather, Giedion's failure seems to me to be symptomatic of a larger problematic within the modernist avant-garde, one with a number of related manifestations. My argument will be that the failure in Giedion's reception points, first, to an internal failure within his efforts to resolve tensions that he claimed to be resolving and that this, in turn, shows how Giedion's history was structured by an *aporia* inscribed into the history of the cultural avant-garde from its inception. To substantiate my claim that Giedion's failure was symptomatic, consider two other instances—first, a tension between Hitchcock and Le Corbusier, and second, Philip Johnson's reading of Giedion's less well-known contemporary, the Viennese private scholar Emil Kaufmann.

* * *

In his book of 1948, *Painting Toward Architecture*,[22] Hitchcock criticized Le Corbusier in a way that stands in curious proximity to the architect's own book of that year, *New World of Space*.[23] Considered together, these books bear witness to a conflict between the desire for a new normative order that the historian

219

continued to call "style"—a broadly binding "visual language" or "pattern" valued for its own sake as an index of a new normative taste appropriate to the historical period called modern—and an equally strong desire for a dimension of architectural experience that might be described as expansive, open and indeterminate, poetic, free, even transcendent. Surely it was no coincidence that the frontispieces of the two books were identical—a still life of 1925 by Le Corbusier (signed Jeanneret) owned by the Herman Miller Company, whose collection of abstract art was the motive and focus of Hitchcock's book. Nor could it be an accident that both focused on the relationship between architecture and painting, with the architect's central theme being the object of the historian's skepticism. Notwithstanding his privileging of Le Corbusier for the frontispiece, Hitchcock held that "the theoretical relationship between painting and architecture has been much more clearly stated [by Walter Gropius] than in the writings of Le Corbusier," and preferred the "*systematic* approach [of the Bauhaus] to the study of design in all fields" over Le Corbusier, who he reproached for simply presuming "that the study of modern painting leads in a somewhat intangible way to the formation of a relevant modern taste in all the arts." [24]

For Hitchcock, "abstract art"—with its systematic and generalizable constructions of lines and planes in two and three dimensions—was the true and legitimate art of the modern era, whose "potential value to contemporary architects" could be understood as instrumental for a company, such as Herman Miller, producing modern furniture for a mass market. It offered the key to a new universality, which nevertheless required the retraining of both artists and viewers, production and reception—the retraining of subjectivity to conform to the apparent objectivity of the emerging new epoch. Correcting the "distortions" of early cubism, whose architectonic quality he considered so obviously suited to architecture, Hitchcock presented abstract art as the common base for nonimitative and nonperspectival modern art and architecture.

For Le Corbusier, on the other hand, the task of architecture was not limited to the realization of a new system. He claimed retrospectively that the relationship between his plastic research and his architecture had, for thirty years, circled around what he called the "miracle of ineffable space" and the "consummation of plastic emotion." While his desire for an architecture of powerful emotions had been a crucial aspect of purist aesthetics, there was no residue of his purist critique of cubism as his prose attempted to portray his experience of an ineffable, inexpressible spatiality—"a boundless depth opens up, effaces the walls, drives away contingent presences." In fact, he now linked this almost religious experience of architecture to the "'magnification' of space that some of the artists of my generation attempted around 1910, during the wonderfully creative flights of cubism. They spoke of the fourth dimension with intuition and clairvoyance." [25] The fourth dimension, he continued, "is the moment of limitless escape evoked by an exceptionally just consonance of the plastic means employed." Neither the fourth dimension nor the experience of ineffable space nor the just consonance of means was seemingly of value for Hitchcock. Yet they were central to that other historian, Sigfried Giedion, whose interpretation of both Le Corbusier *and* Gropius was actually structured by his conception of architecture in space-time. Could *this* have played a role in Hitchcock's curious failure even to acknowledge Giedion's prior treatment of the significance of cubist and post-cubist art for the new architecture, so strategic, after all, to his historical narrative in *Space, Time and Architecture*, published just seven years earlier and so "successful" that a second and enlarged edition would come out the following year?

* * *

Emil Kaufmann too came to the United States in this period, although not for a prestigious lecture series but as an immigrant, leaving Austria after Hitler's takeover in 1938. And Kaufmann too had his American debut at Harvard, although not for Gropius but for the American Society of Architectural Historians meeting in the summer of 1942. For both Giedion and Kaufmann, coming to America was marked by a greater emphasis in their writings on a systemic conception of modernity. While Kaufmann did not affiliate himself with the architects of his generation as actively as Giedion did, nevertheless in the early 1930s he had already mobilized his pioneering research on eighteenth-century French neoclassical architecture and theory to support what he took to be the revolutionary, or at least republican, ambitions of modern architecture, at that very moment being closed down as Hitler dissolved the Weimar Republic.

Informed by the polemical writings of Le Corbusier and his avant-garde contemporaries, Kaufmann's first book, *Von Ledoux bis Le Corbusier: Ursprung und Entwicklung der Autonomen Architektur* (*From Ledoux to Le Corbusier: Origin and Development of Autonomous Architecture*) of 1933,[26] presented Claude-Nicolas Ledoux as a genius struggling in the late eighteenth century to break free from what Kaufmann depicted as the feudal, absolutist order of the baroque (which for him included the Renaissance and neoclassicism), having awakened to the idea of autonomy, individual self-determination, and republican self-government. For Kaufmann, Ledoux was to modern architecture what Kant had been to modern philosophy, Rousseau to modern political theory, and the *Sturm und Drang* to modern German literature. Kaufmann interpreted the forms of Ledoux's architecture and utopian city as structurally homologous to these other manifestations of the idea of autonomy. Individualism, revolution, and republicanism in architecture were seen to be manifest in prismatic building elements (unadorned surfaces, windowless walls, unframed openings, and flat roofs), the display of material integrity (stone had become stone once more), and above all, the pure forms of primary geometry (cubes, pyramids, and spheres). Instead of the melded together cohesion of the baroque, in which parts were subordinated to the whole, he identified a new architectonic system of self-determined, cognitively transparent elements (natural signs) assembled like a toy into geometrically regulated freestanding buildings in which the relationship between parts would similarly be free and immediately legible—the direct, sober, and lawful physiognomic expression of inner necessity (purpose, function, and character). For Kaufmann, taking his cue from Kant, "architecture-in-itself"[27] marked a supersensible freedom from necessity, the conversion of matter into formal self-presentation, which he considered the ultimate form of emancipation. Instead of the pictorialism and organicism of the baroque city, Ledoux's ideal city of Chaux was no longer conceived as spatially bounded or pictorially framed, no longer the heart of a living whole

221

but simply a geometric point around which the parts arranged themselves anorganically as independent subject-citizens (3).

Kaufmann's lecture of 1942, titled "Claude-Nicolas Ledoux: Inaugurator of a New Architectural System," signaled a shift of emphasis away from the authority of absolute forms toward a systematic constitution of architectural modernity.[28] This shift supported a broadening of his historical research to incorporate not only Ledoux's contemporaries in the so-called *Revolutionsarchitektur* in France—especially Etienne-Louis Boullée and Jean-Jacques Lequeu—but ultimately the "architecture of reason" throughout all of Europe, with the exception of Germany.[29] While his earlier writings had already proffered the notion that autonomous architecture entailed a pavilionized and decentralized system of composition, the lecture of 1942 inverted the priority between form and system for the sake of what he called a "new individualism." Adapting his rhetoric to America, he dropped all reference to Kant and Rousseau and instead presented his republican ideals in terms of a constitutional framework for free individuation. He continued to link Ledoux to Le Corbusier, comparing the former's Houses for Peace and Union to the latter's Mundaneum of 1928 on the basis that both aimed to realize Enlightenment ideals. He called Ledoux's Residence of the Surveyors of the River Loue so successful as an *architecture parlante* "that one might easily suppose some present-day expressionist had devised it for an hydraulic power plant."[30] And he observed that Ledoux's spherical Shelter for the Rural Guards, "born of the Revolution" had

been "revived" as the Perisphere by Wallace Harrison "to dominate New York's [1939] Worlds Fair." Yet Kaufmann insisted that "the ultimate goal of the Revolutionists was to set up a new system. . . . Forms themselves are secondary factors. . . . It is the same in social and in artistic life."[31]

The shift from form to system marks a refinement of Kaufmann's efforts to think through the implications of Kant's critical philosophy for architecture. For a contradiction had operated throughout the earlier book between assertions of being and accounts of striving, between stating that "instead of appearances only being was now valid"[32] and citing Friedrich Hölderlin: "We are nothing. What we search for is everything."[33] Despite his apparent codification of autonomous forms, elements, and types, Kaufmann was concerned that autonomy not collapse into mechanism, and that instead (in keeping with Kant) it transform technique and labor into the free play of aesthetic judgment. That he feared the risk of mere technique is clear from this criticism of J. N. L. Durand's mathematization of architecture as an "impoverished schematization."[34] Kaufmann also explicitly refused the false archaism of neoclassicism, which he associated with the political and cultural empire. Winkelmann, Goethe, and Schiller had nothing to say to Ledoux, he wrote, "because what was for them a matter of form, was for him a matter of principle, for them precedents that could be taken as guides, for him the foundations of building itself to

Die bleadstadt Chaux   *in Seite 18*

len Zufahrtsstraßen die Grenze der Residenzstadt markierten, stehen heute
ur zwei noch in ihrer alten Anordnung, die Barrière der Place Denfert-
ochereau und die Barrière du Trône auf der Place de la Nation Zwei
ndere, im Park Monceaux und auf dem Boulevard de la Villette lassen
ire einstige Bestimmung kaum mehr erkennen. Weil Ledoux die schlichten
ollbauten zu großartig ausgestalten wollte und allzu große Mittel bean-
ornchte, weil sein Plan, prächtige „Propyläen" zu schaffen, seinen Auftrag-
ebern nicht genehm war, wurde ihm 1789 die Leitung der Arbeiten, nach
usführung des größten Teiles, abgenommen.
   Der letzte große öffentliche Auftrag, der an Ledoux erging, betraf die
rrichtung von Justizgebäuden in Aix in der Provence. Zur Begutachtung
er dortigen, der Rechtspflege dienenden Bauten hatte man den Architekten
us Paris berufen, der sie, anscheinend in eigennütziger Absicht, in der
offnung, mit einer umfangreichen Aufgabe betraut zu werden, für ab-
ruchreif erklärte. Seine bereits 1785 von der Pariser Bauakademie ge-
illigten Pläne kamen über die Vorarbeiten nicht hinaus. Dann machte die
evolution diesem Projekt, an dem der Architekt besonders gehangen hatte,
nd seiner Bautätigkeit überhaupt ein Ende. Die Wirren der Revolutions-
ahre brachten dem Künstler manchen unruhigen Augenblick. Er selbst
rzählt, wie er infolge einer Namensverwechslung fast unter die Guillotine
ekommen wäre. Doch es war damals ein Doktor der Sorbonne, dem die
hache nationale", wie Ledoux das Instrument des Schreckens nennt, galt.
793 war der Künstler als Royalist in Haft, aus der er erst nach mehreren
fonaten, dank eifrigster Bemühungen seiner Töchter, entlassen wurde. In

7

against the dictate of external nature, speculative reason against empirical matter, the synthetic against the organic, and the godly, enlightened, and pure against the beastly, dark, and corrupt. For Kaufmann, the history of this epochal struggle was not dialectical and produced neither synthesis nor an inexorable teleological movement. Instead, the irresolution of Ledoux's work, his inability to discharge the heteronomous once and for all, was symptomatic of striving for an adequate representation of the formless infinite encountered at the dynamic limits of progressive mathematization—a necessarily incomplete and contingent hermeneutic circling around the mystery of reason striving, yet unable, to achieve transparency unto itself. Every act demanded that the struggle for self-determination be taken up anew, returning incessantly to origins to repeat the founding gesture—a perpetual cultural revolution enacted on a timeless tabula rasa.[37]

In the closing lines of his last and best-known book, *Architecture in the Age of Reason*, published posthumously in 1955, Kaufmann returned to this issue, underscoring its continued significance for him:

> No set of forms nor any definite, all-embracing formula, but the challenge to struggle for new forms and new patterns was the legacy of the Age of Reason. From the moment when a new ideal of configuration arose—a moment which of course can hardly be fixed in time—the battle for its realization began. There was no chance for it ever to attain perfect fulfillment. Yet from it sprang endless tentative solutions, such as at all times have made, and always will make, the life and the history of Architecture.[38]

which he wanted to descend in order to begin, as it were, again at the beginning."[35] In 1942, Kaufmann called this frustrated and unfulfillable striving a "sublime ethics."[36]

None of the reviews of Kaufmann's various writings recognized the extent to which he was driven by this desire to install constitutively an obligation to moral autonomy struggling against native heteronomy. In *Von Ledoux bis Le Corbusier*, this tension had been figured not only in terms of historical periods, but also as opposing forces within the new epoch *and* within the human subject itself—the will to self-regulation struggling

Like Giedion, Kaufmann's writings were generally well received among historians, although he too was consistently criticized for distorting the past for the

223

(4)
Spread from Philip Johnson's "House at New Canaan, Connecticut," showing sources for the house along with details and drawings (*Architectural Review*, September 1950)

sake of his programmatic conception of present tendencies. Where more recently, Hubert Damisch and Monique Moser have interpreted Kaufmann's 1933 book as an almost heroic defense of modern architecture on the eve of its eclipse by fascism[39] marked by the closing of the Bauhaus in Berlin, the construction of Hitler's Haus der deutschen Kunst (House of German Art) by Paul Troost in Munich, and the ascendancy of fascism in Austria—among earlier historians only Peter Collins acknowledged Kaufmann's "invaluable service to contemporary architecture" for showing how "we may appreciate our own problems more acutely by seeing them in an eighteenth-century setting."[40] Others considered his case for Ledoux as a prophet of modernism "not very successful"[41] and "difficult to swallow but not difficult to digest,"[42] or claimed that "the really prophetic works" had been created instead by industrialization[43] and that Kaufmann's preoccupation with modern architecture blinded him to Ledoux's neoclassicism[44] and historicity.

(5)
Spread from Philip Johnson's "House at New Canaan, Connecticut," with views of the house (*Architectural Review*, September 1950)

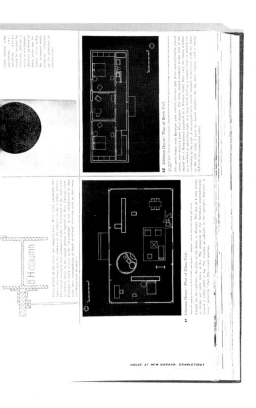

Kaufmann's preoccupation with revolution was called "ideological," [45] "distorting," and "Marxist," [46] his "metaphysics" a dangerous and "unclear theoretical basis." Like Giedion, Kaufmann was admired for his "rich factual research," but rebuked, even by his most sympathetic readers, for failing to account for the concrete historical relationships that operated between architecture and the social and political conditions of the time. Only Paul Zucker commended Kaufmann as being in "the best tradition of thorough European scholarship." [47] Even Meyer Shapiro, who in 1936 introduced Kaufmann's work in America with praise, also observed—with considerable insight, I might add—that Kaufmann's categorical distinction between autonomy and heteronomy was too metaphorical, inadequate to the historical evidence, and presumed that architecture could have such a thing as "a nature" and conform to such things as pure "laws of art," assumptions that ignored the historical contingency of disciplinary self-definitions. [48]

Among architects of the period that concerns this conference, the one notable reception of Kaufmann was by Philip Johnson. As Franz Schulze's biography of Johnson has recounted, the American Society of Architectural Historians convened at Johnson's newly completed Miesian house in Cambridge at around the time of its conference at Harvard in 1942 specifically to hear Kaufmann discuss his untranslated book of 1933, hoping that he would shed light on the work of Le Corbusier. Later, in presenting the sources and thinking behind his well-known Glass House in New Canaan of 1949 (4+5), Johnson used a plate from Kaufmann's book, depicting Ledoux's spherical Shelter for the Rural Guards. Johnson's article in *Architectural Review* [49] offered an assemblage of images accompanied by short texts that served to position his project among elementarist works by Le Corbusier, Mies, van Doesburg, Schinkel, and Malevich. Johnson's caption

225

to Ledoux's sphere explained that the "cubic, 'absolute' forms" of the Glass House and its separation of functional units into pure mathematical shapes came directly from Ledoux, whom he called "the Eighteenth Century father of modern architecture," one of "those intellectual revolutionaries from the baroque" from whom "we" are descended.

While interpretations of the house (beginning with Johnson's own) have tended to focus on its debt to Mies's Farnsworth House of 1946–50, the distinctive achievement of Johnson's design may be more related to his positioning of Mies (and himself) within this elementarist field, which extended and elaborated Kaufmann's historical portrait of the new architectural system. The house itself, then, may be considered a demonstration of the compositional system or "grammar"—site planning by Le Corbusier and Mies considered in relation to van Doesburg's composition of sliding rectangles and Choisy's analysis of the approach to the Acropolis; the principle of absolute form exemplified by Ledoux as a sphere, by Mies as a rectangular glass prism floating above the landscape, and by Schinkel as a cube at the edge of a sharp bluff; and the compositional principle of combining discrete geometric elements demonstrated by Johnson in an assembly of steel sections that make an "open" Miesian corner and in a floor plan that recalls the "interesting" space generated in a suprematist painting, which Johnson considered "even today the strongest single aesthetic influence on the grammar of architecture." As Hitchcock observed in 1966:

[Johnson] was content, then, like most architects before 1750, to accept the established structural methods of his day and, like them, to design in the style of his day, or at least of his youth, the style he had joined with me in defining twenty years before as the International Style. As he told the Harvard students, he did not, like Gropius, "believe in perpetual revolution in architecture." Said he, firmly, "I do not strive for originality," for Mies had once told him: "Philip, it is much better to be good than to be original."[50]

Yet, where Mies's projects worked to elevate or sublate modern rationality into a transcendent self-reflexive artistic construct, Johnson's house shows no evidence of such dialectics. Neither epistemological nor metaphysical (Johnson interpreted Mies's transformation of standard steel sections as the equivalent of decoration, asking if mannerism would be next), Johnson's self-declared derivativeness transformed Kaufmann's system for individuation into a repertoire of forms and relational principles, discharging all obligation to struggle for transparent self-knowledge in cognizance of its limits. He made Kaufmann's endgame of autonomous reason into a language game, whose rules were reductive and stringent but free of universalizing necessity and whose aims returned to the worldliness of a social discourse of pleasure. In reaffirming, or at least making explicit, the culture of taste, style, and imitation that had after all continued into the "new" times, even within modernism, Johnson's house points to an unresolved problem in Giedion's as well as in Kaufmann's writings, one that they inherited from the impossible quest of German rationalist modernism in the 1920s to leave behind what it took to be the inadequate laws of social conventions.

*　*　*

Reiterating a topos from the eighteenth century, rationalists such as Mies, Ludwig Hilberseimer, Gropius, Adolf Behne, and Max Taut rejected not only old conventions and styles but conventionality and style per se— in favor of a utopian striving for a natural lawfulness of construction, designated most often by the notion of *Gestaltung* or form-creation, and later by Giedion's "space-time" and Kaufmann's "autonomy." Among architects, Mies's statements of 1923 against style and formalism, which accompanied his elemental projects in concrete, are perhaps the most well-known examples—"Any aesthetic speculation, any doctrine and any formalism we reject."[51] And "Form is not the goal but the result of our work. . . . Nor do we strive for a style. . . . We have other worries."[52] To avoid the codification and regulation associated with the idea of style, Giedion and Kaufmann, like the architects with whom they aligned themselves, posited the exigency of a higher law that would serve as a regulative ideal for a system of freedom. This, however, harbored the paradox that a regulative ideal cannot, by definition, exist or be known, cannot have properties, and so cannot actually serve as a criterion against which to judge conformance to law. Consequently, characteristics had to be projected from examples already at hand, thereby collapsing claims for natural lawfulness into cultural conventions despite the intentions of architects and historians. It is no accident that these modernists found it necessary to campaign for what should have been automatic. The achievement of nature, reason, or historical necessity was, in the end, contin-gent on retraining and reculturation—on programs that no one was not, after all, obliged to subscribe to. It was the operation of this regulative ideal that engendered the unresolved tension in Giedion's and Kaufmann's histories between completion and incompletion, being and becoming-striving, immanence and transcendence, which for most readers appeared as a seemingly unaccountable disparity between astute accounts of emerging tendencies and perplexing philosophical and aesthetic ideals.

The quest of 1920s rationalist architecture may in turn be understood as responding to a related problematic inscribed into the history of cultural avant-gardism, seeking to resolve the opposition between freedom and system identified by Matei Calinescu as the "irresolvable contradiction between the supposedly courageous nonconformism of the avant-garde and its final submissiveness to blind, intolerant discipline"—the *aporia* of an avant-garde wanting to be free and yet demanding regulation. In his *Five Face of Modernity*,[53] Calinescu recounted that the term "avant-garde" was first introduced in military discourse during the Middle Ages to refer to an advance guard. It was given its first figurative meaning in the Renaissance, but only became a metaphor for a self-consciously advanced position in politics, literature, and art during the nineteenth century. Political overtones accrued in the aftermath of the French Revolution and were transposed to literary-artistic circles by romantic theorists, notably Saint-Simonian social reformers who promoted the artist as the "man of imagination" capable of both foreseeing the future and creating it, as the messianic vanguard in the moral history of humankind. In the 1860s, Charles Baudelaire was the first to point out that this notion of the avant-garde harbored a tension between radical artistic freedom and programmatic political campaigns modeled on war, between critique, negation, and destruction, on the one hand, and dogma, affirmation, and construction, on the other—in short, between freedom and system. This tension gave rise to numerous artistic responses—those that emphasized one side at the expense of the other (Seymour Howard, the student at Harvard, clearly sided with affirmation and regulation); those that attempted to resolve the tension, as Giedion did with his dynamic model; and even those that accepted it as irresolvable, as Kaufmann did at least in part.

Not only did Giedion and Kaufmann operate within the structure of this problematic, but their strategies for resolving its constitutive claims originate in the same historical and theoretical context from which cultural avant-gardism emerged—as Calinescu observed, in romanticism, but also in speculative idealism, both of which were launched by Kant's "opening up of an abyss where a bridge should have been." As Philippe Lacoue-Labarthe and Jean-Luc Nancy have explained, Kant's division between the phenomenal and the noumenal, the "is" and the "ought," differed from the traditional division between the sensible and the intelligible as "a division between forms (*a priori*) of the sensible or intuitive itself" refusing claims to knowledge that belonged properly to a transcendent authority.[54] The effect of this was to empty the subject of substance, reducing it to a pure form that was "nothing more than a function of unity or synthesis." Because for him, the subject could only be defined negatively, as a subject that is not the subject of knowledge, Kant promoted the moral subject—the "as if"—as the ethical condition for the future

"necessary to preserve practical judgment from being a mere appeal to conventions." For Kant, transcendental imagination (*Einbildungskraft*) became the function required to form this unity and to do so as representation or picture, as phenomenon. Even if the moral subject, free and self-conscious, could be posited, there could be no cognition of it.[55]

The crisis inaugurated by Kant's questioning of the subject preoccupied his successors, not only in philosophy but also in art. It launched the efforts of philosophical idealism to reconquer the possibility of effective speculation through the exigency of a desire or "will to system" through which the subject would be able to recognize the Ideal in its own form. The System to which idealism aspired, or more precisely the System-Subject, was understood as a task to be done; it did not and could not yet exist, but remained "the last work of humanity." Kant also opened the way for romanticism to address this philosophical aspiration to unity through art, rather than through theory. More precisely, the romantics pursued it through poetics, or more precisely still *poiesie* or generative production, which aimed to operationalize the System through acts of individuation that strive to be absolutely self-positing, that aspire to the Work-Subject. For romanticism, the work in question was not so much an object but that which works, not so much the organon as that which organizes. It was thought to conjoin the critical dissolution of existing systems with the relentless energy of formation, positing the exigency of a total closure that could never be perfected. By thematizing that which works in the individual as the capacity to produce itself by means of its internal formative force, romanticism set up a dialectical unity between artificial and natural production, for the organic is essentially autoformation, or the genuine form of the subject.[56] The operative criterion for this form (the mark of nature) was the perfection of character, which was announced through the exigency of a "physical" knowledge of "the nature of the soul," for which the science of physiognomy was to serve as objective critic and judge.[57]

Where the idealist philosopher Friedrich Schelling grappled for forty years with the problem of grounding an ungroundable system, the romantic writer Friedrich Schlegel attempted to achieve a new unity through the writing and assembly of fragments and Ideas. As a reader of both Schelling and Schlegel,[58] Giedion devised his distinctive theory of history as operationalizing the production of a new system of freedom, which he called "space-time." Like the romantic fragment or Idea, Giedion took works of art and architecture as working toward the realization of the future system and at the same time already incorporating it. Kaufmann's case for autonomy, first as individuated form and then as a system of individuation, was also located in the shadow of Kant's refusal, and while more neo-Kantian than Giedion, was, as I have argued, not untouched by constitutive claims to the absolute.[59]

Parenthetically, let me note that the tendency to collapse Kant's critical path into a formal language for modern architecture had already emerged within art history and criticism in Germany prior to the First World War, when Kant's unrepresentable *Ding-an-sich* began to be invoked in interpretations of abstract geometric forms whose individuated *Sachlichkeit*, objectivity, simplicity, and primitiveness were taken as visible signs of inner lawfulness. Where critical interpretations of the "new Renaissance" of Peter Behrens after

1904, as well as art historical treatments of the neoclassicism of *um 1800*, emphasized the individuation, purity, and primitiveness of linear, geometric forms—forms for themselves—they did not invoke the Kantian thing-in-itself directly. However, in 1907 Wilhelm Worringer schematized the psychology of form as an opposition between urges for abstraction and empathy, characterizing the former by means of "an audacious comparison" between the primitive and the "thing-in-itself," claiming that after thousands of years of evolution the feeling for the "thing-in-itself" had been reawakened, no longer as instinct but now as "the ultimate product of cognition,"[60] manifest in cubic and crystalline forms. By 1911, Worringer had applied these terms in defending the "*sachlich* self-conscious" young art of Paris (inaugurated by Cézanne, van Gogh, and Matisse).[61] In 1913 similar terms were used by the Czech cubist Vlatislav Hofman in a programmatic statement for a new "revolutionary" cubist architecture of "autonomous" forms,[62] and the following year Adolf Behne described the *ur*-forms and *ur*-elements of Bruno Taut's Monument of Iron (sphere, pyramid, undecorated surface) as a rigorous *Sachlichkeit* that freed architecture from the dictates of convention and use.[63] All three articles appeared in the expressionist journal *Der Sturm*. In the late 1920s, such a Kantian "formalism" may be discerned in Ludwig Hilberseimer's programmatic call for a metropolitan architecture "formed exclusively from itself . . . cubes and spheres, pyramids and cylinders . . . geometric and cubistic elements that do not permit of any further objectification."[64] Later, in the early 1960s, having become a reader of Kaufmann, Hilberseimer even described the main body of modern architecture with the term "Autonomous Architecture."[65]

Without thematizing the constitutive dependence of his conception of autonomy on the exclusion of heteronomy and nature, without acknowledging the extent to which his conception of architectural autonomy

229

depended on models from outside architecture—from philosophy, political theory, and mathematics—and without thematizing the reliance of his tentative materializations of autonomy on formal tropes, Kaufmann was unable to install a sufficiently experimental dynamic into his system to avoid its collapse into mechanism. Similarly, he did not recognize, let alone negotiate, the contradiction between the theory of physiognomic expression (common to both expressionism and functionalism) and the a priori formalism of elemental geometry. Nor did he observe, as Robin Evans recently did, that geometry is not a dead science and that architecture's reliance on it and its reciprocal internalization of architecture has produced a rich and unfinished history of disciplinary self-definition and redefinition through interdisciplinary liaisons.[66]

The failures of Giedion and Kaufmann's histories were symptomatic, then, of the modernist quest for a new normativity that would overturn Kant without returning directly to metaphysical claims to substance. While these failures would in retrospect have to be considered justified, I do not mean to suggest that this problematic be condemned or abandoned. For these avant-garde historians did, after all, leave a significant legacy. They mapped the regulatory matrix of architectural production and reception in the modern period more thoroughly and precisely than anyone had before; they scrutinized its internal contradictions, confused mixtures, and problematic transumption of the past into the system of modern production; and they struggled for an ethical relationship between self and other within it. The irresolutions in

their writings are only failures if we accept the modernist assumption that resolution is the aim. Without this, their projects may be read in other ways, and their unresolved negotiation between immanent and transcendent claims for the constitution of freedom may take on new value.

*   *   *

To close, let me offer a possible point of departure for such a reading. In contemporary critical legal studies, Drucilla Cornell (among others) has argued that Kant's division between the "is" and the "ought" needs to be maintained—not, however, as two divided realms that serve simply to stabilize the traditional dichotomy between nature and freedom—but as an unsurpassable paradox—in law, as the irresolvable tension between law considered as a system of norms (the legal system) and justice considered as the pursuit of an ethical relationship with alterity, which necessarily defers to the beyond of code and precedent.[67] Cornell insists that justice is in fact only possible *within* the *aporia* of being both regulated and without regulation. Not only can this aporia not be resolved, efforts to do so, she argues, necessarily lead to false claims for what amount to "the system's own attempts at 'deparadoxicalization.'"[68] The transcendence of justice cannot be made the immanent end of the internal evolution of any legal system. Yet working within the system of law in the pursuit of justice, that is, deconstructively at its limits, can, she suggests, lead performatively to the transformation of the system in the direction of greater freedom.

Reading Giedion and Kaufmann from the perspective of poststructural theories of mediation would, however, require that they be treated as both targets of critique and precursors—which is admittedly risky and would require confronting the model of history that underpins them. Sixty years before Giedion and Kaufmann came to America, Friedrich Nietzsche had already identified this risk when, in his untimely meditation "On the uses and disadvantages of history for life," he promoted what he called "critical history,"[69] whose echo (albeit distorted) may be found in Giedion and Kaufmann, as well as among other activist historian-critics of their generation—Wilhelm Worringer, Adolf Behne, and Franz Roh.[70] In order to live, Nietzsche had written, it was necessary from time to time to pass judgment on the injustices of the past, to break up and dissolve a part of it by "bringing it before the tribunal, scrupulously examining it and finally condemning it." To cope with the problem of judging one's own origins and distancing oneself from them, Nietzsche posited the idea of a "second nature," which he characterized as artistic and fictive. In the very act of critical destruction, he suggested, latent and constructive potentialities could be found that would make it possible "through a new, stern discipline [to] combat our inborn heritage and implant in ourselves a new habit . . . to give oneself, as it were *a posteriori*, a past in which one would like to originate in opposition to that in which one did originate." Invoking an image of architectural creativity later echoed in manifestos for *neues bauen* around 1919, he argued that while "historical justice is always annihilating [if] the historical drive does not also contain a drive to construct, if the purpose of destroying and clearing is not to allow a future already alive in anticipation to raise its house on the ground thus liberated, if justice alone prevails, then the instinct for creation will be enfeebled and discouraged."[71] And:

When the past speaks it always speaks as an oracle; only if you are an architect of the future and know the present will you understand it . . . only he who constructs the future has a right to judge the past. If you look ahead and set yourself a great goal, you at the same time restrain that rank analytical impulse which makes the present into a desert and all tranquility, all peaceful growth and maturing almost impossible. Draw about yourself the fence of a great and comprehensive hope, of a hope-filled striving. Form within yourself an image to which the future shall correspond.[72]

Arguing that these two moments—critical judgment and utopian hopefulness—could be conjoined in the activity of fabricating what he called a "second nature," Nietzsche's concept of critical history made productive what Baudelaire had identified, in synchronic terms, as the *aporia* of the avant-garde by casting it into time, making it productive in history. But Nietzsche was also quick to warn that judging is fraught with dangers, including the risk of forgetting that we are the products of the "aberrations, passions and errors [of earlier generations], and indeed of their crimes."[73]

231

CIAM

City at the End of History

MITCHELL SCHWARZER

Congrès Préparatoire International d'Architecture Moderne

au Château de la Sarraz

(Canton de Vaud, Suisse)

les 26, 27 et 28 Juin 1928

Ce premier congrès est convoqué dans le but d'établir un programme général d'action ayant pour objet d'arracher l'architecture à l'impasse académique et de la mettre dans son véritable milieu économique et social. Ce congrès doit, dans l'esprit des promoteurs, déterminer les limites des études et des discussions qui, à bref délai, doivent être entreprises par de nouveaux congrès d'architecture sur des programmes partiels. Le présent congrès a pour mission d'établir la série de ces programmes.

La liste défininive du Comité de Patronage sera communiqué à l'ouverture du Congrès

Against the oppositional ardor of the avant-gardes in the years following World War I, CIAM is often depicted as the *rappel à l'ordre* of the modern movement.[1] From its founding in 1928 at La Sarraz, Switzerland **(1+2)**, CIAM (Congrès Internationaux d'Architecture Moderne) set forth to rationalize architecture and adapt it to the prevailing socioeconomic order. The infamous positivist equation of modernism was articulated here as nowhere else; architecture and city planning were to be oriented around a functional ordering of dwelling, work, recreation, and circulation.[2] Through eleven congresses—lasting until its final dissolution in 1959 at Otterlo, the Netherlands—CIAM argued that architects must undertake the complete mechanization of the total built environment.[3]

CIAM occupies a critical presence in the history of the twentieth century because it forged an objective and heroic identity for architecture. True, such gestures are a peculiar specialty of architecture, common to the discipline's classical as well as modern guises. Still, earlier attempts to construct consummate architectural identities, at least in the modern era, had met with shorter-lived success. They were unable to meld convincingly the continuities of machine and imaginative processes with the ruptures brought about by these same actions. CIAM's heroic identity was different. It filled the tautological emptiness of scientific and technological objectivity with a revolutionary spirit of redemption. It solidified an identity for the architect as prophet for the machine age.

In order to begin articulating this identity, it bears mentioning that CIAM (like the contemporaneous League of Nations) represented a partial cessation of nationalist rivalry in architecture, most of all between the French and the Germans. Perhaps because of the Great War and the ensuing divisive political climate, architects like Le Corbusier and Walter Gropius, Victor Bourgeois and Hans Schmidt, worked together toward common design solutions. They were able to do so because of their Nietzschean sense of modernity, their distrust of national architectural academies and competing intellectual traditions. One of the great achievements of CIAM was its recognition of architecture and city planning's dependence upon markets, ideas, and technologies beyond the scope of any single culture or individual.

CIAM gatherings expounded the inevitability of internationalism. The complexities of this endeavor are responsible for intrepid as well as outrageous design prognoses. Whereas myths of the solitary artist or the native genius prevail throughout modern aesthetics, CIAM

235

(1)
Title page of the second program for the Preparatory Congress held at the Château de la Sarraz, Switzerland, June 26–28, 1928

CIAM

designated its myth the international constructor. Allusions here to the international industrialist are not coincidental. CIAM architecture, like its business and technocratic counterparts, sought salvation in an unbounded reality. All too often, prior aesthetic formulas for architecture were limited by nationalistic division, individual alienation, or disciplinary convention. They were compromised by resistance toward political, economic, and cultural integration on a worldwide scale. The CIAM project, like its industrialist counterparts, preached a providential climax to all earlier architectural disunity.

Nonetheless, its architects could not accept the wanton nature of the capitalist city. They sharply critiqued arbitrary, shapeless, and everyday building practices; they opposed the empty deluge of fashion trends as well as the bloated illegibility of bourgeois social posturing. They therefore attacked the garments and aspirations of a commodity culture that made possible internationalism in the first place. The result was a call for utopia from above the concrete city, or what amounted to a transcendentalist rejection of urbanity as random occurrence.

It is here that CIAM's relationship to the frenzied illuminations of the avant-gardes is most pronounced. The goal of creating an international constructor meant plowing through false appearance toward underlying reality: if only the physical characteristics of diseased cities were swept away; if only their oppressed inhabitants were liberated. Needless to say, such wild hopes etched an architecture and urbanity far in excess of the sobriety commonly associated with the cubic building masses and orthogonal platting of the modern movement. The CIAM program lay in creating a sublimely rational metropolis in order to free space for a limitless dreamscape. The physical city of right angles, functional zones, and biological minimums always suggested extremes. It was always a door onto something like the crystal city envisioned earlier by Bruno Taut and Paul Scheerbart, that release from the bounds of all-powerful physical need.

The severe simplicity and rationality of CIAM's material city may then be read as a forecast for magnifying desire beyond physicality, an insatiable and infinite revolution of existence beyond urban geography. The CIAM city intended the creation of a celestial kingdom within earth, a building regime whose dogma of minimal materiality would somehow yield optimal spirituality.

(2)
Official photograph of attendees at the Preparatory Congress, La Sarraz, June 1928

The particularities and perplexities of this project are the subject of my essay. In what follows, I will examine architectural themes at the early congresses—from La Sarraz in 1928 to Paris in 1937—and in narratives by Le Corbusier and José Luis Sert during the early years of World War II.

Bombsights

From 1928 to 1942, CIAM writing was a desperate effort to emerge from the most recent fall of architecture, the previous century's descent into the interminable proliferations of industrial culture. The loss of archè suffered during the nineteenth century was epitomized by the reification of building as commercial exchange and by the dispersal of classical architectural knowledge within a multitude of competing styles. Following the logic of Hegel's dialectic, CIAM architects reasoned that a revalorization of archè could emerge only from a usurpation of the disordered urban marketplace and the diverse elements contributing to its chaos.

Greatly enamored by military science and technology, CIAM's campaign to reorder the city was diagrammed as warfare. This orientation explains why time and time again the organization evoked the martial dominion of architecture over other professional and scholarly disciplines. Most of all, the blitzkrieg through knowledge and practice situated its *Schwerpunkt* within those elements that had over the past century worked to constitute the city as wilderness. By breaking through and encircling the city's bondage within the clutches of irrational relations, CIAM architects hoped to advance urban rationalization beyond that already accomplished by early city-planning efforts of the late nineteenth and early twentieth centuries, and thereby standardize the identities of expertise hitherto occupied by uncoordinated disciplines.

The vastness of CIAM's martial stature implied exacting burdens on architects. They aspired to coordinate the ever-expanding parameters of urban reality, both on the ground and from above. Writing as early as 1924, before the founding of CIAM, Hans Schmidt recognized the insights to be gained regarding the ground (the urban body) from the vantage point of the air (the mechanized mind). The view of Paris from the top of the Eiffel Tower filled Schmidt with both melancholy and exhilaration. Depressingly, from that great height he saw the city as "a great mass without the rhythm of organic authority, a chaos from which various monumental buildings emerge without sense and are soon lost again."[4] At the same time, however, he observed unexpected order. This last point is puzzling and speaks to the heart of CIAM's later fixation with constructing urban reality from abstract (and mechanized) representational devices. Perhaps because of its perceptual distance from actual spaces and forms, or the sense of heightened power it gave Schmidt over what he viewed, the air view supported a myth of universal comprehension. Contrary to actual perceptions of disorder, the air view revisualized a state of incipient order, a revelation of unity from within the delirium of multiplicity.[5] As M. Christine Boyer writes, "The airplane allowed for new orthogonal routes that passed over and through all objects, disregarding political boundaries and flowing like primordial rivers back to the sea."[6]

(3)
Jacket design for the unpublished book *Die Funktionnelle Stadt*

Almost twenty years later, in a quasi-official articulation of CIAM urbanism, *Can Our Cities Survive?* (1942) (3), Sert buoyed a similar myth in the long view from airplanes. Writing just after the greatest air campaign in the history of warfare, the Battle of Britain, Sert discerned the possibility for reordering the city from perceptual bombing. The German *Luftwaffe,* in seeking the wholesale destruction of Britain's urbanscape, had begun to reveal a dehistoricized city, a minimalist environment of building foundations and cadastral (street/block) organization, a city exorcised of its customary state of affairs.

Eerily similarly, the Catalan architect perceived the city for its subhistoric forces and patterns, and its new radical potential to subvert random powers. And as it had for Schmidt, the long view down from the sky revealed oppositions to Sert, a haphazard distribution of buildings and streets and a logical lineament of natural topography and emergent technology. In a gesture harkening back to Italian classicism, Sert exposed the air view for its mission to perceive, erase, and reorganize. The air view was a new urban facade, only horizontal and not vertical.[7] And, like earlier perspectival and bird's-eye views, the new air view reproduced an illusion of urban order through a telescoping of perspective. Much as had been the case in the visual elocution of Renaissance urbanism, the modern movement envisioned its utopian city in contrast to the visual ambiguity and complexity inherent within actual urban conditions. As a result, CIAM representations of the city present us with images of chaos (the first glance at aerial photographs) and order (their deeper levels of meaning) alongside one another; urban acumen is a disjuncture in visual consciousness.[8]

Standard of Revolution

CIAM architects often asked themselves what were the contrasting edges of modern architecture. What, in other words, would constitute the dialectics for the utopian metropolis? In *The Athens Charter* (1943), Le Corbusier noted that building a new city would take architects to the furthest reaches of the material world and the most inward recesses of the psyche. The city, melodramatically, was the site for the realization of modern economic and political relations, technological development, as well as group and individual psychology; it was also a masterful shaper of its surrounding geography, topography, demography, and sociology.[9]

Inasmuch as the fields of expertise proposed by Le Corbusier to constitute the city were vast and discontinuous, he realized that architects needed a single device for unification. His insight, and that of CIAM at large, was the possibility to be gained from harnessing the great creator and disrupter of modern civilization: the industrial machine. Indeed, from the initial statements of 1928, modern architecture was revealed by CIAM as the offspring of the insurgent birth and disruptive adolescence of the machine during the Industrial Revolution. Without any regrets, "l'expression architecturale moderne" was announced at La Sarraz as the consequence of an "evolution machiniste."[10] Over and over it is stated that modern architects must align themselves with this altogether new and complicated evolution, rising to the aspirations of their new epoch by adopting the identity of mechanization.[11] They must become artist-diagnosticians and scientist-surgeons of the city's machine-body.[12]

It is worth mentioning that this prognosis for a mechanized (or functionalized) architectural culture was an outgrowth of nineteenth-century strategies for urban rationalization. Encompassing efforts by physicians, engineers, politicians, and architects, the new field of city planning set the stage for the modern movement's understanding of the metropolis as an integral whole comprised of interrelated functions. What is more, in the twentieth century, this prognosis for functional mechanization was profoundly influenced by several extra-architectural factors: first, dramatic increases in the speed of communications and transportation, which allowed for the concept of a worldwide architectural practice; second, the apparent creation of a supremely comfortable dwelling through a conquest of diverse biotic environments via advanced building technologies, central heating, and air conditioning; and third, release from the drudgery of overwhelming toil through shorter working weeks and the consequent popularization of leisure and foreign travel. As we will see, CIAM's functional focus on transportation, dwelling, and recreation was in large part a response to the inroads of mechanization into these realms.

Forcefully, the view of the city from the air (and its geovisual mapping techniques) or from a sheet of statistics (and their underlying numerical surveys and tabulations) met the challenge of developing a mechanized consciousness. They illustrate the new freedoms of mobility and spatiality to be won from within the machine-body; proposed is a dream of weightlessness, a spiritual freedom engendered as architecture is abstracted into line, plane, and number. In a Platonic sense, all these correspond to a vision of creating the city itself as *logos* and neither as phenomena (the work of human artifice) nor as *eidolon* (the debased copy of artificial reality). The air view evinced a higher, subliminal appreciation of the city, its blocks and arteries "less as a deliberate artefact of man than the natural product of topography, trade routes, and changing technology."[13]

Similarly, visualizing the city from rows and combinations of statistics promised a merger of objective processes with the human imagination. Statistics took on monumental significance in the twentieth century. They were perhaps the most profound imagery of prolonged, total warfare. What image better encapsulates the horrors of the World War II than "the six million"? Statistics was also the modus operandi of the international industrialist, the rationale behind a cumulative crescendo toward ever-increasing production and consumption. Numbers, more than almost any other imagistic device, revealed the potential to reshape the *res extensa* via a mechanized *res cogitans*.

> In any case, why should numbers be any less telling a representation of the city than a drawing, photograph, or immediate perception? Much more than the drawings of historic squares or palace gardens of specific cities, comparative statistics demonstrate the transferable, functional, and abstract qualities of modern urbanity. They tell stories of disease and salubrity, antiquation and renewal, crime and safety, that are easily used as a basis for comparison between different urban locales. Numbers relinquish the separate and the traditional. They indicate a city restructured not only through the international but also through the present. It is no wonder that CIAM architects began to perceive a new language of the city from within modernity's technologized numbers and their sublime and homogenizing powers. In 1929, Le Corbusier wrote with great admiration:

> Statistics are the Pegasus of the town planner. They are tedious things, meticulous, passionless and impassive. All the same they are a jumping-off ground for poetry, the base from which the poet may leap into the future and unknown, although his feet remain planted on the solid groundwork of figures, graphs, the eternal verities.[14]

The new mechanized consciousness of the city was, however, by no means as stable as architects would have hoped. As Le Corbusier later remarked, alongside the potentialities of the machine age was its squalor:

The use of the machine has provoked immense disturbances in the conduct of men, in the patterns of their distribution over the earth's surface and in their undertakings; an unchecked trend, propelled by mechanized speeds, toward concentration in the cities, a precipitate and world-wide evolution without precedent in history. Chaos has entered the cities.[15]

Throughout this and other CIAM documents we are confronted by antithetical terminology: constructive attributes are given to the machine while destructive attributes are given to its social refraction within industrial society. Architects as international constructors were asked to create a city through a synthesis of psychological and technological forces. They were asked to harmonize economic and psychological forces more frequently in conflict than harmony: a modernity torn apart by its magnifying desires. In short, the air view and statistical view, alongside their intimations of a mechanized Platonism, promoted explosive reconfiguration. They indicated a city of both precise expression and exploding limits.

Modern architects, if they were to proceed in harmony with technological evolution, had to become doubles of the machine.[16] Architecture, understood since the eighteenth century as the animation of inanimate material by the human spirit, was thus reconceived as the animator of a new human society through the animation of the inorganic. But what does it mean to become the double of an inanimate object put to life by people in the first place?

This question points to a central fiction of CIAM, the re-creation of identity through a commingling of the lost divine creator and a rationally animated natural world. The metaphor of the machine, in this sense, upholds the destination taken over by aesthetics from eschatology: a reinvolvement of spiritual and natural modes of existence in the ecstasy of collective creation. The machine, much as the first creator, was there to set forth new laws of nature so as to free humanity to be itself. The implication was that humanity could never be free in a world of its own making. Either God or machines were needed for that. For the architects of CIAM, a mechanized regime of rationalizing processes became the setting for the ironic liberation of humanity from demoniac earthly powers.

The ivory severity of Neues Bauen, its aerial ratiocination and digital reason, its expression of the machine's immaculate creation, was the basis of a new identity of forfeiture. To re-create the simplicity of an Adamic age (an age before the fall of humanity from Eden), CIAM

CIAM

(4)

Jacket design for the first edition of *Die Wohnung für das Existenzminimum* (Frankfurt, 1930)

architecture would have to pare the decadent and superfluous features of its quotidian world. Consequently, its architects would be agents of a harsh reform of the antiquated, erotic, and licentious pleasures that separate the labyrinthine historical world from the heights of its divine predecessor and mechanical successor.

Memories Forgotten

The first target was history. CIAM demanded that architects redouble the machine in a way that subverted its extreme horrors through an intensification of its rational continuities. To govern life, machines had to become history and at the same time bring an end to history. As Sigfried Giedion's book *Mechanization Takes Command* (1948) later pointed out, machine consciousness had to replace tradition as the prehistory and posthistory for architecture.

This vision had serious implications for architectural education. In order to establish an analogue between the birth of modern architecture and the machine, architects had to sever the continuum with the past built up over several centuries of academic education. As the medieval guilds had served during the Renaissance, the architectural academy now became the illogical barrier to utopia.

Already at La Sarraz, the academies were described as parasitic and senile forces within the architectural profession.[17] Brooders on baneful tradition, they championed irrelevant notions of symmetry and composition that had constituted architecture in its premechanized epoch. Conservators of outmoded drawing habits, they promoted externalities, such as the outline of the roof or the contours of the facade.[18] Because of this focus, "The objectives of architecture were poorly defined. The problems of habitation were also not clearly exposed."[19] If modernism were to thrive, the past had to be unlearned.

In 1929, at the Frankfurt congress "Die Wohnung für das Existenzminimum" (housing for low-income people) (4+5), Ernst May equated the birth of scientific design with such an unlearning of historical attitudes and academic prejudices.[20] The modern concept of design, according to May, should raise building to the level of a comprehensive construction of dwelling cells, what amounted to the mechanical perversion of those individualistic and aesthetic sensibilities cultivated by the academy. May's statistical cosmology of cellular units was envisioned as the generative element for new being—an image of building as an inverted

CIAM

VERLAG ENGLERT UND SCHLOSSER IN FRANKFURT AM MAIN

11

DAS NEUE FRANKFURT

MONATSSCHRIFT FÜR DIE PROBLEME MODERNER GESTALTUNG / 3. JAHRG. 1929

BILLIGE WOHNUNGEN

III. JAHRGANG · NOVEMBER 1929

(5)

Cover of *Das neue Frankfurt* (November 1929)

development of mental perception and cognition.[21] The cellular notion fastened architecture to the same interlocking and multifarious processes gained by the machine's growing dominion over nature.

A similar program for the architect was announced in Victor Bourgeois's essay at the same congress, "Le Programme de l'habitation minimum." If in classical architecture the architect had studied the aesthetic measure of "l'homme universel" for its correspondence to nature, Bourgeois admonished that modern architects should now study the relationships between rationalized men in their rationalizable environment. Habitation was not a matter of imitating the antique orders in the vain hope of developing natural building as the analogue of visual perspective. Instead, it was a question of how to organize and situate human functions scientifically, how to adapt man to new material conditions, and emergent technology to a new man.[22]

Herausgeber: Internationale Kongresse für Neues Bauen
JULIUS HOFFMANN VERLAG, STUTTGART

(6)
Dust jacket for *Rationelle Bebauungsweisen*

In 1930, at the Brussels congress "Rationelle Bebauungsweisen" (rational building methods) **(6)**, Cornelius van Eesteren extended criticism of academic education from its effects on single buildings to its deleterious role in urban planning. The times had changed from when block and street patterns were dependent upon iterative decisions, he claimed. Whereas such decisions characterized the slow development of the city during the Middle Ages and thereafter, the pace of development ever since the Industrial Revolution mandated that architects turn their glance from older cities and reject outdated living habits. As van Eesteren wrote, "Aesthetics, falsely understood traditional building methods, and old techniques of imitation cannot bring us healthy living quarters. Only rational methods for breaking up old neighborhoods can accomplish this."[23]

A comprehensive master plan ("ein geregelter Gesamtplan") was demanded. And at the epochal fourth congress in 1933, "Die Funktionelle Stadt" (the functional city), CIAM attempted to devise such a plan. Speaker after speaker intoned that the functions of the existing city had become *ungeregelt* (disorderly).[24] Put simply, the city no longer fit its historical costumes and representational devices. The consequences, as intimated earlier by van Eesteren, were radical. Architects should no longer plan the city's future as the outgrowth of successive widening of medieval, Renaissance, or baroque streets. Despite the creation of grand axes and monumental buildings during the nineteenth century, these efforts just disguised the increasingly undifferentiated and arbitrary city pattern emerging as a consequence of industrialism. Much as the Bauhaus strove to excavate the elementary psychology of design, CIAM would exhume the city at its most primordial levels.

Engaged Automatons

Criticism of the academies, historicism, and aesthetics buttressed CIAM's assertion that modern architecture must adapt itself to the motifs of continuity and efficiency of machine civilization. Still, it was not as clear how architecture was to attach itself to the automatic aspects of the machine, to its potential subsumption of individuality and free will. This possibility brought up an image of architectural identity calibrated to technical advance and quantification, one with no place for art and beauty.

The repercussions of this potential sacrifice had preoccupied architects in earlier debates, such as those at the Deutsche Werkbund in 1914. Interestingly, these questions did not dominate CIAM discussions between 1928 and 1939. Whereas the problem formed a major part of postwar CIAM,[25] prewar CIAM avoided it through a sublimation of the conflict of alienated individuality within a proposition for mechanized sociability. The space gained for an orchestration of the revolutionary and objectivist aspects of modern architecture was indebted to the shift in debate from the terms of the individual artist versus the industrialist to those of the creation of a society of international constructors. Individuals would no longer be represented by the centric posture embodied in Renaissance drawing, but through a calibrated liberation of humanity from natural necessity. One effect of this displacement was the orientation of discourse away from the tombs of the imagination and toward the tracks of manufacturing.[26] Again, rather than a dismissal of individuality, many architects saw the automatic workings of the machine society as the basis for a unified society of coordinated singularities.

At the Frankfurt congress, Schmidt's essay "Aufgabe und Verwirklichung der Minimalwohnung" stressed an industrial society concomitant with an advance out of bourgeois individualism. He recognized that the pace and scale of business development favored frequent housing relocation. Likewise, he saw that factory production had splintered the institution of home fabrication into smaller family units. Housing, if it was to adapt to the character of machine life, had to focus on the construction of numerous small dwellings. The dwelling, he wrote, should mimic the machine's standardization of nature: "The dwelling unit had to realize its fundamental objective minimum size exactly according to the model of purpose and sense that went into determining a seating place in a railway coach."[27] As important as the dwelling's three-dimensional qualities was its numerical program.

Gropius echoed these thoughts in the essay "Die soziologischen Grundlagen der Minimalwohnung," also delivered at the Frankfurt congress. Taking a longer view of human evolution, one indebted to the sociologist Ferdinand Müller-Leyer, Gropius wrote of the evolution of humanity through four great epochs: wanderings, family, individuality, and *Genossenschaft* (cooperative association).[28] What characterized the latter two phases, both belonging to the machine age, were the initial birth of individual freedom, the eventual problem of social alienation, and the final promise for voluntary social cohesion. The amalgamation of alienated individuality into free social associations described best the phase of social evolution of the time.

Collapsing the earlier opposed positions of Hermann Muthesius and Henry van de Velde at the Werkbund debate, Gropius saw rational, uniform, machine design as corresponding to the liberation of artistic desire. Architects would become the automatic designers of uniform dwellings which themselves would be flexibly adapted to a wide-ranging set of possible social relations. There was no attack on art within this formula. In the past, architects had been falsely preoccupied with the contours of entablatures and the monuments of form, issues that spoke to nonsystematic individuality. At this later time, by contrast, a new definition of the social architect was proposed; the focus on elementary minimums required by people for space, light, air, and warmth would constitute the architect's creative stance as revolutionizer of standardized habitation.[29] In contrast to the fragmented glances of the alienated bourgeois artist, CIAM architects would introduce the rational and thereby liberating systems of numerical and abstract spatial order into building design.

CIAM

To a large extent, dwelling design became a matter of understanding the parameters that would foster the greatest degree of individualized social interaction. In May's terminology, building was increasingly seen as a rationalized cell for habitation, one that permits a plethora of internal dispositions within standard plans, massing, windows, stairs. Such standard measures would promote individualism within the bounds of reciprocal social interaction. At the same time, by conquering nature's barriers to efficient dwelling, architecture would free the spirit for its higher, and immaterial, aspirations. Minimal architecture would result in unpredictable excess.

Schmidt's and Gropius's emphasis on the vast potential for new social associations brings up the issue of density, so prominent at the Brussels congress. The central question posed at Brussels was whether architects should design low-rise (*Flachbau*) or high-rise (*Hochbau*) cities. By 1930, architects had become aware that rail concentration was giving way to auto decentralization. Mechanized transport was redirecting the organization of human settlement.[30] The problem became whether to accept unplanned decentralization or to combat it as vigorously as unplanned congestion.

In light of the formula established for the evolution of society in Frankfurt, Gropius in Brussels came out in favor of greater density: the high-rise solution. He took this position in order to strike a balance between the needs of individuality and society, the constituent parts of the *Genossenschaft*. Low-rise cities, while attractive to certain individuals because of their salubrious qualities, made neither economic nor social sense for the masses. Because of longer commutes and the higher land costs incurred in developing a larger share of the metropolitan region, living on the periphery was uneconomical for the average person.[31] More seriously, the coupling of individuality with low-density living precluded the possibility of attaining Gropius's critical final stage of free association. Low-density and low-rise suburban living, an outburst against inner-city congestion, was seen by Gropius as a reaction against the irrational conditions of the unregulated city. Yet once urban chaos and disorder were solved, the benefits of higher density and vast populations in rationally designed neighborhoods would become evident.

Neighborhood size was better regulated by the number of dwellings required to create adequate density for the *Genossenschaft*.[32] Density exemplified the dynamic interactions of

CIAM

INTERNATIONALER KONGRESS FÜR MODERNE ARCHITEKTUR

gegründet 1928 in La Sarraz

(Auszug aus den Statuten) Art. 2. — Ziel der Vereinigung ist :
a) das Problem der zeitgemässen Architektur zu formulieren ; b) die Idee der modernen Architektur zu vertreten ; c) diese Idee in die technischen, ökonomischen und sozialen Zirkel einzuführen ; d) die Lösung des Problems der Architektur zu überwachen.

5. KONGRESS IN PARIS

» WOHNUNG und ERHOLUNG «

PARIS, 28. JUNI bis 2. JULI 1937

Patroniert vom :

MINISTER DES AÜSSEREN, MINISTER FÜR NATION-ERZIEHUNG UND KUNST, MINISTER DER LANDWIRTSCHAFT, MINISTER DER ÖFFENTLICHEN ARBEITEN, SEKRETARIAT FÜR SPORT UND ERHOLUNG, ALLGEMEINER KUNSTDIREKTOR.

1. Kongress : La Sarraz 1928, Gründung.
2. — Frankfurt-a.-Mein, 1929, Das › Haus-Mininimum ›.
3. — Brüssel, 1930, Planmässiges Bauen.
4. — Athen, 1933, Die funktionelle Stadt.

1. TAG : 29. Juni.
Grundlegende Lösungen (Wohnung und Erholung).

2. TAG : 30. Juni.
Angewandte Fälle : Die Städte (Wohnung und Erholung).

3. TAG : 1. Juli.
Vorschläge zu den Problemen auf dem Lande (Wohnung und Erholung).

4. TAG : 2. Juli.
Resolutionen.

machine processes, the interlocking of private elements into a systemic unity of numerical relations. In and of itself, density was not the problem. As Gropius wrote: "The goal is a loosening up and not dissolution of the cities."[33] The issue at hand was one of mechanizing density such that it actualized its systemic potentialities for creating community.[34]

Apropos of Market Perfection

At the fifth congress in Paris (7+8), Le Corbusier raised a troubling issue that encapsulates the organization's approach to creating community in the age of capitalism. "Urgent needs" (Aux besoins urgent), he wrote, were a more important consideration for architects than "the demands of the marketplace" (La demande sur le marché).[35] In a similar criticism, Sert later admonished commercial society for contriving to suppress everything not useful to its own ends. The faceless producer of modern cities, real-estate speculation, was castigated as utterly unsympathetic to the social goals of a mechanized architecture. Were the global economy and new mechanized architectural culture somehow out of sync?

Of course, commodity speculation resulted from the same industrialization of the building industry that exposed architects to the possibility for design according to rudimentary rational processes. Any resolution of this paradox would have to explain why an earlier, and unmechanized, building industry and urban structure were better able to meet human needs than the rationalized city of the machine. Moreover, modern urban and economic chaos put into question Adam Smith's rational equation for the future of industrial production: multiplication through division. Smith's formula stated that the division of labor leads first to specialization (division) and then to an increase in production (multiplication). Why, then, did an unequal society, a city without limits, emerge from these rational steps?[36] The investigation became: how could the boundless energy of the marketplace be channeled in such a way as to transform metropolitan chaos into stability, and overwhelming production into consumption for all?

Responses to this problem were in large part determined by the sea change in economic patterns of organization that followed World War I and that made themselves felt in the civilian sector during the European economic revival of the mid-1920s. During that time, European architects became greatly enamored by studies of productivity and optimization undertaken by American industrialists earlier in the century. In the American gospel of rational, mechanized processes, the engineer was in charge. More than any other specialist, the engineer

URBANISME 37

5ᴱ CONGRÈS CIAM PARIS 1937

LOGIS ET LOISIRS

BERTRAND
BÉZARD
BIERBAUER
DELAISI
FAURE
FORBAT
FREYSSINET
GIÉDION
LE CORBUSIER
LENOIR
PY
QUÉTANT
RIVIÈRE
SERT
SYRKUS
TOLWINSKI
VAN EESTEREN
VAUTHIER
WINTER

SOUS LE PATRONAGE : DU MINISTRE DES AFFAIRES ÉTRANGÈRES, DU MINISTRE DE L'ÉDUCATION NATIONALE ET DES BEAUX-ARTS, DU MINISTRE DE L'AGRICULTURE, DU MINISTRE DES TRAVAUX PUBLICS, DU SOUS-SECRÉTAIRE AUX SPORTS ET LOISIRS, DU DIRECTEUR GÉNÉRAL DES BEAUX-ARTS.

(8)
Title page of *Logis et Loisirs* (Paris, 1938)

was the great consolidator of the fragments of the world into an unconscious association, an uninterrupted community of productivity.[37]

Interestingly, the conscious business philosophies of Taylorism and Fordism underlay this engineering gospel. They provided potent examples to architects of how engineering studies of efficiency and optimality could be applied to architectural economy. Rationalization, as understood by Taylor, referred to the widest possible increase in productive efficiency through the systematic deployment of labor. Standardization, in Ford's system, spoke to the potential for the moving assembly line to organize disparate production processes within economical and repetitious norms.[38] Coincident with CIAM's goal of revolutionary functionalism, both American business philosophies called for the greatest degree of industrial change and output through an economy of means.

Rationalization and standardization were touchstones of the CIAM approach to building, reducing building tasks, simplifying functional elements, and generalizing human dwelling habits.[39] Machinelike qualities were the salvation of the building trades: "In order to actualize Taylorism it is necessary to standardize the elements of building."[40] Factory production was similarly recommended to replace "handfertigen Baumethoden" that contradicted machine methods and resulted in poorly made and expensive houses.[41] Finally, it was argued that customary building trades (e.g., masons or carpenters) should be replaced by *les monteurs,* intuitive erectors who actually constituted the engineers of the machine-body of world architecture.

This last point is important. Inasmuch as rationalization and standardization were the engineer's gospel, CIAM thinkers sought to expand them into the instinctual nature of architecture. They went a long way to argue, as, for instance, Giedion did in *Bauen in Frankreich* (1928), that architectural construction, akin to other engineering enterprises, was an inner expression of generalizable life forces (*den allgemeinen Lebensprozeß*). Machines were not, oddly enough, mechanically deterministic; they were unparalleled frameworks for the realization of human desire.

This association of life processes with technology was popular among conservative German thinkers of the 1920s. For them, it represented an attempt to harmonize machines with the anticapitalistic currents of the nineteenth-century *Lebensphilosophie* movement. If engineering could be described through words like *Schöpfung* (creation), *Gestaltung* (formation), and even *Seelentum* (realm of soul and mind), machines could be disassociated from the negative abstractions of bourgeois commerce.[42] Technology could become an organic-rational will to power and form. It could become a celestial force.

Giedion's book, although reconciled to the world of rationality and intellect and not the conservative *Volk* (common people), partook of Spenglerian phrasings of mythic creativity.[43] His remarks on iron's *Ausdehnnung* (extensiveness) and *Zusammenziehen* (connectivity), on its "Durchdringen aller Teile eines Baus" (penetration of all parts of a building) were intended to convince the reader of modern technology's organic ties to all aspects of life.[44] Iron's plasticity and universal applicability were used by Giedion as metaphors for the machine's intuitive (and divine) restructuring of architecture and city planning. Architecture would neither be the production of singularities nor the laboring toward particularities.

Instead, the machine would phenomenalize building. As Giedion remarked in reference to Le Corbusier's houses, architecture is neither spatial nor plastic: instead, it encapsulates the engineer's gospel of *Beziehung* (relatedness) and *Durchdringung* (pervasiveness).[45] And although as distanced from conservative nationalism as Giedion, Le Corbusier too was haunted by the generative primal powers of machine technology. The transcendent systems of Taylorism and Fordism were a formula for elevating architectural identity beyond the problems of economic ownership and political organization. For the critical congresses of 1933 and 1937, Giedion and Le Corbusier shifted debate on the problem of capitalist urban chaos away from the direct challenge to capitalism posed by architects like May, Schmidt, and Mart Stam.[46] Instead of entrusting the reorganization of the building environment to non-architectural forces, they fought for absolute architectural control.

Disembodied Circulation

The ideas of *Lebensphilosophie,* which swept through architectural culture during the 1920s, had the affect of vitalizing an already mechanized design process. By 1933, architects had overseen a program to eliminate all aspects of design that did not conform to the machine's new Adamic language. As we have seen, these included the principal elements of fragmented bourgeois culture: the academies, the individual, real estate commodification. At this later time, on the sea passage to Athens and back, CIAM argued for a language of the city in more patently biological terms, using the word *Stadtorganismus* (urban organicism) to envelop the systemic relationships between the fourfold complex of urban functions.[47]

Few architects, going back to the Renaissance, had not been captivated by the idea of engendering building through an embrace of the body. Modern architects distinguished themselves from earlier formal fantasies through their increasing reduction of the body to successive definitions of mathematized function and their expansion of the corporeal proposition to encompass the entire city. In this regard, they were greatly influenced by successive campaigns for enhanced sanitation and hygiene since the nineteenth century.[48] To a large extent, CIAM continued these efforts toward the city's reincarnation as a spotless organism. But what would be the consequences when the physician-as-architect was also the ruthless rationalizer and standardizer of all the city's organs and circulation systems?

One aftereffect has been that modernist city planning is better remembered for its destruction of the traditional city than its medicinal balms. The vitalism that underwrote Giedion's and Le Corbusier's association of mechanical technology with creative architecture was as predisposed to surgical removal as reconstruction. At the Athens and Paris congresses, proposals for urban renewal were phrased as the eradication of disease. Acknowledgment of failing organs and blocked circulation was the biological counterpart to discussions on the maladies of academic misdirection, individual arbitrariness, and economic inequality. The blame for high death rates, low birth rates, and rampant infectious ailments (like tuberculosis) fell not on the economic system but on architecture: on its lack of attentiveness to mechanistic and organic organization of city building. The cancer of disorderly city design and growth, like poor personal hygiene and manners, was directly to blame for disease and slum conditions.[49] Such massive urban hemorrhaging, the cardiac arrest of discontinuous design, spoke to the inevitability of a last judgment for architecture. Not surprisingly, mechanized reconstruction accented the interlocking and elemental aspects of urban design: Platonic ideas of lot and block, linear street canyon, and planar building volume. All of these measures partook of customary arithmetic and geometry, but through representations of the mechanized statistical and air view.

For example, especially despised by Gropius were clutter and unevenness, epitomized by "the horrible houses built on rear lots of the late nineteenth century."[50] He blamed small lots as well for uncoordinated, pathological development out of which biological norms for habitation were unreachable. They exemplified how piecemeal and arbitrary development of building masses led to biological ills. In place of them was recommended the superblock. Density was not the problem. To be sure, on superblocks density could be accommodated through a restructuring of building mass and circulation. The ratio of building mass to building area could be reduced, while increases in height could allow for greater populations. The prevailing illusion of this theory was that by inverting dwelling from the ground to the sky, the city's organic body would gain a preferable space for its healthful functioning.

Three cardinal points constitute Gropius's vision for the high-rise city: *Licht* (light), *Luft* (air), and *Auslaufsmöglichkeit* (mobility).[51] The high-rise city proposed by him and others argued for a reordering of the city into two discrete dimensions: a sky zone for habitation, which took maximum advantage of light and air; and a ground plane for recreation and circulation. Using this reasoning, Gropius's advocacy for the high-rise had a clear biological component alongside its sociological one. He described the high-rise formula as follows: "the uniting of maximum standards for air, sun, and plant growth with minimum levels of traffic and economic activity."[52]

Le Corbusier likewise equated healthy habitation with high-rise living. The location of high-rise cities in verdant landscapes had been his great project since the early 1920s. It explains his insistence at Frankfurt that the entire surface of the city should be available for circulation. The ground plane, freed from habitation, could then be regulated as a machine for movement: "The mains of a city will be installed like the organs of a machine in a factory: accessible, open, and reparable."[53] At the Paris congress, similarly, *habiter* (*Logis*) and *recréer* (*Loisir*) were to Le Corbusier the most important issues of architectural and urban design. They corresponded most intimately to his vision of new urban order. True habitation only occurs where dwelling is accompanied by recreation, where houses are bathed in sun, space, trees, winds, water, and views of the horizon—all the elements of recreation.[54]

The fetish of functional elements, of urban organs, lies at the heart of CIAM's reconception of circulation and the street. Narrow, abundant streets of the traditional city mimicked all the problems of the small lot. On such streets, circulation was undifferentiated, leading to slow travel times and an inefficient mixing of traffic, vehicular and pedestrian, local and regional. Frequent street/block intersections also led to auto/pedestrian accidents. Finally, the street siting of residential buildings brought noise and pollution directly into the home. All in all, the traditional street epitomized laborious living.

The solution proposed at Athens and Paris was to eliminate the street and to separate residence from circulation through measures beyond merely building skyward. High-rise residential buildings were to be situated on superblocks and separated from traffic arteries via green strips. The street, similarly, was reconceived into the road. Unlike the heterogeneous qualities of the city street, which encompassed most customary urban functions, the road served circulation alone. In the declarations at the Paris congress, new streets were to be dimensioned solely according to "carefully determined static foundations and preparations."[55] Later, Sert summarized the consequences of this proposal: "The actual function of the street, which is simply that of serving as a channel for traffic, might be independent of the orientation of houses."[56] What resulted was a hierarchy for universal circulation: arterial and collector streets for vehicles and unimpeded paths for pedestrian movement through verdant landscapes. The street, freed from the requirements of dwelling (and for that matter, commerce and other forms of social life), became a channel for differential circulation. As was the case with Gropius, Le Corbusier's high-rise city on superblocks opened itself up to maximum circulation in two dimensions: hygienic air and light for the dwelling units, and mobility within a ground plane resplendent with natural landscaping and specialized circulation. By separating functions, by raising dwelling into the sky, however, did CIAM actually reject its biological metaphor? Unlike the braiding of organs by a universal circulation system in the human body, urban functions were separated. How can this obvious divergence be explained?

The remaking of the ground and sky spoke to CIAM's attitude regarding a building nature made divine. It would create the city as successor to the venerated relationship once held between heaven and the Garden of Eden. The formula for high-rise dwelling in a sky as invisible as it was all-encompassing is a clear analogy to heaven. Such dwelling, in contradiction to all the qualifying gestures that architecture had always imposed on habitation on the ground, its *mythoi,* was as immaterial and essential as divine thought, as the *logos.* Likewise, after the hours of God-like existence in the sky, individuals would terrestrialize themselves within the vast reaches of the forests, fields, and paths that surrounded the high-rise complexes. On the ground, nature was restored to its primeval, unfabricated natural essence. Between sky and earth, then, there would no longer exist an artificial human realm. The CIAM city, in a sonnet that makes scant reference to cultural politics or commerce, brought the city backward to its genesis and forward to its prophetic revelation.

After Impact

Forced totalization is the precursor of lightning demolition. CIAM's monopoly on the definition of modernity, for all its staying power into the 1950s, unraveled as spectacularly as it emerged. The mechanized building nature of the early years already began its path into disrepute within the postwar organization. By the time of the ninth congress at Aix-en-Provence in 1954, the functionalist mechanization of the city was largely abandoned.[57] The dissolution of the organization a few years later was testimony to its failed ambitions. To a large extent, the spectacular rise of wealth in both western Europe and the United States during the 1950s no longer supported the minimalist materialism of the interwar CIAM.[58]

Despite the fact that the CIAM claimed mechanized building as a second elemental nature, its texts demonstrate an inconclusive struggle between understanding nature in its universal and particular guises, efficient and degenerate modes of existence. The organization's heroes, Gropius, Le Corbusier, and Giedion, attempted a purification of building along the lines of that paring down of language sought by logical positivist philosophers. Incorporating the machine into a positivistic program for building, however, brought these same architects face to face with the illogical qualities of everyday urban life. It confronted them with the machine's inherent duplicity. The mechanization of building could never be a literal enactment of soulless mechanism, akin to the formalization of language statements called for in Ludwig Wittgenstein's *Tractatus Logico-Philosophicus* (1921).

Instead, the modernist city was a spiritual creation in a secular age, an avant-garde desperation sheathed in the optimistic raiment of business and technology. The mechanization of building speech proposed a second coming of the age of truthful construction that prevailed before humanity's biblical fall from heavenly grace. Central to CIAM's conquest of the title of modernity was its spectral fashioning of the architect as a divine stand-in, an amalgamation of an avant-garde prophet and a pragmatic machine-maker. For a relatively long period in the

CIAM

age of modernity, these actions resurrected the chronic legend of architecture as harbinger of beginnings and ends.

The divine connotations of its mechanization of interlocking building elements were responsible for CIAM's canonization as modern architecture. Liberating functionalism was a credo without which CIAM would never have gained widespread notice. The machine fulfilled every dream of *elementare Gestaltung,* of a mechanism of forming prior to any concretization of form, prior to any strained laboring with materials. Who, after all, other than God (or an architect-prophet), could accomplish this act?

This mechanism of prior forming denied the overshadowing of the mechanical by the intellectual, what amounted to the subordination of the hand to the mind. From antiquity to the modern era, the mechanical arts had been widely regarded as either merely useful or dangerously deceptive. The mechanical arts, fashioning nature by the hand of humanity and not by the will of a deity, were long doomed to the status of artifice. CIAM, in its time, however, formulated a philosophy of mechanical illumination that erased the dichotomy between the liberal and mechanical arts. Architecture would no longer be trapped in imprudent schemes of carnal becoming, or in questionable defenses of its motherland of necessity. Because of CIAM's materialization of soul in the rational machine and engineer, architects could escape the labyrinths posed by their mechanical labors. The moralized and engineered machine became the heavenly sower and harvester of unified expertise, solving the problem of understanding the mechanical nature of industrial culture in spiritual terms.[59]

Still, unraveling and refashioning the city was a rancorous act. It yielded a biblical repetition of rupture and renewal, faith and disloyalty. At the same moment that CIAM modernism promoted the victorious story of the objective forces of Neues Bauen, it rejected the capitalist building industry, folk crafts, aristocratic norms, bourgeois historicism, and popular mass culture. The magnificent parade of mechanized architecture was a funeral march for nonsystematic modes of building, habitation, and psychology.

The birth of a city of Augustinian purity demanded a denial of the personal distraction and product obsolescence common to urbanism in the age of commodity capital. Central to the machine-concept of an interlocking architectural culture was the usurpation of the libidinal desires and outmoded detours that characterize modern life. Neither distracted thoughts nor discarded instruments were allowed to interrupt the international world modern architecture was shaping.

Scandalized especially was the underground nature of industrial culture that accounted for much of modernity's creativity. A transgression of their earlier avant-garde identities, CIAM architects became over time only too eager to sacrifice youthful indiscretions.[60] Like other totalizing modern projects—Soviet communism of the 1920s comes readily to mind—avant-garde radicalism became incompatible with the realist disguises adopted by mature CIAM after 1933. In fact, the virginal austerity of the functional city may be seen as a deliberate cover-up of earlier, darker ecstasies and compulsions. The fetishes of rational numbers, underlying cadastral patterns, crisp lines, and pristine surfaces were gestures in tune with two and a half millennia of Platonic intimidations of the everyday that CIAM was more than happy to incorporate into architecture.

But, of course, CIAM ended up sharing much with the avant-gardes. Like the surrealists, who sought in other ways to grasp the totality of objective nature, its architects were driven toward an elusive unity and purity that existed before historical diffusion at Babel, an immediacy of mind and body preceding the corruptions of historical culture. Similar as well to images of the *flâneur* amid the overpowering crowd, CIAM advocated passive urban experience for the populace. Total control over the shaping of the social city was ceded to architects so as to free immaterialized individual space. Ultimately, and because of its credo of the liberating machine, the modernist city was all about aesthetics, imbued with its secular theology of escape and isolation from the political world. CIAM architects were the *Luftmenschen* of their time, aerodynamic drafters of a city of number, line, and plane intended to dissolve the thick mass of the lived city within the immeasurable space of the mind's wanderings.

CIAM

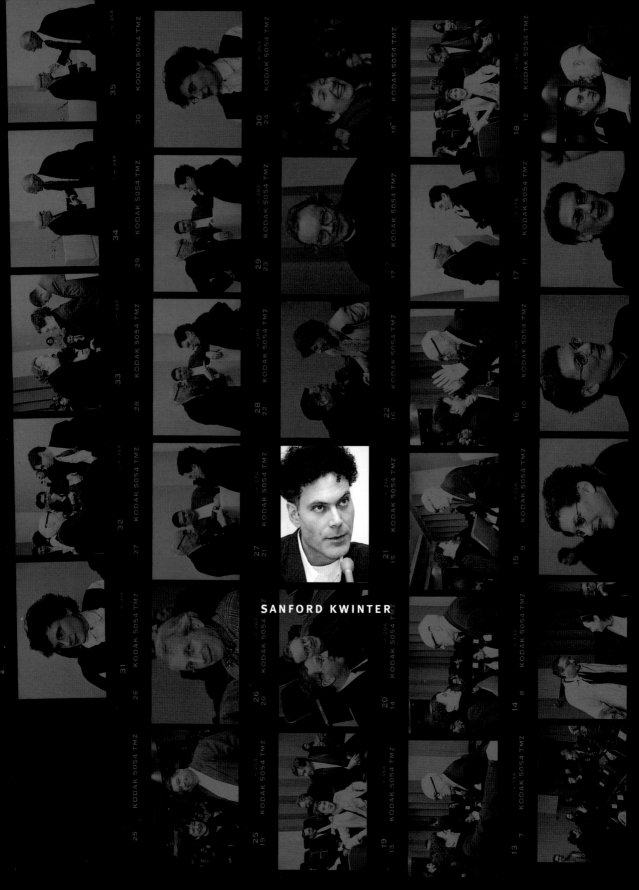

SANFORD KWINTER

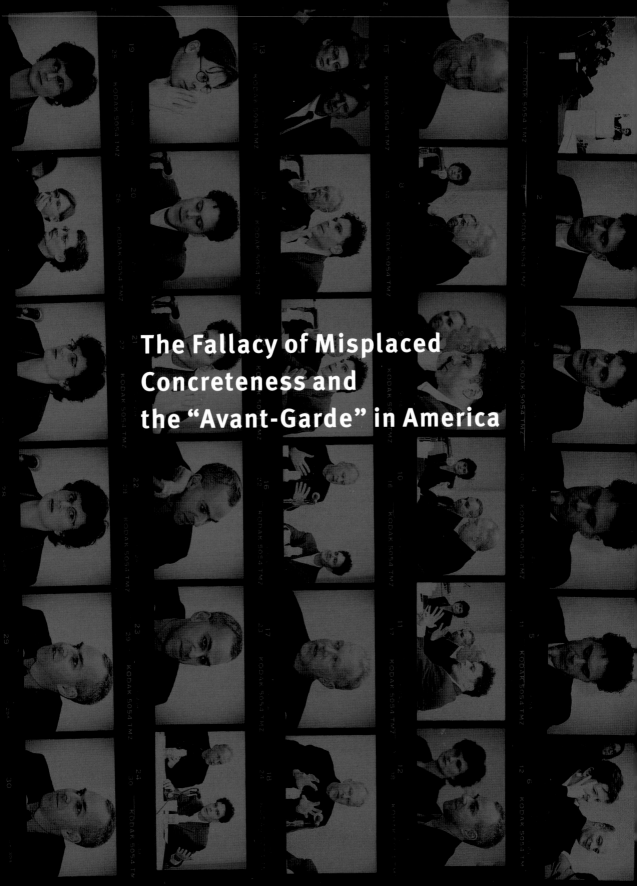

The Fallacy of Misplaced
Concreteness and
the "Avant-Garde" in America

Der Puritaner wollte Berufsmensch sein—wir müssen es sein.
— MAX WEBER, 1921

The early years of the 1920s saw the birth of a plethora of intense new terms and phrases: "montage," the arraying and release of motive images in controlled, modulated succession (1929); the curiously arcane "timbre melodies" and "atonalism" of musical composition (1922–24); "Joycean," a term at once of endearment and of derision in literary circles; "quantum mechanics," which posed as systematic a challenge to epistemology as it did to physical theory (1922); and among these others, probably the first use in English of the adjective "avant-garde" (as an adjective in 1925, as a noun in 1915). These words emerged together in mood, place, and time, and they belong well together, so long, I will argue, as the words "architecture" and especially "America" are kept far away. The 1920s were a time of very profound changes in lifeworld and worldview, and a time of many changes that sought to appear so, but were not. Today, however, we are continually censured when we wish to speak earnestly of an avant-garde—by sterile, know-it-all academics who manage to feel intelligent only when disqualifying what they hold to be illegitimate passions possessed by others—yet to speak of an avant-garde, today, is both a right and a political obligation. This obligation must carry us beyond the claque and ressentiment of revisionist critics and historians; it must carry us to principles, and more important, to fundamental questions. To speak about the avant-garde is therefore more difficult today than formerly; it now entails ethical and metaphysical dimensions, dimensions of intellectual commitment that go beyond mere sociology and aesthetics. The very phrase "avant-garde," after all, represents not only the idea of directed novelty, that is, not the idea of any-novelty-whatever, but specifically novelty in the service of hope. The notion of the avant-garde is useful for us today precisely for its capacity to oppose conceptually these two types of novelty, these two types of historical change: on the one hand, the breaks of fully geological magnitude out of which systematic human transformations become genuinely possible, and on the other, those fully routinized forms of innovation that do little more than mark the onward march of technological, economic, and scientific rationality.

To return to the list of words introduced at the outset: each is drawn from a domain of cultural and scientific research; each marks what might be called an internally troubling development for the context or discipline from which it emerged. These diverse, individual perplexities can be said to have in common a projection into the world of a logic and a set of material givens that are irreducible to, and that fundamentally supersede, the classical framework of their respective traditions that would normally be relied upon to give them sense. James Joyce, for example, quite simply did not write (panoramic) novels, and the world, according to quantum mechanics, is made not of solid particles, but fluxes and waves. What is at stake in each case—and I include here the projection of motion into the culture of the picture and of atonal or dodecaphonic composition into the aural chromatic scale—is a radical transformation of what is seen to constitute fundamental relations in the physical world. The problem of physical existence, expressed simply in the questions "How does a physically existent thing present itself to us, how is it organized, and how is it to be conceived?," clearly goes back to the time of the Greeks (notably to the pre-Socratics, and to Pythagoras), but the question to which our own lived-world forms the fully expressed answer is one that intimately concerns the status of our world's invisible but pervasive armature—embedded mathematics. The relationship between the mathematical and the physical must form the framework against which any modern understanding—aesthetic as well as scientific—must invariably be placed. For the most part, however, this is neither obvious nor conventionally recognized by analytical practice. On the contrary, the real strangeness of this intimate relationship is by now mostly obscured, in fact somewhat insidiously so. Arguably, we would scarcely be aware of it at all were it not, in fact, for the spontaneous emergence of the historical avant-gardes over seven decades ago.

The story, in grossly abbreviated form, unfolds something like this. In the early seventeenth century, a genuine revolution in thought took place that has come to be known as the Scientific Revolution. The Scientific Revolution brought an entirely new conception of nature—already clearly visible in Nicholas of Cusa's fifteenth-century vision of the universe as a mathematical construction of circles, centers, infinities, and spheres—to the work of Galileo, Descartes, Leibniz, Newton, and a great host of others for whom nature would ever after appear as the ordered, mechanical expression of mathematical relationships and laws, and who themselves produced a never-ending, ever-refining stream of numerical formulas to mirror it. Nature was seen, according to the Platonic metaphysics that had newly and effectively superseded the more dynamic and qualitative Aristotelian one that preceded it,[1] as an intricate but unmoving and changeless structure (Descartes' *res extensa*). Thus, as science and philosophy proceeded on their converging and world-building courses, the physical came more and more fully to be identified with the mathematical. It is this fundamental

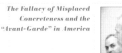

relationship perhaps more than any other that found itself radically destabilized by the cultural and intellectual developments of the 1920s. Among philosophers, Nietzsche, Bergson, and Ernst Mach had anticipated the crisis in scientific knowledge that emerged out of the nineteenth century, but only Alfred North Whitehead, in the 1920s, recognized that the challenge of these transformations could be met only with a total rejection of the metaphysical system upon which modern science had been based since its formation in the seventeenth century. For Whitehead, what had emerged was a pressing, even epochal, need for a new metaphysics of nature.

Whitehead's work between 1919 and 1933—from *Enquiry Concerning the Principles of Natural Knowledge* through *Adventures of Ideas* and comprising the total cosmology of *Process and Reality* and the abbreviated Lowell Lectures given at Harvard in 1925, *Science in the Modern World*—dealt primarily with the metaphysics of physical reality, the status of physical entities, and the specific problem that concerns me here: the question of what constitutes "concreteness." Whitehead's inquiry into concreteness begins with a general critique of the seventeenth century's abstractive notion of space as expressed in what he calls the doctrine of "simple location":

> To say that a bit of matter has *simple location* means that, in expressing its spatio-temporal
> relations, it is adequate to state that it is where it is, in a definite finite region of space,
> and throughout a definite, finite duration of time, apart from any essential reference of the
> relations of that bit of matter to other regions of space and to other durations of time. [2]

A few years earlier, Whitehead had argued that it is a fundamental—and generally unexamined—given of the schema of traditional scientific explanation in terms of time (homogeneous), space (inert), and material (matter, ether, electricity) to be based on the idea of a pure, or material, extension that has as its subtext the principle of *disconnection*. [3] In other words, according to the modern "materialist" view, the physical world is made up of discontinuous substance, isolated points, and univocal relations. To make very clear what he means, I will provide another simple example. Mathematics for Whitehead (coauthor of the *Principia Mathematica* and a mathematical physicist himself) represented an immensely powerful tool of abstraction, allowing the relation of things of concrete fact (*relata*) that are not otherwise relatable through mere intuition or sense data. The person, he points out, who noticed "the analogy between a group of seven fishes and a group of seven days made a notable advance in the history of thought."[4] But at the same time, he stresses, in the concrete reality of immediate experience, that is, among the primary elements of nature, "there is no element whatever which possesses this character of simple location."[5] It is not, of course, that scientific expression is in error; it is simply that science in its essence is a technique of "constructive abstraction." We can indeed, and without inordinate difficulty, arrive at simply located bits of material, *but only in and through constructive logical abstraction*. The problem is that we can never arrive at such simple location in the naturally occurring physical world itself. The fallacy to which this situation almost invariably gives rise, and the one into which the seventeenth century and the subsequent tradition of scientific inquiry categorically fell, was, *in their metaphysics*, to have mistaken what is abstract for what is concrete.

To this conundrum Whitehead gave a label: the Fallacy of Misplaced Concreteness. In essence, it decries the systematic self-delusion on the part of a lengthy, seminal philosophical tradition, the fallacy that space and time are simple, inert, and serve as a detachable substrate to the events that take place on or within them. The theory of motion, for example, was not an easy problem for the seventeenth century. At the very least it necessitated a coherent and defensible theory of *place*, a datum as it were, in relation to which the concept of movement could be extracted as an abstractable numerical value. Thus, the mechanist Descartes could do no better than to describe motion as "the transference of one part of matter or body from the vicinity of those bodies that are in immediate contact with it, and which we regard as in repose, into the vicinity of others."[6] What for Descartes was still just a vestigial potentiality in passive, indeed inert, "repose"—he had, after all, not fully abstracted the difficult concept of place from things—would later, in the hands of Newton, become a total conceptual and immaterial construct, that is, an *absolute*, and a divine one at that.[7] Motion was stripped of any of the qualitative, transformative values with which it was still endowed in the Aristotelian-medieval worldview; its effects were now sequestered within the numerical construct that descriptively linked discrete figure to impassive ground. The schema of the seventeenth century was in this way completed; the enormously efficient feat of abstraction had yielded a functional polarity: *matter* with its simple location in absolute space and time on one side, and *mind* (*res cogitans*), active and functional but entirely placeless and distinct, on the other. This, according to Whitehead, is what our philosophy and popular metaphysics have inherited: a false dichotomy, sterile dualisms, and the

endless confusion introduced by the ascription of misplaced concreteness to what is only the modern scientific epistemological scheme. The Fallacy of Misplaced Concreteness, and the culture of inquiry that grew around it, have placed any possible apprehension of real physical reality beyond the scope of modern thought. Between the terms of this disfiguring dualist (matter/mind) abstraction, however, Whitehead claimed, "lie the concepts of life, organism, function, instantaneous reality, interaction, order of nature, which collectively form the achilles heel of the whole [modern] system."[8]

What then is the actual physical existent? Where does real concreteness lie? It is not hard to guess from the assertion quoted above that it may be found neither in extension nor in mind, neither in space nor in time—for these are but technical abstractions from more primary dynamic phenomena:

> The actual world is a manifold of prehensions; and a "prehension" is a "prehensive occa-
> sion"; and a prehensive occasion is the most concrete finite entity, conceived as what it is
> in itself and for itself, and not as from its aspect in the essence of another such occasion.
> Prehensive unification might be said to have simple location in its volume A. But this would
> be a mere tautology. For space and time are simply abstractions from the totality of prehen-
> sive unifications *as mutually patterned in each other*. Thus a prehension has simple location
> at the volume A in the same way as that in which a man's face fits on to the smile which
> spreads over it.[9]

What does this tell us? Firstly, that "concrescence" comprises the primary activity and fact of nature, that nature's concreteness may legitimately be found nowhere else than in its *activity*. Nature is first and foremost *process*, or rather, it is a structure of evolving processes, here described as the ceaseless formation of prehensive unifications. Now every prehension is a unity, indeed, prehension by definition consists in the very act of forming actual unities from all the possible perspectives distributed within the world's prehensive manifold. Unification should be understood here in terms of "connectedness,"[10] the type of connectedness that may be said to hold between the elements that come together to form a single event. Thus the event in Whitehead's cosmology may be understood as "the emergence into actuality of something." What this something is, and where it comes from, I will explain below. The concrete "event" in Whitehead's cosmology is meant to replace the abstract notions of space, time, and object, while the concept of "organism" is made to represent the "concrete endur-ing entities" that are the full expressions of all concrete occurrence. Whitehead shows that the classical space and time of the modern scientific era are at bottom techniques of separa-tion: things are separated in space as they are separated in time. But things are also *togeth-er* in space and in time, and it is to this aspect that the "prehensive character" of space-time refers. Now in addition to the "separative" and "prehensive" characters, there exists yet a third, the "modal" character, to which we must turn our attention. The modal character con-cerns what I will call a substrate activity of nature or, to speak more loosely (and germanely), of space. This substrate activity has to do with the impossibility of speaking strictly about a point in space-time (simple location) without reference to its embeddedness, that is, its *relations* with other points both distant and near. After all, a volume, as Whitehead points out, cannot be conceived of simply as made up of a multiplicity of points, because points are by definition empty, and a volume is manifestly a concrete fact of experience. Of what, then, is it made up? The answer is that a volume is made up of parts, though not in the sense of a simple aggregate to which things are merely added, but as an entity compounded of a selec-tion of many aspects that impress themselves (within the prehensive event) into every other part. Yet the true concreteness of the volume is not here either, but in its evental appearance as organized or "patterned" at a given place: If A and B are parts of the volume C—for exam-ple, an auditorium—A may be understood eventally as presenting an aspect of itself to C just as B does. But a specific relation also exists between A and B, again comprised of that particular aspect that each volume may be said to have from the standpoint of the other. This relation AB must also be understood as impressing its contour into volume C. The as-pects of A, B, and AB from the standpoint of C contribute to, or partake of, the essence of C by means of what is called their "modal ingression." Now it is important to understand that not every possible aspect of volume A or region B is active in C, but the degree to which some of their potential aspects do ingress, or to which they *enter into composition* with our volume C, they may be said to be *individualizing* entities rather than simply individuated ones. The important thing to grasp here is that they are actively expanding and becoming when grasped or prehended into unity, which is to say, when they burst into actuality by taking on and contributing specific (selected) determinations. The actual(-ized) unity is therefore an *acting* or an occurrence; it is the organism-event understood as the concrete structure or scaffold of interlocked evolving processes. To extend Whitehead's example given above, we might say that what we have to do with here is the reality of the smile onto

which the face is caught, not that of the face from which, in the habitual and disfiguring (so to speak) materialist mode, it would otherwise be said to be abstracted.

Concreteness in the final analysis consists in the process by which general "simples" become realized or expressed in specific prehensive events. The connection between regions of the physical world, of nature, and between the substrate of so-called eternal objects that lie awaiting determination through actualization and the prehensive occasions that receive them, is real. This is the second, and by far the most difficult, meaning of the Fallacy of Misplaced Concreteness. According to this doctrine, metaphysics has mistakenly ascribed concreteness to compound entities rather than to the substrate *activity*, that is, to the realization process or to the "becoming" that shaped them. But the unity of the event is more directly derived from the multiple ingressions or the plurality of modes. To put this more simply: concreteness is rooted in internal relations. [11]

Every prehensive event is an organism. As Whitehead wrote: "Biology is the study of the larger organisms; whereas physics is the study of the smaller organisms." What he means primarily is that the plan of every whole influences the character of its parts by means of the given pattern, the routes, by and through which they interact. The parts in an organism are continually *acting upon* one another. Their relations with one another actually contribute to, and determine, their respective essences. The unity of the prehensive event is a seizing together of aspects or relations between things; everything is determined—by deformation and limitation or selection—by everything else. This interfusion and mutual emendation of events through their compound relatedness is, in fact, our elusive real concreteness in its most simple form. Metaphysics has failed to ascribe concreteness to this, the most fundamental mode of being of the physical world.

In summary then, it is the failure to recognize the primacy of relations, and the failure to recognize the substrate process or agency that ensues from these, that constitute the Fallacy of Misplaced Concreteness, or the failure of traditional metaphysics to account for real physical existence in its dynamic heterogeneity, organicity, and multiplicity. The very concept of an order in nature could, for centuries, not even be posed coherently, let alone the theory that nature might first and foremost be conceived as the locus of organisms in the process of development. [12]

* * *

By the 1920s a new movement, mood, and style, and many lucid proclamations, had emerged in architectural milieus in Russia, France, Italy, Germany, Holland, even in America. The European movements had roots often, yet not always, in political and social developments, but none failed to engage revolutionary ideas of cosmology derived from physics and philosophy, or from the social sciences. Architecture sought emancipation from restrictive historical programs of all types, while modernization was embraced as if it were a salvational religion. Technical innovations, while not the cause, certainly provided much of the fuel—material and intellectual—that drove the movement, and helped confuse what the word "modern" would thereafter come to mean. The modern movement had many chapters and many parts, but collectively, at least for a time, it may be said to have formed a coherent project: the search for new fundamental principles through which the physical world might appear both to us, and for us, as open, changeable, and especially, free. But this program and its clear aspirations cannot be separated from adjacent social and civil developments on the broadest possible scale: to wit, the systematic rise of the modern scientific bureaucracy, the appearance of what the great sociologist of religions and economic historian Max Weber would call that "precision instrument" of formal, technical, and political rationality. Though there is neither the space nor the need to present a full analysis here, I will limit myself to two points that relate to Whitehead's problematic, and to the fate of modernity in America.

Modern bureaucratic organization as it arose in the nineteenth century, and as we have come to understand it through the analysis of Marx as well as of Weber, may be said to be based on the two principles of simple location, that is, on formalisms of separation and abstraction. Bureaucratic organization entails separation in the sense that it both effectuates and exploits what Marx called the separation of "producers from the means of production," but here a more complex and nuanced *civil* separation is implied—that of civil servants and specialized administrators from the means of public administration. Abstraction is played out more obviously as the abstraction of concrete, spontaneous—what Weber would occasionally call "Faustian"—humanity, first into degraded *Berufsmenschen* (specialized or vocational individuals, or etiologically, those subject to divine obligation or "calling"), and finally, by their reduction through abstract regulation and rational calculation, to the status of mere administrated entities or "files." The spread of bureaucratization is inseparable from modern capitalism (indeed its roots are commonly associated with the rise of the money economies from as early as Roman times), inseparable from the secular rationalization process that in the West has focused powerfully on the domains of politics, industry, and most notably, the law. Yet these processes, which can be reduced to a single idea—the rationalization of action—have penetrated in an almost unfettered manner into all spheres of culture, including music, literature, and of course, over and above all others, architecture.

Now this phrase, "the rationalization of action," is not one to be passed over quickly. It tells us that in our cultural world there exist formal entities that are capable of inducing strictly precise behavioral routines and codes of conduct. We are not shocked when told that religious doctrine or systems of belief belong to this category of institution, but we are more surprised to learn that formal structures of social organization as mundane as public administrative apparatuses draw upon, and organize, these same "irrational" or magical forces. [13] Modern bureaucracy, which Weber himself compared to the advent of the industrial machine in recognition of its clear technical superiority over all previous systems of production/organization, is entirely oriented toward submitting social conduct to rationally calculable principles. Such an operation does not merely assume that both objects and humans behave in equally predictable, quantifiable ways; it firmly cultivates and induces such types of predictable behavior. It is, of course, only the *ethic* of Protestantism that is required in order to forge a *spirit* of capitalism; in other words, it is a relationship of dynamic formalisms (even if life-hating ones) whose substantial prescriptions and constraints remain for the most part atmospheric and invisible.

The "rationality" of bureaucracy, among other things, lies in its arguably democratic capacity to regulate *generally*, to transform every *individual* case into an abstract member of a *category*. The reduction of specificity, and the meticulous application of a fixed, preexisting regimen of administrative protocols ("the exact execution of the received order"—Weber), are the social equivalent of numericalization (quantification) in industrial and experimental scientific milieus. Indeed, bureaucratization, insofar as it is rational, is the crowning result of the wholesale penetration of modern science and its mathematical substrate into the social sphere. The transformation of magical or religious belief into the decidedly disenchanted but highly effective rationalistic posture toward the world that characterizes modern capitalist organization represents, however, only a redirection of faith, not its destruction.

Modern social life—with its telephones, high-rises, therapists, ergonomic imperatives, actuarial tables, marketing and entertainment apparatuses, etc.—is fraught to the point of saturation with scientific principles, yet it is not necessary that their equations be explicit or visible to us for our conduct in the world to be entirely governed by our implicit faith in their existence. The world- and event-continuum is quite simply no longer even remotely believed to be made up of mysterious and intractable anomalies, special cases and magical forces; on the contrary, everything—even the flying circus of human existence—is seen to be calculable and hence masterable by virtue of that very calculability.

It is not by accident that the theory of the division of labor is routinely used to describe both modern bureaucratic technique and the advent of the rational juridico-administrative apparatus. All are based on the actual *instrumentalization* of the Fallacy of Misplaced Concreteness and its system of accompanying reductions. Weber continually decried this process as the virtually irresistible tyranny of the enforced "calling" (that Protestant distortion in which we moderns are compelled to recognize our lives) and the ugly, irreversible ascendency of "the bureaucratic ideal."

* * *

In the 1930s three Americans of position or means set out for Europe in search of a style.[14] Like proverbial rubes in the big city, however, they quickly fell dupe to the cardsharps of history, and unwittingly acted out the very script that Alexis de Tocqueville had written for them a century earlier. What they brought home was not European or even remotely "advanced," but rather a hodgepodge of enthusiastic but mostly trivial insights and frivolous infatuations that amounted to no more than reorganizing and aestheticizing a broad set of plastico-material practices whose specificity, meaning, and historical purpose escaped them, yet whose clear, uninflected forms were easily amenable to the cultural logic of the simple, the efficient, and the slightly sadistic but taut mathematical beauty of administrative space. They brought back to America, in other words, store-bought forms that seemed a perfect fit for what American society had already programmatically forged: "elegant" (one of their favorite words of approbation and ironclad legitimation) correlatives of the numerical space of Taylorist "scientific" management and of the dead, but deadly efficient, homogenizing space of Fordist mass-production/mass-consumption loops.[15] The "international" modernism that

The Fallacy of Misplaced
Concreteness and the
"Avant-Garde" in America

they brought home was unconsciously tendentious and may be seen, in the absence of any alternative critical apparatus of reception at the time, as a vulgar aesthetic alibi for a nascent yet burgeoning new type of cultural institution: the industrial-administrative corporation. The business corporation is a peculiarly modern entity, not merely a huge *Fabrik* or manufacturing enterprise, but a massively specialized society of administrative, managerial, and productive technologies that include both implicit and explicit systematized rules of personal conduct, new architectural forms such as the huge, continuous, upright, curtain-walled fields of indistinguishable offices and files, and a program of uniform, global self-presentation within the public sphere. This latter is itself perhaps the most sophisticated and scientific of all bureaucratic activities: the communication and engineering of identity.

While Europe wrestled with these same developments (more highly evolved corporate entities already existed in Germany and Switzerland), its aesthetic and architectural movements, their representatives and their thinkers, never detached themselves from the dynamics of crisis: social, political, or epistemological. It is known that the American shopping expedition rejected works that bore the taint of "expressionism" even when steeped in the most advanced speculations regarding physical matter in movement, decay, or tension: Mendelsohn's extraordinary "spasm" of 1919–22—the Einsteinturm in Potsdam—would have been one egregious example, as would the startlingly inventive but more heterogeneous experiments of the Soviet Constructivists. It is simply no surprise that Lewis Mumford, the only deeply civilized and cosmopolitan imagination to have been involved in the planning of the International Style exhibition, was compelled to withdraw from the project on ethical principles. Americans, as de Tocqueville well knew, were simply not (yet) interested in ideas.

In assimilating the progressive modernist research that was inseparable from Europe's struggle to emancipate itself from traditional forms of social domination to the pragmatic but predatory logic of the emerging international corporate agenda, that is, to the bureaucratic ideal, an entirely retrograde space was put at the service of social engineers, and the speculative imagination of America's young and spectacularly inventive culture was stifled and shunted back to the sterile utilitarian mechanism of the seventeenth century. In other aspects of its culture, in its literature, music, biology, and for a few decades, its cinema, new languages and material intensities began to proliferate steadily, while the New World's architecture remained merely elegant, effete, brutally corrupted, and if not entirely retrograde, then certainly naive.[16] Architecture in America, because of the untimely meddling of dilet-tante aesthetes, served in subsequent decades as a Trojan horse that in both visible and invisible ways hobbled the American social and aesthetic imagination, even while its cities and its industry were becoming the marvels of the Western world. The false and bland con-creteness that these vain yet grand technological monuments passed off as harmonious and universal pattern was little more than what Foucault would have called the "diagram" of the invisible, routinizing cage within which modern humans unconsciously yet unhappily are forced to live their increasingly petty, bullied, and attenuated lives. It should be clear that I am referring here not directly to the physical works of architecture themselves, nor to the alternative possibilities that undeniably lay poised within them, but to the specific physical argument or modulus that they actually delivered into a complex historical calculus of mo-tives, rationales, and instrumentalities. The question is not whether there was a systematic avant-garde spirit in America in the middle decades of the century—the idea, to me at least, is laughable—but whether the American spatial and physical imagination can yet possibly claim to have recovered from the confusion and ineptitude that was visited upon it.[17]

K. MICHAEL HAYS

Abstraction's Appearance (Seagram Building)

The avant-garde in America is an architecture forced into radical contradiction. American architectural culture is deeply locked into the structure of commodification, yet one effect of this is to release architecture into a certain autonomy. Its autonomy allows architecture to stand against the very social order with which it is complicitous, yet the same complicity racks architecture into an agonistic position—combative, striving to produce effects that are *of* the system yet against the system. There is no avant-garde that is not contained, but also enabled, by what it opposes.[1] Writing sometime after 1956, Theodor Adorno put the point this way:

> Art remains alive only through its social power to resist society; unless it reifies itself, it becomes a commodity. What it contributes to society is not some communication with the same but rather something more mediate—resistance. Resistance reproduces social development in aesthetic terms without directly imitating it. Radical modernism preserves the immanence of art by letting society into its precincts but only in dimmed form, as though it were a dream. If it refused to do so, it would dig its own grave.[2]

Between 1919 and 1922, Mies van der Rohe was already working through the determinate dialectic of resistance versus sheer immanence. Take the 1922 skyscraper project (**1+2**). On the one hand, the skyscraper's newly achieved optics of mechanical reproduction is a thorough encoding of post–World War I society's technical advances out of which Weimar culture was to be constructed. The vivid coordination of the reflective and refractive glass surface, the repetitive steel structural elements and floor plates, the contingent plan and aleatory volume, and the technical form of the high-rise building itself attest to architecture's social power of representation, to architecture's "letting society into its precincts." And that same

representation makes its own contribution to the contradictory experience of that society's development, which comprises almost equal measures of euphoria and anxiety, higher consciousness and alienation, and finds its principal location in Berlin.[3] Learning from expressionism's anguished stimulation of the object (itself a projection of subjective disturbances), Mies's glass curtain wall, alternately transparent, reflective, or refractive depending on light conditions and viewing positions, absorbs, mirrors, or distorts the immediate, constantly changing images of city life. The very body of the building contorts to assume the form demanded by the contingent configuration of the site and to register the circumstantial images of the context. But countering expressionism's subjectifying tendencies, the reiterative steel structure mimics the anonymous repetition of the assembly line and poses mechanization as another sort of contextual determinant.

On the other side of Adorno's dialectic, however, on the other side of the mimetic submission to the alienating, reified context out of which it emerges, the skyscraper demonstrates architecture's power of resistance through its autonomy and the independent material existence of the architectural sign. For the other aspect of the project—most apparent in the thick, black, silent elevational drawing—strives toward an immediate materiality of the surface, attempting to oppose and negate the contextual status quo and assert itself as a radically intrusive, non-identical object within an unsatisfactory social and physical fabric, an opaque refusal of the situation that was its sponsor. Mies seems eager here to escape the kinds of interiority bequeathed to aesthetic practice by the traditional bourgeois cultural values from which his early work had emerged—the map of prior experiences drawn by the cultivation of subjective refinements and aesthetic discriminations, the fetishization of experience as a kind of private property, the individualism that substitutes for the life and culture of groups. But he also wants to escape the "incomprehensible triviality" (as Martin Heidegger would say) of the social product.[4] His later work would emphasize again and again its ambition to salvage the purity of high art from the encroachment of mass production, technological modernization, urbanization, in short, of modern mass culture and everyday life. But already in the skyscraper project—or at least in this one of its aspects, the elevational drawing seeming incompatible with the socially "reflective" model—Mies has reserved a dimension of antisociality and refusal. "*Denn wahr is nur, was nicht in diese Welt passt,*" Adorno would say: only what does not fit into this world is true.[5]

The two aspects of Mies's project are, then, the result of the encounter between these contradictory impulses: representation and resistance, submission and refusal, mimesis and expression (mimesis meaning objective dissonance in this case, and expression the subjective attempt to transcribe it). I want to keep this dialectic of Mies's 1922 skyscraper project in the near background for some time for it is a dialectic that he will return to over thirty years later in the high-rise buildings of North America. With this, I offer my preliminary hypothesis: the abstraction of Mies's architecture arises out of a central tension in his overall architectural program, namely, that between the desire to desubjectify the aesthetic phenomena—to displace the subject-centered categories of experience, consciousness, interiority, and the like with the elementary bits and pieces of the object world itself—and the

commitment to produce aesthetic experience—to maintain some last dimension of fully achieved engagement with form that the desubjectifying desire cannot wish to deny. What will happen under this strain is that Mies's aesthetic production will push back toward the ineffable limit-condition of architectural form, to the silence, the abstraction that almost every analysis of Mies ends up declaring.

Fritz Neumeyer's central thesis regarding the reciprocal mediations between art and technology, gravitas and transparency, is not incompatible with what I have claimed for the skyscraper project above. In his study of Mies's writings, Neumeyer has already alerted us to the persistence of their dialectical structure, the "double way to order." Rehearsing a manuscript of Mies's from 1927, for example, Neumeyer notes "a regular two-step of opposites: life and form, inside and outside, unformed and overformed, nothing or appearances, what had been or what had been thought, how and what, classical and Gothic, constructivist or functionalist."[6] Neumeyer continues, interpreting Mies through his underlinings of Romano Guardini's 1925 *Der Gegensatz*: "This conflict of opposites was not resolvable by a redeeming formula. Life could not be thought as a 'synthesis of disparities' nor even as a whole the two sides of which are complementary 'parts.' It exists rather as an elemental form, a 'bound duality.'"[7]

What is more, the oscillations of this same structure mark out the limit-condition of Mies's dialectic (called, for now, a bound

(1)
Ludwig Mies van der Rohe, Glass Skyscraper, Berlin, 1922,
elevation (schematic view)

the aesthetic experience produced in Mies's architecture is different from essences or ideals or some hovering *Geist* waiting to be discovered and made palpable in art form. It is rather an experience well-nigh unprecedented, a blocking together of the aesthetic and the anti-aesthetic: *le fait social mise en architecture*. Mies wrestles with the inescapable contradiction that anything that appears architecturally, thematized through the discipline's signs, risks falling to one side into the net of subjectifying discourse with all its placating aestheticism and visual commodification, and to the other side onto the scabrous surface of the ordinary where it is transformed into a similarly fetishized symptom of objective processes. And yet, architecture cannot abdicate its aesthetic vocation altogether without turning into the unformed; the capacity for representation, fictionality, and imagination is not a supplement to building art but rather its distinguishing feature. Such problems are historicized in Mies's work; they subtend the trajectory of his architectural program begun in 1922 to intersect with another skyscraper in the altogether different time and place of Park Avenue 1954–58, to which we can now turn.

The facts of the Seagram project are well known: Samuel Bronfman and Phyllis Lambert's desire for a building of solid patrician elegance that would rise above the mediocrity of steel and glass in Manhattan; the preeminence of Mies's position in American architectural discourse of the 1950s, surpassing even that of Frank Lloyd Wright and Le Corbusier; the axial, frontal "American"

duality), which is nothing less than *art* itself. But I must be careful with my attributions, for talk of art in general (let's think of it with a capital A) must normally presuppose a primitive accumulation of the capital of aesthetic experience and allude to what you already know about art, must normally make appeals to greatness or the idea or spirit or something similar, and if you don't know about these things already, then no one can tell you. In matters of such art, some would say, there is only the experience itself or its absence, appearance or nothing. I would insist, however (and will try to make the insistence specific shortly), that

(2)
Ludwig Mies van der Rohe,
Glass Skyscraper, Berlin, 1922, model

dialogue of the Seagram Building with McKim, Mead & White's Racquet and Tennis Club, the elementarist "European" play of volumes; and the negative dialogue of the Seagram pink granite plaza with the cavernous streets of New York.[8] I wish only to underscore one of the facts here: that the focus of Mies's attention seems to be—from the start, judging from the documents—the plaza itself, with the building surface understood as a kind of frame or support for that primary clearing in the deadening thickness of the Manhattan grid. The sketch of the plaza is the only drawing "in Mies's hand," as the archival curators say, that sketch and a dozen or so more of sculptures for the plaza.

Look at that sketch (3). Traces of Schinkel are there still, perhaps, attesting to this new architecture's enlightenment pedigree; a Crown Hall project drawing of 1955 is there with its five bays and human figures drawn in and its "universal" space of the clear-span pavilion; the New National Gallery is somehow prefigured, with Giacometti's somnambulators replaced by Mies's own scribbles for sculpture. But mostly there is just the space of the plaza and the few props—edges, planes, and frames—needed for its definition. Critics like Neumeyer would want to see this as a staking out of a "space of contemplation," I suppose, with all the promise for subjective experience that notion holds out. But it is hard for me to understand Mies's *Bilderverbot* as promising anything like experience in its older sense; it attests more to the utter fungibility of subject and object alike.

It is more correct to think of this sketch as Mies's attempt to pass beyond the contradictions of representation and resistance, or mimesis and expression, that are manifest in the two aspects of the 1922 skyscraper project—that is, the model's commitment to the context and the elevational drawing's inexorable autonomy—toward some vanishing point where something

(3)
Ludwig Mies van der Rohe, Seagram Building, New York, 1954–58, perspective of the plaza

like what Hannah Arendt called "space of appearance"[9] and what Mies called "almost nothing" are conjoined and architecture doggedly holds both together in order to deny that either is any longer actually possible by itself. To say it another way: architecture, of course, cannot eradicate appearance altogether (the untranslatable *Schein* being the better formulation for my purposes since it captures the aesthetic artifice or *illusion* of the appearance), cannot become nothing without destroying itself, turning into a reductive materialism, and leaving behind the unmediated symptoms of the unsatisfactory reality it hopes to change. But Mies now regards with distrust any expression (*Ausdruck*), since with that concept comes the nagging worry that what is driving the architectural expression, what is behind the appearance, so to speak, are just those social forces—instrumental technology, the market, the chattering masses, *das Licht der Oeffenlichkeit* (Heidegger)—into whose service architecture is constantly being pressed. This was the lesson Mies learned from the moment of 1910–22, the historical moment of expressionism. If architecture could do away with expression, empty out every trace of agonistic subjectivity, then perhaps some other kind of experience could make an appearance. [10]

This simultaneous production of difference from and integration with the social city, this impossible third term or "bound duality," is what the Seagram plaza, as built, tries to effect. It is a cutout in the city, a literal nothing endowed nevertheless with a positive presence through its material and dimensional precision. What would become the most significant feature of the Seagram Building, its curtain wall of glass and steel, is in the sketch notated by only a hasty, rhythmic zigzag of the pencil. Yet it is necessary that it be notated, for without this veil of matter-to-come, there would be no architectural body to support the aesthetic and social effects, no evocation of any essential truth within the experience of modernity so framed.

Let us then move quickly to consider that matter as it was built (4). This matter, like the curtain wall of 1922, has a mimetic dimension. Here the Seagram's famous I-section steel mullion is crucial; it is the nexus of meaning of the entire building surface: functional, factural, symbolic; utterly commonplace yet raised to representational status in the matrix that is the Seagram's surface; the primary mark out of which the surface's tissue of effects is produced. What is more, the I-section mullion can be construed as the final stage in a set of transformations from a purely technical, instrumental fragment to a new form that organizes the visual exchange between the work and

its reader; that is to say, from the I-section's use as a load-bearing component in some hypothetical steel-frame building to its tectonic role in the trabeated frame and brick infill at IIT (where the I-section still functions as a structural support behind the glass line or embedded in the wall) to the Seagram where the I-section, for one thing, stands as a synecdoche for the steel construction now pushed behind, but by dissolving its factural identity into a mode of address, becomes strikingly more thinglike and present than ever.

But as we move back to view the curtain wall at a distance, the facture of the primal elements is taken over by their visual effect, that is to say, by a logic of surface perception. [11] The series of bronzed-steel mullions now casts shadows on the bronze glass, erasing themselves as figures and the glass curtain wall as ground into a continuous spread of surface. The modulations of the surface—the reticulated grid of welded mullions and panels—as tectonically thick as they are, cannot be read "deeply" like the agonized surface of the 1922 project, which still projects subjective disturbances and contextual dissonances onto the full body of the building. Rather, they can only be scanned for textural information: they are metal-marked calibrations of autonomous vision. Though they trace a manufacture and a certain skill, these marks signal precisely the renunciation of expression and of a controlling agency in favor of an immanent evenness of surface persisting from start to finish as if unencumbered by subjective intent. This, I take it, is Mies's abstraction: the effort to turn subjective experi-

ence into objectivized form and images but that now flow back into the space of experience thus left open.

It is helpful to consider the built wall of the Seagram Building together with Mies's sketches for the sculptures, the wall seemingly come into existence fully conceptualized, with little intermediate development (I could find no developmental drawings in the archives), the sculptures churned out in variation after variation, then finally discarded. The sketches have a kind of hit-or-miss quality: they can be taken as a search or as a catharsis, as if they were never meant to go into production, as if they had flowed from Mies's ruminations over the famous cigar and whiskey in the leisure time still allowed to the social mandarin back in his Chicago apartment. There is this implacable optical field of the building and the unsure plastic figure of the sculpture, the object found *already* and the object not-being-found. And the two make sense only as negations of one another. By 1958, it seems, if there is to be an appearance at all, it will not be built up out of the human body (as the sculptures are, as all of Mies's chosen sculptures were) but rather out of architectural materials already reified, which have already sucked in all corporeality. The abstract field will displace the figurative object, put it in the back pages of the notebook or submerge it in the pools that finally appeared in the plaza in its stead, and then itself take on just enough of the aesthetic substance necessary to remain in experience at all.

One is reminded of Mondrian, who while dancing to his favorite Broadway boogie-woogie, suddenly turned to his partner. "Let's sit down," he said, "I hear a melody." Perhaps Mies's abstraction harbors just this negativity of modernist refusal; perhaps Mies is just like all the others of the avant-garde, only more so. But I think there is more, and we must now push beyond a phenomenological reading of surfaces. The Miesian desire

to build "almost nothing" is at one with his abstraction. If abstraction could finally dispose of any conciliatory melody, but in such a way that you could still dance to it, then architecture might discover some other means of signifying experience;[12] it might put itself in a different sort of relation to the world, create an experience that culture had not yet invented or not yet banalized. "Almost nothing," indeed, because there is not much left to work on.

Abstraction is late-modern architecture's way of working through the social fact, part of its "social power to resist society," to recall the formulation by Adorno with which I began. Manfredo Tafuri, in perhaps the most provocative and most elliptical interpretation of Mies's building in North America, sees the abstraction of its surface—construed as an Adorno-like opposition filtered through Roland Barthes's "white writing"—as the last, desperate non-solution to the historical guilt of modern architecture. Tafuri wrote:

> The "almost nothing" has become a "big glass" . . . reflecting images of the urban chaos that surrounds the timeless Miesian purity . . . in the neutral mirror that breaks the city web. In this, architecture arrives at the ultimate limits of its own possibilities. Like the last notes sounded by the Doctor Faustus of Thomas Mann, alienation, having become absolute, testifies uniquely to its own presence, separating itself from the world to declare the world's incurable malady.[13]

(4)
Ludwig Mies van der Rohe,
Seagram Building, New York, 1954–58

For Tafuri, abstraction is a sign of formal closure and withdrawal in the face of overwhelming historical forces. Architectural abstraction is legitimate precisely because it reproduces the abstraction of the social system of exchange itself, putting the best face on the society's rationalization and planification of the subject, which ultimately disposes altogether with that inconvenience and reduces subjective choice to market desire. At the same time, Tafuri sees in Mies's work a wish to neutralize the social, which is not to say that it succeeded in doing so, or even that such a project makes any sense, for the social will still be found but, for Tafuri, *outside* the work.

I want to modify this account slightly to find the social still inherent in the work. It is therefore important to historicize Mies's effort at Seagram and factor in the anthropological shock of the European mandarin in contact with the new American democracy that is his social surround, and in particular with social practices that assured the destruction of the last remnants of surviving aristocratic forms but came into being independently of the class struggle with an aristocratic *ancien regime*, as had been the case in the Old World. For American popular culture in the 1950s had on its own, so to speak, become as technologically advanced as anything modernism could have hoped for—or better, there was a simultaneous leap forward both technologically and culturally and in which these two developments were consciously linked, resulting in the emergence of what we now call media culture. Unlike in modernism's earlier stages, in America in the 1950s the *image* of mass production and consumption, and the logic of mass advertising and image-reception, were privileged over the mechanical production techniques of the modern "masters." The logic of image reception began to displace that of object production.

Henri Lefebvre articulates for us this new condition as a kind of space that is *produced as it is consumed*. It has a history whose duration is interesting in the present context. "The fact is that around 1910 a certain space was shattered. It was the space of common sense, of knowledge (*savoir*), of social practice, of political power, a space [until then] enshrined in everyday discourse, just as in abstract thought, as the environment of and channel for communications."[14] Around 1910, according to Lefebvre, artists and architects in Europe heralded a new conception of space simultaneous with imperialism, social revolution, a world market, and the explosion of the historical city (and should we not include Mies's 1922 project as one such herald?). By 1950, and most apparently, perhaps, in the United States, the process of global spatialization of society had completely absorbed and superseded the aspects of social life formerly marked by distinctions between city and country, center and periphery, industry and agriculture, commodity and art, and precipitated the passage from the production of things *in* space to the production of space itself.

In Lefebvre's formulation, the production of space is the way in which the society of the commodity maintains itself, creates more room for itself. The space of capitalism depends on global networks of banks and businesses, on highways and airports, on flows of energy, raw materials, and information. "Natural space" and its particularities, such as climates, topographies, and bodies, are irrevocably reduced to exchangeable materials on which society's productive forces operate: ground, underground, air, even light become products that can be manipulated, exchanged, and controlled; space is utilized to produce surplus value; space is consumed in tourism and leisure. Like equipment in factories, the spatial arrangements of buildings, cities, and regions increase production and reproduce the relations of production. Even time is spatialized in capitalism's repetition, circularity, and immobility; distances between things are collapsed and our felt perception of our own place in history is distorted. Lefebvre is explicit about the architectural consequences of this new mode of production: "1. *A new consciousness of space* emerged whereby space (an object in its surroundings) was explored . . . by deliberately reducing it to its outline or plan and to the flat surface. . . . 2. *The facade. . . disappeared.* . . . 3. Global space established itself in the abstract as a void waiting to be filled, as a medium waiting to be colonized . . . by commercial images, signs and objects. . . ." Ultimately, Lefebvre argues (in a harsh criticism of architectural semiotics), "The 'signifier-signified' relationship [dissolved] conflicts into a general transparency, into a one-dimensional present— and onto an as it were 'pure' *surface.* . . ." "Thus space appears solely in its reduced forms. *Volume* leaves the field to *surface*, and any overall view surrenders to visual signals spaced out along fixed trajectories already laid down in the 'plan.' An extraordinary—indeed unthinkable, impossible—confusion gradually arises between space and surface, with the latter determining a spatial abstraction which it endows with a half-imaginary, half-real existence." [15]

Lefebvre's conception of the historical specificity and originality of the production of space—which is lived distinctively and differently from other modes of production, and which finds its ultimate instantiation in America around 1950—counters the standard treatment of space and time as universal, empty containers whose forms structure experience but are not themselves part of that experience. And within his conception, abstraction—very much including its most sophisticated philosophical and architectural equivalents, and especially that of surface—is revealed at another level to be at one with the logic of equivalence and exchange, that is to say, with the logic of the commodity.

The emergence shortly afterward of so-called pop architecture is enough verification of this. And the work of Archigram, the Smithsons, and the Independent Group in Great Britain, and even more so the semiotic surfaces of Robert Venturi and Denise Scott-Brown in the United States are only the most obvious examples of architecture's close involvement with consumer culture and mass advertising and the consequent challenge to the cherished modernist ideals of profundity and autonomy. During the years of the Seagram Building and just after, more intensely than any other time in modern history, architecture itself began to be seen as part of commodity culture generally. Not only does this mean that the aesthetic tastes of the new mass-cultural subject will be different in kind from those of the controlled and more comfortable identities of either the older aristocratic or bourgeois publics; it means, ultimately, the end of any doctrine of aesthetic universals or invariables, the tendency going even so far (as we now know from our postmodern perspective) as to break up the very concept of the aesthetic unity and organicity of the work. It means that aesthetic self-referentiality begins to recede as a possible defense against mass culture.

The reemerging consumer culture of the 1950s that I speak of, with its newly devised strategies of advertising—large-scale color printing on outdoor billboards and electric lighting for advertisement, both on a scale and pervasiveness not imaginable previously—changed the very nature of the experience of urban public space. For now visual reception challenged tactility, and the perception of architectural surfaces began to overtake the experience of urban space in the traditional sense. The extensive development of buildings on the outskirts of the city and the new distribution of services to suburban commercial zones made the control of the quality of urban space through traditional compositional, tectonic, and constructional means more and more difficult. Consequently a split was felt to open between the world of quality building, in the European tradition of *bauen* or *Baukunst*, and the everyday world of the American popular environment; and this would later (with Venturi and others) become a fundamental split in architectural theory.

It is precisely the isolation, self-referentiality, and conceptual opacity of modernist abstraction that has been fixed on by historians and critics as the definitive characteristic of the resistant abstraction of modernism. But I want to suggest that when read through a logic of the surface—a perceptual logic we must now understand as having been given to us by consumer culture itself—self-referential or autonomous is too passive an adjective for Mies's abstraction. Abstraction in its fullest sense as a historically specific mode of organizing both subject and object comes into our perception in forms that are themselves produced by society, not by architecture alone. The experience of abstraction therefore belies architecture's autonomy, pinning that inside and that appearance to its outside, which is the production of space and the nothingness of reification.

I have already made the first of two relevant points about this particular abstraction: that in the Seagram project there is only a visual field so homogeneous, spread out, and intense that one wants to adopt the painting critic's nomenclature and call it optical. There is an aspect of the Seagram that addresses itself to the eye alone, and the result is a new kind of architectural space and experience. But here I am attempting to interpret opticality not as an ontological threshold but rather as a specific cultural response: the surface is the architectural form adequate to the new mode of production—the production of space. A second point is that Mies's use of the tower type, as well as of the grid, here amounts to the appropriation of found forms as if each were a ready-made. Given this second emphasis, this work thus actually shares with pop art and pop architecture a common source—the newly awakened interest in ready-made units and systems—and with that, makes problematic the conventional distinction between the ordinary, functionally and commercially derived object and the rarefied object of high art. And the development of the curtain wall generally is consistent with this dialectic of a ready-made system of enclosure and the production of signs for what amounts to advertising purposes, or in any case, that compare themselves to the surfaces of advertisement. Venturi's famous distinction between the self-referential duck of modernism—a building that speaks antagonistically but only of itself—and the decorated shed of pop—a building that compares itself to other surfaces of the everyday environment—this supposedly definitive and long-held distinction is utterly collapsed. The result is something like what art critics call a "hand-made ready-made"—something that maintains the aspirations of modernism toward a visual logic derived from the qualities of materials and the nature of construction processes but, at the same time, is not impervious to the gritty world of commercial culture that modernism, in its most famous moments, tried to refuse.

The particular experience of this "something," which is at once autonomous and porous, opaque and transparent, which "lets society into its precincts but only in dimmed form," which "reproduces social development in aesthetic terms without directly imitating it" (Adorno), is rather more complex and dialectical than the abstraction that has been fixed on by historians and critics as the definitive characteristic of the resistant abstraction of modernism. For one who would experience this manifestation is encouraged to adopt the perspective of just what is vilified (commodity culture) in order, just maybe, to see its "other." But allow me now to add one more account of abstraction to the list, one that gets at the radical working through of the conjunction of the aesthetic and anti-aesthetic—of art with a capital A *and* advanced technical reification.

In the first chapter of *Dialectic of Enlightenment*, Adorno and Max Horkheimer replay the Sirens episode of the *Odyssey* as homologous struggles of class and aesthetic reception and read the experience of art as a series of cancellations and repressions—the colonization of pleasure by the commodity fetish (experience as the "after-image of the work process"),[16] the denial of happiness yet the holding out of its possible existence in some unrepeatable past, in short, the experience of art not as *bonheur* but rather as only its *promise*:

> He knows only two possible ways to escape. One of
> them he prescribes for his men. He plugs their ears

with wax, and they must row with all their strength. Whoever would survive must not hear the temptation of that which is unrepeatable, and he is able to survive only by being unable to hear it. Society has always made provision for that. The laborers must be fresh and concentrate as they look ahead, and must ignore whatever lies to one side. They must doggedly sublimate in additional effort the drive that impels to diversion. And so they become practical.— The other possibility Odysseus, the seigneur who allows the others to labor for themselves, reserves to himself. He listens, but while bound impotently to the mast; the greater the temptation the more he has his bonds tightened—just as later the bourgeois would deny themselves happiness all the more doggedly as it drew closer to them with the growth of their own power. What Odysseus hears is without consequence for him; he is able only to nod his head as a sign to be set free from his bonds; but it is too late; his men, who do not listen, know only the song's danger but nothing of its beauty, and leave him at the mast in order to save him and themselves. They reproduce the oppressor's life together with their own, and the oppressor is no longer able to escape his social role. The bonds with which he has irremediably tied himself to practice, also keep the Sirens away from practice: their temptation is neutralized and becomes a mere object of contemplation— becomes art. The prisoner is present at a concert, an inactive eavesdropper like later concertgoers, and his spirited call for liberation fades like applause. Thus the enjoyment of art and manual labor break apart

*Abstraction's Appearance
(Seagram Building)*

as the world of prehistory is left behind. The epic already contains the appropriate theory. The cultural material is in exact correlation to work done according to command; and both are grounded in the inescapable compulsion to social domination of nature. . . . Just as the capacity of representation is the measure of domination, and domination is the most powerful thing that can be represented in most performances, so the capacity of representation is the vehicle of progress and regression at one and the same time.[17]

What is produced here for Odysseus alone is nothing less than art itself. Yet, impotent in his bonds, he can only contemplate its contours of pure sound; his experience is utterly hollowed out. ("Not Italy is offered, but evidence that it exists" is the famous phrase from the "Culture Industry" chapter that registers the same domination capacity of representation.)[18] While the oarsmen, like Mies, like the rest of us, whatever closeness to materials and production might be salvaged, can neither hear art's song nor delight in its labor but can only sense that they are missing out on something, *das Unwiederbringliche*, the genuine experience that can never be brought back from prehistory.

But it is important to insist on the thematic integration of what is presented in the quoted passage as two differentiated modes, for the encounters of Odysseus and the oarsmen are but two aspects of the same process, namely, abstraction as the historically emergent form of organizing experience. Marx's painful lesson reappears in Adorno's retelling of the Homeric story, that the experience of the degree of an artwork's concreteness, density, and plenitude, or of its abstraction, dispersion, and impoverishment, ultimately derives from the concreteness or abstractness of the particular moment of society itself (however nonsynchronously it may be periodized). And in modernity, a unified and

substantial center of experience can never be restored but only given as an illusion (*Schein*) through modernism's abstraction. For Adorno, this has everything to do with mass production and the rationalization of the labor process—the equivalence imposed on every dimension of our world—for aesthetic reception itself is structured like the mode of production (even mental processes have been "Taylorized") and the experience of the products of "high" modernism and the culture industry alike is what we might call the reception *of* production at its most advanced. For Lefebvre, it is just the nature of the production of space that it parcel out experience into discrete domains, then homogenize those domains, that it flatten the full volume of experience into surface, then bleach out that surface to form a thin and brittle simulacrum.

But the crucial move of Mies's is to pose abstraction as, at one and the same time, the ultimate achievement of reification—the separation and neutralization of the full range of experience being the precondition of abstract thought—and a historically new experience, the only possible experience adequate to everything we have lost in reification. Here I circle back to the epigraph with which I began: art must submit to reification in order to preserve the possibility of something more true. What results in the Seagram Building is a series of transductions whereby abstraction changes its nature as it passes from the social to the aesthetic and back again. The plaza at Seagram is perhaps the first pulling back from the alienating life of the metropolis, and the assertion of the architectural surface as the support for that space is commensurate with that withdrawal. At this point, however, reification is borrowed back from the social in the form of the volumetric ready-made of the high-rise building and, even more, in the perception of the abstract surface. Then, in a final moment of transfer, reification appears as the experience of abstraction. By *producing* the abstract, architecture acquires a means to escape that same status, to refuse to become a mere thing among things. Abstraction—the pure sound of the Sirens, the organizing absent presence—is the maximal limit of the avant-garde.[19]

Abstraction's Appearance
(Seagram Building)

En⁰/ₐbling Architecture

REM KOOLHAAS

City

The city will always be the screen on which the avant-garde projects its ambitions, against which the avant-garde prepares its (usually futile) stratagems of substitution; who can ever forget Malevich sticking the image of one of his Architectons onto Manhattan's skyline?

But the relationship between "the" city and "the" avant-garde has always been problematic, or rather unilateral—pathetically one-sided. The avant-garde is, almost permanently, in the humiliating position of a lover who is not merely rejected, but worse, not even noticed. The city inspires but it does not respond. In its obliviousness, it casually resists consummation of any of the passions, inspirations, breakthroughs, *transports* that it provokes.

The bottom line is that the avant-garde needs the city but that the city can do very well without the avant-garde.

Mies, 1922

In 1922 Mies designs two tall buildings—one triangular, one formless—with skins entirely of glass which are presented in drawings and models, but in their most memorable versions as photomontages. The aura of the existing city lends both plausibility and genuine shock value to the radicality of his proposals.

Their promise is that out of the stone mass of the nineteenth-century city could rise new crystal forms of transcendent lightness, so light, in fact, that there is no discernible structure in these mutants. They are like glass balloons, dreams.

Le Corbusier, 1922

In 1922 Le Corbusier is working on his Plan Voisin—a series of cruciform glass towers, spaced widely apart. Where Mies projects specific buildings that would revolutionize the city, Le Corbusier proposes a revolutionary urbanism based on generic buildings.

There are two versions of his project: in one his city stands entirely alone—it looks innocent, harmless; in the second a fragment is grafted, again by photomontage, onto the center of Paris, where it looks suddenly ominous, surrealistic, alarming.

Again, the aura of the existing is used to make the speculative come to life, even if the second is programmed to kill and replace the first.

Gropius, 1922

In 1922 Walter Gropius takes part in the competition for the Chicago Tribune Tower with a design of moderately exalted pragmatism. He does not win the competition, even if his tower is eminently realistic.

For Gropius no photomontage, no replacement, no undermining—just presentation drawing, addition, hopefully construction.

Avant-Garde, 1922

The problem for the European avant-garde in the twenties is that it is "inventing" a form that already exists in America—the skyscraper.

Mies ignores it, Le Corbusier denigrates it, Gropius emulates it.

1950s Ties

Thirty years later—which is not long for architecture—three structures conceived by the three great avatars of the prewar European avant-garde go up almost simultaneously in a small section of Manhattan between 53rd and 42nd Streets, Park Avenue and the East River.

Theoretically, these parallel operations present each architect with an opportunity to realize in 1950s America speculations that had originated in the prewar climate of Europe. The coincidence of their coexistence now presents us with a case study of the particularities and practicalities of the "traffic" between avant-garde notion and concrete object—Europe vs. America—that is the theme of this conference, and a rare chance to compare their relative merits.

Each European architect is assisted—but that is not always the word—by American *enablers*, so-called local architects from New York.

Mies builds the Seagram with Johnson as co-architect, Le Corbusier "invents" the forms that Wallace Harrison "steals" to realize the U.N., and Gropius "comes on board" with the American team of Emory Roth to build the Pan Am Building.

Were these three towers the major statements that could be expected? Did hybrids of European genius and American know-how create masterpieces? Were these buildings evidence of modernism's second wind, this time in the New World? Were they an ultimate homecoming for the skyscraper: American impulse, enhanced by European vision, finally fabricated on an island of mythical pragmatism?

U.N. 1950

The tragedy of the U.N. is the beauty of its location. Instead of an aggressive implantation in the grid—a U.N. *anywhere*—the complex is dissociated from the city. But after a long, "fruitless" search, "Le Corbusier" is happy with the "best" site in Manhattan—once a fan of the Acropolis, always a fan. His aggression and contempt for the existing city—the U.N. slab blocks 43rd Street—becomes, on the East River, harmless, marginal, an exercise in Manhattan picturesque.

Just before and during the war, the European avant-garde—puritans and surrealists—had come to America. In Wallace Harrison their influences had been effortlessly amalgamated into a fundamental pragmatism—maybe *polymorphous pragmatism* would describe the expectant recombination with which America was ready to embrace newness in the 1950s.

In the U.N. it is as if Harrison played innocently with the repressions of Le Corbusier's psyche. Is it too much to suggest that the formal promiscuity of the U.N. as realized—a triumph of unconscious smoothness over angular dogma—had an impact on Le Corbusier's later career in the 1950s?

Was Harrison, inadvertently, Le Corbusier's therapist? By letting it all hang out? Or is this the kind of question that never gets asked, because the terminology of the avant-garde itself implies one-way traffic only, from the genius to the hack, from Europe to America, from the source to the compromise?

Seagram

I have a confession to make. There was no building I was more eager to see when I first came to New York than the Seagram and there was no building that left me more baffled. In spite of its obvious beauty, I did not "get" it.

It is only very recently that I have been able to identify possible explanations for the embarrassing moment where what you most *want* to admire somehow underwhelms.

Could the initial disappointment of Seagram have been related to Mies's inexperience? Was he anxious about his first encounter with New York? Would the city yield to truth or would Mies yield to the city?

Seagram is Mies's first office building, the first of his buildings that had to be inscribed within the romantic straitjacket of Manhattan's 1916 zoning law—pyramidal in section, orthogonal in plan. Mies hides the evidence of the obligatory ziggurat behind the vertical thrust of the Seagram's shaft.

There is an *un-Miesian* theatricality to the whole effort, an effect of *mise-en-scène*: not "Look, no hands!"; you *see* the hands. The famous plaza is actually a device that blocks, through the positioning of the pools, visual access to the lower masses that Mies would clearly prefer not to be there.

The cliché is to talk of Mies in terms of monoliths—glass monoliths. There are no urban complexes that I like and admire more than the Federal Center in Chicago and the Toronto Dominion Center—modernist episodes slipped by stealth into the city. The buildings all look *dark* and mysterious. Life is suggested but somehow in recesses, in the depths.

What is the essence of the Miesian monolith? No falsehoods. In such a monolith the core is a massive vertical shaft of travertine, the skin a web of I-beams, the glass a dark shield that spares the world a too-intimate confrontation with what happens inside, and the floors solid sections of presumably of steel and concrete.

In one essential respect Seagram does not conform to the prototype: its ceilings are not massive slabs but light boxes; they destabilize the equation, fragment the monolith. Those luminous ceilings represent an almost exhibitionist display of the false ceiling, and the theoretical Mies—"Beauty is the radiance of Truth"—is incompatible with any kind of falsehood.

Through the combination of electric ceiling and bronze glass, the effect of Mies's other towers—darkish monolith by day, erratic pattern of horizontals by night—is replaced by a twenty-four-hour insistence on the accumulation of vertical plates. The Seagram is always nocturnal, a day-for-night building.

Because of its ceiling, the Seagram is no longer a dark whole. We know that it is a place for serious business, but its ceilings could also exist in a beauty parlor.

Is it Mies? A hidden return to the 1922 crystal mutations? Or is it post-Mies? Johnson speaks, significantly, of a period "before" and "after" Mies's return to Chicago during the Seagram's design in a tone that implies the suspension of a parental regime. Was there mischief? Philip, in his eagerness to accumulate even unflattering interpretations, would probably happily support a reading of himself as a baby-sitter tampering with his charges.

It could be, he suggested only three days ago, that the luminous ceilings, invented by the light expert Kelly, were thought of *after* Mies's departure to Chicago. They were, he remembered, discussed "over the phone."

But maybe assuming Johnson's touch is too simple. From the 1930s when he began "working" with Lily Reich, on, Mies left the theatrical to others—perversion by proxy. From her silk and velvet to Johnson's chain mail in the Four Seasons, what is the connection? Who took advantage?

Pan Am

Whatever its architectural clumsiness—and the details are atrocious—as an organization the Pan Am is the purest realization of a futurist avant-garde diagram: the metropolis as an exhilarating machine for the exacerbation of business on all possible levels. A project that straddles, orients, accommodates flows in a way that we now routinely call Deleuzian.

The largest building in the world is so effortlessly integrated that it is, ironically, both unavoidable and hard to locate. The biggest building in the world leaves no footprint. It is a disappearing act, *an apotheosis of background.*

It is one of those ironies of history that the one operation that could be called revolution-ary—the biggest building in the world on the most congested site in the world, that embod-ies in its section the most fully developed representation of the "metropolitan," that spans the distance between the earth and the sky from the underground trains to the helicopter—has been lost in a fog of indifference, strictly (or can one by now say "merely"?) through its lack of architectural merit.

Conclusion

In this triple confrontation between architects and city we find instructive couplings: Le Corbusier's speculative frenzy rendered useful by the Wasp efficiency of Harrison; the innocence of Mies coupled with the perversity of Johnson—or is it Johnson's innocence and Mies's perversion?—creating a provisional triumph with hovering question marks; the most "spent" of the Europeans coupled with the most "thoughtless" and commercial of American assists producing an unacknowledged, invisible utopia, a section of "pure" avant-garde that we routinely prefer to ignore.

1949

BEATRIZ COLOMINA

Can one really talk about an American architectural avant-garde? And if so, why between 1923 and 1949? What do we understand as "avant-garde," already a problematic category in the architecture of the so-called heroic period, to use the term coined by the Smithsons in their brilliant book *The Heroic Period of Modern Architecture*?

As the invitation to participate in this symposium and book reminds us, "1923 is the year of Le Corbusier's *Vers une architecture,* Mies's project for the brick country house and Lewis Mumford's *Sticks and Stones.*" But Le Corbusier was not American. Despite his serious efforts, with Ozenfant, to come up with an American version of *L' Esprit Nouveau* (the journal where Le Corbusier first published the material later put together in *Vers une architecture*), the project did not take off. It would seem that there was no climate for the reception of his ideas. *Vers une architecture* was not translated into English until 1927 (and in England!). Only a handful of architects here would have known about it in 1923. There was no notice of the book in any American architectural journal. In fact, if one is to take publications seriously, and one should, South Africans knew about Le Corbusier before Americans did. In 1925 the *South African Architectural Record* published an article entitled "The Modern Movement in Architecture." It would take three more years for the American *Architectural Record* to acknowledge Le Corbusier: in an article entitled "Modern Architecture: The New Pioneers," written by Henry-Russell Hitchcock.

Even less known in 1923 must have been Mies's project for the Brick Country House. Indeed, it seems to have passed totally unnoticed, unlike his earlier projects for the Office Building on Friedrichstrasse (1919) and the Glass Skyscraper (1922), which received some attention in the professional journals in America. Their plans appeared in a 1923 issue of the *Journal of the American Institute of Architects* entirely devoted to the skyscraper. While Mies is not mentioned by name in the text, this is the first publication of his work in the United States.[1] In one of the articles in this journal, William Stanley Parker writes that if he were to caption the plan of the Glass Skyscraper it would be "Nude Building Falling Down Stairs."[2] Still in 1930, in an issue of *Architectural Record* devoted to glass architecture, where Mies's Glass Skyscraper and the Glass Industry Exhibit of Stuttgart, designed with Lily Reich in 1927, are featured, neither Mies nor Reich are mentioned by name in the text. As far as I can determine, architects in this country did not have any idea of who Mies was until the exhibition "Modern Architecture—International Style," organized by Philip Johnson and Henry-Russell Hitchcock for the Museum of Modern Art in 1932, which incidentally included the Brick Country House in the catalog.[3]

As for the last reference provided in the invitation, Lewis Mumford's *Sticks and Stones,* under which category does this volume qualify as an avant-garde book?

I could not make sense of the "1923" in the title of the symposium until I read the transcript of a lecture given by Johnson at Barnard College in 1955 entitled "Style and International Style" where, after going on and on about how 1923 was the year in which everything had happened ("there was no style in our times until the year 1923," 1923 was the "magic year"), Johnson says: "I could not, even if I would, tell you just what happened, but I am at home from that year

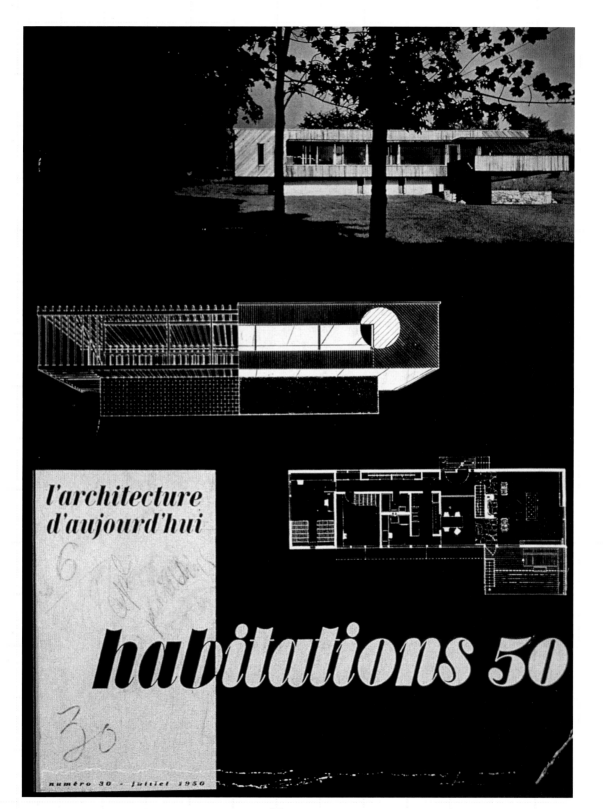

(1)
Cover of *L'Architecture d'aujourd'hui*, July 1950

on."[4] Paradoxically, since all the events of 1923 he cites are European—Mies's Brick Country House, Le Corbusier's Ozenfant House, etc.—Johnson is at home away from home, itself a metaphor for the modern house.

On the other hand, 1949 is a far more promising date for a consideration of the American context, even if we may still have to leave the avant-garde issue suspended. While we are reminded in the invitation of Wittkower's *Architectural Principles in the Age of Humanism,* Hitchcock's *Painting Toward Architecture,* and Johnson's Glass House, all of 1949, only the last reference seems relevant here. It could be argued that 1949 is the year in which things really started to happen in the United States—the year in which the eyes of the architectural world shifted direction. It was no longer America looking at Europe but the other way around. And not just Europe but the rest of the world: all the countries on the edges of the map—Australia, New Zealand, South Africa, etc.—were suddenly looking in this direction. If this is what we mean by avant-garde, then it could be argued that 1949, or in any case, the immediate postwar years, coincides with the beginning of an American architectural avant-garde rather than with the end. Or perhaps it is the beginning and the end: 1949 is simply emblematic of what had happened in architecture in the United States in the immediate postwar years, and what would soon move in a completely different direction.

Take, for example, the July 1950 issue of *L'Architecture d'aujourd'hui,* one of the most—if not the most—widely read architectural

journals in Europe (1). The issue is dedicated to the house, and while practically every country listed has one architect represented, France, naturally, has four, and the United States a total of nine! Moreover, the cover goes to an American house, Marcel Breuer's own house in Connecticut. Breuer got several of his houses published in this issue, including the 1949 House in the Garden in the Museum of Modern Art. Philip Johnson's Glass House was included, Pierre Chareau's Motherwell House, Richard Neutra's Case Study House in Santa Monica and Tremaine Residence in Santa Barbara, Paul Laszlo's residence at Brentwood, several houses by Ralph Twitchel and Paul Rudolph (which is understandable, since Paul Rudolph had in February of the same year edited a famous issue dedicated to the Gropius school at Harvard), and so on.[5] It is a big list, but dominated overall by European émigrés. This is consistent with the standard view that if there is an architectural avant-garde in post-1945 USA it is because of the influx of émigrés. Symptomatically, *L'Architecture d'aujourd'hui* missed the Eames House of 1949, perhaps because, as the editorial announces, the issue was interested in the house as a work of art and not in the question of the mass-produced house. "Such documentation," the editors ask themselves rather rhetorically (if not defensively), "could it be of interest today? . . . We think so. . . . The work of art is gratuitous by definition, but necessary to man."[6] The Eames House would not be covered by *L'Architecture d'aujourd'hui* until December 1953.

It is interesting to note that while the center, France, missed out on the Eames house, for the margins it had an immediate appeal. Reyner Banham wrote:

For most Europeans—and some Africans, Australians, and Japanese to whom I have spoken—the Case Study era began around Christmas 1949. By that time the magazine *Arts and Architecture* had achieved a sufficient degree of penetration into specialized bookstores and architectural libraries for the impact of the first of the steel-frame Case Study houses to trigger—as British architect Peter Smithson said—"a wholly different kind of conversation."[7]

I have experienced a similar kind of reaction. When I went to New Zealand last summer for a conference, they told me how influential the Case Study Houses were in 1950s New Zealand, not just in the schools of architecture but in the profession at large. That fall, I bumped into Robin Middleton in the subway in New York, and he told me that when he was studying architecture in South Africa in the 1950s they used to look at issues of *Arts & Architecture*. In Australia, they reminded me of Harry Seidler. Of course they knew about *Arts & Architecture*—Seidler was published there, he was one of their buddies. In the Netherlands, Max Risselada told me he worked for a year in the Eames office in Santa Monica. So if *Arts & Architecture* and the Case Study Houses had such an enormous impact in the 1950s throughout the world, how come we still know so little about them?

That first steel house that Banham refers to as having triggered, in Peter Smithson's words, a "wholly different kind of conversation" was, of course, the Eames House, number 8 of the Case Study House program in California, into which the Eameses moved on Christmas eve 1949 precisely. The Case Study House program was, as Banham noted, "overwhelmingly Charles and Ray Eames in foreign perception."[8] That explains why for-

eigners thought of the program as starting in 1949, even if it had actually been January 1945, a few months before the end of the war.

Not exclusively a West Coast phenomenon, 1949 was also the year in which the Museum of Modern Art built a house by Marcel Breuer (2–6) in its first sculpture garden of the museum (designed by John McAndrew and in 1939). It is important to note that the house had an independent entrance on 54th Street. The visitor was provided with the address, "4 West 54 Street," and was charged a separate admission fee. The house was intended for the commuter, the museum said, a middle-class man in his thirties, employed in the city, living in the suburbs with a wife and two children.[9]

Was this man likely to own modern art? Not really. But he was nevertheless already tied to the museum through programs such as the "Good Design" products initiated by Kaufmann in 1950, which was preceded by the John McAndrew series of "Useful Objects" exhibitions.[10] Among the many consumptive needs of the postwar family was a house, a suburban house, not a work of art. In fact, the museum went out of its way to solicit bids from construction companies to build the house in different versions in the suburbs of Connecticut, New Jersey, and New York.[11] The plans of the house were made available. It was not a unique art object; it was a prototype.

To some extent, the museum addressing the commuter in this way is the museum undoing itself. While there is some art in the house,[12] the television, which was designed by Breuer and featured a proto–remote control, was clearly more interesting to most reporters and visitors,[13] and there were plenty of them. Seventy thousand people went through the house (6). The event also received enormous publicity from the press, popular and professional, national and foreign.

305

1949

(2–6)
Marcel Breuer, House in the Garden,
Museum of Modern Art, 1949. Views, plans,
visitors to the house

PEEKING into Breuer house playroom. It is barred to keep visitors from toys

308

The Museum of Modern Art had reaimed itself at the middle class immediately after the
war. [14] It is important to assess the influence
of the programs of the war years in the museum. Breuer's house was not "the first architectural structure built for public exhibition in
the Museum's first sculpture garden," as the
official history of the museum claims. [15] In
1941, Buckminster Fuller had a house set up
in the museum garden (7). It was developed
from a standard metal grain storage bin and
completely prefabricated. The museum
called it "Defense House." [16] In September
1941, the *Bulletin of the Museum of Modern
Art* explains the delay in the opening of
"Buckminster Fuller's Demountable Defense
House," which had originally been scheduled
for July of the same year: "Navy priorities
have prevented delivery of the house." [17] The
Bulletin of October 1941 shows Fuller's demountable defense house renamed as "Dymaxion Deployment Unit," installed in the
museum garden.

The Defense House was made up of two deployment units whose interiors were reorganized to accommodate a family of six. The
Bulletin argued that the original unit, twenty
feet in diameter, "may serve as a spacious
living room but may also be divided into
three rooms by means of curtains. The
adjoining fifteen foot unit contains kitchen,
bath and a separate bedroom. Shelves,

lighting equipment, plumbing and closets were built
in." The units that were serving as military barracks,
furnishing sleeping space for twenty-four soldiers on
double-decker cots could, the museum insisted, be
manufactured at the rate of one thousand per day at a
cost of $1,500 each. [18] Barracks had been turned into
mass-produced, infinitely rearrangable, modular
housing units.

The house was extensively represented in newspapers
throughout the country. The similarity between reports
("War Inspired" (9); "Comfortable though Bombed";
and "A Shelter in War—a Beach House in Peacetime"
are some of the repeated headlines in newspapers)
clearly points to one source, the Museum of Modern
Art press release. The museum presented this house as
a bomb shelter of sorts—not totally safe in case of a direct hit, but definitely an improvement over traditional
building. "Its circulate, corrugated, surfaces, deflect
bomb fragments or flying debris; its steel structure is
entirely fireproof and its shape and anchor foundation

render it non-collapsible. A nearby bomb hit might cause it to bounce a few inches."[19] But the biggest advantage by far is that it would be unrecognizable by a bomber. Buildings are square. This house, a reporter says, "could be made to look like a tree, or even a hole in the ground."[20] This building is therefore a house in camouflage. Not by chance, the Defense House in the museum garden was itself camouflaged, covered with shrubbery that disguised it from the traditional galleries. The following year the museum held an exhibition on "Camouflage for Civilian Defense."[21]

WAR-INSPIRED

These circular houses of corrugated steel, formally known as Dymaxion deployment units, were shown recently at the Museum of Modern Art in New York as something new in defense housing, suitable for use as air raid shelters, troop barracks, temporary homes for defense workers, etc. They were devised by R. Buckminster Fuller, who stands in front of one of them with Miss Ann Tredick of the museum.

(9)

"War Inspired," article about Fuller's Dymaxion Deployment Unit in the Saint Louis *Post Dispatch*, October 26, 1941

(8)

"A Peacetime Use for the Quonset Hut," advertisement in *Architectural Record*, 1944

Another precedent of a structure to be built in the museum garden, even if it never materialized, also comes from the war years. According to Peter Galassi, Edward Steichen (later director of the museum's photography department), who had worked as a photographer for the army in World War I and for the navy in World War II, and who had organized at the museum important war exhibitions such as "Road to Victory" (1942) and "Power in the Pacific" (1945), brought a Quonset hut to the museum to be placed in the garden and used as exhibition space. It was part of a program of expansion of the photography department that did not work out. The Quonset hut was in the museum, but in the end it had to be sold at a loss.[22]

Demountable, prefabricated Quonset huts were of course very available in the immediate postwar years. About 170,000 had been produced and erected around the world, many to return to the home front after the war.[23] Already in 1944, *Architectural Record* was printing ads announcing a "Peacetime Use for the Quonset

Hut" (8). And Pierre Chareau used a Quonset hut to build the studio/house for Robert Motherwell in East Hampton in 1948 (a house that appeared in the July 1950 issue of *L'Architecture d' aujourd' hui*).

In fact, the museum garden was occupied by the military in different ways. During the war the garden was used as an entertainment center for troops of all Allied nations.[24] They occupied the garden and the front covers of museum *Bulletin*s at the same time as they occupied theaters of war in Europe. The postwar houses in the garden have to be understood in this context.

The transition from military to domestic is unambiguous in the museum's collaboration with *Ladies' Home Journal* for the exhibition "Tomorrow's Small House," organized by Elizabeth B. Mock, curator of architecture, immediately after the war. The kind of thinking evident in the exhibition "War Time Housing" of 1942 slides into the private construction of suburban houses. The spring and summer 1945 issues of the *Bulletin of the Museum of Modern Art* very starkly mark this transition from war to peace. As the issues appear today in a bound volume, we see, on the left, the last images of war (as represented in the exhibition "Power in the Pacific") and, on the right, the first images of domestic bliss ("Tomorrow's Small House"). Not by chance are the new images for the first time in color.

"War Time Housing," an exhibition organized in collaboration with the National Committee on the Housing Emergency

(shown from April to June 1942), was a multimedia event. As a reporter described it, there were "movies, photographs, models, recorded voices that appear to come from nowhere, sound effects. . . . "[25] A recording of President Roosevelt greeted the visitor at the entrance. The message emphasized that "homes for workers in war industries are an essential element in the whole program of making the weapons of war."[26] The National Housing Administration "spoke with some pride of 'the housing sector of the war front.'"[27] A point brought out again and again is that "wartime housing facilities can be converted to peacetime."[28]

"Tomorrow's Small House" was an exhibition of models, or as they were called, "postwar houses in miniature," which visitors were encouraged to imagine themselves inside (10). As the museum's *Bulletin* puts it: "The danger of realistic models is the easy magic of the medium. The delight of tiny bentwood chairs, workable four-inch lawnmowers and real greenery . . . you must put your eyes just a little above the ground level of the model, then imagine yourself five or six inches tall and walk about each house until you feel quite at home, inside and out."[29] The arrangement of models in the space of the exhibition reinforced that way of reading them. They were installed on high platforms, which brought the floor to eye level.

But who was the museum addressing with this exhibition, with this language? Definitely not to architects, or to the cultivated public that may have seen the International Style show, but to the most general public. Reporters speak of "crowds packing" the exhibition. It opened with eight small houses built to the scale of an inch to a foot, completely landscaped and furnished, all susceptible to prefabrication (except Frank Lloyd Wright's). The architects were George Fred Keck, Carl Koch, Philip Johnson, Mario Corbett, Hugh Stubbins, Plan-Tech Associates, Vernon de Mars, and Frank

Lloyd Wright. Two more models were added later: a house by John Funk and another by Wurster & Bernardi. The original site plan by Vernon de Mars was developed by Serge Chermayeff and Susanne Wasson-Tucker. The exhibition traveled to some department stores, such as Gimbel's in Philadelphia.

Are the houses in this exhibition high art? On the one hand, one finds here architects such as Frank Lloyd Wright and Philip Johnson. Nothing would seem more high art. But then, in the only reference I have been able to find to Johnson's project, Kenneth Frampton accuses it of being "banal."[30] This could, of course, pass as a compliment these days, but the point is that while there are seemingly high-art architects in the exhibition, they do not produce high-art architecture. Proof: these architects do not include these projects in the heroic accounts of their careers.

This helps me to answer a question, a very dumb question I have always had about the house in the garden: why Breuer? Why did Johnson, who had just taken up, again, the direction of the Department of Architecture and Design in the museum, choose Breuer to do this house? Why not Mies, or Le Corbusier? Of course, Breuer had been Johnson's teacher at Harvard, and Johnson has always been sentimental about him. In a recent issue of *GSD News,* Johnson still goes on about how Breuer "was simply the best teacher of architecture [Johnson] ever worked with," about how Breuer was really an "artist in the field of architecture."[31] But he certainly was not Mies or Le Corbusier, was he? Nor was the house admired as a work of art. Indeed, it has

TIPTOE: A pretty homemaker studies an interior

(10)

Visitor peeking into a house model in "Tomorrow's Small House" exhibition, Museum of Modern Art, 1945

311

always been looked down on, even by Breuer himself, who recognized that it was not his best project. What is radical about the house is not the form but its context: the very idea of an exhibition house in the museum's garden designed for a commuter rather than for an art collector (the traditional client of high modern architecture) according to a militarized logic of mass production for a generic upper-middle-class suburb. A house that could be reproduced by anybody, anywhere.[32]

As I have noted, there was another house in the garden of the Museum of Modern Art: Gregory Ain's house of 1950, sometimes referred to as the "Woman's Home Companion" house because of the collaboration of the museum with the magazine *Woman's Home Companion*. In many ways this less-known house is closer to the logic of the exhibition "Tomorrow's Small House" than to Breuer's project. As with "Tomorrow's Small House," the museum collaborated in this project with a women's magazine. Also, Ain's house was smaller and less expensive than Breuer's, which had been criticized even by Eleanor Roosevelt as being "too expensive."[33] We should remember this was the age of the prefabricated house. As Lewis Mumford wrote, "Today almost any vacant corner lot in midtown Manhattan is apt to burgeon with a cozy bit of prefabricated domesticity."[34] In that context, Breuer's house was seen as too exclusive. A few copies were made, one in Chappaqua, another in Princeton. But the house was not for the masses. The one built in the museum's garden was in the end bought by John Rockefeller, not exactly your typical middle-class commuter, who installed it on his estate as a guest house.[35]

Nearly 300,000 people visited Ain's house, which they found furnished down to a black Jeepster in the garage (a Jeepster, Peter Blake, then curator of architecture and design, said, was "a happy adaptation of the wartime Jeep"),[36] grocery bills on the kitchen bulletin board, towels in the bathroom, hangers in the hall closets, and so on.[37] An issue of *Retailing* wrote, "This architecture affects your sales."[38] Sales of various brand-name kitchen products used in the house doubled at Bloomingdale's,[39] and the house was extensively used as the background for advertisements. Newspaper and magazine articles gave complete lists of furnishings along with prices and places to purchase the pieces.[40]

The first color images of Ain's house were presented in the June 1950 issue of *Woman's Home Companion*. The context of the museum was airbrushed to make it look like a regular suburban house. In the article it becomes clear that it was the museum that had approached the journal and not the other way around. The magazine, which calls the house "our house," doesn't push its readers very hard to visit it in the museum: "Even without a visit to New York, you can go through our house on these pages by means of the pictures."[41]

The program of houses in the garden constitutes a shift in the policies of the department of architecture from the prewar years. This shift is perhaps reflected in Johnson's introduction to *Built in the USA: Post-War Architecture,* a 1952 book accompanying an exhibition at the Museum of Modern Art, in which he proclaims:

The battle of modern architecture has long been won. Twenty years ago the Museum was in the thick of the fight, but now our exhibitions and catalogues take part in that unending campaign described by Alfred Barr as "simply the continuous, conscientious, resolute distinction of quality from mediocrity—the discovery and proclamation of excellence."[42]

The department of architecture, in other words, was no longer at war, no longer felt the need to present an avant-garde architecture; it had become a referee. In the tradition of the so-called (by the museum) service exhibitions, initiated in 1938 by John McAndrew and expanded by Edgar Kaufmann in 1950, with the "Good Design" programs, the department's role was simply to point out what was good and what was bad. This pot is good, this one is not. This house is good, this house is not. Can one talk about avant-garde here? Not really. The house in the museum garden is as avant-garde as the pots the institution was endorsing in collaboration with the Merchandise Mart in Chicago.

In his introduction, Johnson was quoting Barr, who had made the point that "the battle of modern architecture is won" in the earlier *Built in the USA: 1932–1944* published in 1944.[43] Understanding the museum's programs as military campaigns was not new. Already in 1931, in his preface to *The International Style,* Barr had identified the project of Johnson and Hitchcock as a military campaign to introduce modern architecture in this country. And when in 1948 Barr opened the symposium "What Is Happening to Modern Architecture?," a symposium organized by the Museum of Modern Art in response to a Lewis Mumford article in *The New Yorker,* he said: "I have read with care Mr. Mumford's piece in *The New Yorker,* which is the basis of tonight's discussion. If we differ this evening, lay to the fact that it is hard for two old soldiers to remember a campaign in exactly the same way."[44]

While this rhetoric is part of a widespread tendency among art historians to use such expressions as "battle of the styles," it takes on a particular resonance when we consider the fact that the so-called modern movement in architecture was born around World War I, and is inseparable from that episode, and also that in 1944, the year that Barr proclaimed victory, the country was at war. The museum was at war, in more than one sense. Not only was it deeply engaged in military programs, but it was also at war with itself. Barr had been fired as the museum's director in 1943. He did not leave, however; he became director of research and in 1947 was rehabilitated as director of museum collections.[45]

The idea of victory pervaded the mid-1940s. From 1942 on, all sorts of advertisements appeared in journals using Vs, from rugs with a big V and three dots and a dash inscribed on them (advertised in *Arts & Architecture*) **(11)** to dresses for victory. And suddenly, looking at the catalog of the 1944 exhibition "Art in Progress," an exhibition commemorating the fifteenth anniversary of the Museum of Modern Art, all I can see is that V, which I never saw before. Could it be unintentional? And back to the Breuer house: what are we to make of that V-shaped roof, particularly when we realize that the first time he introduced this feature (clearly indebted to Le Corbusier's Errazuriz house in Chile of 1930)[46] was in his project for the competition "Design for Postwar Living," organized by *Arts & Architecture* in 1943. Unintentional it may be. But that does not mean that the unconscious is not playing a role.

The way the museum design program emerged out of World War II echoes the relationship between modern architecture and World War I. As I have argued at length elsewhere, architects like Le Corbusier conceived of their architecture as a surrogate military campaign. Architecture is war by other (and more

1919

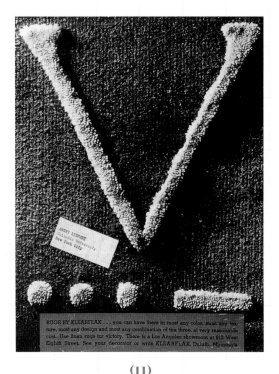

(11)

Advertisement for Klearfax rugs, *Arts & Architecture,* November 1942;
the V and the •••— indicate "victory"

preferable) means. The necessary equipment of modern life was for Le Corbusier that of the soldier. His re-arrangement in the space of a page of *L'Esprit Nouveau* of Hermes bags echoes an image that appeared in the newspaper *L'Illustration* in 1919 showing the equipment of a French soldier during the war.[47] In 1943, the Museum of Modern Art organized "Useful Objects in Wartime," a variant of the series of "Useful Objects" exhibitions, where members of the armed forces provided recommendations on what objects of everyday life were needed in the army.

This mentality of the soldier as client, the civilian as soldier, quickly passed from the wartime exhibitions to peacetime ones. It runs through "Useful Objects in Wartime" to "Wartime Housing" to Fuller's "Defense House" to "Tomorrow's Small House" to Breuer's "House in the Museum Garden" to Ain's house and so on. "Tomorrow's Small House" was the turning point from war to peace. War does not go away. Rather, it is carried out in the consumption of mass-produced spin-offs of military technology and efficiency. The museum's sustained attempt to produce an idealized image of postwar domesticity was, in a way, a military campaign.

This idealized image quickly become a national issue. Indeed, it would become the very issue of the nation, of national identity, as became clear in the "kitchen debates" of 1959. In July of that year, at the peak of the cold war, Richard Nixon (then vice president of the United States) traveled to Moscow to open the American National Exhibition. While there, he engaged in a heated debate with Nikita Khrushchev about the virtues of American life. What is remarkable about this exchange, which has been recently analyzed by Elaine Tyler May, is the focus: "The two leaders did not discuss missiles, bombs, or even modes of government. Rather, they argued over the relative merits of American and Soviet washing machines, televisions, and

(12)

Richard Nixon and Nikita Khrushchev at the American National Exhibition in Moscow, 1959

electric ranges."[48] As a result, the arguments became known as the kitchen debates **(12)**. For Nixon, superiority rested on the ideal of the suburban home, complete with modern appliances and distinct gender roles. He proclaimed that this "model" suburban home represented nothing less than American freedom:

> To us, diversity, the right to choose, is the most important thing. . . . We don't have one decision made at the top by one government official. . . . We have many different manufacturers and many different kinds of washing machines so that the housewife has a choice.[49]

The American National Exhibition was a showcase of American consumer goods. But the main attraction was a full-scale model house, cut in half to allow viewing. In the department-store tradition appropriated by the Museum of Modern Art, it was erected by a Long Island builder and furnished by Macy's. It was in the kitchen of this $14,000, six-room, ranch-style house filled with appliances that the debates began with an argument over automatic washers.

The house that resulted from the war was itself deployed as a weapon in the cold war. How else are we to account for the extraordinary success of the "Good Design" programs in the Museum of Modern Art and of the houses in the museum's garden? The issue, of

course, is the nuclear house: the house for the nuclear family in the nuclear age. Not by accident does the issue of *Life* magazine devoted to the kitchen debates also include an article on a couple who spent their fourteen-day honeymoon in a Miami fallout shelter. They are pictured on their lawn with their provisions spread out around them as "wedding gifts" (13).[50] A couple of years later, *Life* would present the canonic photograph of a cold-war family in their fallout shelter.[51]

The museum programs rehearsed the thinking behind these astonishing images, as did parallel developments on the West Coast. It was precisely the industrialization of the war effort that mobilized the Case Study House program in Los Angeles. When the eyes of the architectural world that had turned to the United States started to see through the East Coast and detect the West Coast experiments, they were still looking at the effects of war. The Case Study House program was sponsored by *Arts & Architecture* magazine under John Entenza.[52] The journal commissioned a number of architects to design houses as prototypes for a new way of living—the postwar way of living. Entenza's assumption was that the soldier returning from war had become a "modern man," a figure who would prefer to live in a modern environment utilizing the most advanced technology rather than return to "old-fashioned houses with enclosed rooms." The twenty-six houses resulting from this program were not only published in *Arts & Architecture* but were, for the most part, built. It was a requirement to have a "real client" and to open the house to the public for six to eight weeks. Each house was

to be completely furnished under an arrangement with manufacturers. Like the Breuer House, the Case Study Houses were exhibition houses. The program was enormously successful both professionally and among the wider public. The first six houses to be opened received almost 400,000 visitors.

The program was preceded by two competitions organized by *Arts & Architecture:* the 1943 "Design for Postwar Living" and a second such competition in 1944, sponsored by the U.S. Plywood Association. These competitions encouraged participants to arrive at a "pattern of living for the American worker" and his family. "This American worker," says the call for entries, "conditioned by the war-time years (including the members of the armed forces who will become a part of the working population) . . . is likely to have an enormous respect for the machine both as creator and as a weapon of destruction . . . and it is very likely that he will not only accept but demand simple, direct, and honest efficiency in the material aspects of the means by which he lives." World War II, *Arts & Architecture* implied, provided the context for the acceptance of modern architecture. It was as if the war had educated the taste, the aesthetic sensibility, of the public.

A historical reference for the Case Study Houses can be found in Le Corbusier's fascination with the technologies developed during World War I and his dream of an architecture that would "recycle" these materials and techniques into the mass production of houses. This was most obvious in his relationship with Gabriel Voisin who, after the war, was looking to transform his war aircraft factories by breaking into the building industry.[53]

The Case Study House program likewise exemplifies the impact of the war on both architectural discourse and the specific techniques and materials employed in

(14)
Plywood leg splint, designed by Charles and Ray Eames, in use, 1943

the production of housing. On the one hand, the industry was recycling the products and techniques that it had developed and tested at war. On the other hand, and this is what was new, the architects themselves had been involved in the development of these military products.

During the war, Charles and Ray Eames had formed a company with John Entenza to mass-produce plywood war products. In 1941–42 they developed a molded plywood splint for the U.S. Navy to replace a metal leg splint used in the field, which did not sufficiently secure the leg and led to gangrene **(14)**. The navy accepted the Eames prototype and, with the financial support of Entenza and the help of other architects such as Gregory Ain (who later became involved in the Case Study House program), designed the equipment needed for mass production, and eventually put 150,000 units into service. The splint performed very well in the field and was praised for its life-saving features. In addition, the company designed and developed a plywood body litter and an arm splint, molded plywood aircraft

parts, and so on. By 1945 the Eameses were producing lightweight plywood cabinets and molded plywood chairs and tables with the technology they had developed for the military. A photograph of the plywood lounge chair of 1946 shows Charles Eames reclined on it, the position of his leg indicating that he had not forgotten where it comes from (15). In addition, the Eameses produced molded plywood children's furniture, molded plywood animals, and even plywood Christmas decorations from leftover splints.

Military equipment had become the basis of domestic equipment.

This obvious displacement from war to architecture can be found throughout the Case Study House program in more subtle forms. The very idea of standardization, for example, was very much part of the program's agenda. Every component of the Eames House was selected from a steel manufacturer's catalog and bolted together like a Meccano set (16). It took a day and a half to get the structure of the Eames House up. The house for John Entenza, designed by Charles

Eames and Eero Saarinen, was built from the same standardized elements but was very different architecturally.

One is reminded again of Le Corbusier who, in relation to his potential collaboration with Voisin, had written (with Ozenfant) in *L' Esprit Nouveau:*

> Houses must go up all of a piece, made by machine tools in a factory. . . . It is in aircraft factories that the *soldier-architects* have decided to build their houses; they decided to build this house like an aircraft, with the same structural methods, lightweight framing, metal braces, tubular supports.[54]

From that point of view, the Eames House represents the realization of Le Corbusier's dreams. Like Le Corbusier, Charles Eames was an avid reader of catalogs on marine and avia-

tion equipment. He later said about the house that he regretted having stuck so close to the building industry, neglecting several outside offers, and that if he were to do the house all over again he might treat it more as a job of "product design," less as architecture in the traditional sense. Less as architecture in the traditional sense? And we all thought this house was just like one of their plywood cabinets blown up in scale! Off-the-shelf components, assembled from the back of a truck, in just over one day. How more radical can you get?

Perhaps nobody was so captivated by the Eameses, and more lucid about their work, than their friends Peter and Alison Smithson. In a 1966 issue of *Architectural Digest* devoted exclusively to the Eameses and prepared by the Smithsons, they write:

There has been much reflection in England on the Eames House. For the Eames House was a cultural gift parcel received here at a particularly useful time. The bright wrapper has made most people—especially Americans—throw the content away as not sustaining. But we have been brooding on it—working on it—feeding from it. [55]

The house as an object, a gift all wrapped up in colored papers. This comment reflects so much of the Smithsons' obsessions, so much of what they saw as new in the Eameses: the attention to objects (objects they understand as "remnants of identity"), the love of ephemera, of gifts, of colored wrapping paper, and so on.

The idea that the house was a gift also points to the constant shift in scale in the Eameses' work: from the house to the cabinets, to children's furniture, to toys, to miniatures. Even the architectural models were treated like toys, played with by excited architects and clients acting like curious children (17). In this architecture, everything is a toy, everybody is a child. Perhaps this

(18)

Billy and Audrey Wilder on their honeymoon, photographed by Charles Eames

explains the constant presence of children in the Eames images. Since when have there been so many children in architecture?

The Eameses saw everything through the camera. This explains the astonishing continuity in their work in so many different scales. If the eye is the eye of a camera, size is not fixed, but continuously shifting. The Eameses used to shoot at everything. This was surely not just an obsession with recording everything. There is that, no doubt, but they also made decisions on the basis of what they saw through the lens.

There is a curious letter in the Eames Archives from Ludwig Glasser (the letterhead is from the Museum of Modern Art), who tells the Eameses that late one night, when leaving the museum, he had seen Charles inside the Newton show of 1974, and caught him photographing the installation before the opening: "It only happens once a year that I am carrying my camera with me on my way to or from the office. I am particularly happy that it was the night before the opening of the Newton show, and that I could photograph the designer in the act of photographing." The letter includes two black-and-white prints. The exhibition appears unfinished. Is he documenting the different stages of the exhibition or still making decisions about where things go? Eames replies: "Caught in the act indeed—and I thought no one could see into that fish bowl. You were most thoughtful to send the evidence." What is this? "It only happens once a year": this was not intentional. And "caught in the act," "I thought no one could see," thanks for the "evidence." Evidence of what precisely?

What is it that the camera eye of the Eameses is so furtively trying to catch?

I have always been fascinated by a picture of Billy Wilder and his wife, Audrey, taken from the back seat of a fast car (18). They were on their honeymoon. And the photographer? Charles Eames. Believe it or not, the Eameses accompanied the Wilders on their honeymoon trip to Lake Tahoe in June-July 1948, photographing, they said, Virginia City and Lake Tahoe.

They were friends. Arriving in California in 1941, Charles Eames had worked as a stage designer for the MGM movie studio under Billy Wilder. Eames later said that "he had learned more about design by watching Billy Wilder than from working with any architect."[56] To think about the Eameses' architecture is to think about this extraordinary intimacy with film, an intimacy that marks a distinct shift from the productions of the historical avant-garde. This shift can be seen between the first and second version of the Eames House. The first version, the so-called Bridge House, published in *Arts & Architecture* in 1945, was obviously based on Mies's sketch of a glass house on the hillside of 1934. The scheme was rejected in 1947, after Charles came to the Museum of Modern Art to photograph the Mies exhibition in which the sketch was first exhibited. Charles already knew the sketch. In fact, he said that he didn't see anything new in the projects that were exhibited, but he was impressed by Mies's design of the exhibition itself. Shortly afterwards, the Eameses came up with a new scheme for their house.

In this house, the camera eye that organized the architecture of the historical avant-garde has been displaced by a multiplicity of zooming eyes. Not by chance, the Eameses' film *House: After Five Years of Living* of 1955 is made up entirely of thousands of slides. Every aspect of this house is scrutinized by these all too intimate eyes. The camera moves up close to every surface, every detail. But these are not the details of the building as such; they are the details of the everyday life that the building makes possible. It is their own life, of course. And they were always recording it.

In the last few months I have been going through boxes of documents belonging to the Eames Archives (now in the Library of Congress), shuffling through their papers, peeking into their correspondence, going through their so-called publicity file (where they kept track of every notice of their work in the press, in professional journals, in catalogs, in advertisements), and so on. I thought, having spent so much time at the Foundation Le Corbusier, that Le Corbusier was the most compulsive filer one could find, that only he could keep track of "everything." That was before I encountered the Eameses. With the Eameses, all the stuff of everyday life enters the archives. They kept track of such mundane things as what they ate at the office during a particular week (menus, with two choices for each course, were typed), or the clothes they were taking on a trip (lists of items to take are first scribbled on scraps of paper, then typed), even the memos of who called on what day, at what hour, with what message. The same mentality organizes the film about their house.

Le Corbusier considered film the best medium to represent his architecture. In his movie with Pierre Chenal, *L' Architecture d' aujourd' hui* (1929), he moves through the space of his houses (Villa Savoye, Garches, Villa d'Avray) without removing his jacket. In *House:*

After Five Years of Living, the Eameses take the opposite approach. Everything, as the title indicates, is about living in the house. The focus is extremely close: flowers, bugs, eggs, pots and pans, crockery, etc. While Le Corbusier had included figures to provide scale, and perhaps to insist that he was just visiting, in the Eames film there are no figures, only traces of ongoing life.

Le Corbusier's film is all horizontal panning—like the modern house that frames a horizontal view. The Eames film is just a collection of slides. This is consistent with the house itself. It is impossible to focus in the Eames House in the same way that we do in a house of the 1920s. Here the eye is that of a television watcher—not the 1950s viewer but closer to the one of today—multiple screens, some with captions, all viewed simultaneously. It helps to follow more than one story at once.

To some extent, the Eameses pioneered this mode of viewing. They were experts in communications. In 1959, they brought "Glimpses of the U.S.A." to Moscow, with its seven screens suspended within Buckminster Fuller's geodesic dome **(19)**. As many as 2,200 still and moving images (some from Billy Wilder's *Some Like it Hot*) presented the theme of "A Day in the Life of the United States." Fuller said that nobody had done it before and that advertisers and filmmakers would soon follow.

Unfortunately, the Wilder House, which was modular in plan and assembled out of prefabricated off-the-shelf parts, was not built.

Indeed, it was one of the last architectural commissions that the Eameses would undertake. When asked, in a 1972 interview, why he turned away from the practice of architecture, Charles said:

> That's partially the result of my chickening out. Architecture is a frustrating business. You work on an idea, but standing between you and the event are many traps. The finance committee, the contractor, the subcontractor, the engineer, even politicians— all of them can really cause the concept to degenerate. Going into furniture or film is a deviation of a sort, but at least we had a more direct relationship with the end product—a better chance to keep the project from degenerating. That's why architects design furniture—so you can design a piece of architecture that you can hold in your hand.[57]

While leaving building behind, Charles Eames continued to think of himself as an architect, insisting that even film and graphic design are forms of architecture: "I think of myself functionally as an architect. I can't help but look at the problems around us as problems of structure—and structure is architecture. A good film needs structure as much as a good front page does."[58] Charles Eames became an architect who no longer built. Ray Eames became an artist who made architecture.

In the meantime, the number of architects chickening out of building is increasing by the hour. It would seem that experimental work in architecture today is rarely found outside the gallery or the university. The American avant-garde architect, if we still want to use the term, and I am not sure that we do, has become some kind of installation artist or writer.

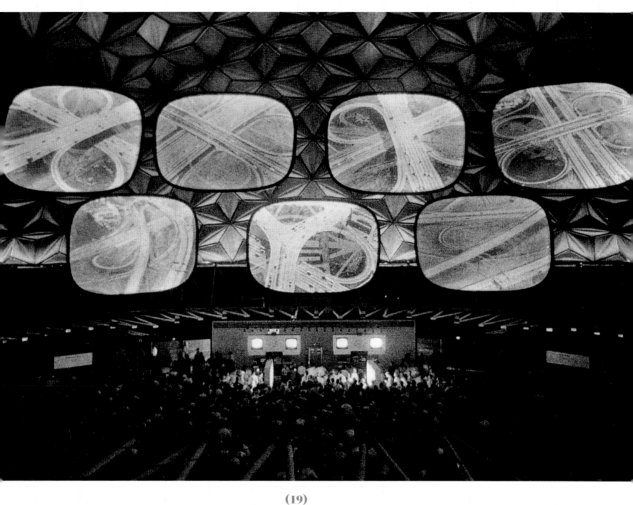

(19)
"Glimpses of the U.S.A.," seven screens in
Buckminster Fuller's geodesic dome at the
Moscow Fair Auditorium, 1959

Notes

Introduction: Columbia University

BERNARD TSCHUMI

1 All of the quotations in this introduction were taken from the publication celebrating the hundredth anniversary of the Graduate School of Architecture, Planning, and Preservation at Columbia University: Richard Oliver, ed., *The Making of an Architect 1881–1981* (New York: Rizzoli, 1981), specifically the essays "Modernism Rears Its Head—The Twenties and Thirties" by Rosemarie Haag Bletter, "History IV: 1933–1935" by Judith Oberlander, "History V: 1935–1959" by Diane Boas, and "Slouching Toward Modernity: Talbot Faulkner Hamlin and the Architecture of the New Deal" by Kenneth Frampton.

Statement of Editorial Withdrawal

R. E. SOMOL

1 See Maurice Berger's *Labyrinths: Robert Morris, Minimalism, and the 1960s* (New York: Harper & Row, 1989). The issue of proper title with regard to *Litanies* apparently did not preclude later contracted exchanges between the two, as suggested in the following remarks of Morris, though a concern emerges about the ultimate effectiveness of the work's new conditions of display: "If it can't be handled through one of those distribution systems, either the media or the museum, then I think the work is in real trouble; it's going to disappear; and I think those pieces have in a way. I mean Philip Johnson owns one of those pieces. He keeps it in a little corner. So it's like a little postcard of what it was, and when I first showed it people weren't sure whether they could go into the room or not." Benjamin H. D. Buchloh, "Three Conversations in 1985: Claes Oldenburg, Andy Warhol, Robert Morris," *October* 70 (Fall 1994): 54. For diverse accounts of the effect of such distribution systems on architecture in the period under consideration and beyond, see the essays by Phyllis Lambert and Beatriz Colomina included in this volume.

2 For Grassi, see "Avant-Garde and Continuity," *Oppositions* 21 (Summer 1980): 24–33, where he contends that "the avant-garde position in architecture contradicts the very definition of architecture; that is to say, it is contrary to architecture's most specific characteristics" (25). In writing on the work of the New York Five, Tafuri asserts that "there is nothing new to the fact that American culture is possessed of a deep sense of nostalgia for that which it has never had," and claims that the Five represent "a desperate attempt to recapture those avant-gardes which America experienced only in its superficial aspects." See "American Graffiti: Five x Five = Twenty-five," *Oppositions* 5 (Summer 1976): 37.

3 Benjamin H. D. Buchloh, "The Primary Colors for the Second

Time: A Paradigm Repetition of the Neo-Avant-Garde," *October* 37, 52. He concludes more explicitly, if pessimistically, that "the very same strategies that had developed within modernism's project of enlightenment now serve the transformation of the bourgeois public sphere into the public sphere of the corporate state, with its appropriate forms of distribution (total commodification) and cultural experience (the spectacle)."

4 Somewhat ironically, this dismissal contends that architecture has at once succumbed to "fashion" and, at the same time, is insufficiently engaged in popular culture.

5 This distinction recalls a comment by Paul Virilio: "I don't believe in sociology. It's a mask. Sociology was invented in order to forget politics. For me, all that is social, sociology, doesn't interest me." Virilio, *Pure War* (New York: Semiotext(e), 1983), 10.

6 See Colin Rowe's *As I Was Saying*, vol. 1, ed. Alexander Caragonne (Cambridge, Mass.: MIT Press, 1996), 14, for this evaluation, which is similar to the one offered in his contribution to this collection.

7 E.g., see Gilles Deleuze, *Difference and Repetition*, trans. Paul Patton (New York: Columbia University Press, 1994), and *The Logic of Sense*, trans. Mark Lester (New York: Columbia University Press, 1990), esp. 261–66.

8 It is precisely the economy of theft and gift that Rowe consistently denigrates in his sympathetic references to Samuel Johnson. See, e.g., *Collage City* (Cambridge, Mass.: MIT Press, 1978), 148, and "On Conceptual Architecture," in *As I Was Saying*, vol. 2 (Cambridge, Mass.: MIT Press, 1996).

9 Craig Owens, "Philip Johnson: History, Genealogy, Historicism," *Philip Johnson: Processes* (catalog, Institute for Architecture and Urban Studies), 3–11.

10 Something of this sort was no doubt sensed by Reyner Banham in his conclusion to *Theory and Design in the First Machine Age* (Cambridge, Mass.: MIT Press, 1980): "The architect who proposes to run with technology knows now that he will be in fast company, and that, in order to keep up, he may have to emulate the Futurists and discard his whole load, including the cultural garments by which he is recognised as an architect" (329–30). This may go some way toward explaining Eames's "confession," particularly given Colomina's presentation of his and Ray's diverse affiliations. For an account of Duchamp's abandonment, see Thierry de Duve, *Pictorial Nominalism: On Duchamp's Passage from Painting to Readymade* (Minneapolis: University of Minnesota Press, 1991).

Kirstein's Circle
Cambridge, Hartford, New York,
1927–1931

PHYLLIS LAMBERT

1 William Innes Homer, *Alfred Stieglitz and the American Avant-Garde* (London: Fecker & Warburg, 1977), 235.

2 Homer, *Alfred Stieglitz*, 239.

3 Lincoln Kirstein, *Mosaic: Memoir* (New York: Farrar, Straus and Giroux, 1994), 160.

4 Kirstein, *Mosaic: Memoir*, 161.

5 W. McNeil Lowry, "Profiles: Conversations with Kirstein II," *New Yorker* (Dec. 15, 1986): 55.

6 Lowry, "Profiles," 55.

7 Kirstein, *Mosaic: Memoir*, 169.

8 Kirstein, *Mosaic: Memoir*, 172.

9 Kirstein, *Mosaic: Memoir*, 163.

10 Kirstein, *Mosaic: Memoir*, 170.

11 Kirstein, *Mosaic: Memoir*, 170.

12 Kirstein, *Mosaic: Memoir*, 170.

13 Kirstein, *Mosaic: Memoir*, 172, 173.

14 Nicholas Fox Weber, *Patron Saints: Five Rebels Who Opened America to a New Art, 1928–1943* (New York: Alfred A. Knopf, 1992), 102.

15 Prospectus, Harvard Society for Contemporary Art, 1929 (microfilm, Library of the Museum of Modern Art, New York).

16 "A Summary of the Activities of its First Year," Harvard Society for Contemporary Art, Feb. 1930 (microfilm, Library of the Museum of Modern Art, New York), unpaginated.

17 Kirstein, *Mosaic: Memoir*, 175.

18 Weber, *Patron Saints*, 66.

19 Weber, *Patron Saints*, 66.

20 Kirstein, *Mosaic: Memoir*, 186.

21 Kirstein, *Mosaic: Memoir*, 101.

22 Kirstein, *Mosaic: Memoir*, 201.

23 Kirstein, *Mosaic: Memoir*, 103.

24 "Announcement," *Hound & Horn: A Harvard Miscellany* I, no. 1 (Sept. 1927): 6.

25 Kirstein, *Mosaic: Memoir*, 186.

26 Henry-Russell Hitchcock Jr., "The Decline of Architecture," *Hound & Horn* I, no. 1 (Sept. 1927): 34.

27 Hitchcock, "The Decline of Architecture," 34.

28 Henry-Russell Hitchcock Jr., "Four Harvard Architects," *Hound & Horn* II, no. 1 (Sept. 1928): 47.

29 "Announcement," *Hound & Horn* I, no. 1 (Sept. 1927): 6.

30 "Comment," *Hound & Horn* III, no. 1 (Oct.–Dec. 1929): 5.

31 Kirstein, *Mosaic: Memoir*, 181.

32 Leonard Greenbaum, *Hound & Horn: The History of a Literary Quarterly* (The Hague: Mouton, 1966), 57.

33 Bandler, Kirstein and Hyatt Mayor, cited in Greenbaum, 59.

34 Weber, *Patron Saints*, 136, 139.

35 Henry-Russell Hitchcock Jr., "A. Everett Austin, Jr. and Architecture," in *A. Everett Austin, Jr.: A Director's Taste and Achievement* (exhibition catalog, Sarasota and Hartford, 1958), 40.

36 Hitchcock, "A. Everett Austin, Jr.," 39.

37 Weber, *Patron Saints*, 140–50 passim.

38 Hitchcock, "A. Everett Austin, Jr.," 39–40.

The Avant-Garde Revisited

COLIN ROWE

1 Peter Medawar, *The Art of the Soluble* (London, 1967), 99. Medawar's presentation of science as *the art of the soluble* is probably connected with Edmund Burke's definition of politics as *the art of the possible*.

2 "*Architecture is the will of the epoch translated into space, living, changing, new.*" This is surely one of the most laconic, poetic, potent, and alluring definitions of architecture ever provided. It is interesting and entertaining to compare it with Gropius:

> Modern architecture . . . [is] the inevitable consequential product of the intellectual, social, and technical conditions of our age.

This is a statement again involving a chronological criterion, "*our age*"; but it is entirely lacking in Mies's concentration and Hegelian pungency. Published after Gropius's protracted residence in the United States, one might suppose that some extra intellectual baggage had been taken on. However, this does not seem to be evident. It is interesting to speculate what Gropius might have said twenty-five years earlier in Berlin; but one can only imagine that it would not have been anything so condensed as Mies's.

And, then, from Le Corbusier:

> The architects' task consists in coming into agreement with the orientation of their epoch. Their works should express the spirit of their time.

And the much less pedestrian:

> Architecture, which is the expression of the spirit as an epoch, delivered an ultimatum.

And again:

> Architecture is a unity of principles animating all the works of an epoch, the result of a state of mind which has its own special character.

And in this last quotation, as I remember the French text, Corbu himself does not talk about a "state of mind." He talks about "un état d'ame," *a state of soul*; and this is, clearly, somewhat different. But then, *why* did the English translator mistranslate? Is it his opinion that to talk about *a state of soul*—in English—might provoke derision? However, apropos "un état d'ame," it is Henry Millon's suggestion that present-day French usage now prefers "une mentalité."

So as with Mies and Gropius, these three statements of Corbu's all exhibit the traces of a Hegelian affiliation: the first very pallid, the second threatening, the third adequate; and it should be amusing to compare them with the Mies statement of 1923—this because particularly the first reads like a very washed-out rendition of Mies. So did Corbu "crib"? Or to be more polite, did Corbu "borrow"? Or is there a common source shared by both? Or is it a case of Hegel's ideas being highly pervasive? On the whole, this is more likely to be the case with Corbu, in Paris rather than in Berlin. For from the intensity and compression of his wording, one can very well guess that Mies enjoyed a far more direct confrontation with the Hegelian message.

But this still leaves unconsidered Corbu's most famous definition:

> L'architecture est le jeu savant, correcte et magnifique des volumes assemblés sous la lumière (Architecture is the learned, correct, and magnificent game of volumes assembled under light).

No trace of zeitgeist here!; and a classically French presumption that "correctness" *must* exist? It is an atemporal definition involving simply visible and morphological criteria, and the proximity of date should insist upon comparison with the wholly different content of the Mies statement of 1923. For in this comparison, the indications of a frontier between very different cultures are very acute; and one might wonder whether cards of identity are not required to proceed from the one to the other!

3 I attempted a discussion of this issue in *Neo-"classicism" and Modern Architecture,* two articles, written 1956–57 but not published until 1973. This was in *Oppositions;*

it was through the agency of Peter Eisenman; and this long delay might be a commentary on the predicament of moderately serious architectural discourse in the 1950s. It had no "market" and was difficult to publish—at least for me.

The two articles are *not* profound; they are moderately lucid; they do not parade "difficulty"; and they are not, excessively, "intellectual." However, in those days, they must have seemed all too cerebral for popular consumption—this according to the standards of journalistic judgment then. That, nowadays, they might be considered not cerebral enough is, I think, entirely a result of the publishing interventions of *one* person.

To my understanding, perhaps since the days of the New Deal, architectural discourse in the United States had become increasingly fatigued, to reach a condition of almost extinction during the regime of Dwight D. Eisenhower; and its resuscitation—though it may be invidious to say it—I believe is entirely the work of Eisenman. It must be his primary achievement; he has contrived to inject ideas into criticism; and though I don't always like them, this is why, with reference to architectural discourse since World War II, I perceive a crucial division of time. Like the Christian division of history into B.C. and A.D., myself makes a division of time into B.P. and A.P.—acronyms for *Before Peter* and *After Peter*.

Strange all the same that that, though the leading inference of *Neo-"classicism,"* is what I am here about to contend—that in any conflict between "the spirit of the age" and "the spirit of the law," the culture of the United States will always opt for "the spirit of the law"—that such argument seems to have been completely overlooked or, when noticed, in some quarters even been considered meretricious. Strange also (see *ANY* 7–8) that these pieces of 1956–57 should be interpreted as

yet further exhibitions of exclusively morphological analysis, still further evidence of that unregenerate "formalism" to which their author is, so superficially, addicted.

4 In 1825 William Hazlitt published a collection of biographical essays upon certain contemporaries: Bentham, Coleridge, Southey, Byron, Scott, Washington Irving, etc. It was entitled *The Spirit of the Age;* and this is, probably, the first prominent and "modern" use of such a term in the English language. The older usage—as in Wren—the older sense—as in Dryden—had been either more cautious or more passive. In the older usage and sense "the age" had not yet become an exacting and prescriptive presence, not an emanation that might require an "obedience" in the interests of a "freedom" and certainly, not something that could only be ignored at the risk of cultural confusion.

This transformation of meaning and emphasis, only incipient in Hazlitt, has received little attention from those who, at the present time, envisage themselves as the more active agents of the zeitgeist; but it has, of course, been widely recognized by historians of ideas as part of a general inflammation of consciousness more specifically related to late-eighteenth-century Germany: to *Sturm und Drang* and to the philosophical systems that evolved from the highly pregnant intuitions of a romantic sensibility.

And the influence of these intuitions on those who did their thinking in terms of the more prosaic categories induced by the English language?

By the early 1820s there had already begun that long academic procession of Harvard boys to German universities. Apparently, the Americans—some of them—went out to get their German intuitions straight from the source; but if the English picked up their own more by hearsay, more as intimations that were "in the air," for all this absence of adventure, it was still

in London that *The Spirit of the Age* emerged as a title for what, in fact, was a brilliant work of journalism.

And what *was* "the spirit of the age" all about? To an older generation, nurtured upon the principles of the Enlightenment, even in Germany it must have seemed an affair of inexplicable hocus-pocus; but to the young and the enthusiastic, it was evidently a voice—both ancestral and new—something of an oracle that transcended the artificial mechanisms of simple logic, both obscure and illuminated—and published at Bamberg in 1807, might be accepted as a crucial utterance.

For here, Napoleon was pronounced to be a "*World-Soul,*" and at the same time, it was proclaimed that "*a new epoch has arisen*" (shades of Mies and Corbu?); and with this sense of a new dispensation of time (fairly recent in its birth?), Hegel could continue:

> It seems as if the World-Spirit had now succeeded in freeing itself from all foreign objective existence and finally apprehending itself as absolute Mind.

And then, the following (italics mine):

> Those who are said to have genius have acquired some special aptitude by which they render *the general shapes of the nation* their *own* work. . . . What they produce is not *their* invention, but the invention of *the whole nation;* or rather, what they find is that the whole nation *has found its true nature.* Each, as it were, piles up his stone. So too does the artist. Somehow he has the good fortune to come *last,* and when *he* places *his* the arch stands *self-supported.*

Incredible rhetoric! And no wonder that its intoxication came to saturate almost all nineteenth-century thought. Allow later sophistication (Hegel's own) to substitute *epoch* for *nation* and you have the whole cultural/psychological setting for a stage! No wonder that it became absorbed—as we are always told—

by Karl Marx! Very strange though, that in no "introductions to" or "pioneers of" modern architecture does Hegel—so far as I am aware—figure as *preeminent precursor*!

Could this be because, in Hegel's estimation, the artist had "the good fortune to come *last,*" whereas around 1900, by inflammation and inversion of Hegelian dogma, it was now "the good fortune" of the artist to come *first*—and maybe even a bit sooner than *that*? Or could it, after 1918, have been that disturbing emphasis on *the nation,* strange to the avant-garde of seventy years ago and, to the mentality of the present day, downright bizarre?

However, as a Württemberger, *what,* in 1807, did Hegel mean by *the nation*? Was it a political entity? a spiritual one? an ethnic condition? And there must be a bit of ambivalence here—as there always is. But to consider the historical occasion: Hegel had been teaching at Jena, in the territory of Saxe-Weimar; and in 1806, it was at Jena that Napoleon—that World-Soul—had inflicted appalling defeat upon the Prussians. But was this a *national calamity*? Or merely a *Prussian* catastrophe? Down in Bamberg or Stuttgart—so close and yet so distant—there may have been a period of doubt and confusion, so that it was not until a few years later that emphatic pan-German patriotism became more completely definable. This was in that great insurrection of the Germanic lands, the Befreiungskrieg, the almost maniacally propelled German War of Liberation of 1813, that culminated, in October of that year, with Napoleon's pretty shattering defeat at Leipzig and his rapid return to Paris. This was the crucial event; and it may be suggestive to think of some of the boys in those armies—students from Berlin or Jena, perhaps students of Hegel himself?—inflamed by the ideas of the French Revolution ("a new epoch has arisen") and, simultaneously, appalled by French imperialist domination (determined to free themselves "from all foreign objective existence"?). And since it seems to have been that kind of war, it might be further suggestive to think of a few of them—just a very few—carrying along Hegel's *Phänomenologie des Geistes*—for purposes of light reading?—and perhaps being killed, as so many were, but still expiring in the happy knowledge that, as agents of the World-Spirit in action, they had finally "apprehended" themselves as Absolute Mind!

But to return to "the spirit of the age" and to its career in the English language. In London in 1813, with the news from Leipzig, there must have been, if not the wildest transports of joy, at least feelings of the deepest satisfaction. For after all, with the exception of the two years 1802–4, London, and the Bank of England, had fought the French since 1792 with a persistence—indomitable or self-serving—no longer easy to comprehend. They had fought on sea and on land (*and* by the issue of stock) first the Revolution and then Napoleon. The Revolution, in the words of Edmund Burke, had been "a wild, enthusiastic, nameless thing"; and then there was Napoleon: a Corsican ogre, a self-styled "emperor" with impossible dreams of a personal hegemony. And to defeat these two "menaces," both different but both French, London had organized, and the bank had subsidized, an apparently opportune series of coalitions, none of them very successful. Of course, in 1812 there had been the Russian check at Moscow; but Napoleon had still been able to rally. However, with this sudden, almost spontaneous, German upsurge, perhaps London and the Bank of England had finally succeeded. Perhaps the Germans, unexpectedly united, had delivered the goods.

And about this, *who* could have been disappointed? Apart from a few disgruntled "poets and intellectuals" (not to be relied upon), probably not very many. But apart

from Byron, Shelley, and the generally discontented, still sympathetic to Enlightenment principles, in this winter of 1813–14, even among the Tories, there was much to reflect upon. For what had occurred, in that crazy collection of little German principalities, was very strange, and for connoisseurs of English politics, it lay beyond their sphere of calculation. They could understand the French—*and* fight them; they had made a point of this for hundreds of years; but what had happened in the Germanic lands was something different. Fashionable and political London could continue as ever—debates, dinners, and *bals masqués;* but there was still an ineffable *something* that had entered to disturb the glitter and the aplomb of the established social facade.

Perhaps among those who were concerned to give concentrated attention to the Battle of Leipzig (and there couldn't have been very many), among those who were able to think about it in terms of its *meaning* (i.e., as other than a French defeat), only Samuel Taylor Coleridge (1772–1834) was equipped to do so. Often said to be the most penetrating English critic of his time, Coleridge enjoyed the most intensive exposure to the contemporary German intellectual scene. According to René Wellek's *History of Modern Criticism,* it was Coleridge who introduced into English—from Kant, Schelling, Schlegel, and Goethe—such distinctions as those between "mechanical regularity" and "organic form" (A. W. Schlegel), between the romantic and the classical, the statuesque and the picturesque, reason and understanding, genius and talent, the objective and the subjective. . . . Astonishing to think that all these critical categories were admitted so late; but they are *not* Italian and *not* French. And with Coleridge thoroughly conversant with German romantic philosophy, with Sturm und Drang, might the Befreiungskrieg have been envisaged as a case of Sturm in full working operation? Perhaps he did

so regard the Battle of Leipzig, as a physical triumph of German *Geist* over the diminished forces of French *raison.* And if so, his "understanding" would have been reciprocated by Germaine de Stael, that other great proponent of German thought whose *D'Allemagne* had been published in English translation in that same year, 1813, and who, as a celebrity, was herself in London in 1814 for the arrival and reception of the Allied princes.

In any case, I suggest that it was in these contexts—and probably in the winter of 1813–14—that, as an explanation of German events, "the spirit of the age," essentially the zeitgeist, made its first significant—energetic and "modern"—appearance in the English language; and then, with all those Allied princes around—and nearly all of them German and waiting to be entertained—it must quickly have entered fashionable usage.

And hence Hazlitt's *The Spirit of The Age* of 1825, which as René Wellek points out, is only superficially to be considered as a work in the older, and mostly empirical, English tradition; but in which, instead, the title's emphasis upon *the age* is frequently affirmed within the text. For instance: the "poet can do no more than stamp the mind of his age upon his works"; "the human mind floats on the tide of mighty *Circumstance*"; no single mind can resist "the vast machine of the world"; and on Shakespeare, "His age was necessary to him," "He overlooks and commands the admiration of posterity, but he does it from the tableland of the age in which he lived."

Rather tedious clichés of criticism at the present day!; but in 1825, they must have been among the more startling revelations of the romantic movement in Germany, and they may serve to illustrate why so many Harvard graduates went off to Germany to study. For in Germany, this kind of perception must have been far more strenuously maintained; and thus, at

Leipzig, for many students it must have seemed that Hegel's World-Spirit had been in complete control, that a metaphysical hypothesis had become a palpable reality, that, virtually, the battle had been a vindication of Hegel's *Phänomenologie.*

So the story of Hegel's continuing influence is almost a platitude of the history of ideas. His influence on Marx, his influence on Jakob Burckhardt and the continuing course of art history, his influence (somewhat warped) on such twentieth-century characters as Benito Mussolini (1883–1945) and Adolf Hitler (1892–1945)—all this is announced, or conceded. But then, to bring into this intellectual genealogy such persons as Walter Gropius, Ludwig Mies van der Rohe, Hannes Meyer? And there ensues an utter silence. . . .

And *why* is this? Because these persons were architects and therefore had no use for abstract thought? Or because they were *originals* and therefore could be related to no systems of abstract thought before their own appearance? Neither question is very satisfactory and the second is extremely ludicrous when so much energy has been invested in providing the "new" architecture with so widely advertised a technological and formal pedigree.

Which is not intended to demonize Gropius, Mies, Corbu, et al., but only to call attention to what *should* seem to be a serious *lacuna.*

For in the frenzied search for "ancestors," for proofs of "legitimacy," Hegel's absence from the genealogical tree surely represents the most glaring failure of acknowledgment. Both Nikolaus Pevsner and Sigfried Giedion, for instance, were the authors of historical texts in which the influence of Hegel is highly overt; but anxious to drag into their accounts every possible (and impossible) pioneer and hero, they neglected to introduce the pioneer and hero of the very methods and historical schematics they themselves employed.

329

Note to page 54

Indeed, for the Pevsners and Giedions of this world, Hegel had become invisible. His conjectures as to "world" and "historical" structure had come to seem entirely concurrent with "empirical" reality. He had become transparent; and the achievement of his genius was, correspondingly, eclipsed. For all its outstanding brilliance, for very many, the shattering revolution of German thought during the approximate years 1770 to 1830 was simply not available for notice. Its fallout had become so pervasive, so diffused throughout all thought, so popularized, that, like a natural element, it had ceased to be obtrusive. And thus a version of Hegel was *inhaled,* as though Hegel was a given *natural* datum and not a superb *mental* construction, not an "invention" but an organic emanation of "time" and "folk."

And therefore, the curiosity of histories such as those provided by the likes of Pevsner and Giedion: they itemized details and failed to apprehend the *Gestalt* of the whole; the *fons et origo* was just *not* to be observed—only the miscellaneous artifacts that floated down the lower reaches of the stream; they were more or less archaeologists digging in the lava of Pompeii without directing *any* notice to the presence of Vesuvius; or, to be crudely provincial, *they couldn't see the forest for the trees.*

This absence of *consciousness* was, of course, understandable—the precursive figure had effectively disguised his own intervention; but this lack of *consciousness* has also lead to the most baneful results—both for the making of architecture and the thinking about it. And most notably, it has perpetuated a number of related illusions:

- *that* between artist and artifact there is no screen of ideas in the case of architecture is (or should be) the neutral agent of some essence of time or essence of science.
- *that* such terms as avant-garde and zeitgeist are completely perspicuous, that they are innocent of

any iconography of their own.
- *that* to make an act of choice is, somehow, a moral error. This illusion is very prevalent among academics; and though this prejudice is often dissimulated, it is still evident that a simple, overt act of choice may arouse the most rabid of passions. Most characteristically, an act of choice is found to be self-indulgent, a yielding to temptation, somewhat intellectually depraved, and—in extreme cases—a specimen of collusion with the most dubious institutions of a liberal-bourgeois-capitalist-"contractualist" society. And significantly, this illusion flourishes with the greatest profusion when the act of choice is related to any issue of style. For then, the most extravagant vituperation is likely to follow.

Briefly stated thus, of course the vehemence of these illusions will not be believed; and therefore, it becomes necessary to seek specific indication of the *odium theologicum* which they may elicit. But a case is readily available. In *ANY* 1 (July-Aug. 1993), a small resort town in the panhandle of Florida was the topic of discussion, and the divisive mudslinging that resulted can only exceed the capacities of imagination. It was almost as though the fate of nations was dependent upon the work of Andres Duany and Elizabeth Plater-Zyberk at Seaside. Thus, irrespective of the merits or demerits of what they had built, they were assaulted and damaged in every possible way. They were too good looking (!), they were insufficiently prone to angst, they were playing the media, they lacked contact with "the spirit of the age" . . . but why go on? It was almost as though a new commandment had been added to those ten already delivered by God to Moses: Thou shall not commit a sin against the zeitgeist.

Indeed, for a retarded late modernism that, desperately, still conceives of itself to be ahead of the more stupid, a "sin" against a category of Hegelian philosophy (however dimly understood) must

be far more appalling than any "offense" against the Holy Ghost. . . .

P.S.
The issue here implicit (Duany and Plater-Zyberk have failed to respond to the promptings of the World-Spirit, have violated the dictates of historical necessity) may, for purposes of amusement, be thrown into prominence by an alleged declaration of Benito Mussolini. In 1943, on learning that the Allies had landed in Sicily, Mussolini is reputed to have said: *History has taken us by the throat.* Melodramatic? However, not at all the sort of thing that the great Duce *ought* to have said, nothing about *blood, toil, tears, and sweat;* but all the same, in its invocation of the "inevitable," a curiously Hegelian reaction that really means: *I didn't bring it about. It was the zeitgeist that played me a dirty trick.*

But *is* this so very different from an architect's claim just to be serving *the will of the epoch*—even anticipating it—and then explaining a lack of success in exactly the same terms? For active collaboration with a figment of the romantic imagination may very easily become passive subservience to it.

Nevertheless, and in spite of these reservations about the propulsive idea of the historical avant-garde, in that ecstatic motivation and elemental fever that distinguished the psychology of a generation maturing toward 1910, with those architects, as with Georg Friedrich Wilhelm Hegel, one may still feel compelled to salute a genuinely heroic dimension.

P.P.S.
American historian George Bancroft, 1800–1891, was ambassador "minister" to London in the mid-1840s and to Berlin for a few years around 1870; but perhaps more interesting than that, he was possibly the first of the Harvard boys to do graduate work in Germany. He went in 1817 and remained for several years, returning to the United

States to become involved with the Round Hill School at Northampton, Massachusetts. But this is just two years after Waterloo and only four years after Leipzig, and Bancroft could well have attended Hegel's lectures. I owe this information to Henry-Russell Hitchcock himself, though the likely Hegel connection has no interest for him; but Russell was Bancroft's, I think, great-grandson. Anyway, so much for the allure of recent German thought at very early-nineteenth-century Harvard. . . .

5 Dominick La Capra, *Soundings in Critical Theory* (Ithaca, N.Y.: Cornell University Press, 1989), 17–18. I am indebted to Brian Kelly for reminding me of this observation.

6 Claude Levi-Strauss, *The Savage Mind* (London, 1966; New York, 1969), 30.

7 Ernst Gombrich, "Icon," review of *Three Essays on Style* and *Perspective as Symbolic Form,* by Erwin Panofsky, *New York Review of Books,* Feb. 15, 1996, 29.

8 As the agent in London for the colony of New York, rather than advise active interference in its affairs, it was Edmund Burke's judgment that the British government should pursue a policy of "salutary neglect." Did he also speak about "benign neglect"? Some years ago when Henry Kissinger, with reference to I-don't-know-what, proposed an equivalent policy (I think without citing Burke), I remember there were noises of conscientious protest.

9 Matthew Arnold, *Poetry and Prose,* 1865, ed. John Bryson (Cambridge, Mass.: Harvard University Press, 1954), 400, 366.

10 Alexis de Tocqueville's *Democracy in America* has a chapter entitled "Why the Americans Show More Aptitude for General Ideas than their Forefathers the English."

11 Katherine deKay Bronson of Providence, Rhode Island, makes an appearance, *incognita,* in Henry James, *Italian Hours,* where she comes on as something "very special." She is a "lady" who lives in Venice — and has lived there for quite a time. She inhabits part of a palazzo not far from the location where now is to be found Harry's Bar; and of course — but wouldn't you expect it? — she is almost inscrutably refined. She is also "sympathetic," a little elusive, a persistent hostess to visiting — and resident — Americans and English; and I like to imagine her, on her part of the canal, as a pendent to Dan and Ariana Curtis along by Campo S. Stefano and the bridge of the Accademia: Bostonian Dan Curtis, who had punched some minor character on the nose in a streetcar, who had quit the United States in a consequent disgust, who had acquired the Palazzo Barbaro, who couldn't quite afford it, who, therefore, rented it out every other summer to Isabella Stewart Gardner, who, along with his English wife and their son and daughter-in-law, was painted by John Singer Sargent in the *gran' salone* of his not so little house, also — of course — frequented by Henry James.

But enough of this. Though the sub-Proustian involutions of late-nineteenth-century American expatriate society have a faded charm all their own, though this society may excite the curiosity of the frivolous, perhaps it should be considered as *not* totally devoid of a "heavier" sociological interest. A sociology of the poor-rich, of quasibohemianism among the American high bourgeoisie in the years down to 1914?

And I ask this question very cautiously; but might it not have been the foreign existence of such American specimens as these that provided at least *one* of the preconditions of a later American avant-garde (if there was one)? For it is, after all, from the culturally estranged that avant-garde demonstrations are likely to proceed.

But how about Mrs. Bronson and her English connections? Well, it was at Asolo, in the early sixteenth century, that Cardinal Bembo, for the diversion of Caterina Cornaro, ex-Queen of Cyprus, is said to have invented the verb *asolare;* and it was at Asolo, in the late nineteenth century, that Robert Browning, for the pleasure of Katherine Bronson, proceeded, in his *Asolando,* to conjugate this same verb. And then, in Asolo, there were the neighbors from almost next door, and it was from one of these, who died only the other day at an immense age, that I was able to learn a little more — even as late as 1964. It was Freya Stark who talked to me about Katherine deKay Bronson's last days and of how she clung, in something like desperation, to a string of pearls. . . . But she has also described this scene in the first book of her autobiography, *Traveller's Prelude.*

Then, from Providence, Rhode Island, there was the other deKay daughter, Katherine Bronson's sister:

> [It was] on June 1, 1877, at Miss Helena deKay's studio [that] Saint-Gaudens, Easton and Shirley organized the Society of American Artists. . . .

Interesting this event: for it would seem that this was the kind of get-together that, fifty years later, might have been called an avant-garde manifestation; and with Helena deKay become by marriage Helena Gilder, and with her son married to the daughter of Louis Comfort Tiffany, it may be seen how the plot for a prehistory of the American avant-garde (again if there was one) may seem to thicken.

Germane to my experience in Hartford-Farmington? Its relevance, I think, is both direct and indirect; but it must certainly have been this line of connection — deKay, Gilder, Bronson, Rucellai — that made it possible for Russell Hitchcock to observe the quantity of bathrooms that American appetite had caused to be inserted into Alberti's palace of about 1450–60.

On the organization of the Society of American Artists, see *The Reminiscences of Augustus Saint-Gaudens,* edited and amplified by Homer Saint-Gaudens, vol. 1 (New York: Century Co., 1913), 186. At this time Helena deKay "was a student . . . first at the Cooper Institute and then at the Academy School. Later she belonged to the new Art Students League, which was a revolt from the Academy School. Just then the old Academicians were carrying things with a pretty high hand. . . ." Or in other words, the time was ripe for a demonstration. From a letter (no date, c. 1910?) of Richard Watson Gilder to Homer Saint-Gaudens. A long time later he still felt about it. However, in this case, one understands . . . and funny the way this grabs both Cooper Union and the Palazzo Rucellai. . . .

P.S.
In *Praxis: A Journal of Cultural Criticism* 6 (1982), published by U.C.L.A., there is a very remarkable article: Nikos Hadjinicolaou, "On the Ideology of the Avant-Garde," translated by Diane Belle James. This should be compulsory reading for anybody who proposes to talk about the concept and the history of the avant-garde. Sources used are mostly French and American; and it may be inferred that the author lives in Paris, writes in French, and has spent some time — not evident how long — in the United States.

This article is exceptionally penetrating; but I don't receive the impression that any of the contributors to the colloquium were aware of it. Otherwise it would have inevitably altered the tone of discourse.

In my case the article was brought to my attention too late for me to use it in my paper.

[1] Russell Lynes, *Good Old Modern: An Intimate Portrait of the Museum of Modern Art* (New York: Atheneum, 1973), 286. In the context of the present essay, it is worth recalling that Gertrude Stein was a prime pupil of Pragmatist philosopher William James. On Stein's affinities to Pragmatist thought, see the foreword by Robert Bartlett Haas to Gertrude Stein, *What Are Masterpieces* (Los Angeles: Conference Press, 1940), 7–22.

[2] Peter Bürger, *Theory of the Avant-Garde,* trans. Michael Shaw (1974; Minneapolis: University of Minnesota Press, 1984), 54.

[3] Alexander Dorner, *The Way Beyond "Art" — The Work of Herbert Bayer,* Problems of Contemporary Art, no. 3 (New York: Wittenborn, Schultz, 1947). A major section of the book was devoted to a monographic essay on Herbert Bayer. A revised edition was published by New York University Press in 1958, a year after Dorner's death, significantly without the section on Bayer (see below), and with a brief introduction by Charles Kuhn, but in other respects little changed from the original edition. All citations to *The Way Beyond "Art"* in the present paper are to the original edition unless otherwise indicated.

[4] Dorner, *Way Beyond "Art,"* 18–19. Dorner apparently had no knowledge of Pragmatism prior to leaving Germany. On the reception of American Pragmatism in Germany, largely a history of inattention, lack of sympathy, and misreading, see Hans Joas, "American Pragmatism and German Thought: A History of Misunderstandings," in Joas, *Pragmatism and Social Theory* (Chicago: University of Chicago Press, 1993), 94–121. A comment by Theo van Doesburg typifies general European reaction to Pragmatist thought in the 1920s, bound up for many, including some members of the avant-garde, with fears of Americanization: "As a result of the pragmatis-

331

tic conception of life, America found an overdevelopment of the technical-materialistic needs of life. The psychic and esthetic values were reduced to dollar-values. . . . Although the influence of America upon Europe is important, it only goes into breadth, not into depth." See Eugène Jolas, ed., "Inquiry among European Writers into the Spirit of America," *Transition* 13 (Summer 1928). However, a shared belief in the centrality of science would occasion a convergence between American Pragmatism and logical positivism in the 1930s, when the most important members of the Vienna circle of philosophers emigrated to the United States and were warmly received by Dewey's followers. See note 44 below and Herbert Feigl, "The Wiener Kreis in America," in *The Intellectual Migration: Europe and America, 1930–1960*, vol. 2 of *Perspectives in American History* (Cambridge, Mass.: Charles Warren Center for Studies in American History, 1968), 63–73. Dorner's discovery of Pragmatism parallels this convergence but is only indirectly related to it.

5 Dorner Archives, Busch-Reisinger Museum, Harvard University, Box G. I wish to express my appreciation to Peter Nisbet and Emily Norris of the Busch-Reisinger for facilitating my research for this paper.

6 Goldschmidt was the first German art historian to come to the United States for an extended period after World War I, teaching medieval sculpture as a visiting professor first at Harvard and later at New York University. According to Colin Eisler, "Goldschmidt, with his mistrust of the generalization, his suspicion of the German penchant for elaborate theorizing, while not viewed in the Fatherland as one of the crown princes of art history, was an especially happy choice for instruction in America. . . . His enthusiasm for America included Hollywood, of which he was a devoted fan." Colin Eisler, "*Kunstgeschichte* American Style:

A Study in Migration," in *The Intellectual Migration*, 556. Goldschmidt's enthusiasm for the movies was shared by Dorner, likewise a fan of this form of American popular culture.

7 Samuel Cauman, *The Living Museum: Experiences of an Art Historian and Museum Director—Alexander Dorner* (New York: New York University Press, 1958), 45. Cauman's book, written in close association with Dorner, was published the year after Dorner's death and has the flavor of being the work of a disciple. Cauman (later to collaborate with H. W. Janson on a textbook history of art) describes *The Living Museum* as "less the biography of Alexander Dorner than the story of museums in our day as seen through his eyes and lived through his experience" (ix).

8 Cauman, *Living Museum*, 36; John Elderfield, *Schwitters* (London: Thames and Hudson, 1985), 125–26, 162. An early exchange between Dorner and Schwitters, uncomplimentary on both sides, took place on the occasion of an exhibition of Schwitters' work at the Von Garvens Gallery in 1922; Schwitters' reply to Dorner, republ. in *Manifeste und kritische Prosa*, vol. 5 of *Kurt Schwitters. Das literarische Werk* (Cologne: DuMont, 1973–81), 118–19, appeared in the magazine *Tran*. On Hanover in the 1920s see Henning Rischbieter, ed., *Hannover. Die zwanziger Jahre in Hannover. Bildende Kunst—Literatur—Theater—Tanz—Architektur, 1916–1933* (Hanover: Kunstverein Hannover, 1962), and Wieland Schmied, *Wegbereiter zur modernen Kunst: 50 Jahre Kestner-Gesellschaft* (Hanover: Fackelträger-Verlag, 1967). Also see Willy Rotzler, *Constructive Concepts: A History of Constructive Art from Cubism to the Present* (Zurich: ABC Edition, 1977), 90–93. More generally on relations between German museum directors, gallery owners, art critics, and the avant-garde, see Henrike Junge, ed., *Avantgarde und Publikum: Zur Rezep-*

tion avantgardistischer Kunst in Deutschland 1905–1933 (Cologne: Böhlau Verlag, 1992), with an essay on Dorner's activity in Hanover by Monike Flacke, 51–58.

9 Cauman, *Living Museum*, 106; Eisler, "*Kunstgeschichte* American Style," 594.

10 Dorner, *Way Beyond "Art,"* 18; Cauman, *Living Museum*, 41.

11 See Monike Flacke-Knoch, *Museumskonzeptionen in der Weimarer Republik. Die Tätigkeit Alexander Dorners im Provinzialmuseum Hanover* (Marburg: Jonas Verlag, 1985), 36–38.

12 Alexander Dorner, "Die Erkenntnis des Kunstwollens durch die Kunstgeschichte," *Zeitschrift für Aesthetik und Allgemeine Kunstwissenschaft* 16 (1922): 216–22.

13 Erwin Panofsky, "Über das Verhältnis der Kunstgeschichte zur Kunsttheorie: ein Beitrag zu der Erörterung über die Möglichkeit 'kunstwissenschaftlicher Grundbegriffe,'" *Zeitschrift für Aesthetik und Allgemeine Kunstwissenschaft* 28 (1925): 129–61; republ. in Panofsky, *Aufsätze zu Grundfragen der Kunstwissenschaft* (Berlin: Bruno Hessling, 1964), 49–75. On the debate between Dorner and Panofsky, see Cauman, *Living Museum*, 41, and also Manfredo Tafuri, *Theories and History of Architecture* (New York: Harper & Row, 1979), 190–91.

14 Cauman, *Living Museum*, 93–95; cf. Flacke-Knoch, *Museumskonzeptionen*, 33–34. Swarzenski was later to come to the Museum of Fine Arts in Boston. See also Dorner's article "La Raison d'être actuelle des musées d'art," *Cahiers d'art* 7 (Paris, 1932): 365–66.

15 Alexander Dorner, "Die neue Raumvorstellung in der bildenden Kunst," *Museum der Gegenwart. Zeitschrift der deutschen Museen für neuere Kunst* 2 (Berlin, 1931): 30–37; Alexander Doerner [sic],

"Considérations sur la signification de l'art abstrait," *Cahiers d'art* 6 (Paris, 1931): 354–57. Citations of both these articles appear in the bibliography compiled by Beaumont Newhall for Alfred Barr's catalog *Cubism and Abstract Art* (New York: Museum of Modern Art, 1936), with the *Cahiers d'art* publication being singled out as particularly important. See also two other articles by Dorner: "Zur Raumvorstellung der Romantik," *Zeitschrift für Aesthetik und Allgemeine Kunstwissenschaft* 25 (Stuttgart, 1931): 130–44, and "Zur abstrakten Malerei. Erklärung zum Raum der Abstrakten in der Hannoverischen Gemäldegalerie," *Die Form. Monatsschrift für gestaltende Arbeit* 3, no. 4 (April 1928): 110–14.

16 Dorner, *Way Beyond "Art,"* 34–36.

17 "Malerei im Zeitganzen," *Neue Zürcher Zeitung*, June 28, 1932, 5 (Giedion's emphasis); cited in Sokratis Georgiadis, *Sigfried Giedion: An Intellectual Biography* (Edinburgh: Edinburgh University Press, 1993), 92. Giedion similarly states in another essay of the same date: "At the fourth Congress for Aesthetics (Hamburg, 1930), Alexander Dorner (Hanover) demonstrated to the astonishment of his academic colleagues that Cubism—optically speaking—represents the greatest revolution since the Renaissance"; Giedion, "Picasso als Erfinder," *Information* 5 (Zurich, 1932); republ. in Dorothée Huber, ed., *Sigfried Giedion: Wege in die Oeffentlichkeit. Aufsätze und unveröffentlichte Schriften aus den Jahren 1926–1956* (Zurich: GTA/Ammann, 1987), 166, my translation. For the relevant passages in *Space, Time and Architecture*, see the subsections "The Dissolution of Perspective" and "Space-Time"; *Space, Time and Architecture: The Growth of a New Tradition* (1941; 3rd ed., Cambridge, Mass.: Harvard University Press, 1954), 431–32.

18 Flacke-Knoch, *Museumskonzeptionen*, 191. Cf. statement

by Valentiner published in Cauman, *Living Museum,* 106. After completing this paper, I came across a catalog published in 1940 by the Museum of Living Art, a pioneering American collection of abstract art established by A. E. Gallatin in 1927 and housed at New York University until 1943, when it was moved permanently to the Philadelphia Museum of Art. Beyond the fact that in 1938 Gallatin acquired two paintings for his collection that had once hung in Dorner's Abstract Cabinet in Hanover (a Mondrian and a Lissitzky), I was struck, apropos of Dorner, by the name of the collection. In an introduction to the catalog written by James Johnson Sweeney, I discovered the following passage: "Space, up to [the time of Cubism], had been conceived as seen from a fixed point of view. The picture was, as it were, a window-into-space. Objects took their places with an apparent three-dimensionality in this space in strict keeping with the rules of linear perspective: volume masked volume, or offered a surface or a fragment of a surface to the observer as the fixed point of view dictated. This conception of space according to the Cubists was onesided. From it no true sense of space as such—that is to say its extension in all directions—could be had. To provide this they claimed it would be necessary for the painters' vision to move about within the picture-space, not merely to regard it from outside. Then by a depiction of various disparate aspects of the picture-space, which arranged side by side on the canvas would be seen simultaneously, the painter might hope to give the observer a genuine realization of three-dimensionality. . . . Yet this was merely a beginning. Cubism in the strict sense of the word was only a critical fingerpost. . . . [Once] the spectator imagines space as something which, on the principle of relative perspective, can be looked into and out from at the same time—when the convex view and the concave view of a body may be depicted side by side— mass in the usual sense will cease

to have any necessary existence. On the one hand, matter need no longer be represented as opaque— for example, in Lissitzky's or Moholy-Nagy's work where surfaces appear as transparent and interpenetrable; on the other, it may be decomposed into simple surfaces or simple lines, as with Mondrian . . ."; James Johnson Sweeney, "Painting," *Museum of Living Art: A. E. Gallatin Collection* (New York: New York University, 1940), n.p. [27–29]. This introduction was actually reprinted from an earlier catalog of the Gallatin Collection, published in December 1933, and it would appear for a third time in a catalog of 1954 published by the Philadelphia Museum of Art. Sweeney, a fledgling art critic in the early 1930s, also recycled portions of the same text in the chapter on cubism in his book *Plastic Redirections in Twentieth Century Painting* (Chicago: University of Chicago, 1934), a precocious publication that established his reputation. Sweeney's text may be compared line by line to Dorner's essay in its original French: "L'espace y est considéré d'un point de vue fixe, absolu comme une étendue infinie, homogène, à trois dimensions, et les parties qui s'y distinguent, comme les volumes (massifs ou transparents), nettement délimités et se recouvrant mutuellement dans la vue qu'on a. Cette représentation de l'espace, objectivée par la construction en perspective, reste fondamentale jusqu'à nos jours. Le tableau est toujours ce que l'on découvre par une fenêtre; la portion de l'espace s'étend devant nous comme une scène considérée d'un point de vue fixe. . . . La nouveauté décisive du cubisme est la substitution du point de vue relatif au point de vue absolue. . . . Les artistes [cubistes] jugent la vision que l'on s'est faite jusqu'alors de l'espace limitée et unilatérale; ils sentent que de la sorte l'essentiel de l'espace, à savoir *son étendue réelle dans tous les sens,* n'est pas saisi, et qu'il faut se mouvoir dans l'espace pour prendre vraiment conscience des trois dimensions. . . . *Mais la forme*

abstraite n'est qu'un moyen pour parvenir à une fin, elle n'est pas fin en soi et l'essentiel. C'est une conséquence naturelle du renversement de la représentation de l'espace, que . . . *on cesse de représenter la matière conçue comme mass opaque* . . . car d'un point de vue relatif, le spectateur doit imaginer les parties de l'espace comme s'il envisageait à la fois du dehors et du dedans. Elles sont à la fois convexes et concaves. . . . La matière se décompose finalement en simple surfaces et en simples lines, comme il en avait été auparavent chez Mondrian, où les plans sont juxtaposés et n'entrent en mouvement qu'en vertu de leurs oppositions de couleurs, ou bien se font transparents et se pénètrent les uns les autres (V. fig. Lissitzky)." Dorner, "Considérations sur la signification de l'art abstrait," 354 (Dorner's italics). To my knowledge, this instance of plagiarism has not been remarked before. Cauman mentions Sweeney as being a friend of Dorner's (Cauman, *Living Museum,* 122).

19 Dorner, *Way Beyond "Art,"* 230. Manfredo Tafuri offers the following comment on the Dorner-Giedion relationship: "The opposition between Dorner and Giedion is interesting because it illustrates the clash between two types of operative criticism; Dorner's position is more within the new dimensions dictated by contemporary movements, while Giedion's is halfway between Dorner's and a more traditional evaluation"; Tafuri, *Theories and History of Architecture,* 167. In other words, while both Giedion and Dorner were proselytizers for modernist aesthetics, Dorner's position is avant-gardist while Giedion's is ultimately classicizing. This philosophical difference also comes to the fore in a review of *The Way Beyond "Art"* published in 1949 in the Swiss journal *Werk.* The author, Carola Giedion-Welcker, art historian and wife of Sigfried Giedion, criticizes Dorner for his excessive positivism, implicitly sharing her husband's view: "Das Ineinander-

fließen von Tradition und Verwandlung, von 'spirit of change and spirit of conservation' . . . wie es der englische Philosoph A. N. Whitehead in seinem Buch *Science and the Modern World* zusammenfassend präzisierte, wird hier völlig negiert und durch die Auffassung der pragmatischen Philosophie des Amerikaners J. Dewey ersetzt mit dem Leitgedanken: 'Growth itself becomes the only moral end.' . . . Bedenklich ist, daß der Verfasser immer noch mit einem unbeirrbaren Fortschrittsgedanken argumentiert." C.G.–W., *Das Werk* 4 (1949): 50.

20 Sigfried Giedion, "Lebendiges Museum," *Der Cicerone* 21, no. 4 (1929): 103–6, passage quoted, 106. Partial transl. in Sophie Lissitzky-Küppers, *El Lissitzky: Life, Letters, Texts* (Greenwich, Conn.: New York Graphic Society, 1968), 378–79. Further contact between Giedion and Dorner would take place two years later when Giedion enlisted Dorner's collaboration in the establishment of an international "Congrès du Musée Contemporain," which he hoped to convene on a regular basis at La Sarraz, Switzerland, under the patronage of Hélène de Mandrot. In June 1931 a questionnaire with a cover letter signed by Giedion, Dorner, and Pierre Andry-Farcy (a progressive museum director from Grenoble) was circulated to an international group of artists and museum administrators. Despite Giedion's strong interest in the project, which was modeled on CIAM, the response was disappointing, and the Congresses of the Contemporary Museum failed to materialize. See Huber, *Sigfried Giedion: Wege in die Oeffentlichkeit,* 66–73.

21 Cauman, *Living Museum,* 108.

22 Johnson suggests that he saw the room in "the late twenties" in his retrospective letter to Dorner (see below), but his biographer does not place him in Hanover until 1930. Franz Schulze, *Philip Johnson: Life and Work* (New York: Alfred A. Knopf, 1994), 63.

23 El Lissitzky, "Proun Room, Great Berlin Art Exhibition, 1923," *G,* July 1923; transl. in Lissitzky-Küppers, *El Lissitzky: Life, Letters, Texts,* 361. Although critical of the decorative tendencies of de Stijl, Lissitzky was strongly influenced at this date by Mondrian in his conception of an evolutionary and environmental relationship between painting and architecture. Mondrian considered architecture—the "total nonnatural environment"—the ultimate realization of neoplasticism. See two essays by Mondrian, "The Realization of Neo-Plasticism in the Distant Future and in Architecture Today" (1922) and "Is Painting Inferior to Architecture?" (1923), in Harry Holtzman and Martin S. James, *The New Art— The New Life: The Collected Writings of Piet Mondrian* (Boston: G. K. Hall, 1986), 164–74.

24 El Lissitzky, "Exhibition Rooms," trans. in Lissitzky-Küppers, *El Lissitzky: Life, Letters, Texts,* 362 (orig. undated typescript in Sprengel Museum Archives, Hanover).

25 Giedion, "Lebendiges Museum," 105. Lissitzky had originally also intended to "create effects" through periodically changing electric lighting, but no circuitry was ever installed for this. The most detailed description of the Abstract Cabinet is given by Flacke-Knoch, *Museumskonzeptionen,* 64–77.

26 Lissitzky, "Exhibition Rooms," 362.

27 See Yve-Alain Bois, "El Lissitzky: Radical Reversibility," *Art in America,* Apr. 1988, 160–81.

28 Dorner, *Way Beyond "Art,"* 116. Christopher Phillips has noted the similarity to Benjamin's language in "The Judgment Seat of Photography," *October* 22 (1982); reprinted in Annette Michelson, Rosalind Krauss, Douglas Crimp, and Joan Copjec, eds., *October: The First Decade, 1976–1986*

(Cambridge, Mass.: MIT Press, 1988), 271.

29 Alexander Dorner, "Das Ende der Kunst?" in *Lübeckische Blätter,* Feb. 1929, 280–81. English translation and underlining by Dorner, Dorner Archives, Box K.

30 Benjamin H. D. Buchloh, "From Faktura to Factography," *October* 30 (1984); reprinted in Michelson et al., *October: The First Decade, 1976–1986,* 97.

31 Republ. in Andreas Haus, *Moholy-Nagy: Photographs and Photograms,* trans. Frederic Samson (New York: Pantheon, 1980), 47.

32 On this exhibition and its reception, Dorner Archives, Box K; Flacke-Knoch, *Museumskonzeptionen,* 100–110; Cauman, *Living Museum,* 113–15.

33 Similar proposals had been made earlier in Germany and elsewhere in connection with plaster casts and metal reproductions of sculpture. In the United States a debate had also occurred during the last third of the nineteenth century over the artistic status of chromolithographs, the technology for which became widely available at this time. The outcome was a compromise: "chromos" were deemed suitable for hanging in the home, while only originals were admissible in the imposing new metropolitan temples of art. On the reception of chromolithography in the United States, see Michael Clapper, "The Chromo and the Art Museum: Popular and Elite Art Institutions in Late-Nineteenth-Century America," in Christopher Reed, ed., *Not at Home: The Suppression of Domesticity in Modern Art and Architecture* (London: Thames and Hudson, 1996), 33–47.

34 Comment by Dorner, Dorner Archives, Box K.

35 For the debate, see *Hannoverscher Kurier,* "Original oder Reproduktion," June 9, 1929, supple-

mentary section, with article by Dorner, "Das Lebensrecht des Faksimiles," as well as contributions by Wilhelm Hausenstein (Munich), Max Sauerlandt (Hamburg), and Carl Georg Heise (Lübeck); and "Original und Faksimile," *Der Kreis, Zeitschrift für künstlerische Kultur* 7, no. 3 (Hamburg, 1930): 157–68, with articles by Dorner, Panofsky, Sauerlandt, Arthur Haseloff (Kiel), Gustav Pauli (Hamburg), and the architect Fritz Schumacher (Hamburg). A longer article of 1930 on the subject by Sauerlandt, Dorner's major antagonist in the debate and a staunch opponent of facsimiles, is republished in Heinz Spielmann, ed., *Max Sauerlandt: Ausgewählte Schriften,* vol. 2 (Hamburg: Verlag Hans Christians, 1974), 313–41.

36 Alexander Dorner, "Was sollen jetzt Ausstellungen?" *Das neue Frankfurt* 6 (1930); English translation here taken from rough translation by Dorner in Dorner Archives, Box K.

37 On the Room of Our Time, see Flacke-Knoch, *Museumskonzeptionen,* 77–99; Cauman, Living Museum, 102–3, 109. The correspondence between Dorner and Moholy-Nagy is published in the catalog *Malewitsch-Mondrian, Konstruktion als Konzept. Alexander Dorner Gewidmet* (Ludwigshafen: Wilhelm-Hack-Museum, 1977), 7–14.

38 Flacke-Knoch, *Museumkonzeptionen,* 11–17.

39 Carl Buchheister to Helmuth Rinnebach, Mar. 12, 1934, in *Carl Buchheister, 1890–1964: Ausgewählte Schriften und Briefe,* ed. Gerhard Charles Rump (Hildesheim: Gerstenberg, 1980), 40–41.

40 Cauman, *Living Museum,* 108.

41 See Troels Andersen, ed., *Malevich: Catalogue raisonné of the Berlin exhibition 1927* (Amsterdam: Stedelijk Museum, 1970), 57–58; George Rickey, *Constructivism: Origins and Evolution*

(New York: George Braziller, 1967), ix, 84–85. Cf. Cauman, *Living Museum,* 118–19.

42 Andreas Huyssen, *After the Great Divide: Modernism, Mass Culture, Postmodernism* (Bloomington: Indiana University Press, 1986), 8.

43 This discussion cannot be entered into here. However, Lissitzky's work and writings of the 1920s, as well as the testimony of his wife and others, suggest that even if he was myopic about the realities of Stalinism, he remained strongly committed to the long-term realization of a communist society. For a discussion of the problem of continuity in Lissitzky's work, see Bois, "El Lissitzky: Radical Reversibility."

44 The philosopher Charles W. Morris, in the late 1930s an associate professor at the University of Chicago, taught at the New Bauhaus and its successor school, the School of Design. Seeking to reconcile American Pragmatism, the logical positivism of the Vienna circle, and scientific empiricism, he advocated a synthesis of science and philosophy called "Unity of Science." A staunch supporter of Moholy-Nagy's pedagogical program, he declared in the New Bauhaus's 1937–38 prospectus, "The integration and interpenetration of the characteristic human activities of the artist, scientist, and technologist is a crying need of our time." Morris's statement, "The Contribution of Science to the Designer's Task," is republished in Hans M. Wingler, *The Bauhaus: Weimar, Dessau, Berlin, Chicago* (Cambridge, Mass.: MIT Press, 1969), 195. Initial contacts between the Bauhaus and the Vienna circle took place in Dessau in 1929, when Herbert Feigl was invited to lecture there. On the relationship between the Vienna circle and the American Pragmatists, see Daniel J. Wilson, "Fertile Ground: Pragmatism, Science, and Logical Positivism," in Robert Hollinger and David

Depew, eds., *Pragmatism: From Progressivism to Postmodernism* (Westport, Conn.: Praeger, 1995), 122–41. I am grateful to John Rajchman for drawing my attention to connections between Pragmatism, logical positivism, and the Bauhaus.

45 See James Sloan Allen, *The Romance of Commerce and Culture: Capitalism, Modernism, and the Chicago-Aspen Crusade for Cultural Reform* (Chicago: University of Chicago Press, 1983), 35–77; and Alain Findeli, "Design Education and Industry: The Laborious Beginnings of the Institute of Design in Chicago in 1944," *Journal of Design History* 4, no. 2 (1991): 97–113.

46 *Herbert Bayer: Painter, Designer, Architect* (New York: Reinhold, 1967), 40.

47 Dorner, *Way Beyond "Art,"* 179.

48 Kurt Kranz, cosigner of this work, was a graduate of the Bauhaus and Bayer's closest associate at Dorland. Arthur A. Cohen has been the major apologist for Bayer's Nazi involvements. He writes, "Bayer in those days was a political ingenue. Like many others of the most talented artists to work in Germany, he was too occupied with his work to be much interested in the political events of the day. He did not believe that National Socialism would thrive and only late in the day as the hold of the party tightened did he become aware that the artists could not survive unaffected. The two catalogues of 1936 [*sic*] demonstrated to him that the ministry of propaganda intended precisely that—to insure that every publication made its contribution to the national political will as conceived by the Nazis. Even after Bayer had emigrated, designs he had left in his office were used by others to serve political ends, one—a drawing of springtime—being forced to bear the most odious of Nazi slogans, 'Arbeit macht Frei' [*sic*], and signed completely without his knowledge

with his design stamp." Arthur A. Cohen, *Herbert Bayer: The Complete Work* (Cambridge, Mass.: MIT Press, 1984), 404. Buchloh, who first published the "Deutschland Ausstellung" montage in his article "From Faktura to Factography," offers a much stronger indictment of that work; Michelson et al., *October: The First Decade,* 112–13. The plate from "Das Wunder des Lebens" is published without commentary by Stanislaus von Moos in his article "'Modern Art Gets Down to Business': Anmerkungen zu Alexander Dorner and Herbert Bayer," in Hans M. Wingler and Magdalena Droste, eds., *Herbert Bayer: Das künstlerische Werk 1918–1938* (Berlin: Bauhaus-Archiv, 1982), 103. Cohen writes of this image: "A brilliant catalogue Bayer had designed for Das Wunder des Lebens exhibition organized by the Messenamt in Berlin in 1936 was stopped on press, and under pressure from the ministry of propaganda a small photograph of Adolf Hitler was inserted" (41).

49 In *The Romance of Commerce and Culture,* James Sloan Allen does an admirable job of recounting the story of Paepcke's relationship first to Moholy-Nagy in the context of the Bauhaus in Chicago and then to Bayer at Aspen. Apropos of the spectrum we are suggesting here, the following passage from his book is noteworthy: "Even more than Moholy-Nagy, Bayer was the kind of artist, if not quite so much the kind of man, that Paepcke appreciated. Darkly handsome, deep-voiced, contemplative, and familiar with the ways of commerce, Bayer, despite his frequent melancholy, was the one artist who caused Paepcke no discomfort in the shared company of businessmen. Lacking Moholy-Nagy's heady ambitions as teacher and cultural reformer (Bayer disliked teaching and shunned metaphysical claims for art) and possessing a gift for integrating abstract visual form and practical communication, Bayer could quickly grasp commercial imperatives and translate them into powerful yet elegant layouts

and graphics; as Gropius had said, with complimentary intent, 'Bayer had mastered the language of propaganda'" (128).

50 On Dorner's activities at the Rhode Island School of Design Museum of Art, see Cauman, *Living Museum,* 129–65; and Carolyn E. MacDonald, "Museum Resources for Teachers" (Ed.D. diss., Columbia University Teachers College, 1944), esp. 3–5. MacDonald was head of the museum's educational programs during Dorner's tenure there.

51 Cauman, *Living Museum,* 162.

52 Article in *Boston Herald,* September 5, 1941. I wish to thank Scott Duncan for help in locating this document.

53 Dorner, *Way Beyond "Art,"* 223. Also cited by von Moos in "'Modern Art Gets Down to Business,'" 105. Von Moos' perceptive essay is the only recent writing I have come across to deal critically with the relationship between Dorner and Bayer and to offer an interpretation of *The Way Beyond "Art."*

54 Dorner, *Way Beyond "Art,"* 119.

55 The monograph on Bayer in the end constituted less than one-third of the 230-page book. According to Cauman, the Bayer project outgrew its original scope as Dorner turned *The Way Beyond "Art"* into a much broader and more ambitious theoretical statement (146–47).

56 Alexander Dorner, "The Background of the Bauhaus," in Herbert Bayer, Walter Gropius, and Ise Gropius, eds., *Bauhaus 1919–1928* (New York: Museum of Modern Art, 1938), 9–13. The 1938 exhibition served the purpose of reidentifying the "Bauhaus idea" with the values of American freedom and democracy. However, the catalog stops well short of a full-scale condemnation of Hitler. In fact, Gropius, concerned about stirring up Nazi wrath against friends and

family still in Germany, proposed to include a statement—ultimately omitted—that read, "In 1933 the Bauhaus was closed by the National Socialist Government. Because the Bauhaus had developed during the Social Democratic regime, the National Socialists felt that it was related to the German Democracy and therefore should be excluded from the 'Third Reich.' Actually the Bauhaus under Gropius and Mies van der Rohe had always been deliberately non-political in character. Its radical innovations took place in the fields of art and education and they were never related to any political party program." He also persuaded Barr not to include a statement specifying the number of Jewish faculty who had taught at the school; Barr for his part was apparently concerned about rumors that the exhibition was "Jewish." See Reginald Isaacs, *Gropius: An Illustrated Biography of the Creator of the Bauhaus* (Boston: Little, Brown, 1991), 239–40. The Bauhaus' original reputation as a group of left-wing radicals was in the late 1930s clearly more dangerous to it than the recent flirtations with fascism by some of its members (including, in addition to Bayer, Mies van der Rohe, whose accommodations to the Third Reich have been well documented, and Schawinsky, a Jew who left Germany for Italy, where he used his graphic talents to glorify Mussolini before fleeing to the United States).

57 See Lynes, *Good Old Modern,* 181–82. Cf. "Bauhaus Exhibition," *Bulletin of the Museum of Modern Art* 6, vol. 5 (Dec. 1938): n.p. For Philip Johnson's reaction, also negative, see Schulze, *Philip Johnson: Life and Work,* 172. Johnson, in Germany during the summers of 1938 and 1939 and immersed in right-wing politics throughout this period, seems not to have seen the exhibition, although he receives a thank you from Barr in the preface to the catalog for volunteering assistance in its preparation.

58 Dorner, *Way Beyond "Art,"* 215.

59 Herbert Bayer, "Fundamentals of Exhibition Design," *P.M.* [Production Manager] *Magazine*, Dec.–Jan. 1939–40, 17. Cited in *Way Beyond "Art,"* 200–201.

60 In fact, the motif of the hand—his own—appears repeatedly in Bayer's work, most often as a token or fetish of artistic creativity. A surrealistic photomontage of 1932, *Lonely Metropolitan*, in which two disembodied hands, each bearing an eye, float in front of a building facade, typifies this preoccupation.

61 Dorner, *Way Beyond "Art,"* 118.

62 Dorner, *Way Beyond "Art,"* 180–81.

63 John Dewey, "Pragmatic America," *New Republic*, Apr. 12, 1922; republ. in Gail Kennedy, ed., *Pragmatism and American Culture* (Boston: D. C. Heath and Company, 1950), 59.

64 Cf. Cohen, who stresses that Bayer was "thoroughly nonpolitical in his viewpoint" and harbored no interest "in advancing a public collectivity or a socialist sensibility," elaborating, "Although . . . Bayer's conception of 'total design' has considerable social consequence and significance, since it depends for its viability on the receptiveness of the public to its own visual reeducation, the intent of Bayer's vision is neither Marxist nor collectivist. . . . His recognition that the large corporation is the single institution of modern economic life with the power and, where guided by enlightened and socially responsible management, the efficient will to effect visual communication and to institute a program of total design, is an acknowledgment, *faute de mieux*, of the dominance of a capitalist market system. Bayer passes no judgment on this state of affairs. As a pragmatist he adapts to it." Cohen, *Herbert Bayer: The Complete Work*, 410.

65 *herbert bayer: painter, designer, architect*, 7; Bayer's lower-case orthography. Cohen writes: "The exaggerated claims Dorner had made for Bayer's art in early drafts of *The Way Beyond 'Art'* had made the artist uneasy. Bayer encouraged Dorner to soften his enthusiasm; nonetheless, the book as it was finally published remains one of the finest examples of interpretive advocacy and makes clear Dorner's sense of Bayer as an artist who conceived of art in all its domains as the achievement of a concrete and transmissible grammar of visual communication. *The Way Beyond 'Art,'* despite its occasional excess and tendentiousness, is the first exposition of the artist as communicator of a total system of visual signs, encompassing without discrimination of 'high' and 'popular' the arts of painting and graphic design." Cohen, *Herbert Bayer: The Complete Work*, 410.

66 Rosamund Frost, "This Business Ties Art into a Neat Package," *Art News*, May 15–31, 1945; cited in Allen, *Romance of Commerce and Culture*, 71.

67 Dorner, *Way Beyond "Art"* (rev. ed., New York: New York University Press, 1958), 7.

68 Dorner Archives, Box H.

69 Dorner, *Way Beyond "Art,"* 123.

70 Adelbert Ames Jr., "Sensations, Their Nature and Origin: A Synthesis of the Findings of the Hanover Institute Experiments in Visual Perception," *Trans/Formation: Arts, Communication, Environment* 1, no. 1 (1950): 11. On Dewey's involvement with Ames, see Hadley Cantril, ed., *The Morning Notes of Adelbert Ames, Jr., Including a Correspondence with John Dewey* (New Brunswick, N.J.: Rutgers University Press, 1960). Ames's experiments with spatial perception also made a passing impression on Giedion and Barr when they saw him present them at Princeton and the Hanover Institute respectively. Sigfried Giedion

and Alfred H. Barr Jr., "Notes on the Ames Demonstrations: Art and Perception," *Trans/Formation: Arts, Communication, Environment* 1, no. 1 (1950), 8–9. Also see Adelbert Ames Jr., "Architectural Form and Visual Sensations," in Thomas H. Creighton, ed., *Building for Modern Man* (Princeton: Princeton University Press, 1949), 82–88.

71 Letter from Ames to Dorner, April 15, 1947, Bennington College Library.

72 Dorner Archives, Box R.

73 Letter from Dewey to Dorner, April 1, 1947, Bennington College Library. I wish to express my appreciation to Professor Muriel Palmer of Bennington College, a former acquaintance of Dorner's, for providing me with a copy of this letter as well as other information and reminiscences.

74 Dorner, *Way Beyond "Art,"* 10.

75 John Dewey, *Art as Experience* (New York: Minton, Balch & Company, 1934), 8.

76 Dorner, *Way Beyond "Art,"* 231.

77 Dorner, *Way Beyond "Art,"* 232–33.

78 Cauman, *Living Museum*, 178.

79 Cauman, *Living Museum*, 87.

80 Cauman, *Living Museum*, 186.

81 Cauman, *Living Museum*, 187.

82 See André Malraux, "Museum Without Walls," in *The Voices of Silence* (1951; Garden City, N.Y.: Doubleday, 1953), 13–127.

83 Malraux, "Museum Without Walls," 16 (translation modified).

84 Theodor Adorno, "Valéry Proust Museum," in *Prisms* (Cambridge, Mass.: MIT Press, 1981), 173.

85 Cited in Benjamin Ives Gilman,

Museum Ideals: Of Purpose and Method, 2nd ed. (Boston: Museum of Fine Arts, 1923), 128.

86 Gilman, *Museum Ideals*, 128.

87 Dorner, *Way Beyond "Art,"* 232.

88 Copy of letter, dated January 19, 1955, Dorner Archives, Box P. Published (without date) in Cauman, *Living Museum*, 106.

89 Dorner, *Way Beyond "Art,"* 232.

Wild Kingdom
Frederick Kiesler's Display of the Avant-Garde

MARK LINDER

1 Ada Louise Huxtable, "Architecture on TV: 'Greatest Non-Building Architect of Our Time' Expounds His Ideas." *New York Times*, March 27, 1960, section 2, 13.

2 Lisa Phillips, "Environmental Artist," in *Frederick Kiesler*, ed. Lisa Phillips (exhibition catalog, New York: W. W. Norton & Co., 1989), 108. Despite Phillips' emphasis on Kiesler's multidisciplinarity, the essays in the catalog she edited tend to reinforce disciplinary boundaries and stylistic categories. (The Whitney exhibition was first staged in Vienna at the Museum des 20.Jahrhunderts from April 26 to June 19, 1988, for which Dieter Bogner edited a more elaborate, but similarly organized, catalog.)

3 Robert Pincus-Witten, "Thinking About Kiesler," *Frederick Kiesler (1890–1965) Galaxies* (New York: Alfred Kren Gallery Jason McCoy, 1986), unpaginated.

4 Thomas Creighton, "Kiesler's Pursuit of an Idea," *Progressive Architecture*, July 1961, 115. Phillips does name Kiesler's idea: "the concept of spatial continuity—of endlessness." Lisa Phillips, "Architect of Endless Innovation," in Phillips, *Frederick Kiesler*, 13.

5 Creighton, "Kiesler's Pursuit of an Idea," 115–16. Kiesler mentions six projects: "in the *mobile* interior of *The Emperor Jones*; in the endless *continuity* of the exhibition-method of the L. & T.; in my *galaxial* mural consisting of manifold units of paintings in the year 1918 and continued in 1950; in the 'Space-House' of 1936 [1933, *sic*]; in the galaxy or '*environmental sculpture*' of 1947 or the one owned by Philip Johnson (both sculptures '*to live in and with*'); in the eighteen functions of the one chair of the Peggy Guggenheim gallery, certainly an extension and variability of a simple core."

6 Creighton, "Kiesler's Pursuit of an Idea," 110.

7 For the Vienna exhibition, Kiesler devised his "L + T" installation system, an interchangeable combination of twelve-to-fifteen-foot-tall linear units, composed of horizontal and vertical suspended wooden members painted red, black, and white, which could display both flat and three-dimensional objects.

8 For the New York exhibition, Kiesler reproduced the Vienna catalog in English as the winter 1926 issue of the *Little Review*.

9 Although he began to attack the Bauhaus and functionalism in the early 1930s, Kiesler would not fully renounce de Stijl until 1957: "The venerable Bauhaus-Tradition AND the de Stijl—are dead." Frederick Kiesler, "Design in Continuity," *Architectural Forum*, Oct. 1957, 127. His association with individuals such as van Doesburg, Mondrian, and Oud continued to be supportive into the thirties, and as Kiesler admits in *Contemporary Art Applied to the Store and Its Display* (New York: Brentano's, 1930), the facade of his Film Guild Cinema (1929) has an obvious resemblance to Oud's Café de Unie (1925).

10 Frederick Kiesler, "Vitalbau—Raumstadt—Funktionelle Architektur," *De Stijl* 6, no. 10–11 (1925), 141–47. Based upon the success of the Vienna exhibition, Josef Hoffmann selected Kiesler to design the Austrian theater section of the 1925 Exposition International des Arts Décoratifs et Industriels Modernes. There, Kiesler displayed his City in Space, at once a utopian urban concept and a practical exhibition system that refined the L + T system he developed for the Vienna show. The installation was at the time one of the most ambitious architectural applications of de Stijl. It earned the praise of van Doesburg and Mondrian as well as the derision of Le Corbusier, who had constructed his Pavillon de l'Esprit Nouveau and exhibited his Plan Voisin at the exposition. Of course, Kiesler's City in Space remained a fantasy, as Le Corbusier could well have predicted. Recounting their meeting in his

1961 *Progressive Architecture* interview, Kiesler first praises the Plan Voisin as Le Corbusier's "great contribution . . . adopted by town planners the world over." But then, with more than a hint of resentment, he plays Le Corbusier as a fool: "When I explained to Le Corbusier the 'City in Space' in 1925 in Paris (he came with Léger to the Grand Palais), he asked me, 'Do you intend to hang the houses from Zeppelins?' I said: 'No.' 'Well how then are you going to suspend the City in Space?' 'By suspension in tension,' I answered. His pilotis came later." As he did so often, Kiesler then reiterates his 1925 manifesto.

11 Andreas Huyssen characterizes autonomy as a trait of "modernism" (as espoused by either Adorno or Greenberg), which he opposes to "the avant-garde's intention to merge art and life." Andreas Huyssen, "Mapping the Postmodern," *New German Critique* 33 (Fall 1984): 21.

12 See Kiesler, *Contemporary Art Applied to the Store*, 111.

13 In the remainder of the decade, Kiesler would design a state-of-the-art theater complex in Brooklyn, devise his "telemuseum," and build the Film Guild Cinema, a total cinematic environment where images could be projected on three walls as well as on the ceiling.

14 As is perhaps appropriate for a translator, Kiesler's status in the development of American modernism remains indistinct and undervalued, despite his prolific efforts. As Paul de Man has written, "the translator, per definition, fails. . . . Any translation is always second in relation to the original, and the translator as such is lost from the very beginning. He is per definition underpaid, he is per definition overworked, he is the one history will not retain as an equal." Paul de Man, "Walter Benjamin's 'The Task of the Translator,'" *The Resistance to Theory* (Minneapolis: University of Minnesota Press, 1986), 80.

15 George Nelson, "Introduction," in *Display*, ed. George Nelson (New York: Interiors Library, 1953), 7, 8. Nelson also writes: "The fleeting nature of designs for display has an extraordinary effect on the architect and designer: here, he realizes, he can do his work without the fear that posterity may mock him for his ineptness, and thus freed from the censure of generation unborn he can take a chance, try something out; and in a word, relax. . . . The designer can ease up a bit and enjoy himself. The result can be fun. It is surprising how often it is significant fun" (8–9). Nelson includes none of Kiesler's work in his book.

16 Robert Pincus-Witten reports that Kiesler was in Jungian analysis for at least five years. He is known to have attended a lecture by Jung (Oct. 2, 1936), and had numerous books on psychoanalysis in his library, including several by Freud (in German and English), Karen Horney's *Self Analysis* (1942), as well as *Les Psychoses* (1958), the fourth volume of *La Psychanalyse*. Kiesler worked on what he called a "vision machine" from 1937 to at least 1941, when he formed a formal "advisory committee" at Columbia University. In 1942 he published "Some Testimonial Drawings of Dream Images," *VVV* 1 (June 1942): 27–32. I am suggesting that Kiesler's connection to surrealism is distinct from that expressed in Hans Arp's homage to the Endless House in his 1947 essay "L'oeuf de Kiesler et la Salle des Superstitions," *Cahiers de Art* 22 (1947): 281–86. Arp reiterates Breton's notion of a unifying and transformative surrealism that spans the difference between objective and subjective representations. Pushing the presumptions of impressionism and cubism to their limit, Breton proposed that: "we [surrealists] have succeeded in *dialectically* reconciling these two terms—perception and representation—that are so violently contradictory for the adult man, and . . . we have thrown a bridge over the abyss that separated them. Surrealist

painting and construction have now permitted the organization of perceptions with an objective tendency around subjective elements." André Breton, "Surrealist Situation of the Object" (1935), *Manifestoes of Surrealism*, trans. Richard Seaver and Helen Lane (Ann Arbor: University of Michigan Press, 1969), 278.

17 Kiesler professed notions of artistic genius, stoic individualism, and egoistic subjectivity later in his life. Abandoning the notion of the artist as a participant in a grand, cooperative social experiment, he professed in a 1958 lecture ("Art is the Teaching of Resistance," *College Art Journal* 18 [Spring 1959]: 237) that "the so-called artist must learn only *one thing* in order to be creative: *not to resist himself*, but to resist, without exception every human, technical, social, economical factor that prevents him from being himself." In a passage dated July 3, 1960, from *Inside the Endless House*, a "journal" of his life between 1956 and 1965, Kiesler expressed a keen admiration for what he called the "tripartite artist," an individual who forces an original integration and similitude of painting, sculpture, and architecture. Kiesler specifically names Giotto and Michelangelo (Philip Johnson once described him as "our Leonardoesque man"), and one might infer that he wanted to be remembered similarly. Most accounts do characterize him that way: as a uniquely and diversely talented individual who avoided stylistic or theoretical classification, introduced and explored ideas that would later be more fully developed by others, and attempted odd artistic combinations by willfully breaking disciplinary boundaries. Such a description certainly applies to Kiesler's last projects, such as his 1964 show at the Guggenheim Museum, "Environmental Sculpture," or his posthumously exhibited installation "Us, you, me." Those exhibitions were by far the most extensive presentation of his ideas and efforts toward the combination of

sculpture, architecture, and painting, and as a result it firmly established Kiesler's reputation as a multidisciplinary artist.

18 In 1950, Drexler (as architectural editor) published an article on the Endless House in *Interiors* magazine. That same year Johnson purchased an early model of the Endless House for the Museum of Modern Art. That project was developed in collaboration with the sculptor David Hare for a 1950 show titled "The Muralist and Modern Architecture" at the Kootz Gallery.

19 Huxtable, "Architecture on TV," 13. Kiesler's rhetoric, with its ample measure of neologisms and hyperbole, was concerned less with dissimulation than distraction: it is a supplement which effectively reorients the work's reception and enacts its display.

20 Huxtable writes in "Architecture on TV": "The basic fallacy is that Mr. Kiesler's concept of architecture is not really architectural. He is primarily interested in sculpture, for which he has exceptional sensibility, and he camouflages abstract sculpture as a kind of building." Kiesler takes the inverse attitude toward the relationship of architecture and sculpture. In 1930 he wrote: "Modern sculpture is abstract architecture." Kiesler, *Contemporary Art Applied to the Store*, 28. In 1966 he commented on the Guggenheim Museum and Ronchamp: "The giant hollow space of the interior only comes to life when filled with visitors on festive occasions. . . . The people are transformed into sculptures ever moving at different speeds of coordination." Frederick Kiesler, "The Future: Notes on Architecture as Sculpture," *Art in America* (May–June 1966): 63. In a statement printed on the announcement for his 1954 exhibition "Galaxies," at the Janis Gallery (Sept. 27–Oct. 19), Kiesler claimed that in his work "the traditional division of the plastic arts into painting sculpture and architecture, is transmut-

ed and over-come; and their fluid unification is now contained within rather than combined from without. If a reassessment of values in these times is of necessity for each and all of us, one is convinced that the artist's work too can no longer be placed in isolation; that art must strive again to become part of daily existence. It seems, therefore, that painters, sculptors and architects must conceive their work technically and ideologically as not apart but as part of the world we live in, or better, the world we desire to live in. Hence, the artist's work will foster a new plastic environment no matter what craft he belongs to." Huxtable was certainly aware of Kiesler's friendship with Robert Rauschenberg and Duchamp and her reaction was likely colored by a skepticism toward the rhetoric of neo-dada art.

21 Quoted in Phillips, "Architect of Endless Innovation," 13.

22 The term "navel" originated in 1900 in Freud's *The Interpretation of Dreams*, S.E. 5, 530. "Even in the best interpreted dreams, there is often a place that must be left in the dark, because in the process of interpreting one notices a tangle of dream-thoughts arising which resists unraveling but has also made no further contributions to the dream-content. This, then, is the navel of the dream, the place where it straddles the unknown. The dream-thoughts, to which interpretation leads one, are necessarily interminable and branch out on all sides into the net-like entanglement of our world of thought. Out of one of the denser places in this network, the dream-wish rises like a mushroom out of its mycelium." Jacques Lacan, in 1964, extended the concept to the unconscious and to discourse in general: "It is not without effect that, even in a public speech, one directs one's attention at subjects, touching them at what Freud calls the navel—*the navel of dreams*, he writes, to designate their ultimately unknown center—which is

simply, like the anatomical navel that represents it, that gap [*béance*] of which I have already spoken." Lacan, *The Four Fundamental Concepts of Psycho-Analysis*, ed. Jacques-Alain Miller, trans. Alan Sheridan (New York: W. W. Norton, 1977), 23. Samuel Weber in *The Legend of Freud* (Minneapolis: University of Minnesota Press, 1982), 75–82, offers an interesting comparison of Freud's and Lacan's concepts of the navel, in effect "straddling" the difference between them.

23 One event in particular has recognized the complexity of this moment. In 1987, Janet Kardon organized the exhibition "1967: At the Crossroads" at the Institute of Contemporary Art of the University of Pennsylvania (Mar. 13–Apr. 26). See Janet Kardon, ed., *1967: At the Crossroads* (exhibition catalog, Philadelphia: Institute of Contemporary Art, 1967). The catalog includes the essay "1987/1967" by Hal Foster, who organized a symposium of (almost) the same name at the Dia Center. See Hal Foster, ed., "1967/1987: Genealogies of Art and Theory," *Discussions in Contemporary Culture: Number One* (Seattle: Bay Press, 1987), 55–119. The year 1967 marks what Foster calls the "crux of minimalism," a moment that can be traced in a cluster of essays written between 1965 and 1967: Donald Judd's "Specific Objects" (1965), Robert Morris's "Notes on Sculpture" (1966), and Michael Fried's "Art and Objecthood" (1967).

24 Jacques Lacan, "The Transference and the Drive," in *Four Fundamental Concepts*, 143. It was first published as *Le Seminaire de Jacques Lacan, Livre XI, "Les quatre concepts fondamentaux de la psychanalyse"* (Editions du Seuil, 1973). This seminar was held from January to June 1964.

25 As Donald Judd would write, the new art fell into two categories: objects that would later be described as minimalist and work that is "more or less environmental." Donald Judd, "Specific Objects," *Arts Yearbook* 8 (1965): 74–82.

26 Peter Bürger, *Theory of the Avant-Garde*, trans. M. Shaw (Minneapolis: University of Minnesota Press, 1984), 87.

27 Huyssen, "Mapping the Postmodern," 20.

28 Hal Foster, "The Crux of Minimalism," *Individuals: A Selected History of Contemporary Art, 1945–1986* (New York: Abbeville Press, 1986), 170.

29 Sometime in 1936 or 1937 Kiesler distributed a five-page, typed pamphlet titled "Correalism" as the first in what he planned as a series of "pamphlets, books, and articles, from time to time, dealing with architectural topics and the interdependence of science, art and industry." Archive of American Art, microfilm 127: 652–56.

30 Kiesler had access to German and French books through his wife, Steffi, who worked at the foreign language desk of the New York Public Library from 1927 to 1959. Portmann's *Zoologie und das neue Bild des Menschen* (Rowolts deutsche Enzyklopädie, vol. 20, Hamburg, 1956) was originally published as *Biologische Fragmente zu einer Lehre vom Menschen* (Basel, 1944) and has been translated as *A Zoologist Looks at Humankind*, trans. J. Schaefer (New York: Columbia University Press, 1990). Portmann's theory of self-display is presented in *Die Tiergestalt: Studien über die Bedeutung der tierischen Erscheinung* (Basel, 1948; *Animal Forms and Patterns: A Study of the Appearance of Animals*, trans. Hella Czech, New York: Shocken Books, 1952). In the 1960s Portmann published numerous articles in English on aesthetic topics. See, for example, his essay "Color/Structure/ Pattern in the Animal Kingdom," published in *The Structurist* 8: titled "Light/ Color/Space/Structure in Art and Nature" (1968): 78–87, or his introduction to the catalog *Form in Art*

and Nature*, eds. George Schmidt and Robert Schenk (Basel: Basilius Press, 1960), 15–17.

31 Adolf Portmann, "The Living Thing as Pre-Arranged Relationship," *Essays in Philosophical Zoology by Adolf Portmann: The Living Form and the Seeing Eye*, trans. R. Carter (Lewiston, N.Y.: Edwin Mellen Press, 1990), 25 (originally published as "Das Lebendige als vorbereitete Beziehung," *Eranos-Jahrbuch* 1955, 485–506). Also see Portmann, *Animal Forms and Patterns*, 220: "All around us are forms of life, small or large, in which have been realized other possibilities of existence than those found in our own lives. At times, the sight of these organic forms makes us feel as if we are faced with the uncanny materialization of our dream life, the products of our fantasy. . . . Today as never before the creative artist pays attention to the interplay of these hidden workings within us."

32 Adolph Portmann, *New Paths in Biology*, trans. A. Pomerans, vol. 30 of *World Perspectives*, ed. Ruth Anshen (New York: Harper & Row, 1964). The quotation is from Wölfflin's "Die Kunst der Renaissance," *Italien und das Deutsche Formgefühl* (Munich, 1931), 111. Also see Portmann, "What Does the Living Form Mean to Us?," *Essays in Philosophical Zoology* [originally published as "Was bedeutet uns die lebendige Gestalt," *Neue Sammlung Göttinger Blätter für Kultur und Erziehung* 6, no. 1 (Jan.–Feb. 1966): 1–7]: "living forms, inside, build according to rules which differ from those which they use to build their outward appearances—that is, we perceive that in nature a facade has a certain value and that appearance is not a deception but an element of manifestation and, in particular, of the manifestation of a being whose source is hidden from us. . . . No one denies the importance of the work concerned with preservation in the game of life; it is also present in the organs of appearance. Still, prior to all functions in the

service of bare preservation, prior to all this sort of activity which has gained so much attention, we are faced with the straightforward appearance as self-representation in the living being. And thus, time and time again, the fathoming of form leads beyond the realm in which research shows us the structures which are merely functionally significant."

33 Adolf Portmann, "What Does the Living Form Mean to Us?," 151. An earlier, less explicit example occurs in his 1948 book, *Die Tiergestalt*: "When functional connections are set forth [in evolutionary theory] they tend to be confined to certain examples in which there is a specially striking unity between shape and function. . . . This utmost purposiveness, this perfect agreement between form and function, is considered to be the way in which Nature really works and which man as an artistic creator must imitate. It has not been adequately noticed that this theory works backwards by encouraging us to take note almost exclusively of such 'technical' forms of life, i.e. of specially adapted organisms, and thus creates a privileged class. The 'other' organisms then are rabble or vermin, monsters or abortions, worms or maggots, a collections of monstrosities from which just a few groups are separated off to receive a one-sided aesthetic respect." Portmann, *Animal Forms and Patterns*, 209–10.

34 See, for example, Kiesler's "Design Correlation: Architecture and Animals," *Architectural Record*, Apr. 1937, 87–92. Also see note 43, below.

35 Frederick Kiesler, "Pseudo-Functionalism in Modern Architecture," *Partisan Review* 16 (July 1949): 733–42. At one point Kiesler writes: "At this stage we need not greatly concern ourselves with the future ears, hands and other functional organs of the body of the house . . . these elements are available; they can be had for money. What cannot be bought is the character of the species" (734).

36 Kiesler, "Pseudo-Functionalism in Modern Architecture," 738.

37 Portmann, *Animal Forms and Patterns*, 214.

38 Portmann, *New Paths in Biology*, 99.

39 Despite their different approaches to philosophy and psychology, both Portmann and Lacan were significantly indebted to the other's sources. Lacan studied phenomenology at the Ecole des Hautes Etudes, and the writings of Maurice Merleau-Ponty serve as a proximate discipline for dialogue and a means of critical exchange throughout his career, as is evident in the seminars of 1953–54 and 1964. Portmann was associated with psychoanalysis through Carl Jung, with whom he was acquainted as a member of the Eranos group, an interdisciplinary symposium that has met each August since 1933 in Ascona, Switzerland. Meetings that both Jung and Portmann attended were in 1946, 1948, and 1951. On the psychoanalysis of display see Roger Caillois, "Mimicry and Legendary Psychasthenia," *October* 31 (Winter 1984): 17–32 (originally published as "Mimetisme et psychasthénie légendaire," *Minotaure* 7, 1935) and Jacques Lacan, "The mirror stage as formative of the function of the I as revealed in psychoanalytic experience," *Écrits: A Selection*, trans. Alan Sheridan (New York: W. W. Norton, 1977; originally published in the *Revue francaise de psychanalyse* 4, Oct.–Dec. 1949, 449–55; first version presented in 1936). In the sixties, both Caillois and Portmann were critics of the Batesian "mimicry hypothesis." See Adolph Portmann, *New Paths in Biology*, 97–99, and Roger Caillois, *The Mask of Medusa*, trans. George Ordish (New York: Clarkson N. Potter, 1964), 55–102 (originally published as *Méduse et Cie*, Paris: Librairie Gallimard, 1960).

40 In his 1944 book, *Biologische Fragmente zu einer Lehre vom Menschen* (the book of which

Kiesler owned a later edition), Portmann presented an alternative explanation of the unusual development of humans in their first year (one that is entirely compatible with Lacan's theory of the mirror stage). Portmann presented a synopsis of that explanation in his presentation at the 1946 Eranos conference: "human development in the womb is not prolonged proportionately to the complexity of our order, as is the case with the other higher mammals. It is approximately a year too short, if we take mammals for our norm. The time needed for adaptation to the obligatory social world is thus prolonged not only through postponement of sexual maturity and the late termination of growth, but also, most significantly through our early birth. Why is this so significant? Because the circumstance transfers a stage of development which in the higher mammals occurs in the womb, a constant environment poor in stimuli, to a shifting social world, rich in stimuli. It is precisely in this year that is snatched away from the uterine period that the faculties of standing, speaking, and thinking are developed—and in ways that can be shown to be peculiarly human: by a combination of maturation processes which constitute an obligatory primary system no part of which can be changed without totally vitiating the subsequent development." Adolph Portmann, "Biology and the Phenomenon of the Spiritual," *Spirit and Nature: Papers from the Eranos Yearbooks* (Princeton N.J.: Princeton University Press, 1982), 355–56. In the seminar of 1953–54, Lacan uses the phenomenon of sexual selection in animals to introduce the role of the imaginary in the formation and functioning of the human ego. "Let's start with the animal, an animal which is also an ideal . . . [which] gives us a vision of completeness, of fulfillment, because it presupposes the perfect fit, indeed the identity of the *Innenwelt* and the *Umwelt*. That's what makes this living form seductive, as its appearance harmoniously

unfolds. . . . Let us simplify matters and consider this functioning solely at one given moment. The male or female animal is captivated, as it were, by a *Gestalt*. . . . Let us say that, in the animal world, the entire cycle of sexual behavior is dominated by the imaginary." Lacan then enters into an elaborate explanation of optics, virtual images, and displacement. Jacques Lacan, *The Seminar of Jacques Lacan: Freud's Papers on Technique,* trans. John Forrester (New York: W. W. Norton, 1988), 137–38.

41 In *Four Fundamental Concepts*, Lacan offers one of his more precise, yet enigmatic, statements, characterizing psychoanalysis as an attempt "to embody psychical reality without substantifying it" (72). As Freud offered an alternative to the behavioral and idealist conceptions of "mind," Lacan offers an alternative to the substantive notions of cognition and consciousness. While his work leaves us no identifiable *object* of study (no accessible "real" presented in the appearance of things), be it artifactual, metaphysical or psychological, those same writings (including the formulas, diagrams, and dialogues embedded therein) are unequivocal on the *subject* of study. Lacan explains (later in *Four Fundamental Concepts*), "Psychoanalysis is neither a *Weltanschauung*, nor a philosophy that claims to provide the key to the universe. It is governed by a particular aim, which is historically defined by the elaboration of the notion of the subject" (77). Yet the Lacanian subject is not only "unsubstantified." In a kind of mock repetition of Solomonic judgment, Lacan proposes a splitting of the subject as well, and begins to structure a model, or schema, of the subject that is riven by a deep gap, or seam. Lacan's formulas and diagrams convey the order of this split subject most vividly in the figure known as the Schéma L, in which the subject is divided into a *moi* (an irretrievable ideal ego of identifications) and a *je* (a speaking subject, an ego-ideal governing imaginary

identifications), both of which enter into structural and unconscious relations with others. But like Kiesler's diagrammatic drawings of houses, devices, and installations, Lacan's schemas remain puzzling and allusive. As Ellie Ragland-Sullivan explains, "Lacan's schemata are to be taken as didactic. Their relation with structure is one of analogy that is itself inadequate. That is, the graphs neither ground reality nor retain anything measurable. They are reduced, like the real, to representatives of a given fantasy of which a point or cut provides the structure itself. . . . The schemata are, Lacan said, a way by which to fix ideas that call forth a weakness in our discursive abilities." Ragland-Sullivan, *Jacques Lacan and the Philosophy of Psychoanalysis* (Urbana: University of Illinois Press, 1986), xxi.

42 Harry Adsit Bull, *International Studio* 97 (Dec. 1930): 84. The quotation is from page 20 of Kiesler's book.

43 Kiesler's ability both to participate and to distance himself from the Museum of Modern Art proved to be an effective strategy until at least 1950 when Johnson purchased the Endless House model. This posture would begin to explain why, until 1950, Kiesler's best patrons would be galleries and independent collectors such as Katherine Dreier and Peggy Guggenheim. Kiesler was not part of the Museum of Modern Art's International Style exhibition of 1932, and while Alfred Barr included him in the "Cubism and Abstract Art" show of 1936, he selected minor projects in three different disciplines: theater (the set for *R.U.R.*), architecture (the City in Space), furniture (a lighting fixture). In "Design Correlation: Architecture and Animals," Kiesler lampooned the presumed functionalism of Tecton's modern architecture at the London Whipsnade Zoo, published in Hitchcock's book *Modern Architecture in England*, which was published by the Museum of Modern Art. He chastises Hitchcock for writing "It could be

objected that the penguin pool was not in the fullest sense architecture, but rather a large object or a permanent stage setting." Kiesler replies: "Which it is exactly (see Tatlin Tower, Space-Stage, Meyerhold-Theater)" (89). Not by chance, the previous issue of *Architectural Record* was titled "Architectural Practice and Design in England" and guest-edited by H. de Cronin Hastings of *Architectural Review*. Eventually, Kiesler praises the English modernism: "But: It is very much to the credit of England to have driven on many roads to the center of architecture, namely, to correlative planning, rather than concentration on unique form." Despite his own International Style design for "An American Bauhaus," published in 1934 (see E. M. Benson, "Wanted: An American Bauhaus (Architectural Plans by Frederick J. Kiesler)," *American Magazine of Art* 27, June 1934: 307–11), Kiesler reveals his animosity toward Hitchcock and particularly Johnson who, Kiesler remarks in a footnote, "Quit in 1935 post as Curator of Architecture at the Museum of Modern Art to join forces with the late Senator Huey P. Long" (88). He also implies that zoos are to animals what museums are to art. Thus might be inferred his advocacy of "the ecological abstraction of [nature] if the natural surroundings cannot be provided. . . . Such planned *Correlation-design* is practical in the very meaning of the word" (90–91).

44 Kiesler, "Pseudo-Functionalism in Modern Architecture," 737. Ten years earlier, in "On Correalism and Biotechnique: A Definition and Test of a New Approach to Building Design" (*Architectural Record,* Sept. 1939, 66), Kiesler had bluntly labeled as "scholastic" Barr's attempts to trace specific connections between architecture and painting. Barr wrote: "Purist paintings were designed architectonically so that they were appropriate decorations for the new architecture which Le Corbusier was just developing. Furthermore they were exercises in color which

Le Corbusier was to use so subtly in his architecture. . . . This is not to say that Le Corbusier's architecture is an outgrowth of his Purist painting: they were, rather, interdependent developments united by the same aesthetic and the same immaculate taste." Alfred Barr, *Cubism and Abstract Art* (New York: Museum of Modern Art, 1936), 166.

45 *La Mariée mise à nu par ses célibataires, même*, ed. Rose Sélavy (Paris, 1934). Duchamp's letter was dated June 25, 1937. Six months later (in January 1938), Kiesler lectured on the *Large Glass* at the Art Students League. In 1937 Kiesler bought and sold at least two works of Duchamp's. It is likely that Kiesler had seen André Breton's essay on the *Large Glass* in *Minotaure* 6, 1935 (translated and republished in *View*, 1945.)

46 It is also unavoidable to compare Kiesler's gallery to Duchamp's installation earlier in 1942 in New York for the exhibition "First Papers of Surrealism." Duchamp lived with the Kieslers for a year, beginning in October 1942. See Jennifer Gough-Cooper and Jacques Caumont, "Frederick Kiesler and *The Bride Stripped Bare* . . . " in *Frederick Kiesler, 1890–1965*, ed. Yehuda Safran (London: Architectural Association, 1989), 64. But according to Lisa Phillips's chronology in *Frederick Kiesler*, Duchamp lived with the Kieslers from June 26, 1942, when he returned to New York, until October. (According to a typescript at the Museum of Modern Art, Kiesler had begun the design of the gallery in March, and the plans were finished in April.)

47 Kiesler, *Contemporary Art Applied to the Store*, 66. Some of Kiesler's later store-window designs for Saks were published in the September 1930 issue of *Architectural Record*.

48 Kiesler, *Contemporary Art Applied to the Store*, 67. Four years later, in a sense, Kiesler's prediction, came true. In his 1934

lectures at the Chicago Merchandise Mart's Clinic of Modern Design on "The Difference Between Good and Bad Modern Design," Kiesler advocated the importance of nonskid bathtubs. His opinion was reported in over forty newspapers, many in small towns in the Midwest—the Madison, South Dakota, *Leader;* the Abilene, Texas, *Reporter News* (two articles)—as well as in Philadelphia, New York, Seattle, and Los Angeles. See Lillian Kiesler, "Frederick Kiesler: Bibliography of Articles by and about Frederick Kiesler" (typescript, 1980), 49–51.

49 Kiesler, *Contemporary Art Applied to the Store*, 70.

50 Kiesler, *Contemporary Art Applied to the Store*, 66, 68. Kiesler was by no means alone in his fascination with commercial displays. As Jerrold Seigel notes in *The Private Worlds of Marcel Duchamp: Desire, Liberation, and the Self in Modern Culture* (Berkeley: University of California Press, 1995), 29: "In France before World War I there was much discussion about how modern commerce sought to harness the powers of desire and fantasy for the lowly purpose of selling goods. Merchandise displays of all types—department stores, international expositions, and the salons of individual products like automobiles—all enveloped things in search of buyers in an aura of exoticism and sexual suggestion."

51 In a late review of the Art of this Century Gallery, Edgar Kaufmann Jr. criticized this approach, and compared Kiesler's design unfavorably to Wright's as yet unbuilt Guggenheim Museum. Kaufmann was clearly taking a shot at Kiesler, who claimed to have devised the idea of a spiral-ramped museum. Compare Kiesler's "Notes on the Spiral Theme in Recent Architecture," *Partisan Review* (Winter 1946): 98–104, to Kaufmann's "The Violent Art of Hanging Pictures," *Magazine of Art* 39 (Mar. 1946): 108–13.

52 See "Inheritors of Chaos," *Time*, Nov. 2, 1942, 47.

53 Clement Greenberg, "Cubist, Abstract, Surrealist Art. Guggenheim Collection. Art of this Century Gallery," *Nation*, Jan. 30, 1943, 177.

54 Less than two years later, in 1944 (the year of Mondrian's death), Greenberg published both an explicit defense of "abstract art" and a vicious two-part attack on surrealism. See Clement Greenberg, "Abstract Art," *Nation*, Apr. 15, 1944, 450–51, and "Surrealist Painting: Parts I and II," *Nation,* Aug. 12 and 19, 1944, 192–93, 219–20.

55 In 1948 Greenberg explicitly presented the problem: "There is a persistent urge, as persistent as it is largely unconscious, to go beyond the cabinet [or easel] picture, which is destined to occupy only a spot on the wall, to a kind of picture that, without actually becoming identified with the wall like a mural, would *spread* over it and acknowledge its physical reality. I do not know whether there is anything in modern architecture itself that explicitly invites this tendency. But it is a fact that abstract painting shows a greater reluctance for the small, frame-enclosed format. Abstract painting, being flat, needs a greater extension of surface on which to develop its ideas than does the old three-dimensional easel-painting, and it seems to become trivial when confined within anything measuring less than two feet by two. Thus, while the painter's relation to his art has become more private than ever before because of a shrinking appreciation on the public's part, the architectural and, presumably, social location for which he destines his product has become, in inverse ratio, more public. This is the paradox, the contradiction, the master-current of painting. Perhaps the contradiction between the architectural destination of abstract art and the very, very private atmosphere in which it is produced will kill ambitious painting in the end. As it is, this contradiction, whose ultimate causes lie outside the autonomy of art, defines specifically the crisis in which

painting now finds itself." Clement Greenberg, "The Situation at the Moment," *Partisan Review*, Jan. 1948, 83–84.

56 Greenberg would always dismiss Duchamp. In his review of Art of this Century, he merely remarks that Duchamp's "little quasi-cubist paintings, [are] shown here—with less success—in a glass cage."

57 Frederick Kiesler, "Design Correlation: a column on exhibits, the theater and the cinema," *Architectural Record* (Feb. 1937): 10.

58 Kiesler, "Design Correlation: A Column on Exhibits," 11.

59 As Kiesler tells the story (see Creighton, "Kiesler's Pursuit of an Idea," 114), the exhibit included the work of "sculptors, painters, and architects who had made common projects." Kiesler explains that he had asked Hare to make a sculpture for the Salle de Superstition at the 1947 Exposition Internationale du Surréalisme at Gallerie Maeght in Paris, so for the 1950 show Hare "was gallant, and as a sort of *revanche* he asked me to design a house for him." But Kiesler insisted on showing the Endless House and asked Hare to do a staircase. In the end, Hare exhibited a larger-scale model of the stair in tandem with Kiesler's model.

60 Frederick Kiesler, "The Space-House: Annotations at Random," *Hound & Horn* 7 (Jan.-Mar. 1934): 292.

61 "Walls Are Made into Pictures," *Architectural Record*, Sept. 1936, 235.

62 Kiesler, "Design Correlation: A Column on Exhibits," 12.

63 Frederick Kiesler, "Design Correlation: Certain Data Pertaining to the Genesis of Design by Light (Photo-Graphy), Part 1," *Architectural Record*, July 1937, 90. In the second part Kiesler writes: "Industry will gradually adopt the progress made by the avant-garde.

By manufacturing on a large scale, devices for light design recording will become available to a more popular public. Still-photography is already within the reach of everyone. Ciné-machines are now available for amateurs. In not too distant a future tele-senders and receivers will become just as prevalent as radio amateurs. The cycle of technical creation terminated in reaching the masses. Photo-graphy is *pro*-social. Easel-Painting remains *a*-social." Frederick Kiesler, "Design Correlation: Certain Data Pertaining to the Genesis of Design by Light (Photo-Gra-phy), Part 2," *Architectural Record*, Aug. 1937, 84.

64 Barbara Lesnak, "Visionary of the European Theater," in Phillips, *Frederick Kiesler*, 40.

65 R. L. Held, *Endless Innovations: Frederick Kiesler's Theory and Scenic Design*, vol. 23 of *Studies in the Fine Arts: The Avant-Garde*, ed. Stephen C. Foster (Ann Arbor, Mich.: UMI Research Press, 1982), 11–16.

66 Kiesler, *Contemporary Art Applied to the Store*, 121. Kiesler's "telemuseum" was not ready for the International Exhibition of Modern Art—organized by Dreier and Duchamp—held at the Brooklyn Museum in late 1926. A more modest version was constructed at the Anderson Gallery in early 1927.

67 Kiesler, *Contemporary Art Applied to the Store*, 121.

68 In a 1938 sketch Kiesler described the problem of the vision machine as related to the X-ray: "The short-coming of human sight—: the inability of penetrating objects of different densities with the eye-ray. It proves that we see only the reflec-tion, namely the *surface* which is opposite our eye, which acts as a mirror of what is in front of it. We cannot see behind object or behind each other. We have therefore only a frontal and not a space-dimen-sional sight. We cannot *see space* therefore. What appears to be space

is an illusion of it, namely a succes-sion" (Phillips, *Frederick Kiesler*, 150). At the same time he was con-ceiving the vision machine, he was also researching the electroen-cephalogram. In 1941, when his Design Laboratory was threatened with closure, Kiesler formed an "advisory committee" for the vision machine consisting of several Columbia University faculty.

69 Rosalind Krauss, "Photography in the Service of Surrealism," *L' Amour fou: Photography and Surrealism*, eds. Rosalind Krauss and Jane Livingston (New York: Abbeville Press, 1985), 31.

70 Krauss, "Photography in the Service of Surrealism," 27.

71 *Minotaure* 7 also contained photographs by Man Ray, Breton's "La nuit de tournesol" with photo-graphs by Brassai, and Dalí's "Psychologie non-euclidienne d'une photographie." Also, the copy of *La Psychanalyse* in Kiesler's library included Lacan's essay, "D'une question préliminaire à tout traitement possible de la psychose" (1–50), as well as a positive review by J. P. Pontalis of the first meeting of Group Processes, an "interdisci-plinary conference" on the relation-ships between psychology and ani-mal ethology (297–303).

72 Caillois, "Mimicry and Leg-endary Psychasthenia," 23.

73 Of the connection between Caillois and aesthetics, Rosalind Krauss writes: "The peculiar con-ception of the visual that Caillois depicted and Lacan went on to develop most immediately in his theory of the mirror stage both coincides with the primacy that modernist art gave to pure visuali-ty and conflicts with the utopian conclusions that the theorists of modernism drew from this idea of optical power." Krauss, "Corpus Delicti," *L' Amour fou*, 78.

74 Krauss, "Corpus Delicti," 74.

75 Kiesler, *Contemporary Art Applied to the Store*, 67.

76 Frederick Kiesler, "Design Correlation: [From Brush-Painted Glass Pictures of the Middle Ages to 1920s]," *Architectural Record*, May 1937, 54–55.

77 Kiesler, "Design Correlation: [From Brush-Painted Glass]," 57. On the final page of his article, Kiesler would provide both positive and negative examples of innova-tions in the use of glass, including (as in his 1930 book) a photograph of "Big plate glass in metal frame used as room partition by Mies van der Rohe" as well as promotional images from industry with coinci-dental similarities to the *Large Glass:* an image of rifle shots un-able to penetrate bulletproof glass (recalling Duchamp's "nine shots"), a young woman (the "bride") behind a "nine and one-half inch thickness of Lucite," and five execu-tives ("bachelors") "standing on Herculite tempered plate glass" (60). As Kiesler wrote earlier in the article, "Those who think only in 'practical' meanings . . . would do well to turn to the very last page of this section" (55).

78 Kiesler, "Design Correlation: [From Brush-Painted Glass]," 56.

79 Extending the developmental logic of the mirror stage, Lacan presents his use of optical systems as a means to contrast his notion of the gaze with Merleau-Ponty's phenomenology of vision. Lacan confronts Merleau-Ponty's belief that vision, as epitomized in paint-ing, is a "cohesion" and a "concre-tion" of "two extremities": one "reaches the eye directly [*de face*]" and the other "reaches it from below—the profound postural la-tency where the body raises itself to see—and . . . from above like the phenomena of flight, of swimming, of movement, where it participates no longer in the heaviness of ori-gins but in free accomplishments." For Merleau-Ponty, the subject conjoins these two extremes and "vision encounters, as at a cross-roads, all aspects of Being." But Lacan presents another characteri-zation of vision's path to an under-

standing of reality: he suggests that psychoanalysis stands at an entirely different crossing. That place, or juncture, maps a particu-lar split in the subject: that be-tween the eye and the gaze. For Lacan, traditional philosophy as-sumes vision is unmediated (a "fundamentally ideic [*sic*] percep-tion"), while the Lacanian subject's encounter (*tuché*) with "facticity" is ever disturbed and confounded by the interchangability of virtual and real images. When Merleau-Ponty argues that "the stirring of the 'appearance' does not disrupt the evidence of the thing" he sug-gests that certain *eidetic* percep-tions are commensurable with "worldly" things. In this way, with-out actual consciousness or cogni-tion of "things," the individual is able to share with others the "un-justifiable certitude of a sensible world common to us that is the seat of truth." Instead of seeking a common ground (the immanence of things in the world), Lacan dwells upon what is missing and what is confusing in the perceptual field. He theorizes a crossroads other than the reflexive "chiasm" Merleau-Ponty describes in *Le visi-ble et l' invisible* ("a reversability of the seeing and the visible . . . always immanent and never real-ized in fact"). For Lacan, the virtual and the real are necessarily mis-taken and vision is not reflexive but apparently doubled—"con-sciousness, in its illusion of *seeing itself seeing itself*, finds its basis in the inside-out structure of the gaze." This begins to explain Lacan's statement that "it is not between the visible and the invisi-ble that we have to pass."

80 In Lacan's words, the real presents "itself in the form of that which is *unassimilable* in it—in the form of the trauma." Lacan, *Four Fundamental Concepts*, 55.

81 This development might be de-scribed as a transition from immer-sion to identity, from undifferenti-ated self-containment to an ability to imagine one's own body as a container. Yet this imaginary iden-

tification is marked by anticipation; the subject is ever fantasizing
its totality as well as continually
questioning the veracity of its own
"contents"—that is, subjective
perceptions, sensations, images,
and ultimately, knowledge of the
world. This uncertainty confronts
the subject with the necessity of
enduring the real and the virtual
emptiness of the (not simply concave, but involuted) container. The
body is the foremost container, yet
in regarding every other container,
the subject remains in doubt. "To
be capable of enduring [the perceived container's] emptiness is,
in the end, to identify it as truly a
human object, that is to say, an
instrument, capable of being detached from its function." With this
celebration of the human capacity
to identify (with) emptiness, Lacan
distinguishes the aporia of psychoanalysis from the latent humanism
of phenomenology, which knows
fullness only in detachment. Lacan,
The Seminar, Book I, 104.

82 Lacan, *Four Fundamental Concepts,* 147.

83 Lacan, *Four Fundamental Concepts,* 161. In common-sense
terms, Lacan subverts what appears to be a fundamental and
phenomenal dialectic between the
inside and outside of the subject.
The seeming obviousness of the
dialectic is precisely what Lacan
aims to disturb, and he does so
most directly and demonstrably in
the schema he calls the "interior
8," a figure that articulates "the
topology of the subject." The interior 8 is not a representation in any
conventional sense; Lacan calls it a
"sign" and remarks that it cannot
"actually be made" (155). In other
words, the diagram properly belongs to the realm of the symbolic,
but is insistently invaded by the
imaginary. It both denotes and
depicts the subject, organizing the
conflicts engendered by such a
double functioning.

84 "It is not a question of eyes,
but of something shining, big,
motionless, and circular, carried by

a living creature and which, in
effect, seems to be watching even
though it is not an eye." Caillois,
Mask of Medusa, 91.

85 Lacan says a painting solicits a
"laying down of the gaze" (that is,
an entering into vision that slyly
screens out others' coinciding
vision and appearance) But this
does not include expressionist
painting, which *satisfies* a gaze.
Trompe l'oeil, on the other hand, is
the triumph of the gaze, the given-
to-be-seen overwhelming vision,
the production of an illusion that is
effectively real: a lure. "The point is
not that painting gives an illusory
equivalence to the object, even if
Plato seems to be saying this.
The point is that the *trompe l'oeil* of
painting pretends to be something
other than what it is" (*Four Fundamental Concepts*, 112). Lacan's
comments on painting are likely
prompted by Merleau-Ponty's essay
"Eye and Mind" in which he discusses the same issues, including
Plato's remarks on painting and
Caravaggio's famous realistic
grapes that attracted birds.

86 Lacan, *Four Fundamental Concepts,* 107.

87 Lacan, *The Seminar, Book I*, 215.

88 Kiesler, *Contemporary Art
Applied to the Store*, 102.

89 Kiesler, *Contemporary Art
Applied to the Store*, 79.

90 Kiesler, *Contemporary Art
Applied to the Store*, 78.

91 Kiesler, *Contemporary Art
Applied to the Store*, 79.

92 Kiesler, *Contemporary Art
Applied to the Store*, 93. The influence of Loos (who Kiesler claimed
to have worked for on housing
projects in 1920) is apparent in the
book. Although Kiesler does not
mention any of his store designs,
he extends Loos's notion of the
Raumplan and repeats his opinions
on ornament and decoration.
"Chapter Twenty. Architecture and

Decoration. There is no line of demarcation between architecture
and decoration. Decoration, or
what is called decoration, such as
painted ornaments, printed wall
paper, carved cornices, hanging
draperies, has been ruled out as
superfluous by contemporary
architecture. . . . It is of course in
most cases less expensive to re-
decorate than to rebuild. Especially is this true in the case of stores.
Therefore, 'modern art' and 'modern thought' slipped in as decoration, not as architecture. It is less
expensive. It is easier of comprehension by the public" (143).

93 In *Contemporary Art Applied to
the Store,* Kiesler advocated a "kinetic window" that would be operated by "a pushbutton system"
that allowed viewers to control the
display and purchase merchandise
in a manner similar to an automat
(110). He also advocated using
large photographs of paintings for
backgrounds, formed into a funnel
or forced perspective (114).

94 Kiesler, *Contemporary Art
Applied to the Store,* 70.

95 The note was first published in
A l' Infinitif [The White Box], trans.
Cleve Gray, 1966, 74.

96 This English version of the note
includes revisions in the translation by Jerrold Seigel and appears
in his book *The Private Worlds of
Marcel Duchamp: Desire, Liberation, and the Self in Modern Culture* (Berkeley: University of California Press, 1995), 29–30. The
phrase "s'en mordre les pouces"
(literally translated as "to bite
one's thumbs") is a French idiom
meaning "regretting it bitterly."

97 Kiesler, "Design Correlation:
[From Brush-Painted Glass]," 54.

98 Kiesler, "Design Correlation:
[From Brush-Painted Glass]," 53.

99 Frederick Kiesler, "Les Larves
d'Imagie d'Henri Robert Marcel
Duchamp," *View* 5, no. 1 (Mar.
1945): 24–30.

100 Kiesler's explanatory text
reads: "The interior of the Triptych
contains: a) Ceiling hook and 'Cro-
chet de la Mariée . . .'; b) 3 window
rectangles 'pistons de courant
d'air'; c) leather piece and 'voie
lactée'; d) 2 saws, suspended
lamp, cords and 'pendu-femelle';
e) chessboard with large rectangle;
f) below: 2 filter-'Tamis'; g) above
head: Mitre; h) pipe 'ready made';
i) 'Moulin à film et à eau'; j) film
band and 'glissière'; k) chair leg
and 'chassis Louis XV'; l) chess-
lion. Left panel: Bottle of Coverde-
sign; one 'stoppage-étalon'; window 'Bagarre d'Austerlitz.' Right
panel: window rectangles 'Fresh
Widow'; Theme 'Descente.' Back-
side of Triptych: Duchamp's left
hand; the 'Machine d'Eros'; chess
constellation of R. Roussel: Fou.
Cavalier et Rois; center panel:
'réseau des stoppages' painting;
Salon surréaliste, New York 1942;
left panel: 'ciseau de la broyeuse
de chocalat'; 'Témoins occultistes';
Backplate of chocolate grinder.
The 2 flaps interlocked assume the
shape of the 'livreur de grand mag-
asin,' one of the 'moules malic.'"

343

1 Oscar Wilde, *The Importance of Being Earnest* (1895; reprint, *Complete Works of Oscar Wilde*, Glasgow: Harper Collins, 1994), 357.

2 Oscar Wilde, *Importance of Being Earnest*, 363, 389, 406.

3 I am grateful to Joel Barkley for sharing with me his Princeton University master's thesis in architecture. Barkley proposed the addition of a tower to the Museum of Modern Art that he generated from plans of the Breuer House. The perspective that Barkley developed from his new tower inspired my own lamination of the Breuer House onto the Johnson courtyard.

4 *Architectural Forum*, May 1949, 98.

5 Oscar Wilde, *Importance of Being Earnest*, 357.

6 Mario Praz, *An Illustrated History of Furnishing: From the Renaissance to the Twentieth Century*, trans. William Weaver (New York: Braziller, 1964), 65.

7 Philippe Jullian, *Prince of Aesthetes: Count Robert de Montesquiou, 1855–1921*, trans. John Haylock and Francis King (New York: Viking, 1967), 109.

8 Russell Lynes, *The Tastemakers* (New York: Grosset and Dunlap, 1954), 130.

9 Oscar Wilde, *The Picture of Dorian Gray* (1890; reprint, *Complete Works of Oscar Wilde*, Glasgow: Harper Collins, 1994), 101–2.

10 Oscar Wilde, "The House Beautiful" (reprint, *Complete Works of Oscar Wilde*, Glasgow: Harper Collins, 1994), 916.

11 Martin Fido, *Oscar Wilde* (New York: Viking, 1973), 6.

12 Fido, *Oscar Wilde*, 6.

13 Wilde, *Picture of Dorian Gray*, 47. Lord Henry's full statement reads: "My dear boy, no woman is a genius. Women are a decorative sex. They never have anything to say, but they say it charmingly. Women represent the triumph of matter over mind, just as men represent the triumph of mind over morals."

14 Wilde, *Picture of Dorian Gray*, 31, 35, 66.

15 Wilde, *Picture of Dorian Gray*, 106.

16 Barbara Spackman, *Decadent Geneaologies: The Rhetoric of Sickness From Baudelaire to D'Annunzio* (Ithaca, N.Y.: Cornell University Press, 1989), ix.

17 Cesare Lombroso, *The Man of Genius* (orig. *Genio e degenerazione*, Palermo: Remo Sandro, 1897; English ed., New York: Scribners, 1910), 13.

18 Spackman, *Decadent Geneaologies*, vii.

19 Spackman, *Decadent Geneaologies*, vii.

20 Spackman, *Decadent Geneaologies*, 30, 20.

21 Debora Silverman, "A Fin de Siècle Interior and the Psyche. The Soul Box of Dr. Jean-Martin Charcot," *Daidalos: Soul Boxes* 28 (June 1988): 25.

22 Friedrich Nietzsche, *The Birth of Tragedy and the Case of Wagner*, trans. Walter Kaufmann (New York: Random House, 1967), 172.

23 Nietzsche, *Birth of Tragedy*, 166.

24 Nietzsche, *Birth of Tragedy*, 166.

25 See *Designs for the Dream King: The Castles and Palaces of Ludwig II of Bavaria* (New York: Cooper-Hewitt Museum, 1978).

26 Hans Mayer, *Richard Wagner in Bayreuth 1876–1976*, trans. Jack Zipes (New York: Rizzoli, 1976), 19.

27 Nietzsche, *Birth of Tragedy*, 184, 176.

28 Susan Buck-Morss, "Aesthetics and Anaesthetics: Walter Benjamin's Artwork Essay Reconsidered," *October* 62 (Fall 1992): 6.

29 Buck-Morss, "Aesthetics and Anaesthetics," 10.

30 Nietzsche, *Birth of Tragedy*, 176.

31 Nietzsche, *Birth of Tragedy*, 170, 175, 176. Nietzsche writes that the Goncourt brothers "are quite generally pertinent to Wagner's style" (170).

32 Mario Praz, *The Romantic Agony*, trans. Angus Davidson (London: Oxford University Press, 1933), 343.

33 J. K. Huysmans, *Against Nature (A Rebours)*, trans. Robert Baldick (Baltimore: Penguin, 1959).

34 Wilde, *Picture of Dorian Gray*, 109.

35 Wilde, *Picture of Dorian Gray*, 96.

36 Huysmans, *Against Nature*, 17.

37 Huysmans, *Against Nature*, 32.

38 Huysmans, *Against Nature*, 171.

39 Silverman, "Fin de Siècle Interior," 26.

40 Jullian, "Prince of Aesthetes," 101, 109, 113. As Edgar Munhall writes, "Long before Proust utilized him as a model, Karl Huysmans had done so with the character of des Esseintes in *A Rebours*, Jean Lorrain with *Monsieur de Phocas*, Georges Duhamel with the Marquis de Fonfreyde in *Le Désert de Bièvres*, perhaps even, as some believe, Oscar Wilde with *The Picture of Dorian Gray*." Edgar Munhall, *Whistler and Montesquiou: The Butterfly and the Bat* (New York: Frick Collection, 1995), 13.

41 According to Munhall, Stéphane Mallarmé visited Montesquiou's apartment on the quai d'Orsay. "Mallarmé in turn gave a description of what he had seen to a younger writer, then unknown, Joris Karl Huysmans (1848–1907). The latter adapted what he had learned about Montesquiou and his apartment to create the character of the Duc Jean Floressas des Esseintes" (35). Regarding the interior of this apartment, as Robin Middleton writes, Montesquiou "used objects he had inherited with imported novelties, oddities and bric à brac in the interiors he created for himself on the Quai d'Orsay and the Rue Franklin. Not to shock or to create visual effects of untoward incongruity, but rather to provoke thoughts and feelings that would stir the inner realms of the mind, and would penetrate even to the world of the unconscious and perhaps, even for a fleeting moment, make it present." Robin Middleton, "Glimpses: Rue Franklin, Paris: Robert de Montesquiou," *Daidalos: Soul Boxes* 28 (June 1988): 33.

42 See Jean-François Bastide, *The Little House: An Architectural Seduction*, trans. Rodolphe El-Khoury (New York: Princeton Architectural Press, 1996).

43 Middleton, "Glimpses: Rue Franklin, Paris," 49.

44 Patrick Mauriès, "Serebriakoff: The Beistegui Episode," *FMR* 9, no. 45 (Aug. 1990): 112.

45 John Richardson, "Despot of Decoration," *HG*, Dec. 1991, 140.

46 Clive Aslet, "Château de Groussay: The Home of Juan de Beistegui," *Country Life*, June 1987, 160.

47 Mauriès, "Serebriakoff: The Beistegui Episode," 118.

48 Mauriès, "Serebriakoff: The Beistegui Episode," 118.

49 Mauriès, "Serebriakoff: The Beistegui Episode," 116.

50 Aslet, "Château de Groussay: The Home of Juan de Beistegui," *Country Life*, June 1987, 162.

51 Philip Johnson, "House at New Canaan, Connecticut," *Architectural Review,* Sept. 1950, 152–59.

52 Reyner Banham, "Ateliers d'Artistes: Paris Studio Houses and the Modern Movement," *Architectural Review* 120 (1956): 76. Stanislaus von Moos also summarizes the significance of the artist's house for domestic space, writing, "One of the sources for the Citrohan idea was the Parisian artist's studio and workshop: a type of building that had vernacular origins—as Banham has shown—and that received a number of sophisticated modern interpretations by architects such as François Lecoeur, Auguste Perret, and later André Lurçat. The type is simple: a long, often split level studio-space lit by a large picture window. There was, however, another and possibly more important source. A small tavern, the bistro 'Legendre' opposite Ozenfant's studio on the rue Godot-de-Mauroy, seems to have played a decisive role. The bistro was a regular haunt of Le Corbusier and Ozenfant." It featured a kitchen in the back with a balcony on its top. *Le Corbusier: Elements of a Synthesis* (Cambridge, Mass.: MIT Press, 1979), 75.

53 As cited by Hilary Lewis and John O'Connor in *Philip Johnson: The Architect in His Own Words* (New York: Rizzoli, 1994), 68.

54 Johann Gfeller, "La Casa-studio di Le Corbusier per Ozenfant a Parigi," *Case d'artista: Dal Rinascimento a oggi* (Torino: Bottati Boringhieri, 1992), 237.

55 Gfeller, "La Casa-studio," 235.

56 Banham, "Ateliers d'Artistes," 76.

57 Gfeller, "La Casa-studio," 239.

58 Lynes, *The Tastemakers,* 19.

59 Paul R. Baker, *Stanny: The Gilded Life of Stanford White* (New York: MacMillan, 1989), 274.

60 Michael Macdonald Mooney, *Evelyn Nesbit and Stanford White: Love and Death in the Gilded Age* (New York: William Morrow, 1976), 46.

61 Mooney, *Evelyn Nesbit and Stanford White,* 50.

62 Klaus Herdeg, *The Decorated Diagram: Harvard Architecture and the Failure of the Bauhaus Legacy* (Cambridge, Mass.: MIT Press, 1983), 5. Writing on Harvard's influence—personified by figures such as Edward Larrabee Barnes, John Johansen, Philip Johnson, I. M. Pei, etc.—Klaus Herdeg explains and critiques the transformation of the European avant-garde into North American modernism. He writes: "With their *Architectural Record* House of the Year and AIA awards these architects became bright young heroes to the students of the fifties and early sixties. To their professional colleagues they became legitimizers of the modern movement, for they knew how to domesticate the new, largely European demands on architecture as a social and political force. To prospective clients, who had read about them and their work in *House and Home* or *House and Garden,* they made contemporary architecture respectable. A client could bask in the rays of the avant-garde without the risk of sunburn" (3). Similarly, Mark Jarzombek discusses the issue of the American house in relation to European modernism, writing: "In 1952 *Architectural Record* published a list of 'eighty-two distinctive houses' in an effort to document and lend support to what the editors confidently called a 'revolution' in American architecture. Modernist principles, so it was pointed out, had coalesced with the time-honored virtues of domestic design to create an architecture so convincing as to seem to exemplify the way of the future." Regarding the Breuer House, Jarzombek writes: "The Museum of Modern Art in New York was also actively engaged in keeping the consumer from 'going astray.' In 1951–52, it held an exhibit entitled *Good Design* that was no less an exhibit than a glorified trade show 'educating' Americans to the new architecture and its furnishings. . . . To make sure Americans knew that their new furniture required a house, the Museum of Modern Art commissioned Marcel Breuer in 1949 to build an exhibition house in the gardens of the museum." Mark Jarzombek, "'Good-Life Modernism' and Beyond," *The Cornell Journal of Architecture* 4 (New York: Rizzoli, 1991), 77, 79.

63 *The Museum of Modern Art Bulletin* 16, no. 1 (1949).

64 As quoted in *The Museum of Modern Art Bulletin* 16, no. 1 (1949).

65 As cited in Lewis and O'Connor, *Philip Johnson: The Architect in His Own Words,* 62.

66 Franz Schulze, *Philip Johnson: Life and Work* (New York: Knopf, 1994), 157.

67 Schulze, *Philip Johnson: Life and Work,* 214.

68 Schulze, *Philip Johnson: Life and Work,* 214.

69 As cited by Schulze. The full quotation reads: ". . . are you in fact earnest? a charlatan? a montebank? a juggler?—that are the very stuff of which architectural magazines are made." Robin Middleton, "Open Letter to Philip Johnson," *Architectural Design,* Mar. 1967, 107. Pertinent to this discussion on the Museum of Modern Art sculpture garden, Middleton also critiques Johnson's museum projects, writing: "Each of your buildings is imbued with great wealth. I'm not thinking alone of those elegant and expensive houses that you have designed, but even of your museums (no less than five) that should, one imagines, have provided opportunities for a display of a specifically public architecture. Instead, they are conceived in the tradition of the great palace museums of Europe: they are remote repositories of treasures, designed to emphasize as firmly as possible the distinction between those who can afford to buy and endow such collections and those who are graciously permitted to view them, but may never aspire, either socially or even physically, to the style of life of which they are a token" (107). Even more pertinent to this discussion on style and sincerity, Middleton strategically deploys the anti-effeminate language that was directed at Wilde and other homosexuals, writing: "The movement you seem to represent has grown horribly in power. And it seems so prissily opposed to all the buoyancy and vigour that is represented to us by the USA itself. In an exuberantly active and expansive country you have the determination and courage, at least, to be effete" (107).

70 Colin Rowe, "Chicago Frame," *The Mathematics of the Ideal Villa and Other Essays* (Cambridge, Mass.: MIT Press, 1956), 99.

345

The Avant-Garde Is Not at Home
Richard Neutra and the American Psychologizing of Modernity

SYLVIA LAVIN

1 Reyner Banham, "A Home Is Not a House," *Art in America*, Apr. 1965, 109–18. Republished with introduction in Joan Ockman, ed., *Architecture Culture 1943–1968* (New York: Rizzoli, 1993), 370–78.

2 Polly Adler, *A House Is Not a Home* (New York: Rinehard & Co., 1953), 318.

3 Philip Johnson first proclaimed himself to be a whore in 1982 at a conference at the University of Virginia. See Franz Schulze, *Philip Johnson: Life and Work* (New York: Knopf, 1994), 376.

4 The rapidity with which the significance of the phrase "a house is not a home" was transformed and softened between 1953 and 1965 reveals just how turbulent domesticity was during the postwar period. The flexibility of the idiom has implications not just for American erotic life but also for the relations between the public and private spheres, the place and nature of female labor, the nomadism of modern life, and many other important issues not immediately germane to my argument.

5 Although psychoanalytic interpretations of architecture abound, and despite Foucault's major studies, the rich historical relationship between psychology and modern architecture has been little excavated. Yet as the broad outlines of modern psychology were being established, spatial culture immediately became a site that registered and explored this new line of thinking. Perhaps the best-known examples are the links between associationism and the picturesque; Camillo Sitte in relation to agoraphobia in the modern metropolis; surrealism and psychoanalysis. On these examples and others in the nineteenth and twentieth centuries, see Sylvia Lavin, "Sacrifice and the Garden: Watelet's *Essai sur les jardins* and the Space of the Picturesque," *Assemblage* 28 (1995): 16–33; George R. Collins and Christiane Collins, *Camillo Sitte: The Birth of Modern City*

Planning (New York: Rizzoli, 1986); Anthony Vidler, *The Architectural Uncanny* (Cambridge, Mass.: MIT Press, 1992); Esther da Costa Meyer, "La Donna è mobile," *Assemblage* 28 (1995): 6–15; Mark Jarzombek, "Describing the Language of Looking: Wölfflin and the History of Aesthetic Experientialism," *Assemblage* 23 (1994): 28–69.

6 There is a large and growing literature on the role of the military in postwar American architecture, the treatment of which is beyond the scope of this essay. For some recent writings on the subject, see Donald Albrecht, ed., *World War II and the American Dream: How Wartime Building Changed a Nation* (Cambridge, Mass.: MIT Press, 1995), and Beatriz Colomina, "Domesticity at War,"*Assemblage* 16 (1991): 14–41 and her "1949" in this volume.

7 For some recent histories of psychoanalysis and psychology in America, see Nathan G. Hale, Jr., *The Rise and Crisis of Psychoanalysis in the United States: Freud and the Americans, 1917–1985* (New York: Oxford University Press, 1995); Ellen Herman, *The Romance of American Psychology: Political Culture in the Age of Experts* (Berkeley: University of California Press, 1995); and Philip Cushman, *Constructing the Self, Constructing America: A Cultural History of Psychotherapy* (Reading, Mass.: Addison Wesley, 1995).

8 Herman describes the development after the war as follows: "Psychological help was so broadly defined that everyone needed it. Because mental health became a prerequisite to social-welfare and economic prosperity, and not merely a state of individual well-being, virtually no aspect of U.S. life, private or public, remained out of clinicians' reach." Herman, *Romance of American Psychology*, 311.

9 All research on the life and work of Richard Neutra must begin with the essential biography by Thomas

S. Hines, *Richard Neutra and the Search for Modern Architecture* (Berkeley: University of California Press, 1982). I rely largely on Hines for the biographical and other basic data in this essay, including the central facts of Neutra's association with Freud. I would also like to thank Professor Hines for the generous support and encouragement he has given to my work on Neutra, which has extended far beyond the requirements of collegiality.

10 Neutra, "Inferiority-Nightmare," typescript manuscript, 1942. This and all subsequent discussions of unpublished material refer to documents housed in the Richard J. Neutra Archive, Special Collections, University Research Library, University of California, Los Angeles, hereafter referred to as Neutra Archive.

11 Richard Neutra, *Nature Near: The Late Essays of Richard Neutra*, ed. William Marlin (Santa Barbara: Capra Press, 1989), 13–15.

12 For some recent literature on Wundt, see Wolfgang G. Bringmann and Ryan D. Tweney, eds., *Wundt Studies: A Centennial Collection* (Toronto: C. J. Hogrefe, 1980); Daniel N. Robinson, "Wilhelm Wundt," *Toward a Science of Human Nature* (New York: Columbia University Press, 1982), 127–72; and "First Among Equals: Wundt" in Morton Hunt, *The Story of Psychology* (New York: Doubleday, 1993), 127–43.

13 Biological realism remains a completely unexplored aspect of Neutra's work. Nevertheless, given the new emphasis historians are placing on the relationship of Wundt to Freud and on the role of biology in the history of psychoanalysis, biological realism raises interesting questions. Moreover, recent interests in the sciences and psychologies of the body further suggest both a means of and a reason for investigating this concept. A few of Neutra's texts concerned with biological realism include

Survival Through Design (New York: Oxford University Press, 1954) and *Life and Human Habitat* (Stuttgart: Verlagsanstalt Alexander Koch, 1956).

14 The basic literature on Rank includes James E. Lieberman, *Acts of Will: The Life and Work of Otto Rank* (New York: Free Press, 1985); Esther Menaker, *Otto Rank: A Rediscovered Legacy* (New York: Columbia University Press, 1982); Jessie Taft, *Otto Rank* (New York: Julian Press, 1958).

15 The Committee refers to the secret inner circle of Freud's younger colleagues established in 1912. Members of this group, also called the Ring, included Sandor Ferenczi, Ernest Jones, and Karl Abraham.

16 Otto Rank, *The Trauma of Birth* (New York: Robert Brunner, 1952).

17 This accusation was most elaborately developed by Ernest Jones, Rank's primary competitor for Freud's affection and Freud's biographer. See Jones, *The Life and Work of Sigmund Freud*, vol. 3 (New York: Basic Books 1953, 1955, 1957), 44–77.

18 See, for example, the chapter "Rank as a Precursor of Contemporary Psychoanalysis" in Peter L. Rudnytsky, *The Psychoanalytic Vocation: Rank, Winnicott and the Legacy of Freud* (New Haven: Yale University Press, 1991), 46–69.

19 Rank wrote that "the analysis finally turns out to be a belated accomplishment of the incompleted mastery of the birth trauma." See Rank, *Trauma of Birth*, 5.

20 Interestingly, this step in Rank's development was, according to Freud himself, a consequence of Americanization: "It cannot be denied that Rank's train of thought was bold and ingenious, but it did not stand the test of critical examination. It . . . was designed to accelerate the tempo of analytic therapy to suit the rush of American life."

Cited in Ernest Jones, *Life and Work of Sigmund Freud*, vol. 3, 77.

21 Otto Rank, *Art and Artist: Creative Urge and Personality Development* (New York: W. W. Norton, 1989), 185.

22 Rank frequently cites German art historians, such as Wölfflin, Worringer, and Riegl, all of whom were involved in the spatial implications of form-psychology. The connection between space and anxiety was developed and suppress by these writers, particulary in relation to the subject's anxiety of dissolving into space, of losing definition as an autonomous entity. For example, in analyzing ancient architecture Riegl wrote that "the ultimate goal of the visual arts during all of antiquity thus was the representation of external objects as clear material entities . . . by strictly following its responsibility, [ancient art] had to negate and suppress the existence of space because it constituted an obstacle for the clarity of the absolute individuality of external objects." See Riegl, *Late Roman Art Industry*, trans. Rolf Winkes (Rome: Giorgio Bretschneider Editore, 1985), 21. Worringer's *Abstraction and Empathy: A Contribution to the Psychology of Style*, trans. Michael Bullock (New York: International Universities Press, 1963) similarly describes the general condition of humanity's psychic dread of space. These links between Rank and art history and between Neutra and Rank raise the question of Neutra's relation to this art historical tradition. For example, and in addition to the question of spatial anxiety, Neutra wrote frequently about the role of empathy not only in the perception of objects but in the design process as well. It is interesting to consider how, and if, Neutra's concept of empathy relates to Worringer's. On the German tradition, see *Empathy, Form and Space: Problems in German Aesthetics, 1873–1893*, ed. and trans. Harry Francis Mallgrave and Eleftherios Ikonomou (Santa Monica, Calif.: Getty Center for the History of Art and the Humanities, 1994.)

23 Copy of letter from Betty H. Rourke to Richard Neutra, dated April 1952, Neutra Archive.

24 Mrs. Rourke, three typescript pages recounting her memories and thoughts of the Neutra house, May 3, 1977, Neutra Archive. The article in *Time*, which concerns Neutra as well as modern houses in the United States generally, does not fully identify the Rourke House and refers to the clients only as Mr. and Mrs. B. See *Time*, Aug. 15, 1949, 58–66.

25 Menaker, *Otto Rank*, 66.

26 Rank, *Trauma of Birth*, 85–87.

27 Richard Neutra, "Human Setting in an Industrial Civilization," in Ockman, *Architecture Culture*, 283, originally published in *Zodiac* 2 (1958).

28 Neutra, "Human Setting in an Industrial Civilization," 283.

29 Discussing symbolic adaptation, for example, Rank defines the room as "the space, which for the Unconscious regularly symbolizes the female genitals. And, indeed, ultimately it symbolizes the womb as relating to the only female genital known to the Unconscious, and the places in which before the birth trauma one was protected and warmed." Rank, *Trauma of Birth*, 86. For additional discussions by Rank about space, see the chapter on artistic idealization, especially 147ff.

30 Rank considered Greek art to have been an idealizing and compensatory reaction to an "all too maternal attachment." He explained this in terms of the forced migration of the Dorians away from the motherland. He wrote, "This compulsory separation from the native land seems, in the sense of a repetition of the birth trauma, the violent severance from the mother, to have determined the entire further development of Greek culture." Rank, *Trauma of Birth*, 160ff. Neutra had similar ideas about

immigration and cultural habits. On April 8, 1939, he gave a lecture to the German Culture Society. After describing the various difficulties inherent in being an immigrant, Neutra wrote in his lecture notes, "This again has its striking parallels in the daily professional experience of the architect. A person who goes into the hardship of indebting himself for the next 15 years to build a new house does so because he or his wife (or in some rare cases both!) feels that they have outgrown their to date environment. He wants to surround himself with a new one, still consciously and even more subconsciously he is conditionned [*sic*] thoroughly by the old one in which he has grown up." Neutra Archive.

31 A single immovable glass panel between the living room and balcony further dismantles conventional definitions of windows and their role in defining both spatial movement and visuality.

32 Here Neutra seems to be joining Frank Lloyd Wright's stress on the exaggerated roof overhang with the Miesian tradition of the glass house.

33 Neutra goes on to write, "It must have influenced the entire upper brain development with much too late and therefore unstable conditionings. To learn of sex in the litter when one is two or four years old is a milder impact than to learn it outside of the family from school fellows, pornography clandestinely passed, or from the 'True Love Story' magazines. . . . Now they [humans] sleep segregated, never in the family beds of the U.W. Lodge, but in daytime they are crowded in interiors, school rooms, offices, shops, assembly lines." Neutra, "Ideas," typescript manuscript, 1946, Neutra Archive.

34 This letter from Neutra to Shulman, dated March 3, 1947, in the Neutra Archive, also rules that furniture should not be included in the image. For an account that emphasizes a different aspect of the

photographic history of the Kaufmann House, see Simon Niedenthal, "'Glamourized Houses': Neutra, Photography, and the Kaufmann House," *Journal of Architectural Education*, Nov. 1993, 101–12.

35 Richard Neutra, letter to Mr. Bernard of Hollywood, May 19, 1947, Neutra Archive.

36 On this point see Arthur Drexler, "The Architecture of Richard Neutra," in Drexler and Thomas Hines, *The Architecture of Richard Neutra: From International Style to California Modern* (exhibition catalog, New York: Museum of Modern Art, 1982), 52.

37 For Rank on the anxiety produced by small animals and insects, see *Trauma of Birth*, 13–17.

38 For a detailed discussion of one such questionnaire, see Hines, *Richard Neutra*, 153ff. The article in *Time* (Aug. 15, 1949, 65) also emphasized the importance of these documents, both to Neutra's design process and to the clients.

39 Neutra, "The Architect Faces the Client and his Conditionings–'The Layercake,'" typescript manuscript, Mar. 19, 1957, Neutra Archive.

40 Richard Neutra, "Client Interrogation–An Art and A Science," *AIA Journal*, June 1958, 285–86.

41 Freud wrote that "young and eager psycho-analysts will no doubt be tempted to bring their own individuality freely into the discussion . . . I have no hesitation in condemning this kind of technique as incorrect. The doctor should be opaque to his patients and, like a mirror, should show them nothing but what is shown to him." Sigmund Freud, *Therapy and Technique* (New York: Collier Books, 1963), 123–24.

42 This perception of Neutra's work as emphatically depersonalized was one that he actively cultivated and disseminated through

his control over photographic reproductions. His desire to exclude furniture and personal objects from the photographs of the Kaufmann House, for example, extended to the Kaufmanns themselves. In explaining why he did not want the clients in the pictures, Neutra wrote that the house was a "typical problem and typical technical solution and artistic approach" rather than "a special story that conveys just how the Kaufmanns live." Letter from Neutra to Mr. Barnard dated May 29, 1947, Neutra Archive. On Neutra's relationship with Shulman and their debates about architectural photography, see Joseph Rosa, *A Constructed View: The Architectural Photography of Julius Shulman* (New York: Rizzoli, 1994), 42–54.

43 From the notes to a lecture Neutra gave to the Women's University Club on May 4, 1940, in the Neutra Archive.

44 Neutra's reliance on fantasy and other psychological material to fill in missing details and to personalize architecture found its most effective expression and restaging through photography. Here the architectural and filmic screens collapse into psychic projection machines. Neutra's great success with middle-class residential clients after World War II may derive from his capacity to make viewers of photographs of his work feel that they could be at home in the image. These images are advertisements of a sort, where nothing too personal to an "other's" domestic life intrudes upon the viewers. An important study of postwar American architecture, not yet undertaken, would examine architectural photography in relation to psychological manipulation developed primarily in the arena of advertising. On advertising, see Jackson Lears, *Fables of Abundance: A Cultural History of Advertising in America* (New York: Basic Books, 1994).

45 Neutra, "Woman Makes Man

Clear," typescript manuscript, Nov. 13, 1953, Neutra Archive.

46 See the rather surprising inclusion of an article by Neutra, "Human Habitation Under New Conditions," in the third revised edition of Greta Gray's *House and Home: A Manual and Textbook of Practical House Planning* (Chicago: J. B. Lippincott, 1935), 194. Neutra describes his own pre-Oedipal relation to architecture as follows: "First I had learned about it [architecture], subconsciously, as a baby, sitting with a bare bottom on a splintery parquetry floor, digging dirt out of the cracks and licking the brass hardware of my toy cupboard. These, and my playing under the grand piano as well, had been preverbal experiences, but they were so deep as to deserve a most thorough analysis." Neutra, *Life and Shape* (New York: Appleton-Century-Crofts, 1962), 48.

47 Neutra, "The Architect Faces the Client."

48 Rank was speaking in particular of Expressionism, and used its "embryonal" forms to argue that "all form goes back to the primal form of the maternal vessel, which has become to a large extent the content of art; and indeed in an idealized and sublimated way, namely as form, which makes the primal form, fallen under repression again acceptable, in that it can be represented and felt as 'beautiful.'" See Rank, *Trauma of Birth*, 160.

49 In Nelson's operating rooms in particular, one sees psychoanalytic treatment being added to the "therapeutic" interventions made by architecture as described by Foucault in *The Birth of the Clinic.* On Nelson, see *The Filter of Reason: Work of Paul Nelson*, eds. Terence Riley and Joseph Abram (New York: Rizzoli, 1990).

50 Saarinen added at this point in his discussion that pulling your legs into the womb chair was "something which women seem

especially to like to do. . . . The chair should also be a flattering background when someone is in it–especially the female occupant." *Eero Saarinen On His Work* (New Haven: Yale University Press, 1962), 68. The chair was designed in 1946 and produced by Knoll.

51 The Rourke House, for example, except for a few unidentified images in *Time* and in Neutra's own *Life and Human Habitat*, 170–75, has not previously been published.

52 Singling out the domestic architect for the upper-middle-class client as an example of "avocational counseling," David Reisman wrote in his book, *The Lonely Crowd: A Study of the Changing American Character* (New Haven: Yale University Press, 1950), 364, that "with the architects' encouragement and help, it is possible that people are becoming willing to have a house fit them. This requires that they find out who they are."

53 Donald Woods Winnicott characterizes the holding environment as "not only the actual physical holding of the infant, but also the total environmental provision prior to the concept of 'living with.' In other words, it refers to a three-dimensional or space relationship." In further analyzing maternal care during this stage of infant development, and the merger that takes place between mother and child, Winnicott argued that "the holding environment therefore has as its main function the reduction to a minimum of impingements to which the infant must react with resultant annihilation of personal being." See Winnicott, "The Theory of the Parent-Infant Relationship," *International Journal of Psycho-Analysis* 41 (1960): 585–905. Republished in Winnicott, *Maturational Processes and the Facilitating Environment: Studies in the Theory of Emotional Development* (New York: International Universities Press, 1965), 37–55. See especially 43–46.

54 The belief that this fusion is not only possible but desirable persists

today both in the popular imagination and in academia. See for example University of California, Berkeley, professor Clare Cooper-Marcus, *House as a Mirror of Self: Exploring the Deeper Meaning of Home* (Berkeley: Conari Press, 1995).

55 A good example of this kind of demonization is Tom Wolfe's *From Bauhaus To Our House* (New York: Farrar, Straus and Giroux, 1981.) On the other hand, the identification of the many non-architectural elements that contributed to the demolition of Pruitt-Igoe, for example, suggests that this tendency may be abating. See Katherine G. Bristol, "The Pruitt-Igoe Myth," *Journal of Architectural Education* 44 (May 1991): 163–71.

348

System and Freedom

Sigfried Giedion, Emil Kaufmann, and the Constitution of Architectural Modernity

DETLEF MERTINS

I would like to thank George Baird, Alan Colquhoun, Louis Martin, Andrew Payne, Georges Teyssot, and Mark Wigley for their insightful criticisms and helpful suggestions during the writing of this paper.

[1] Sigfried Giedion, letter to Walter Gropius, Oct. 25, 1937 (Gropius Archive, Houghton Library, Harvard University, bMS GER208–778), trans. author.

[2] For the significance of the German distinction between *Zivilisation* and *Kultur*, see Norbert Elias, *The History of Manners*, trans. Edmund Jephcott (New York: Pantheon Books, 1978).

[3] See Jill E. Pearlman, "Joseph Hudnut and the Education of the Modern Architect" (Ph.D. diss., University of Chicago, 1993). See also Winfried Nerdinger, "From Bauhaus to Harvard: Walter Gropius and the Use of History," in *The History of History in American Schools of Architecture, 1865–1975*, eds. Gwendolyn Wright and Janet Parks (New York: Temple Hoyne Buell Center for the Study of American Architecture, 1990), 89–98.

[4] Walter Gropius, letter to Sigfried Giedion, Dec. 23, 1937 (Gropius Archive, Houghton Library, Harvard University, bMS GER208–778), trans. author.

[5] Sigfried Giedion, *Space, Time and Architecture* (Cambridge, Mass.: Harvard University Press, 1941).

[6] Kenneth John Conant, review of *Space, Time and Architecture*, by Sigfried Giedion, *Journal of Aesthetics and Art Criticism* 2–3 (Fall 1941), 128–29.

[7] Elizabeth Coit, review of *Space, Time, and Architecture*, by Sigfried Giedion, *Architectural Record*, Apr. 1941, 28.

[8] John A. Hartell, "Wither Architect? *Space, Time and Architecture*," *ARTnews*, Nov. 15–30, 1941, 36.

[9] Henry-Russell Hitchcock, review of *Space, Time and Architecture*, by Sigfried Giedion, *Parnassus*, Apr. 1941, 179–80.

[10] Philip Johnson, "Architecture in 1941," *Philip Johnson Writings* (New York: Oxford University Press, 1979), 57–60. The article was not published at the time of its writing in 1942.

[11] Sokratis Georgiadis has reviewed Giedion's conception of space-time extensively in relation to prior scientific, art historical, and artistic theories. See Sokratis Georgiadis, *Sigfried Giedion: An Intellectual Biography*, trans. Colin Hall (Edinburgh: Edinburgh University Press, 1993), esp. 97–150. For Alexander Dorner's treatment of space-time, see Joan Ockman, "The Road Not Taken: Alexander Dorner's Way Beyond Art," in this volume.

[12] Georgiadis has discussed Schmarsow's theory of *Raumgestaltung* in relation to Giedion's space-time, these two notions already being conflated, prior to Giedion, in Theo van Doesburg, *Grundbegriffe der neuen gestaltenden Kunst* (Frankfurt am Main: Oehms, 1925; reprint, Mainz: Florian Kupferberg, 1966) and László Moholy-Nagy, *Von Material zu Architektur* (Passau: Passavia, 1929; reprint, Mainz: Florian Kupferberg, 1968).

[13] Giedion, *Space, Time*, 50–55, 86–89, 188–91, 204–9, 401–4, 408–16.

[14] Sigfried Giedion, *Bauen in Frankreich. Bauen in Eisen. Bauen in Eisen-Beton* (Leipzig: Klinkhardt & Biermann, 1928; *Building in France. Building in Iron. Building in Ferro-Concrete*, trans. J. Duncan Berry, Santa Monica: Getty Center for the History of Art and the Humanities, 1995).

[15] Turpin C. Bannister, review of *Space, Time and Architecture*, by Sigfried Giedion, *Art Bulletin*, Mar. 1944, 134–38; Douglas Haskell, review of *Space, Time and Architecture*, by Sigfried Giedion, *Nation*, Aug. 16, 1941, 145.

[16] Giedion, *Space, Time*, 6.

[17] John Summerson, review of *Space, Time and Architecture*, by Sigfried Giedion, *Architectural Review*, May 1942, 126–27; Nikolaus Pevsner, review of *Space, Time and Architecture*, by Sigfried Giedion, *Burlington Magazine for Connoisseurs*, Jan.-Dec. 1943, 25–26.

[18] Giedion writes, "This living from day to day, from hour to hour, with no feeling for relationships, does not merely lack dignity; it is neither natural nor human." Giedion, *Space, Time*, 7.

[19] Much earlier than Giedion, Wilhelm Worringer had suggested that the urge to abstraction and the urge to empathy both entailed self-alienation, albeit from diametrically opposed directions, and that this need for self-alienation was the essence of aesthetic experience. See Wilhelm Worringer, *Abstraction and Empathy* (1907; trans. Michael Bullock, New York: International Universities Press, 1953), 24–25.

[20] H. Seymour Howard Jr., review of *Space, Time and Architecture*, by Sigfried Giedion, *Task* 2 (1941): 37–38.

[21] Sigfried Giedion, "To the Editors of Task," *Task* 2 (1941): 38–39.

[22] Henry-Russell Hitchcock, *Painting Toward Architecture* (New York: Duell, Sloan and Pearce, 1948).

[23] Le Corbusier, *New World of Space* (New York and Boston: Reynal & Hitchcock/Institute of Contemporary Art, 1948).

[24] Hitchcock, *Painting*, 38–40; my emphasis.

[25] Le Corbusier, *New World*, 8.

[26] Emil Kaufmann, *Von Ledoux bis Le Corbusier: Ursprung und Entwicklung der Autonomen Architektur* (Vienna: Rolf Passer, 1933; reprint, Stuttgart: Gerd Hatje, 1985).

[27] Kaufmann, *Von Ledoux*, 51.

[28] Emil Kaufmann, "Claude-Nicolas Ledoux: Inaugurator of a New Architectural System," *Journal of the American Society of Architectural Historians* 3, no. 3 (July 1943): 12–20.

[29] In his review of *Architecture in the Age of Reason*, Alfred Neumeyer questioned this absence, writing "One wonders whether the complete absence of Germany in his discussion might not also be based on bitter personal experiences." See Alfred Neumeyer, review of *Architecture in the Age of Reason*, by Emil Kaufmann, *Journal of Aesthetics and Art Criticism* 15 (Mar. 1957), 365–66.

[30] Kaufmann, "Claude-Nicolas Ledoux," 19.

[31] Kaufmann, "Claude-Nicolas Ledoux," 17–18.

[32] Kaufmann, *Von Ledoux*, 19.

[33] Kaufmann, *Von Ledoux*, 24.

[34] Kaufmann, *Von Ledoux*, 17–18.

[35] Kaufmann, *Von Ledoux*, 39.

[36] Kaufmann, "Claude-Nicolas Ledoux," 20.

[37] An alternative formulation of this idea was later put forward by Ernst Bloch when he interpreted Kaufmann's presentation of Ledoux's ideal city as a multifarious utopia of crystalline geometric order, a nonorganic and empty frame waiting to be penetrated with "stimulus, humanity, and fullness," the frame or "horizon of peace" in which "the ornament of the human tree of life is the only real content of that overall peace and clarity." See Ernst Bloch, "Building in Empty Spaces," (1959), in *The Utopian Function of*

349

Art and Literature: Selected Essays, trans. Jack Zipes and Frank Mecklenburg (Cambridge, Mass.: MIT Press, 1988), 195–99.

38 Emil Kaufmann, *Architecture in the Age of Reason* (New York: Dover, 1955), 215.

39 See Hubert Damisch, "Ledoux avec Kant," in Emil Kaufmann, *De Ledoux à Le Corbusier. Origine et dévelopment de l'architecture autonome* (Paris: Editions l'Equerre, 1981), 11–22; and Monique Moser, "Situation d'Emil K.," in *Origines de l' Architecture Moderne* (exhibition catalog, Arc-et-Senans: Edition Fondation C.-N. Ledoux, 1987), 84–89.

40 Peter Collins, review of *Architecture in the Age of Reason*, by Emil Kaufmann, *Royal Architectural Institute of Canada Journal* 34 (May 1957): 184–55.

41 S. Lang, review of *Three Revolutionary Architects, Boullée, Ledoux, and Lequeu*, by Emil Kaufmann, *Royal Institute of British Architects Journal* 61 (Dec. 1953): 70.

42 H. A. N. Brockman, review of *Architecture in the Age of Reason*, by Emil Kaufmann, *Royal Institute of British Architects Journal* 63 (Aug. 1956): 430.

43 Fiske Kimball, review of *Three Revolutionary Architects, Boullée, Ledoux, and Lequeu*, by Emil Kaufmann, *Art Bulletin*, Mar. 1954, 77.

44 Thomas J. McCormick Jr., review of *Three Revolutionary Architects, Boullée, Ledoux, and Lequeu*, by Emil Kaufmann, *Journal of the Society of Architectural Historians* 12, 31–32.

45 Neumeyer, review of *Architecture in the Age of Reason*, 365–66.

46 Ilaria Toesca, review of *Architecture in the Age of Reason*, by Emil Kaufmann, *Burlington Magazine for Connoisseurs*, Oct. 1957, 351–52.

47 Paul Zucker, review of *Architecture in the Age of Reason*, by Emil Kaufmann, *Progressive Architecture*, Mar. 1956, 204–22.

48 Meyer Shapiro, review of *Kunstwissenschaftliche Forschungen*, by Emil Kaufmann, *Art Bulletin* 18, no. 2 (June 1936): 258–66.

49 Philip Johnson, "House at New Canaan, Connecticut," *Architectural Review*, Sept. 1950, 152–59.

50 Henry-Russell Hitchcock, introduction to *Philip Johnson Architecture 1949–1965* (London: Thames and Hudson, 1966), 10.

51 Mies van der Rohe, "Bürohaus," *G* 1 (July 1922): 3. Ludwig Mies van der Rohe, "Office Building," trans. Mark Jarzombek, in Fritz Neumeyer, *The Artless Word: Mies van der Rohe on the Building Art* (Cambridge: MIT Press, 1991), 241.

52 Mies van der Rohe, "Bauen," *G* 2 (Sept. 1923): 1. Ludwig Mies van der Rohe, "Building," trans. Mark Jarzombek, in Fritz Neumeyer, *Artless Word*, 242.

53 Matei Calinescu, *Five Faces of Modernity: Modernism, Avant-Garde, Decadence, Kitsch, Postmodernism* (Durham: Duke University Press, 1987). The first edition was published as *Faces of Modernity* (Bloomington: Indiana University Press, 1977). See "The Idea of the Avant-garde," 97–148.

54 Philippe Lacoue-Labarthe and Jean-Luc Nancy, *The Literary Absolute: The Theory of Literature in German Romanticism*, trans. Philip Barnard and Cheryl Lester (Albany: State University of New York, 1988).

55 Lacoue-Labarthe and Nancy, "Overture: The System-Subject," *Literary Absolute*, 27–37.

56 Lacoue-Labarthe and Nancy, *Literary Absolute*, 48–49.

57 Lacoue-Labarthe and Nancy, *Literary Absolute*, 112–19.

58 As a student of Heinrich Wölfflin and an admirer of the Viennese school of art history, Giedion assumed a neo-Kantian orientation toward the systemic analysis of historical periods, with idealist overtones. Sokratis Georgiadis has noted Giedion's interest in Friedrich Schelling around 1936 in his "Giedions Versuch einer ästhetischen Theorie der Moderne," in *Sigfried Giedion 1888–1968. Der Entwurf einer modernen Tradition* (exhibition catalog, Zurich: Ammann, 1989), 22–23. Yet Giedion had cited Friedrich Schlegel on the title page of his first book, *Spätbaroker und Romantischer Klassizismus* (*Late Baroque and Romantic Classicism*) of 1922: "Once there is talk of a comprehensive transformation (*Umgestaltung*), one must not forget that architecture provides the firm ground and common basis for all the other formative arts, and that the renewal must take its start from here." As this quotation announced, Giedion took architecture to be a thoroughly historical work, the putting-into-form of a comprehensive transformation through artistic production. Where this first book concerned the transformation that occurred around 1800 in its relationship to the past, Giedion spent the next twenty-five years elaborating his understanding of its implications for his own time. Offering his own resolution to the *aporia* of the avant-garde in a synthetic mixture of romanticism's generative work and idealism's auto-system—Georgiadis has pointed to the "artistic" character of Giedion's project—Giedion made the writing of history itself into a work of critically reproducing the architectonic system and, reciprocally, made architecture into an ongoing work of operationalizing the historical transformation through which the system-subject would be materialized and made available to consciousness. He described historical artifacts as indices of their time, testimony for the historian to decode and judge, and took it as his moral responsibility to distinguish between those things that were incompatible with

the work ("transitory facts") and those that were compatible with the system ("constituent facts"), not the so-called systematic ordering of an ensemble, but in the romantic sense—which Lacoue-Labarthe and Nancy, paraphrasing Benjamin with Heidegger in mind, characterized as "that by which and as which an ensemble holds together and establishes itself for itself in the autonomy of the self-jointure that makes its 'sytasis' to use Heidegger's term" (*Literary Absolute*, 46). Not only does this conception of system rehearse Giedion's notion of space-time, but it also resonates with his appreciation of Jacob Burckhardt's treatment of the totality of the Renaissance by assembling fragments of its daily life "so skillfully that a picture of the whole forms in his readers' minds" (*Space, Time*, 3)

59 Neo-Kantianism was the most pervasive intellectual orientation in German-speaking countries in the decades around 1900. Quite varied, it included several distinct schools and many singular philosophical projects. See Klaus Christian Köhnke, *Entstehung und Aufstieg des Neukantianismus. Die deutsche Universitätsphilosophie zwischen Idealismus und Positivismus* (Frankfurt am Main: Suhrkamp, 1986). See also Jürgen Oelkers, Wolfgang K. Schultz, and Heinz-Elmar Tenorth, eds., *Neukantianismus. Kulturtheorie, Pädagogik und Philosophie* (Weinheim: Deutscher Studien, 1989). In English, see Thomas E. Willey, *Back to Kant* (Detroit: Wayne State University Press, 1978).

60 Worringer, *Abstraction and Empathy*, 18.

61 Wilhelm Worringer, "Zur Entwicklungsgeschichte der modernen Malerei," *Der Sturm* 2, no. 75 (Aug. 1911): 597–98.

62 Vlatislav Hofman, "Der Geist der Umwandlung in der bildenden Kunst," *Der Sturm* 4, no. 190–91 (Dec. 1913): 146–47. Hofman's fellow Czech cubist, Josef Capek, also

published a manifesto for modern architecture in *Der Sturm*, calling for a "pure architectonic language" whose expressions would be "sublime"; see Josef Capek, "Moderne Architektur," *Der Sturm* 5, no. 3 (May 1914): 18–19.

63 Adolf Behne, "Bruno Taut," *Der Sturm* 4, no. 198–99 (Feb. 1914): 182–83.

64 Ludwig Hilberseimer, *Groß-stadtarchitektur* (Stuttgart: Julius Hoffmann, 1927; reprint, 1978), 100.

65 See Ludwig Hilberseimer, *Contemporary Architecture: Its Roots and Trends* (Chicago: Paul Theobald and Company, 1964), 104–31. Under the title "Autonomous Architecture," Hilberseimer assembled what he referred to as Le Corbusier's revived classicism, Russian constructivism, Dutch neoplasticism, German expressionism, and the "structural" architecture of Mies van der Rohe. "The architecture of the 'Twenties," he wrote, reiterating not only Kaufmann but also his own writings from that time, "was characterized by its objectivity, its directness, and its simplicity. Its trend was toward architectural autonomy. It aimed to free itself from all external influences, from all traditional bonds, to be self-determined, and to realize its goals by the true means of architecture" (104).

66 See Robin Evans, *The Projective Cast: Architecture and Its Three Geometries* (Cambridge, Mass.: MIT Press, 1995), xxxvi–xxxvii.

67 See Drucilla Cornell, *The Philosophy of the Limit* (New York: Routledge, 1992), especially chapter 5, "The Relevance of Time to the Relationship between the Philosophy of the Limit and Systems Theory: The Call to Judicial Responsibility," 116–54.

68 Cornell, *Philosophy of the Limit*, 133.

69 Friedrich Nietzsche, "On the

Uses and Disadvantages of History for Life," 1874, in *Untimely Meditations*, trans. R. J. Hollingdale (Cambridge: Cambridge University Press, 1985), 57–124, 75–76.

70 See Wilhelm Worringer, *Form Problems of the Gothic* (New York: G. E. Stechert, 1910), 18; Adolf Behne, *Zur neuen Kunst* (Berlin: Der Sturm, 1915; reprinted in *Sturm-Bücher,* Nendeln/Liechtenstein: Kraus reprint, 1974), 32; Franz Roh, *Nach-Expressionismus. Magischer Realismus. Probleme der neuesten Europäischen Malerei* (Leipzig: Klinkhardt & Biermann, 1925), 5–6; Sigfried Giedion, *Building in France,* 85.

Despite the absence of Nietzsche's radicality in Giedion's text, and despite Giedion's emphasis on developmental history and organic growth—both of which Nietzsche eschewed—the imprint of Nietzsche's historiographic invention remains legible. Giedion's self-reflections on the task of history continued to be structured in this way, as evident in the introductory section of *Space, Time and Architecture*, which he titled "History A Part of Life." Even Nietzsche's insistence on the critical judgment of history for "those who suffer and seek deliverance" finds its distorted echo in Giedion's therapeutic conception of resolving the tragic, schizophrenic experiences of the chaotic and unstable modern world through the self-consciousness proffered by history.

That the historians' participation in the formation of the present was welcomed by artists and architects is attested to by an editorial in the 1926 issue of the elementarist pan-avant-garde magazine *G*, whose circle included the architects Mies, Hilberseimer, and Hugo Häring as well as the critic Walter Benjamin, who would soon take up the project of history. Probably written by the filmmaker Hans Richter (the journal's editor), "History is what happens today" cried out against the art history of connoisseurship, taste, and psychology and urged historians to place their work into

the moving forces of the epoch, arguing that "the truth of history will not be read from the 'facts,' rather it will be constructed." It continued:

> Let your manuscripts be pulped!
> Write manifestos for us!
> Live for what is objective today—
> so far as you see it.
> Learn to see it—so far as you want
> and
> Learn to want it.

See "Geschichte ist das, was Heute geschieht," *G* 5–6 (Apr. 1926): 131.

71 Nietzsche, "On the Uses and Disadvantages," 95.

72 Nietzsche, "On the Uses and Disadvantages," 94.

73 Nietzsche, "On the Uses and Disadvantages," 76.

1 Martin Steinmann observes a change in architectural publishing around 1928: "The necessity to obtain commissions not only from progressive and wealthy clients but also an increase of commissions from the state began to have an effect on the architectural theory of the modern movement about 1928. It revealed itself in the fact that pertinent statements, full of technical assertions took the place of proclamations, and that former polemical periodicals were replaced by publications as *Das Neue Frankfurt*." Martin Steinmann, "Political Standpoints in CIAM: 1928–1933," *Architectural Association Quarterly* 4 (Oct.-Dec. 1972): 49.

2 "Die Erklärung von La Sarraz," in *CIAM: Dokumente 1928–1939,* ed. Martin Steinmann (Basel: Birkhäuser, 1979), 29.

3 On the history of CIAM, see Auke van der Woud, *CIAM: Volks-huisvesting, Stedebouw/Housing, Town Planning* (Delft: Delft University Press, 1983); and Eric Mumford, "CIAM Urbanism after the Athens Charter," *Planning Perspectives* 7 (1992).

4 Hans Schmidt, *Beiträge zur Architektur, 1924–1964* (Berlin: Verlag für Bauwesen, 1965), 17: "Eine Masse, ohne den Rhythmus des organisch Befügten, in Chaos, aus den die verschiedenen Hauptgebäude sinnlos auftauchen und wieder verschwinden."

5 The air view was utilized most spectacularly at the fourth congress of 1933, which took place aboard the steamship *Patris II* as it sailed from Marseilles to Athens and back. Here orthographic representation of same-scale plans, based in large part on aerial photography, provided a universal basis for a comparison of thirty-three different world cities.

6 M. Christine Boyer, "Mobility and Modernism in the Postwar City," *CENTER* 5 (1989): 88.

351

7 José Luis Sert, *Can Our Cities Survive? An ABC of Urban Problems, Their Analysis, Their Solutions (Based on Proposals Formulated by the CIAM)* (Cambridge, Mass.: Harvard University Press, 1944), 2.

8 On this note, Sigfried Giedion wrote: "The book [*Can Our Cities Survive?*] was written and published because people do not yet recognize that city life as we now know it blocks them from achieving essential vital values." Sigfried Giedion, "On CIAM's Unwritten Catalog," *Journal of the Society of Architectural Historians* 3 (Jan.-Apr. 1943): 44.

9 Le Corbusier, *The Athens Charter*, trans. Anthony Eardley (New York: Grossman Publishers, 1973), 43.

10 "Das erste Programm für einen Internationalen Kongress für Neues Bauen," in Steinmann, *CIAM: Dokumente*, 12.

11 "Das erste Programm," 12–13.

12 As described by Sert, the architect-planner was envisioned as head of a team of specialists to lay out the city, a student of the various organs that perform urban functions. *Can Our Cities Survive?*, 222, 224.

13 Peter Buchanan, "City as Natural Habitat vs. City as Cultural Artefact," *Architectural Review*, Dec. 1984, 64.

14 Le Corbusier, *The City of To-morrow and its Planning* (1929), trans. Frederick Etchells (New York: Dover, 1987), 107.

15 Le Corbusier, *The Athens Charter*, 49.

16 For example, construction methods had to be adapted to vast progress in technology. Rural areas had to be integrated into the process of civilization. In Paris, at the congress "Logis et Loisirs" (1937), Szymon Syrkus argued that technological evolution and progress must be furthered. Architects must create a plan encompassing science, techniques, arts in order to rid the world of chaos. Szymon Syrkus, "Rapport no 3 — Cas d'application: régions et campagnes," in Steinmann, *CIAM: Dokumente*, 196, 199.

17 "Das zweite Programm des 1. Kongresses," in Steinmann, *CIAM: Dokumente*, 21.

18 "Das zweite Programm," 18.

19 "Das zweite Programm," 21: "Les devoirs de l'architecte sont mal définis. Les problèmes de l'habitation ne sont pas clairement exposés."

20 Ernst May, "Die Wohnung für das Existenzminimum," in Steinmann, *CIAM: Dokumente*, 41.

21 Günther Uhlig, "Town Planning in the Weimar Republic," *Architectural Association Quarterly* 11, no. 1 (1979): 32.

22 Here the Belgian architect argued: "Il devient en quelque sorte un observateur et un administrateur de toutes les valeurs utiles." Victor Bourgeois, "Le Programme de l'habitation minimum," in Steinmann, *CIAM: Dokumente*, 50.

23 Cornelius van Eesteren, "Rationelle Bebauungsweisen," in Steinmann, *CIAM: Dokumente*, 109: "Kein falsch verstandener Heimatschutz, der alte Bauweisen nachahmen läßt, keine Aesthetik bringt uns gesunde Wohnviertel. Rationelle Aufschließungsmethoden allein können es."

24 "Die Festellungen des 4. Kongresses 'Funktionelle Stadt,'" in Steinmann, *CIAM: Dokumente*, 160–61.

25 The sixth congress at Bridgwater in 1947 took up the previously ignored issues of aesthetics, avant-garde art, and monumentality. As Giedion summarized after the congress, aesthetic problems and emotional expression were to be of increasing importance to CIAM after this time. Sigfried Giedion, ed., *A Decade of New Architecture* (Zurich: Editions Girsberger, 1951), 40.

26 Hendrik Petrus Berlage first spoke out against bourgeois individualism, and against the errors of pure formalism that resulted from its arbitrary and accidental temperament: "Der heute auszufechtende Kampf ist der Kampf der Allgemeinheit gegen den Individualismus." Hendrik Berlage, "Der Staat und der Widerstreit in der modernen Architektur," in Steinmann, *CIAM: Dokumente*, 25. Berlage's articulation of a new society was limited, however, by his complete rejection of bourgeois individualism. His keen interest in past communal forms of society outweighed the obvious reality that individualism was an integral aspect of machine commerce and civilization.

27 Hans Schmidt, "Aufgabe und Verwirklichung der Minimalwohnung," in Steinmann, *CIAM: Dokumente*, 48: "Die Wohnung hat genau wie der Platz in Eisenbahnabteil ein aus ihrem Zweck und Sinn heraus begründetes sachliches Minimum zu erfüllen: Minimal Wohnung oder Standardwohnung." This point had been remarked upon a couple of decades earlier by Karl Scheffler, who likewise saw the future of housing development as one of uniformity for the purposes of liberated movement.

28 Walter Gropius, "Die soziologischen Grundlagen der Minimalwohnung," in Steinmann, *CIAM: Dokumente*, 56.

29 Gropius, "Die soziologischen Grundlagen," 58.

30 As Sert later wrote: "The ties which previously held urban populations together into closely packed communities have been dissolved. This has come about because of the presence of new factors, expressed in the mobility of power (electricity), labor (mobilized transportation), and goods (distribution via cars, bus, railway)." *Can Our Cities Survive?*, 114.

31 Walter Gropius, "Flach-, Mittel- oder Hochbau?" in Steinmann, *CIAM: Dokumente*, 93.

32 As Sert also commented, neighborhoods must house a sufficient number of people to support civic activities (i.e., elementary schools). Sert, *Can Our Cities Survive?*, 72.

33 Walter Gropius, "Flach-, Mittel- oder Hochbau?," 97: "Auflockerung und nicht Auflösung der Städte ist das Ziel."

34 These questions resurfaced after World War II in the guise of the question of the center or core. In particular, the eighth congress, "The Heart of the City," held at Hoddesdon in 1951, was devoted to the issue of rebuilding the physical and spiritual heart of devastated European cities.

35 Le Corbusier, "Rapport no 1 — Solutions de principe," in Steinmann, *CIAM: Dokumente*, 183.

36 Susan Buck-Morss, "Envisioning Capital: Political Economy on Display," *Critical Inquiry* 21 (Winter 1995): 448–49.

37 Charles S. Maier, "Between Taylorism and Technocracy: European Ideologies and the Vision of Industrial Productivity in the 1920s," *Journal of Contemporary History* 5 (1970): 28, 46–47.

38 Standardization encompasses several subcategories. *Vereinheitlichung* meant standardization in all its aspects. *Normalisierung* applied only to its constituent parts, whereas *Typisierung* took in the entire product. Richard Pommer and Christian Otto, *Weissenhof 1927 and the Modern Movement in Architecture* (Chicago: University of Chicago, 1991), 216, n.21.

39 "Die Erklärung von La Sarraz," in Steinmann, *CIAM: Dokumente*, 28.

40 "Das erste Programm," 12: "Pour pouvoir tayloriser il faut avoir standardisé une partie des éléments du bâtiment."

41 Sigfried Giedion, "Die Wohnung für das Existenzminimum," in Steinmann, *CIAM: Dokumente,* 38.

42 On the association of machine technology with *Lebensphiloso-phie* and conservative nationalism, see Jeffrey Herf, *Reactionary Modernism: Technology, Culture, and Politics in Weimar and the Third Reich* (Cambridge: Cambridge University Press, 1984).

43 The organic and mythic metaphors in *Bauen in Frankreich* were made in the service of internationalism and not of nationalism. They made their way into a CIAM discourse that made a plea for an international yet unique technical language of building that would replace various national building languages. At Frankfurt, for instance, Ernst May wrote that, in spite of differences in climate and living conditions around the world, the progress of technology is making the world smaller and puts all people on a new, common playing field.

44 Sigfried Giedion, *Bauen in Frankreich: Eisen, Eisenbeton* (Leipzig & Berlin: Klinkhardt & Biermann, 1929), 17, 22.

45 Giedion, *Bauen in Frankreich,* 85.

46 The leftist German architects asserted the importance of the collective nature of society and class conflict. By contrast, Le Corbusier believed that mechanization could transform society. Giorgio Ciucci, "The Invention of the Modern Movement," *Oppositions* 24 (1981): 75, 78.

47 Earlier, at the Frankfurt congress, Gropius had already advocated this development "in the future of a biologically truthful dwelling image for the urban industrial population." "Die soziologischen Grundlagen," 59: "ein

biologisch bedingtes echtes Zukunfts wohngebilde für die städtische Industriebevölkerung."

48 After the Garden City movement of the late nineteenth century, and its direct references to the empirical science of physiology, architects engaged in proposals to respace the elements of the city in order to provide for a seamless and healthful organicism. During the 1920s, the Siedlungen movement and its *Zeilenbau* system for housing layout developed a notion of urban design calibrated to the effects of sunlight and orientation, air ventilation, temperature, hygiene, and noise on the collective population.

49 Sert wrote that disease in the city had to be treated like disease in the body: "The only remedy for this condition is the demolition of the infested houses and the reconstruction, upon the reclaimed land, of sanitary buildings surrounded by open areas, so that air and sunshine can penetrate into their rooms without hindrance." *Can Our Cities Survive?,* 24.

50 Gropius, "Flach-, Mittel- oder Hochbau?," 96: "Furchtbaren Hinterhäuser der Gründerzeit."

51 Gropius, "Flach-, Mittel- oder Hochbau?," 93.

52 Gropius, "Flach-, Mittel- oder Hochbau?," 96: "ein relatives maximum an Luft, Sonne, und Planzenwuchs mit einem minimum an Verkehrswegen und an Bewirtschaftungsaufwand vereint."

53 Le Corbusier and Pierre Jeanneret, "Analyse des éléments fondamentaux du problème de la maison minimum," in Steinmann, *CIAM: Dokumente,* 62: "Les canalisations de la ville seront installées comme les organes d'une machine dans une usine: accessibles, visitables, réparables."

54 Le Corbusier, "Rapport no 1," 184.

55 "Die Feststellungen des 4.Kongresses," 162: "Sorgfältiger statistischer Grundlagen und Vorbereitungen."

56 Sert, *Can Our Cities Survive?,* 48.

57 In a recent article on later CIAM, Ignasi de Solà-Morales argues that existentialism assumed a much greater dominance after World War II. Metaphysical notions, like dwelling, habitation, community, and the core, replaced former functionalist verities. "Architettura e esistenzialismo: una crisi dell'architettura moderna," *Casabella* 55 (Oct. 1991): 38–40.

58 Criticism in the postmodern era has been no less forgiving. For instance, Manfredo Tafuri and Francesco Dal Co write that the Athens Charter represented a simplification and a compromise in that it fixed a minimum common methodological denominator on the basis of very different experiences; set up in advance analytic instruments and parameters of intervention that were only apparently objective; affirmed once again a generic faith in the regenerative role of modern technology; and put on record all the contradictions deriving from the capitalist system of land ownership and control without pointing to any solutions. *Modern Architecture,* vol. 2, trans. Robert Erich Wolf (New York: Rizzoli, 1979), 219.

59 Equally, machine civilization's tangible materiality—of steel and concrete—was an icon with which to wish away matter and overcome its dualism with spirit. For this reason, CIAM writings placed little emphasis on the factories and productive industryscape that were most responsible for the modernist city. They engendered buildings as ends and not means.

60 The CIAM members had histories in academic architectural culture as well as avant-garde movements. They were peculiarly comfortable fashioning a new architectural language from a collage

of rule and subversion. Thus, it may be argued that CIAM's *rappel à l'ordre* referred to the academic objectivities of architectural *ordonnance* as well as to the avant-garde's challenge to false articles of faith. Likewise, CIAM subsumed avant-gardist depositioning in bureaucratic, technocratic, and centric realms characteristic of the academy. Finally, it may be said that the organization's ostensibly rational language of design was in actuality a recuperation of opposition and reversal into rule of method.

353

1 The concept of physical existence in Aristotelian metaphysics was based on actualization—*energeia*—of inbuilt potential, and on *kinesis*, where motion is conceived as a principle of internally driven change, transformation, or becoming that resides within the existent itself, and that is not reducible to mere translation or change of position.

2 Alfred North Whitehead, *Science in the Modern World* (New York: Free Press, 1925), 58.

3 Alfred North Whitehead, *Enquiry Concerning the Principles of Natural Knowledge,* chapter 1, section 1.2.

4 Whitehead, *Science in the Modern World*, 20.

5 Whitehead, *Science in the Modern World*, 58.

6 Descartes, *Principles of Philosophy*, part 2, principle 25.

7 Newton could not bear the idea that vicinities or places themselves might be movable because this would render precise measurement impossible. In the first Scholium of his *Principia Mathematica* he grants the existence of absolute, immovable places and calls the sum of these places space (*spatium*). Yet ascribing real "concreteness" to this mathematical construct was, curiously, for him philosophically untenable. He is thus led to summon a god to serve as the creator of all places. The activity of his ceaseless creating becomes the universal substrate he calls "space." See Ivor Leclerc's strikingly original analysis in *The Philosophy of Nature*, vol. 14 of *Studies in the History of Philosophy* (Washington, D.C.: Catholic University of America Press, 1986), 140.

8 Whitehead, *Science in the Modern World*, 57. Whitehead claimed that his philosophy was an attempt to produce an "organic mechanism."

9 Whitehead, *Science in the Modern World*, 71.

10 Whitehead, *Enquiry Concerning the Principles of Natural Knowledge*, chapter 1, section 1.5.

11 The "internal relations" school of philosophy is associated with the work of F. H. Bradley, J. McTaggart, and other British neo-Hegelians of their generation. It seems clear to me that Whitehead's work issues from theirs, though I have seen no confirmation of this at the present writing.

12 Whitehead, *Science in the Modern World*, 73.

13 This is Weber's most famous thesis. See *The Protestant Ethic and the Spirit of Capitalism* (New York: Scribner and Sons, 1958).

14 Alfred Barr Jr., Henry-Russell Hitchcock Jr., and Philip Johnson. Possessed undeniably of genuine curiosity and zeal they were apparently the first Americans to feel at least professionally concerned by new European developments. However, they were all (with the partial exception of Barr, who had significant understanding of and not only acquaintance with European painting) too deeply entrenched in the nineteenth-century parlor traditions of connoisseurship and refined appreciation to sustain any concern with social, historical, or philosophical aesthetic issues. Hitchcock's writings, for example, particularly his defenses of the International Style exhibition that was the ultimate issue of their trip, are comical in their confident displays and defense of vapid sensibility over principle and idea, all the more so when read against the intellectual standards of modern times. In addition, we now know from Franz Schulze's biography of Philip Johnson that for a time he was an acquaintance of Whitehead and his wife during his undergraduate years at Harvard despite having failed to impress Whitehead intellectually or even to pass his course successfully. It seems that this was an important turning point in Johnson's life, since it convinced him that he was not particularly

well endowed for intellectual work and so could more usefully turn his energies and attention to promotion, alternately of fascism and of design. Johnson, who later signed and paid for the exhibition's essay, and to which he may have contributed some editing, was, by his own admission, primarily a booster along for the ride.

15 The Model T of 1914 represents a quantum leap in the bureaucratic mastery of social routines: workers are transformed from producers to consumers, the market penetrates even the factory floor, and workers' wages are recycled as revenue through the repurchase of products they themselves produce. The increasingly motorized workforce permits the steady transfer and refinement of mechanical expertise from workplace (machines) to leisure modalities (automobiles) and back in a mutually reinforcing loop that will soon become so comprehensive that it will disappear from view. Optimization of productive locales (factories) in relation to housing, secondary and correlative markets, and the total reshaping of urban environments according to rational economic principles overcame a major inertial obstacle in social space through the so-called democratization of mobility with the affordable (as it were) automobile.

16 Rem Koolhaas's seductive, career-long apologia for this architecture notwithstanding, it represents less a recovery of than a corrective to the tradition legitimized by the Museum of Modern Art exhibition group. Koolhaas's is a European's salvaging of a European tradition that Europe, in its weariness, could not sustain alone. America's modernism, one might say, was Europe's *Aufhebung* in action.

17 The third section of this essay was adapted shortly before the conference in order to address more appropriately the conference's last-minute change in title and focus toward the Philip Johnson legacy.

1 I shall not enter into a discussion, primarily semantic, of whether there is an avant-garde in America, but rather stipulate that the transformation of certain experiments originating in the historic European avant-garde was played out by émigrés in North America during the period in question.

This is an expanded version of a paper first published as a response to a symposium held in 1992 and documented in Detlef Mertins, ed., *The Presence of Mies* (New York: Princeton Architectural Press, 1994).

2 Theodor Adorno, *Aesthetische Theorie* (Frankfurt am Main: Suhrkamp, 1970), 335–36. The fragmented notes that make up this work date from 1956 to 1968; it was published posthumously. Of course, Adorno was speaking generally, not just about American art. Nevertheless, it is correct to say that his views on the culture of the commodity were forged by American experiences.

3 In this context one cannot but invoke, by way of analogy to Mies's project, Georg Grosz's 1919 interpretation of the Friedrichstrasse and Georg Simmel's characterization of the city's mental life, both of which are enclosed by the same boundaries of time and place as Mies's architectural representation and both of which analyze what Adorno, following Simmel and Georg Lukács, called reification—that epistemic anomie resulting from the systematic fragmentation, quantification, and depletion of every realm of subjective experience.

4 Hannah Arendt writes, "Heidegger described with uncanny precision in those paragraphs of Being and Time that deal with 'the they,' their 'mere talk,' and generally everything that, unhidden and unprotected by the privacy of the self, appears in public. . . . There is no escape, according to Heidegger, from the 'incomprehensible triviality' of this common everyday world except by withdrawal from it into

354

that solitude which philosophers from Parmenides and Plato have opposed to the public realm. . . . [T]he sarcastic, perverse-sounding statement '*Das Licht der Öffentlichkeit verdunkelt alles*' went to the heart of the matter." Hannah Arendt, *Men in Dark Times* (New York: Harcourt Brace & World, 1968), ix. I owe this reference to George Baird who, in turn, owes it to Rebecca Comay.

5 Adorno, *Aesthetische Theorie*, 93.

6 Fritz Neumeyer, *The Artless Word*, trans. Mark Jarzombek (Cambridge, Mass.: MIT Press, 1991), 197; Mies's manuscript is presented in Appendix I, 12.

7 Neumeyer, *The Artless Word*, 200.

8 See Franze Schulze, *Mies van der Rohe: A Critical Biography* (Chicago: University of Chicago Press, 1985), 270ff.

9 "Action and speech create a space between the participants which can find its proper location almost any time and anywhere. It is the space of appearance in the widest sense of the word, namely, the space where I appear to others as others appear to me, where men exist not merely like other living or inanimate things but make their appearance explicitly." Hannah Arendt, *The Human Condition* (Chicago: University of Chicago Press, 1958), 198–99.

10 On the dialectics of appearance and expression, see Adorno, "Schein und Ausdruck," *Aesthetische Theorie*, 154–79. For an analysis, see Fredric Jameson, *Late Marxism: Adorno, or, the Persistence of the Dialectic* (London: Verso, 1990), 165ff.

11 This two-stage reading was inspired by Rosalind Krauss's reading of the drawings of Agnes Martin. See Rosalind Krauss, "The Grid, the /Cloud/, and the Detail," in Mertins, *Presence of Mies*.

12 Marilyn Wood staged such a "dance" on the plaza of the Seagram Building in September 1972.

13 Manfredo Tafuri and Francesco Dal Co, *Modern Architecture*, trans. Robert Erich Wolff (New York: Harry N. Abrams, 1979), 342.

14 Henri Lefebvre, *The Production of Space*, trans. Donald Nicholson-Smith (Cambridge: Blackwell, 1991), 25.

15 Lefebvre, *Production of Space*, 125, 145, 313. Emphasis in original.

16 Max Horkheimer and Theodor Adorno, *The Dialectic of Enlightenment* (New York: Continuum, 1988), 137.

17 Horkheimer and Adorno, *Dialectic of Enlightenment*, 34–35.

18 "The new ideology has as its objects the world as such. It makes use of the worship of facts by no more than elevating a disagreeable existence into the world of facts in representing them meticulously. This transference makes existence itself a substitute for meaning and right. Whatever the camera reproduces is beautiful. The disappointment of the prospect that one might be the typist who wins the world trip is matched by the disappointing appearance of the accurately photographed areas which the voyage might include. Not Italy is offered, but evidence that it exists." Horkheimer and Adorno, *Dialectic of Enlightenment*, 148.

19 In 1959 a then almost unknown Frank Stella presented at the Museum of Modern Art four huge canvases projected out from the wall into a room painted mechanically with a regular repetitive pattern of black stripes in commercial enamel with a house painter's brush. The influence on young artists who were to become the minimalists and the pop artists was profound. For Stella seems to have forced the conceptualization of some maximal limit between painting as the high art of vision and the production of

an ordinary object. Just short of implying some existence of a 1950s zeitgeist, I have tried to suggest that Mies, similarly, constructs a new modality of working through (*Durcharbeitung*), in which the architecting subject gives passage to a condition it cannot yet even know—the production of space. One will insist at this point that any mode of production will use art and subjectivity in the ways it sees fit and that the very idea of art resisting such incorporation or constructing alternative subjectivities is pie in the sky. Fair enough. But it is precisely that recognition that led Mies to his "almost nothing," an architectural object on the very edge of the category "Architecture." If we were to continue to reflect on the question of whether there is an *American* avant-garde, we should investigate the shift of paradigms from Stella and Mies to Warhol and Venturi. It is in the space of that shift, I believe, that answers might be found.

1 *Journal of the American Institute of Architects,* Sept. 1923. The issue includes articles by George C. Nimmons, "Skyscrapers in America," and Walter Curt Behrendt, "Skyscrapers in Germany." George Nimmons dismisses the plans of the Glass Skyscraper as "too fantastic and unuseable for offices or apartments."

2 *Journal of the American Institute of Architects,* Sept. 1923, 372.

3 It was also Hitchcock who introduced Mies to the readers of *Hound & Horn* in December 1931, with an article on the Berlin Building Exhibition. He notes the collaboration of Mies and Lilly Reich on the exhibition of materials and states that "the work of Mies van der Rohe stands out like that of Schinkel in old Berlin." "Architectural Chronicle—Berlin; Paris: 1931," *Hound & Horn* 5, no. 1, 94–97. While Hitchcock refers to Mies as one of the "New Pioneers" in his *Modern Architecture: Romanticism and Reintegration* (New York: Payson & Clarke, 1929), the only illustration of his work in the book is the House at Guben of 1926.

4 Philip Johnson, "Style and International Style," speech at Barnard College, Apr. 30, 1955, *Philip Johnson Writings* (New York: Oxford University Press, 1979), 75.

5 Gordon Drake, Ralph Rapson, and John van der Meulen are the other American architects included in this issue. *L'Architecture d'aujourd' hui,* July 1950.

6 *L'Architecture d'aujourd' hui,* July 1950, 1.

7 Reyner Banham, "Klarheit, Ehrlichkeit, Einfachheit . . . and Wit Too!: The Case Study Houses in the World's Eyes," *Blueprint for Modern Living: History and Legacy of the Case Study Houses,* ed. Elizabeth Smith (Los Angeles: Museum of Contemporary Art; Cambridge, Mass.: MIT Press, 1989), 183.

355

8 Banham, "Klarheit, Ehrlichkeit, Einfachkeit," 183.

9 Breuer described the house as "for the commuter who has personal views in selecting his land, probably at least an acre." The house was designed for building in two stages: "The first phase . . . contains a living-dining room, two bedrooms, children's playroom, bath, kitchen and utility room. . . . Later on, when the children are older, the garage will be added, with a new master bedroom, bath and sun deck above it, giving the parents complete privacy." *Architectural Record,* Feb. 1949, 26.

10 About these exhibitions see Terence Riley and Edward Eigen, "Between the Museum and the Marketplace: Selling Good Design," *The Museum of Modern Art at Mid-Century* (New York: Museum Of Modern Art, 1994), 150–79.

11 The following prices were listed: "Three-bedroom house. Similar to the House in the Museum Garden $27,475. Same three-bedroom house. Wall, ceiling and floor finished of alternate materials $25,110. Two-bedroom house; without garage and third bedroom. Wall ceiling and floor finishes similar to the House in the Museum Garden $21,960. Same two-bedroom house. Wall, ceiling and floor finishes of alternate materials $19,975." "The House in the Museum Garden," *The Museum of Modern Art Bulletin* 16, no. 1 (1949). This issue of the *Bulletin* served as the exhibition catalog for "The House in the Museum Garden," organized by the Department of Architecture and Design, exhibited from: April 14 to October 30, 1949.

12 There was not much art in the Breuer house. Most journalists did not even remark on it, except for an isolated complaint: "Nothing in the art world these days is where you expect to find it. In a museum we find pots and pans. In a commercial movie we find art. [The House in the Garden of the Museum of Modern Art] is shown complete

with knives, forks, pots and pans and even art books on the book shelves. But on the walls there are only two small pictures. In one bedroom is a small, modest, chaste, Juan Gris abstraction. In another, is a similar work by Leger. A wooden abstract relief by Hans Arp on a stairway wall, an African negro fetish on the fireplace and a Calder metal construction clinging like a huge and fascinating bug to one outside wall. . . . Here is the MoMA presenting a model home almost devoid of fine arts." *New York World Telegraph,* May 2, 1949.

13 Marcel Breuer designed for the house a "radio-television-phonograph" in two units: "A table height unit supported on metal legs houses the screen, radio and phonograph mechanisms, as well as the storage place for records. A completely separate coffee table in front of the sofa is fitted with remote control panels so the viewer can switch programs and mediums without moving from his seat. At the back of the coffee table are shelves for books. Both pieces are lacquered black with polished metal supports." The units were produced in sample form by Philco. "Ultramodern House will Open in New York," *Retailing Daily* (New York), Apr. 8, 1949.

14 John Elderfield, preface to *The Museum of Modern Art at Mid-Century,* 6–11.

15 Sam Hunter, introduction to *The Museum of Modern Art: The History and the Collection* (New York: Harry N. Abrams and The Museum of Modern Art, 1984), 28.

16 For a more comprehensive analysis of the house, see Beatriz Colomina, "DDU at MoMA," *ANY* 17 (1997): 48–53.

17 *Bulletin of the Museum of Modern Art* 8, no. 6 (Sept. 1941): 9.

18 *Bulletin of the Museum of Modern Art* 9, no. 1 (Oct. 1941): 17.

19 "Buckminster Fuller Invents a

Dymaxion Deployment Unit," *Eagle* (Pittsfield, Mass.), Oct. 18, 1941.

20 "The Totem Pole," *Herald Express* (Los Angeles), Feb. 21, 1941. An article in the *Philadelphia Inquirer,* entitled "Sheltering Art from Bombs" (Nov. 23, 1941) showed Buckminster Fuller's "shelter" as it would look to a bomber.

21 The museum's first exhibition of camouflage was prepared in connection with the exhibition "Britain at War" (1941). "Camouflage for Civilian Defense" of 1942 emphasized civilian and industrial defense. "The Museum and the War," *Bulletin of the Museum of Modern Art* 10, no. 1, (Oct.-Nov. 1942): 8.

22 Peter Galassi, "Two Stories," *American Photography 1890–1965: From the Museum of Modern Art, New York* (New York: Museum of Modern Art, 1995), 34.

23 See Peter S. Reed, "Enlisting Modernism," *World War II and the American Dream: How Wartime Building Changed a Nation,* ed. Donald Albrecht (Washington, D.C.: National Building Museum; Cambridge, Mass.: MIT Press, 1995), 25.

24 The Museum of Modern Art held fourteen fortnightly parties in its garden for "fighting men": "sailors, soldiers, marines, merchant marine, and airmen of the United Nations." They were attended by 4,115 men. "They arrived at seven o'clock for a buffet supper in the Museum's penthouse or garden and went on until 11pm with games, sing-songs, dancing, motion pictures from the Museum's Film Library collection, or were entertained by professionals such as Ruth Draper, Gracie Fields and many others." "A Museum's War Program, An Editorial," *American Artist,* Nov. 1942, 30.

25 *New York Times,* April 22, 1942.

26 *New York Times,* April 23, 1942.

27 *New York Times* April 22, 1942.

28 *New York Times,* April 22, 1942.

29 "Tomorrow's Small House," *Bulletin of the Museum of Modern Art* 7, no. 5 (Summer 1945): 5.

30 Kenneth Frampton, "The Glass House Revisited," *Philip Johnson: Processes* (catalog 9, New York: Institute for Architecture and Urban Studies, 1978), 51(?).

31 Philip Johnson, "Breuer: An Artist in Architecture," *GSD News,* Harvard University Graduate School of Design, Fall 1995, 33.

32 While the plan of the house "assumed a suburban location on at least an acre of land," Breuer insisted that "with minor changes it could be adapted to a lot in a suburban development." Antoinette Donelly, "Chatter," *News,* Jan. 15, 1949. As if to reinforce that point, many articles in newspapers and magazines airbrushed the context of the museum.

33 "Museum Model House is New but Expensive," *New York World Telegraph,* June 24, 1949. The headline of this article is a direct quote from Eleanor Roosevelt, who had visited the house the day before.

34 Lewis Mumford, "The Sky Line: Design for Living," *New Yorker,* June 25, 1949.

35 Incidentally, Fuller's Deployment Unit was advertised by the museum as a bomb shelter for now, a guest house for peace time.

36 "In announcing selection of the Jeepster, Peter Blake, museum curator of architecture and design, explained: 'When we were looking for a small car to use with the MoMA–Woman's Home Companion Exhibition house, we sought a car that was handsome, in addition to having good performance. We have long felt that the original war-time Jeep was probably the best looking, mass-produced American car of the past eight or ten years. We like its

clean, unpretentious lines; we like its honest proportion; we like its rugged and serviceable look; and we think all its elements combine to make it a first-rate piece of industrial design.' Referring to the Willys Sports phaeton, Mr. Blake said that 'The Jeepster, which is a happy adaptation of the war-time Jeep, has retained all these features without adding to them the "juke box" treatment with which we are becoming increasingly familiar.'" *Morning Sun,* May 29, 1950.

37 *Herald Tribune,* May 19, 1950.

38 "This Architecture Affects Your Sales," *Retailing* (New York), June 27, 1950.

39 *Brooklyn Height Press,* June 22, 1950.

40 *New Yorker,* July 22, 1950.

41 "Our House: With a View to the Future," *Woman's Home Companion,* June 1950.

42 Philip Johnson, preface to *Built in the USA: Post-War Architecture,* ed. Henry-Russell Hitchcock and Arthur Drexler (New York: Museum of Modern Art, 1952), 8.

43 "As Alfred Barr has said: 'The battle of modern architecture in this country is won but there are other problems with which the Department has concerned itself. . . . Above [all] is the one unending campaign which involves not merely the Department of Architecture but the Museum as a whole. This is simply the continuous, conscientious, resolute distinction of quality from mediocrity—the discovery and proclamation of excellence.'" Philip L. Goodwin, preface to *Built in the USA: 1932–1944,* ed. Elizabeth Mock (New York: Museum of Modern Art, 1944), 8.

44 Alfred H. Barr, "What Is Happening to Modern Architecture?," *The Museum of Modern Art Bulletin* 8, no. 3 (Spring 1948): 5. An excerpt of Lewis Mumford's article in the *New Yorker,* Oct. 11, 1947, is published in this *Bulletin,* 2.

45 Galassi, *American Photography 1890–1965,* 33.

46 For a comparison between Le Corbusier's project for the Errazuriz House and Breuer's House in the Garden, see Klaus Herdeg, *The Decorated Diagram: Harvard Architecture and the Failure of the Bauhaus Legacy* (Cambridge, Mass.: MIT Press, 1983), 5–11.

47 Beatriz Colomina, *Privacy and Publicity: Modern Architecture as Mass Media* (Cambridge, Mass.: MIT Press, 1994), 168–69.

48 Elaine Tyler May, *Homeward Bound: American Families in the Cold War Era* (New York: Basic Books, 1988), 16. See also Karal Ann Marling, *As Seen on TV, The Visual Culture of Everday Life in the 1950s* (Cambridge, Mass.: Harvard University Press, 1994).

49 Quoted in May, *Homeward Bound,* 17. For transcripts of the debate see "The Two Worlds: A Day-Long Debate," *New York Times,* July 25, 1959, 1–3; "When Nixon Took on Khrushchev," a report of the meeting and the text of Nixon's address at the opening of the American National Exhibition in Moscow on July 24, 1959, printed in "Setting Russia Straight On Facts about U.S.," *U.S. News and World Report,* Aug. 3, 1959, 36–39, 70–72; "Encounter," *Newsweek,* Aug. 3, 1959, 15–19; and "Better to See Once," *Time,* Aug. 3, 1959, 12–14.

50 "Their Sheltered Honeymoon," *Life,* Aug. 10, 1959, 51–52.

51 "Containment at Home: A Cold War Family Poses in their Fallout Shelter," *Life,* 1961.

52 About the Case Study House program see Esther McCoy, *Modern California Houses* (1962), reprinted as *Case Study Houses 1945–1962* (Los Angeles: Hennessey & Ingalls, 1977); and Smith, *Blueprint for Modern Living.*

53 Colomina, *Privacy and Publicity,* 159.

54 Le Corbusier–Saugnier, "Les Maisons 'Voisin,'" *L' Esprit Nouveau* 2 (Nov. 1920): 214.

55 Alison and Peter Smithson, "Eames Celebration," *Architectural Design,* Sept. 1966, 432.

56 Quoted by James A. Moore, "From Idea to Place: An Interpretation of the Role of Technology in the Architectural Development of the Post-War Single-Family House" (Ph.D. diss., University of Pennsylvania, 1986).

57 Digby Diehl, "Q&A: Charles Eames," *Los Angeles Times WEST Magazine,* 1972, 16. Reprinted in Digby Diehl, *Supertalk* (New York: Doubleday, 1974). In the transcript of this interview, now in the Library of Congress, Eames elaborates: "The architect really does have a tough time. When Eero [Saarinen] was still alive, I naturally thought that he was really accomplishing something in architecture, but then he'd come out to our home and bemoan the fact that he wasn't able to give that kind of attention to detail in the studio. Even when he was interested in doing furniture, because at least if he did a chair, he would have the opportunity for one minute to do a small piece of architecture, which wasn't quite so apt to get out of hand."

58 Diehl, "Q&A: Charles Eames," 14.

BEATRIZ COLOMINA is associate professor in the School of Architecture at Princeton
University. She is the author of *Privacy and Publicity: Modern Architecture as Mass
Media* (1994) and editor of *Sexuality and Space* (1992) and *Architectureproduction*
(1988). She is currently working on a book on the relationship between war and
modern architecture.

FRANCESCO DAL CO, architectural historian and critic, teaches at the Istituto Universitario
di Architettura di Venezia. He is also the architectural editor of Electa and the
editor of *Casabella*. Among his many book are *The American City, Modern
Architecture* (with Manfredo Tafuri), and *Figures of Architecture and Thought:
German Architecture Culture 1780–1820*.

PETER EISENMAN, principal of Eisenman Architects, is the Irwin S. Chanin Distinguished
Professor of Architecture at the Cooper Union. His buildings include the Wexner
Center for the Arts in Columbus, Ohio, the Nunotani Office Building in Tokyo, and
the Aronoff Center at the University of Cincinnati.

K. MICHAEL HAYS is professor of architectural theory and director of the Ph.D. program
at the Harvard Graduate School of Design. He is the author of *Modernism and
the Posthumanist Subject* and *Unprecedented Realism,* and editor of *Hejduk's
Chronotype* and the forthcoming *Architecture Theory Since 1968*.

PHILIP JOHNSON, principal of Philip Johnson, Ritchie and Fiore Architects, has played
a decisive role in American architecture in the twentieth century. Through his
designs, writings, and teaching, he has helped to define the theoretical discourse
and built form of architecture in the last sixty-five years. As founder and director
of the Department of Architecture and Design at the Museum of Modern Art,
he mounted the landmark 1932 exhibition "Modern Architecture—International
Style" with the architectural historian Henry-Russell Hitchcock. His buildings
include the Seagram Building with Mies van der Rohe and his own Glass House.

JEFFREY KIPNIS is associate professor of architecture at Ohio State University. He was formerly the director of the graduate design program at the Architectural Association
in London. His latest book is *Chora L Works*.

REM KOOLHAAS is a founder of the Office for Metropolitan Architecture in Rotterdam, which has built the Netherlands Dance Theater in The Hague, the Villa Dall'Ava in Paris, housing in Fukuoka, Japan, and the Kunsthal in Rotterdam, and has designed the master plan for the Centre International d'Affaires in Lille, France. He is the author of *Delirious New York* (1978) and *S,M,L,XL* (1996).

SANFORD KWINTER is a writer based in New York. He is a cofounder and editor of the journal *Zone* and associate professor at Rice University.

PHYLLIS LAMBERT, architect and critic, is the director and founder of the Centre Canadien d'Architecture/Canadian Centre for Architecture, Montréal, internationally the leading museum and study center devoted to the art of architecture and its history. She has received numerous awards for various projects and has contributed major essays to numerous exhibitions catalogs, including *Canadian Centre for Architecture: Buildings and Gardens* (1989) and *Opening the Gates of Eighteenth-Century Montréal* (1992). Lambert is also adjunct professor in the School of Architecture, McGill University, and associate professor in the Faculté de l'Aménagement, Université de Montréal.

SYLVIA LAVIN is chair of the Department of Architecture and Urban Design at the University of California, Los Angeles, and an associate professor of architectural history and theory. She is the author of *Quatremère de Quincy and the Invention of a Modern Language of Architecture* (1992). Her current projects include the forthcoming *Richard Neutra and the Psycho-Sexualization of the American House* as well as a more general study of architecture and the American psychologizing of modernity.

MARK LINDER is a doctoral student at Princeton University and teaches at the Rhode Island School of Design, the Harvard Graduate School of Design, and Rensselaer Polytechnic Institute. His publications include *Scogin, Elam and Bray: Critical Architecture/Architectural Criticism* (1990) and numerous articles in *AA Files, A+U, Assemblage, Documents,* and *Journal of Architectural Education*. His design work has been exhibited in Chicago, Philadelphia, Atlanta, and Paris.

DETLEF MERTINS, architect, historian, and critic, is assistant professor of architecture at the University of Toronto. He is the editor of the book *The Presence of Mies.* Recent essays have appeared in *Assemblage, ANY, AA Files, Alphabet City, Monolithic Architecture,* and *Architecture and Cubism,* and his introduction to the translation of Walter Curt Behrendt's *The Victory of the New Building Style* is forthcoming.

JOAN OCKMAN is director of the Buell Center for the Study of American Architecture and adjunct associate professor at Columbia University's Graduate School of Architecture, Planning, and Preservation. She has also taught recently at the University of Pennsylvania and the Graduate Center of the City University of New York. Ockman writes on the history and theory of twentieth-century architecture. Her publications include the award-winning *Architecture Culture 1943–1968: A Documentary Anthology* (1993).

TERENCE RILEY is director of the Department of Architecture and Design at the Museum of Modern Art. His exhibitions and publications include *Paul Nelson: The Filter of Reason, Frank Lloyd Wright, Architect,* and *Light Construction.* Educated as an architect, Riley has been in practice with John Keenen since 1984.

COLIN ROWE is professor emeritus at Cornell University School of Architecture and the 1995 RIBA Gold Medalist. He has recently published a three-volume set of his collected writings and projects entitled *As I Was Saying.*

MITCHELL SCHWARZER is associate professor of architectural history at California College of Arts and Crafts in San Francisco. He is the author of *German Architectural Theory and the Search for Modern Identity* (1995) and guest editor of *ANY* 14, "Tectonics Unbound" (1996).

PAULETTE SINGLEY is an assistant professor at Iowa State University's School of Architecture. Her published works include *Architecture: In Fashion* (1994) and "Moving Solids" (in *Monolithic Architecture,* 1995).

R. E. SOMOL teaches design and theory in the Department of Architecture and Urban Design at the University of California, Los Angeles, and is a member of the editorial board of *ANY* magazine. He is currently completing a manuscript on misreadings of the avant-garde in contemporary architecture. Somol also maintains a design practice in Los Angeles with Linda Pollari.

BERNARD TSCHUMI is dean of the Graduate School of Architecture, Planning, and Preservation at Columbia University. He is the architect of several award-winning projects, including Parc de la Villette in Paris, and the author of *Manhattan Transcripts* and *Architecture and Disjunction*.

All photographs of the conference and its participants and attendees were taken by Dorothy Alexander (except the small photograph on page 198).

Page 61, bottom: Giuseppe Mazzotti. *Palladian and Other Venetian Villas* (London: Alec Tiranti, 1958). Page 175 (no. 232), "Villa Ferretti Angeli at Dolo, Venice," relief halftone, image 16.4 x 21.4 cm. Collection Centre Canadien d'Architecture/Canadian Centre for Architecture, Montréal

Page 91: From *Der Cicerone*, 1929

Page 93: Sprengel Museum Archives, Hanover

Page 96: Sprengel Museum Archives, Hanover

Page 105: Bauhaus-Archiv

Page 106: Collection of Joan Ockman

Pages 158, 161, 164–66, 169, 172, 173, 176, 177: Still-life sets by Christine Magar

Pages 186–89, 191, 192: © Julius Shulman

Page 198: Dida Biggi

Pages 214–15: Sigfried Giedion, Switzerland; Lengnau 1888–Zurich 1968. *Space, Time and Architecture: The Growth of a New Tradition* (Cambridge, Mass.: Harvard University Press; London: Oxford University Press, 1949, second edition). Pages 282–83, "Balloon Frame; Windsor Chair, Balloon Frame House designed by Richard Neutra," illustrations relief halftone and letterpress, 24.6 x 34.9 cm (page). NA2599.8.G454.A73 1949. Collection Centre Canadien d'Architecture/Canadian Centre for Architecture, Montréal

Pages 216–17: Sigfried Giedion, Switzerland; Lengnau 1888–Zurich 1968. *Space, Time and Architecture: The Growth of a New Tradition* (Cambridge, Mass.: Harvard

University Press; London: Oxford University Press, 1949, second edition). Pages 220–21, "Two Views of the Eiffel Tower; Painting of the Eiffel Tower by Robert Delauney," illustrations relief halftone and letterpress, 24.6 x 34.9 cm (page). NA2599.8.G454.A73 1949. Collection Centre Canadien d'Architecture/Canadian Centre for Architecture, Montréal

Page 223: Emil Kaufmann, Austria and the United States; Vienna 1891–Cheyenne, Wyoming 1953. *Von Ledoux bis Le Corbusier: Ursprung und Entwicklung der Autonomen Architektur* (Stuttgart: Verlag Gerd Hatje, 1985, facsimile reprint of edition first published in 1933 by Verlag Dr. Rolf Passer, Vienna and Leipzig). Page 7, "Die Idealstadt Chaux, Claude Nicolas Ledoux, Architect," offset lithograph, image 8.5 x 12.6 cm. ID 87-B15347. Collection Centre Canadien d'Architecture/Canadian Centre for Architecture, Montréal

Page 224–25, top: *The Architectural Review* (London) 108, no. 645 (Sept. 1950). Pages 154–55, "Philip Johnson's Presentation of his Glass House in New Canaan, Connecticut, with its Design Models," illustrations relief halftone and letterpress, 30.3 x 47 cm (pages). Collection Centre Canadien d'Architecture/Canadian Centre for Architecture, Montréal

Page 224–25, bottom: *The Architectural Review* (London) 108, no. 645 (Sept. 1950). Pages 156–57, "Philip Johnson in his Glass House in New Canaan, Connecticut," illustrations relief halftone and letterpress, 30.3 x 47 cm (pages). Collection Centre Canadien d'Architecture/Canadian Centre for Architecture, Montréal

Page 234: International Congress for Modern Architecture. Martin Steinmann, ed. (Switzerland; b. 1942), *CIAM: Dokumente 1928–1939* (Basel: Birkhäuser, 1979, Gta (Series); 11). Page 15, "Title Page of the Second Program for the Preparatory Congress Held

at the Château de La Sarraz, Switzerland, June 26–28, 1928," offset lithograph, 24.3 x 28.4 cm (page). Collection Centre Canadien d'Architecture/Canadian Centre for Architecture, Montréal

Page 237: International Congress for Modern Architecture. Martin Steinmann, ed. (Switzerland; b. 1942), *CIAM: Dokumente 1928–1939* (Basel: Birkhäuser, 1979, Gta (Series); 11). Page 26, "Official Photograph of Congress Attendees, La Sarraz, June 1928," offset lithograph, 24.3 x 28.4 cm (page). Collection Centre Canadien d'Architecture/Canadian Centre for Architecture, Montréal

Page 239: International Congress for Modern Architecture. Martin Steinmann, ed. (Switzerland; b. 1942), *CIAM: Dokumente 1928–1939* (Basel: Birkhäuser, 1979, Gta (Series); 11). Page 167, "Design for the Dust Jacket of the Unpublished Book *Die Funktionnelle Stadt*," offset lithograph, 24.3 x 28.4 cm (page). Collection Centre Canadien d'Architecture/Canadian Centre for Architecture, Montréal

Page 244: International Congress for Modern Architecture. Martin Steinmann, ed. (Switzerland; b. 1942), *CIAM: Dokumente 1928–1939* (Basel: Birkhäuser, 1979, Gta (Series); 11). Page 70, "Dust Jacket from the First Edition of *Die Wohnung für das Existenzminimum* (Frankfurt, 1930)," offset lithograph, 24.3 x 28.4 cm (page). Collection Centre Canadien d'Architecture/Canadian Centre for Architecture, Montréal

Page 246: International Congress for Modern Architecture. Martin Steinmann, ed. (Switzerland; b. 1942), *CIAM: Dokumente 1928–1939* (Basel: Birkhäuser, 1979, Gta (Series); 11). Page 70, "Cover of *Das neue Frankfurt* (Nov. 1929)," offset lithograph, 24.3 x 28.4 cm (page). Collection Centre Canadien d'Architecture/Canadian Centre for Architecture, Montréal

Page 247: International Congress for Modern Architecture. Martin Steinmann, ed. (Switzerland; b. 1942), *CIAM: Dokumente 1928–1939* (Basel: Birkhäuser, 1979, Gta (Series); 11). Page 107, "Dust Jacket from *Rationelle Bebauungsweisen*," offset lithograph, 24.3 x 28.4 cm (page). Collection Centre Canadien d'Architecture/Canadian Centre for Architecture, Montréal

Page 251: International Congress for Modern Architecture. Martin Steinmann, ed. (Switzerland; b. 1942), *CIAM: Dokumente 1928–1939* (Basel: Birkhäuser, 1979, Gta (Series); 11). Page 180, "Program for the Fifth International Congress for Modern Architecture, Paris, 1937," offset lithograph, 24.3 x 28.4 cm (page). Collection Centre Canadien d'Architecture/Canadian Centre for Architecture, Montréal

Page 253: International Congress for Modern Architecture. Martin Steinmann, ed. (Switzerland; b. 1942), *CIAM: Dokumente 1928–1939* (Basel: Birkhäuser, 1979, Gta (Series); 11). Page 202, "Title Page from *Logis et Loisirs* (Paris, 1938)," offset lithograph, 24.3 x 28.4 cm (page). Collection Centre Canadien d'Architecture/Canadian Centre for Architecture, Montréal

Page 280: Mies van der Rohe, Ludwig. "Glass Skyscraper," 1922, elevation (schematic view), Berlin, Germany. Charcoal, brown chalk, crayon on brown paper, 54 1/2 x 32 3/4" (138.5 x 83.2 cm). The Mies van der Rohe Archive, Museum of Modern Art, New York, gift of George Danforth, Chicago, © 1996 The Museum of Modern Art, New York

Page 281: Mies van der Rohe, Ludwig. "Glass Skyscraper," 1922, model, Berlin, Germany. Photograph courtesy the Mies van der Rohe Archive, Museum of Modern Art, New York

362

Page 282: Mies van der Rohe, Ludwig. "Seagram Building," 1954–58, plaza, perspective, New York City. Pencil on note paper, 9 x 11 3/4" (22.9 x 29.8 cm). The Mies van der Rohe Archive, Museum of Modern Art, New York, © 1996 The Museum of Modern Art, New York

Page 284: Mies van der Rohe, Ludwig. "Seagram Building," 1954–58, New York City. Photograph courtesy the Mies van der Rohe Archive, Museum of Modern Art, New York

Pages 306 top left and bottom and 307 bottom: Photographs by Ezra Stoller. From "The House in the Museum Garden," *The Museum of Modern Art Bulletin* 16, no. 1 (1949)

Page 306 top right: From "The House in the Museum Garden," *The Museum of Modern Art Bulletin* 16, no. 1 (1949)

Page 307 top: From a newspaper article in the Museum of Modern Art scrapbooks

Page 308: From *Bulletin of the Museum of Modern Art,* Nov. 1941

Page 309 right: From the Museum of Modern Art scrapbooks

Page 311: From a newspaper article in the Museum of Modern Art scrapbooks

Page 315: Wide World Photo

Pages 318–22, 325: Lucia Eames dba Eames Office © 1989, 1997 www.eamesoffice.com